Managing U.S.
Nuclear Operations
in the 21st Century

Managing U.S. Nuclear Operations in the 21st Century

Edited by
Charles L. Glaser
Austin Long
Brian Radzinsky

Brookings Institution Press
Washington, D.C.

The Brookings Institution is a private nonprofit organization devoted to research, education, and publication on important issues of domestic and foreign policy. Its principal purpose is to bring the highest quality independent research and analysis to bear on current and emerging policy problems. Interpretations or conclusions in Brookings publications should be understood to be solely those of the authors.

Library of Congress Cataloging-in-Publication data has been applied for.

ISBN 9780815739616 (pbk)
ISBN 9780815739623 (ebook)

9 8 7 6 5 4 3 2 1

Typeset in Adobe Garamond and Hypatia

Composition by Cynthia Stock

The authors and editors dedicate this book to the work, memory, and legacy of Janne E. Nolan.

Contents

Foreword

Walter B. Slocombe

In 1987, Brookings published *Managing Nuclear Operations*. Since then, the world has changed greatly; unfortunately, however, the challenge of maintaining nuclear deterrence is still with us. This book analyses and explicates the elements of meeting that challenge in contemporary conditions. The foundational principle is still that for deterrence to be successful, it is a necessary, though not sufficient, condition that the United States has nuclear forces that are unquestionably capable of executing the attacks on the prospect of which deterrence depends, and that that capability is demonstrable to adversaries and allies—and the American public—alike.

This book addresses the spectrum of what must be done to confidently meet that requirement. It begins with explaining basic doctrine and facts and proceeds to address other essential elements: ensuring that the military's operational plans faithfully implement doctrine, and assuring the survivability and effectiveness of the overall system, including command and control, target selection, and development of the immensely complex specific elements of detailed plans for execution. It also—and innovatively—examines the human factors, such as civilian-military collaboration, that make civilian control effective while respecting the essentiality of military expertise; the importance of having "the right people" in both groups; the special challenges of military leadership of the men and women at all ranks on whose discipline, skills, dedication, and reliability the whole system of deterrence depends; the moral and legal standards that apply to the formulation and implementation of deterrence policy and practice; and the integration of military deterrence with diplomacy and political relations, including arms control and relationships with allies and adversaries.

The book has been reviewed to ensure that nothing in it compromises national security, but by no means has excised the candid criticism and details of facts, history, and processes. As such the book presents in readily accessible form information that otherwise resides only in human memory or would be available with considerable difficulty, if at all. (The chapter notes alone comprise a comprehensive compilation of scholarship and recently released documentation.)

Managing U.S. Nuclear Operations in the 21st Century is the product of a remarkable collaboration of ten chapter authors from a wide range of experience and perspectives, including senior civilian officials both career and political, senior military officers, academics, and technical experts. In this respect the book replicates the life and work of Janne Nolan, who took the initiative for its creation and whose ability to convene people of very different views and experiences, along with her own outstanding—and often iconoclastic—scholarship, was the mark of her too-short life. She was a true friend to many, and this book is a tribute to her and part of her legacy.

Acknowledgments

This work would not have been possible without the generous support of many people. The editors wish to thank the main contributors to this volume, who have dedicated a great deal of time and effort to clearly capture their knowledge and experience so that future generations can benefit from the expertise they gained during their many years of public service. This is no easy feat. For participating in this endeavor, and doing so with grace, patience, and good humor, they have our deep gratitude.

We also thank Stephen Del Rosso and the Carnegie Corporation of New York for the generous funding that made this edited volume possible. Thanks are also due to the John D. and Catherine T. MacArthur Foundation, which similarly supported Janne Nolan's efforts to rebuild common ground and consensus in U.S. strategic policy.

This book emerged from a series of working group meetings convened to discuss gaps in public understanding of, and discourse on, U.S. nuclear policy and operations. This work would not have succeeded without the insights of the participants in these initial meetings. Thanks are due to Paul Bernstein, Lt. Gen. John Castellaw, Mary Chesnut, the Hon. Madelyn Creedon, Anya Fink, Rebecca Hersman, Lt. Gen. Arlen "Dirk" Jameson, the Hon. Frank Klotz, Susan Koch, Tom Mahnken, Brad Roberts, the Hon. Frank Rose, Jacquelyn Schneider, Grant Schneider, Erin Simpson, the Hon. Walt Slocombe, Caitlin Talmadge, Vic Utgoff, Jane Vaynman, Lt. Gen. Jack Weinstein, and Greg Weaver. We also thank the experts who participated in our 2020 authors' workshop and provided excellent comments and suggestions on draft chapters: Adm. Cecil Haney, Ambassador Rose Gottemoeller, Douglas Lawson, Stephen Lewia, and Walt Slocombe. Mike Albertson, Brad Roberts, and Walt Slocombe are owed additional thanks for their helpful comments on drafts of this book. Special thanks are due to Lt. Gen Dirk Jameson, who freely contributed his deep expertise and insight to this project before passing away in 2021. Finally, Austin and Brian would like to thank Charles Glaser for his tireless work in shepherding this project to completion after Janne Nolan's untimely passing.

Dedication

The authors and editors dedicate this book to the work, memory, and legacy of Janne E. Nolan. Janne Nolan was a brilliant scholar and practitioner of U.S. foreign policy, although with her characteristic wit and modesty, she might have objected to being described in such lofty terms. A senior national security staffer for the U.S. Senate and an adviser to the Clinton administration at a time when few women held such positions, Nolan had an intuitive grasp of both the power and the limitations of the U.S. government.

After her time in government, Nolan joined the Brookings Institution, where she applied her perspective on public service to the challenges of the final years of the Cold War and the era that followed. Her many books and articles—which addressed an impressive range of issues, including ballistic missile proliferation, U.S. nuclear strategy, intelligence, terrorism, and the ethics of leadership—document the efforts of highly capable, well-intentioned public servants to navigate the intricate politics of U.S. foreign and defense policy. Employing her sharp analytic eye and nuanced understanding of individuals, Nolan explains successes and failures in managing complex bureaucracies, these bureaucracies' inability to anticipate the shortcomings and unintended consequences of their policies, and the moral dilemmas that arise when these factors converge.

Although Nolan was a principled believer in the moral necessity of nuclear disarmament, she engaged freely and eloquently with those she disagreed with. Ethically, she opposed nuclear weapons and abhorred nations' reliance on nuclear deterrence. But pragmatically and politically, she was an institutionalist who believed that forging a path to a world without nuclear weapons would require the emergence of a stable domestic and international consensus around a different approach to security. Devising such an approach would require careful thought. Nolan's work at Brookings evinces her efforts to grapple with this intellectual challenge in the milieu that emerged after the fall of the Soviet Union.

Nolan left the Brookings Institution for a series of other organizations, finally joining the faculty of the Elliott School of International Affairs at George Washington University. There, she dedicated her efforts to challenging what she saw as the collapse in bipartisan consensus on foreign policy and national security matters, and the commensurate rise of a hyper-partisan, highly politicized, and poorly informed approach to public policy, especially in the areas of nuclear arms control and nonproliferation. With her humor, grace, and deep commitment, Nolan engaged multiple facets of this challenge simultaneously.

Through her Nuclear Security Working Group, Nolan brought together bipartisan groups of experts to share their unvarnished (but informed) views on a range of politicized issues, from the Iran nuclear agreement to the New Strategic Arms Reduction Treaty with the Russian Federation. These efforts revealed Nolan's preference for pragmatic, institutionally robust solutions to nuclear dangers, while also responding to pent-up demand among congressional staff and the press for nonpartisan, expert insight. This book was one such response to this demand.

Nolan also focused her efforts on the next generation, securing funding from the John D. and Catherine T. MacArthur Foundation for several projects that aim to rebuild informed pragmatism in foreign policy by creating a fellowship for younger national security professionals to spend a year or two working in the U.S. Congress on some aspect of U.S. nuclear and defense policy.

Nolan cared deeply about the ethical education of future policymakers. Her last book explored the ethics of public service and the perils of a government ethos that can sometimes suppress dissenting views. She worked closely with the Elliott School of International Affairs to create an ethics curriculum and spoke eloquently about the need for public servants to approach their work with conviction and moral clarity.

In early 2019, Nolan passed away from a brief but intense battle with cancer. She is deeply missed by her extraordinarily broad professional network, the numerous scholars and practitioners whom she wisely mentored, and the many true friends that she made over the course of her career. This book was in the drafting stage when she passed. The editors and the authors agreed to finish the project as a tribute to Janne Nolan and her legacy.

CHAPTER 1

Introduction

Charles L. Glaser
Brian Radzinsky

Nuclear weapons are once again at the forefront of foreign policy and national security. China's nuclear forces are raising concerns not just for the United States and its Asian allies but for Europe as well.[1] Russia continues to modernize and improve its nuclear forces.

Both Russia and China loom large in debates over how the United States should manage its own arsenal. In a time of tightening budgets, members of Congress and the general public are reassessing the costs and benefits of sustaining U.S. nuclear forces into the twenty-first century. The United States plans to spend roughly $1 trillion over the next thirty years modernizing its arsenal of intercontinental ballistic missiles (ICBMs), nuclear-powered submarines carrying ballistic missiles (SSBNs), submarine-launched ballistic missiles (SLBMs), and strategic bombers equipped with air-launched cruise missiles (ALCMs) and gravity bombs.[2] Successive administrations have sought opportunities to reduce both the risks of nuclear war and the financial burden of nuclear deterrence through negotiated arms agreements with Russia and China. But despite a five-year extension of New START (the New Strategic Arms Reduction Treaty) with Russia, it is uncertain whether the United States and Russia will reach a follow-on agreement, possibly one including China.

Debates about U.S. nuclear policy tend to focus on a small set of high-level issues, including the number and types of U.S. nuclear weapons and their cost, U.S. nuclear declaratory policy, and the structure of arms control agreements.[3] While these are certainly important, U.S. nuclear policy entails

1

much more. Beyond declaratory policy, which provides a high-level public overview, U.S. nuclear strategy is composed of many elements, including internal policies on the conditions under which the United States would consider nuclear use, private communications and agreements with allied countries, and much more. One important element, for instance, is the policies and plans for when and how the United States would employ nuclear weapons if the need arose. For these plans to support national policy objectives, military planners need detailed guidance that establishes the objectives the United States would pursue if deterrence failed. Once established by civilian leaders, this guidance must be translated by the military into targeting plans that account for a range of potential scenarios and circumstances.

Beyond deploying forces and developing war plans, the United States needs to ensure the capability to carry out these plans, especially forces and supporting systems that can survive crises and war. The United States accomplishes this in a number of ways, for example, by increasing forces' "alert rate"—changing where forces are deployed and how quickly they can be launched. Planning and carrying out military operations involving nuclear forces also requires the development and sustainment of military organizations with the technical capabilities to perform these functions.

This broad range of activities and capabilities is referred to as nuclear operations. Because they are essential, no analysis of nuclear deterrence and U.S. nuclear strategy is complete without an understanding of nuclear operations.

This book provides an overview of U.S. nuclear operations: how the United States plans, oversees, and controls its nuclear forces. The chapters that follow address many of the central challenges and activities involved in effective nuclear operations, including the development of U.S. strategy, civilian oversight, war planning, the exercise of authority, the capabilities for exercising effective command and control, and the interaction of nuclear operations with other areas of U.S. nuclear policy, namely allies and arms control efforts. Each chapter addresses a number of important and largely unanswered questions about U.S. nuclear policy.

First, how has the process of crafting U.S. nuclear strategy changed over time? How have different presidential administrations overseen the development of nuclear plans, operational concepts, and nuclear command and control? What roles do civilians and military officers play in the development of strategy, and how has this changed over time? How have these factors influenced U.S. relationships with its allies and the negotiation and form of arms control agreements?

Second, how is high-level U.S. nuclear policy guidance translated by Department of Defense personnel into targeting guidance and war plans that are well matched to the purposes of U.S. nuclear strategy? Targeting must take into account whether a target is mobile or concealed, whether destroying the target is urgent or can happen further in the future, and how to limit collateral damage while ensuring that a target will be destroyed. In addition, U.S. war plans are required to include a spectrum of preplanned attack options and the ability to quickly create new attack options.

Third, how does the United States ensure the performance of its nuclear forces under a range of very challenging wartime conditions? Nuclear forces must be able to perform their missions despite a variety of potential threats, especially surprise or preemptive attacks by potential adversaries. Survivability refers to measures to protect nuclear weapons from such threats. Decisions about how best to ensure survivability can result in significant differences between how nuclear forces are operated on a day-to-day basis and in severe crises or wars. These differences reflect different levels of alert status.

Fourth, how do U.S. leaders exert control over nuclear forces in peacetime, crises, and war? National leaders and military personnel must be able to communicate with forces reliably and in a manner that ensures that orders directing those forces can be authenticated. The United States has long sought to ensure that its nuclear forces will perform when asked to do so, no matter what foreseeable and unforeseen challenges its adversaries may generate. Because the United States gives only the president the authority to order the use of nuclear weapons, secure communications between the president and the chain of command are essential. At the same time, the United States strives to guarantee that its nuclear weapons are never used when not ordered, whether by accident, unauthorized use, or intrusion into the U.S. command-and-control system. Balancing these requirements for use and nonuse creates complicated trade-offs because measures to achieve the latter could reduce the likelihood of achieving the former. The U.S. nuclear command-and-control system is designed to ensure that these communications and procedures can be carried out. It is also responsible for providing warning of attack and conveying orders during war.

Finally, how do U.S. military nuclear commanders lead the personnel in charge of the day-to-day management of U.S. nuclear weapons? In the United States, as in other nuclear powers, military organizations and individual personnel play a critical role in managing and securing nuclear weapons in peacetime and delivering nuclear weapons in war. Military commanders exercise oversight of the force while bearing responsibility for training and motivating the personnel who operate U.S. nuclear forces. How the United States selects, trains, and supports the people responsible for operating nuclear forces significantly influences their ability to faithfully carry out their assigned peacetime and wartime missions.

What Do We Already Know about Nuclear Operations?

The subject of nuclear operations was first comprehensively addressed by an important book published in 1987: *Managing Nuclear Operations.*[4] This volume was remarkable both for the breadth of experience represented by its contributors and for the range of subject matter covered by the book. Chapters in this volume address almost every aspect of U.S. nuclear operations as practiced in the 1980s, including peacetime operations, protections against unauthorized use, the system for alerting nuclear forces, the technical capabilities and vulnerabilities of U.S. nuclear communications systems, the systems in place for initiating the use of the U.S. nuclear weapons reserved for delivery by NATO forces, the psychology of military commanders involved in commanding nuclear forces, and a range of other strategic and operational challenges confronting the United States at that stage of the Cold War.

Managing Nuclear Operations remains an indispensable guide to U.S. nuclear policy, in part because many of topics discussed are still relevant. The United States still takes the same basic approach to preventing unauthorized use of nuclear weapons as discussed in Donald R. Cotter's chapter, "Peacetime Operations," for example. Many of the conceptual discussions are still highly relevant to today's international environment, although some of the examples and details are less so. For instance, Ashton Carter's chapter, "Sources of Error and Uncertainty," provides important insight into how the unique features of operating nuclear forces, compared with conventional forces, can introduce different risks into nuclear operations in a crisis environment. Carter's discussions in his chapter, "Assessing Command System Vulnerability," are also still timely at a basic level, although today's command system is not identical to the one he analyzed in 1987. General Russell Dougherty's chapter, "The Psychological Climate of Command," is also still relevant to understanding the unique incentives and mindsets of military professionals in charge of nuclear missions. The discussion in Albert Wohlstetter and Richard Brody's chapter,

"Continuing Control as a Requirement for Deterring," is also still highly relevant and provides important insights, as do many other chapters.

On the other hand, much has changed since the publication of that book. Broadly speaking, some of the analyses in *Managing Nuclear Operations* have been overtaken by changes in international politics, strategy, and the state of military technology. These changes have had significant impacts on the role of nuclear weapons in protecting the security of the United States, its allies, and its competitors, on the likely pathways to nuclear war and on the requirements surrounding nuclear use and nonuse.

First, the international political environment has undergone sweeping changes. The Cold War ended, and the United States and the newly formed Russian Federation embarked on a long and arduous process of trying to remake their relationship. As a result of both bilateral treaties and unilateral measures, both countries made major changes to their nuclear forces, retaining some, retiring some, and modernizing others. Both sides also embarked on a series of efforts to reduce the risk of a nuclear accident.[5]

Commensurate with the disappearance of the Cold War threat, the United States turned its attention toward a radically different security environment, one in which U.S. nuclear weapons did not play a central role. The United States' focus shifted from active development and testing of nuclear weapons to stewardship, with the United States anticipating a need for a smaller nuclear arsenal in the post–Cold War environment.[6]

President Barack Obama's commitment to work to create the conditions for nuclear disarmament included a commitment to ensuring the safety, security, and reliability of the existing arsenal while forgoing major changes to U.S. nuclear forces, in the calculated hope of generating an international effort to create the conditions for lasting nuclear disarmament.[7] This effort yielded some successes while also highlighting the reluctance of the other nuclear-armed powers to fundamentally change the role of nuclear weapons in their national security policies.[8]

In the past decade, however, deterioration of the U.S. security environment—most important, growing political strains in relations with both China and Russia combined with improvements to their nuclear arsenals— has refocused attention on the requirements of U.S. nuclear forces and the adequacy of its overall nuclear policy.

Second, technology has changed in dramatic ways. Communications technologies have grown exponentially in capability and sophistication. Carter's chapter on "Communications Technologies and Vulnerabilities" focuses on radio transmission, with overall bandwidths in the range of 1,000 kilohertz.[9] Today, each of the United States' advanced EHF (extremely high frequency) satellites operates in the extremely high frequency or super-high frequency bands, with bandwidths ranging from 20 to 44 gigahertz, a difference of four orders of magnitude. The revolution in information technologies, built largely on continuing increases in computing power allows for richer communications involving the transmission of large amounts of information. As a result, the U.S. government and military now operate with far more detailed and frequent real-time information exchanges and data processing than was feasible in the past.

As a result, the enormous increase in information and computing power in military operations has changed the potential character of armed conflict, including nuclear conflict. Military operations can be planned faster and with less advance notice than in the past. Decisionmakers can now communicate face to face in real time to assess developments in a crisis or war and consider courses of action. During the Cold War, such discussions would have taken place over the telephone or not at all. At the same time, the use of massive amounts of data and reliance on computers for communication create new potential vulnerabilities. Maybe most prominent is the possibility of cyberattacks that degrade or confuse communications, which is now a potential major vulnerability that the U.S. nuclear command-and-control system must address.

Technological change is also affecting the military use of outer space, with significant implications for nuclear operations. For roughly two decades, from the end of the Cold War until the early years of this century, the United States saw space as a relatively secure domain in which to locate key supporting infrastructure for its nuclear forces. Today, however, critical enabling capabilities are vulnerable to disruption or destruction by malign actors. Because some U.S. space systems support both conventional and nuclear operations, potential adversaries could significantly disrupt or damage U.S. nuclear command-and-control assets unintentionally while attempting to gain advantage in conventional wars.[10] In addition, given the potential role of space-based surveillance in supporting U.S. nuclear targeting, adversaries are exploring ways to disrupt U.S. space-based command-and-control capabilities. Russia, for example, is developing mobile ground-based laser systems that are capable of blinding U.S. imagery satellites.

Finally, simply because decades have passed, some key topics need to be updated. As a result of the above and other changes, there have been some significant changes to U.S. nuclear strategy and war planning since the late 1980s. Major reorganizations have been done to the elements of the U.S. military tasked with the nuclear mission. The nature of civil-military relations in the planning process has also evolved. As time has passed, the role of nuclear operations in post–Cold War alliance strategy and relations has also changed, as has the arms control landscape.

Overview of the Book

The chapters that follow draw on the knowledge of experts with extensive experience overseeing, drafting, implementing, and analyzing U.S. nuclear policy. These experts provide the necessary context and background for moving beyond analyses of forces to advance understanding of how the United States implements its nuclear strategy. No such effort has been attempted since the publication of *Managing Nuclear Operations.*

The present book was written in an iterative process. In 2017 Janne Nolan, a nuclear policy expert who had a long career in government and the analytic community, convened a group of experts to discuss ways to assess the quality of nuclear policy debate in Washington and other world capitals in light of the controversies surrounding the Trump administration's Nuclear Posture Review.

The initial review found that the quality of debate could be improved by including more authoritative information about the rationales for long-standing U.S. policies. More broadly, Nolan's assessment of the state of debate found that the corpus of available published works on U.S. nuclear operations was increasingly in need of updating. The review group identified those aspects of U.S. nuclear policy that had the least clarity and the weakest factual basis and then identified experts who could speak authoritatively and intelligibly on those subjects. Through periodic meetings, and with support from research assistants at George Washington University, these experts refined their contributions.

The book roughly follows the hierarchy of nuclear oversight in the United States, beginning at the level of presidential guidance and moving down the chain of command to discuss nuclear planning, military expertise and leadership, command and control, the role of nuclear operational planning and capabilities in assuring U.S. allies, and the nexus between nuclear arms control and nuclear capabilities and plans.

Where necessary, chapters have also been reviewed by the Departments of Defense and Energy to ensure that the authors have not inadvertently revealed classified information. Each chapter speaks for itself and only for itself. Although the contributors to this volume have worked hard to accommodate feedback from expert reviewers, the views expressed are those of the individual authors and are not the views of the broader group, the editors, or their employers and any organizations with whom they are affiliated or have been in the past.

In chapter 2, Charles Glaser and Brian Radzinsky provide a substantive foundation for engaging the chapters that follow. They review deterrence theory and its application to nuclear strategy, the core elements of the U.S. nuclear posture, basic alert and deployment practices, the core concepts underlying the command and control of nuclear forces, and U.S. nuclear doctrine and targeting. Most of this material will be familiar to readers who have studied nuclear weapons extensively; the chapter is geared toward readers who are newer to this subject.

Chapter 3 by Franklin C. Miller sets the stage for the rest of the book with a historical overview of the relationship between the White House and the nuclear planners within the Pentagon and the military services and commands. Miller draws on his decades of government service to describe efforts by the Carter, Reagan, and George H. W. Bush administrations, including his personal efforts, to fully implement the strategy of flexible response. Miller's narrative deepens our understanding of what we now know to be the case from other historical works: that for many years, U.S. nuclear operational plans poorly reflected the priorities and policy guidance of successive presidential administrations. Miller himself was instrumental in rectifying this situation during the Reagan and Bush administrations. His efforts have had a lasting effect on the Defense Department and the broader U.S. nuclear policy apparatus.

In chapter 4, James N. Miller carries forward this narrative, focusing on the Obama administration's second term review of nuclear employment guidance. Miller's account stands as a sharp contrast to previous eras in which there were persistent challenges in communicating presidential-level guidance to planners. Miller also provides an overview of the Obama administration's nuclear policymaking that contrasts in notable ways with other histories of that period.[11] He describes a process that was productive and involved close collaboration between military planners, Defense Department officials, and the president's closest advisers. This chapter provides a fascinating and overdue account of an important period in the history of U.S. national security and nuclear policy.

In chapter 5, Mike Elliott describes the process for translating presidential nuclear employment guidance into detailed war plans for the use of nuclear weapons, focusing on nuclear planning since the end of the Cold War. Elliott gives an overview of the process that turns presidential guidance into a range of nuclear employment plans and shows how such plans are reviewed by civilian leaders in the Defense Department. He also describes some of the major considerations that affect nuclear employment planning as well as the tools that planners use to develop robust plans that meet U.S. deterrence requirements. The chapter has significant implications for ongoing debates about U.S. nuclear policy and the role of military planners.

In chapter 6, General Robert Kehler, a former commander of U.S. Strategic Command, describes the core responsibilities and dilemmas facing U.S. nuclear commanders, particularly the dual responsibilities of leading nuclear operators and providing advice to the commander in chief. The chapter also discusses the difficulties encountered in sustaining the motivation and effectiveness of the nuclear force. Kehler provides a unique perspective on the considerations that go into a presidential decision to employ nuclear weapons.

In chapter 7, John Harvey and John Warden provide an overview of the nuclear command-and-control (NC2) system, delineating its key functions and explaining how specific components of the system enable those functions. The chapter describes how a system that was developed and fielded to meet Cold War security requirements might need to change to address twenty-first century deterrence and conflict. Harvey and Warden consider the kinds of demands that the evolving security environment might impose on the NC2 system and identify a number of considerations that should influence command-and-control modernization.

Chapters 8 and 9 explore two critical areas that influence U.S. nuclear operations and planning. In chapter 8, M. Elaine Bunn discusses how the United States has navigated the operational challenges that have arisen from its alliance security commitments. Bunn observes that in extending a nuclear umbrella to its allies, the United States has necessarily created additional requirements for its nuclear forces. Which forces are to be committed in support of an ally? How should the United States balance the requirement to safeguard critical information about nuclear technology and plans with the desire to reassure its allies that it has developed effective plans for its defense? How would the United States consult with its allies in reaching the decision to initiate the use of nuclear weapons on their behalf? Bunn reviews the U.S. approach to these questions in the decades after the end of the Cold War, focusing on U.S. alliances in Europe and Asia. She then argues that operation-level factors are critically important to U.S. alliance relationships, but they are ultimately secondary to the quality of the relationship itself.

Finally, in chapter 9, Linton Brooks considers the intersection of arms control and nuclear operations. Brooks's point of departure is the observation that the requirement for effective operations determines the kinds of arms controls that a state is willing to accept. This has been the case for both the United States and, as far as is known, the Soviet Union and Russia. The chapter provides an incisive guide to the fundamental logics of past United States–Russia arms control efforts and discusses the operational considerations that would bear on future arms control with Russia, China, or other nuclear-armed states. Brooks evaluates the ability of arms control to help mitigate various risks arising from current or future capabilities and operating practices. He also considers the potential implications of future arms control for key aspects of U.S. military operations.

Key Insights

Although rich insights abound in this volume, three warrant particular attention. First, civilian involvement in nuclear planning, especially in the review of nuclear targeting, has increased significantly since the 1980s. Nuclear planning has in large measure become driven by U.S. strategy, reflecting civilian efforts to have plans flow from national policy. The legitimacy of civilian involvement has been increasingly accepted by the military. In part, this successful civilian–military interaction has depended on the participation of deeply knowledgeable and experienced civilians. It has also depended on personal relationships, trust, respect, and iterative planning and interactions. The process has required that information flow in both directions— from the military to civilians and conversely. The commander of the U.S. Strategic Command plays a critical role in facilitating this communication, alongside the Secretary of Defense, the Undersecretary of Defense for Policy, and the Chairman of the Joint Chiefs of Staff.

Second, in the post–Cold War era, U.S. nuclear planners have faced a more complex international environment that places greater demands on U.S. strategy and plans. Regional contingencies, which are more unpredictable than the canonical Cold War scenarios of a surprise nuclear attack or escalation to all-out nuclear war, have increased the need for flexibility and adaptive planning, which have required changes in U.S. nuclear command and control. Yet NC2 has also been shaped by the fact that for most of the post–Cold War era the United States has not experienced intense military competition with nuclear powers capable of posing a major threat to U.S. territory or U.S. forces. Cold War NC2 systems were retired and replaced by more capable but arguably less resilient systems, in keeping with the diminished major-power challenge. Today, there is consensus that U.S. NC2 must be capable of dealing with a conflict involving nuclear-armed major powers. But there is less consensus on the likeliest threats or the kinds of challenges that could emerge during a future crisis or conflict.

Third, while U.S. NC2 is due for modernization in any event, political and technological changes are influencing the shape it will need to take. Regional contingencies and the related requirement for adaptive planning create new demands for integration of NC2 systems. In addition, potential emerging threats could pose new challenges to NC2, including cyberattacks that could undermine the U.S. ability to provide national leaders with accurate information about the operating environment and to communicate with the force; advanced sensors with faster processing that might enable an adversary to identify and locate airborne command posts; hypersonic cruise missiles that might make possible attacks with very short warning times; and increasing overlap between nuclear and conventional military operations that could damage NC2 in a conventional war and create pressures for escalation.

Notes

The views expressed here are the personal views of the authors and should not be attributed to their employers, the U.S. government, Lawrence Livermore National Laboratory, or its sponsors.

1. "Brussels Summit Communiqué, issued by the Heads of State and Government participating in the meeting of the North Atlantic Council in Brussels, 14 June 2021," NATO press release, June 14, 2021, www.nato.int/cps/en/natohq/news_185000.htm.

2. Amy F. Woolf, *U.S. Strategic Nuclear Forces: Background, Developments, and Issues,* Congressional Research Service Report RL33640 (Washington, D.C., December 10, 2020), https://crsreports.congress.gov/product/pdf/RL/RL33640.

3. *Declaratory policy* is the public presentation of how the United States addresses fundamental questions, including the role and purpose of nuclear weapons, the military requirements of nuclear deterrence, the potential targets of U.S. deterrent efforts, and the conditions under which the United States would consider nuclear use. Declaratory policies can sometimes be in tension with how the United States would actually plan to use nuclear weapons, although as discussed in this book, the degree of tension has changed over time. In the past, declaratory policies took the form of presidential memorandums, public statements, or national strategy documents, such as the Eisenhower administration's now-famous New Look policy; see National Security Council, "Statement of Policy by the National Security Council: Basic National Security Policy," in *Foreign Relations of the United States,* 1952–1954, National Security Affairs, vol. 2, pt. 1, edited by Lisle A. Rose and Neal H. Petersen (Government Printing Office, 1984), Document 101, https://history.state.gov/historicaldocuments/frus1952-54v02p1/d101. Since 2010, U.S. declaratory policy has been most clearly articulated in public Nuclear Posture Review documents (2010 and 2018, with 2021–2022 anticipated). Because Nuclear Posture Reviews conducted prior to 2010 were not released publicly, U.S. declaratory policies were conveyed through a mix of presidential statements and other government statements and publications.

4. Ashton B. Carter, John D. Steinbruner, and Charles A. Zraket, eds., *Managing Nuclear Operations* (Brookings, 1987). Other important books on nuclear command and control that were published during this period include Bruce Blair, *Strategic Command and Control: Redefining the Nuclear Threat* (Brookings, 1985); Bruce Blair, *The Logic of Accidental Nuclear War* (Brookings, 1993); Paul Bracken, *The Command and Control of Nuclear Forces* (Yale University Press, 1993); Peter Feaver, *Guarding the Guardians: Civilian Control of Nuclear Weapons in the United States* (Cornell University Press, 1992); and Janne Nolan, *Guardians of the Arsenal: The Politics of Nuclear Strategy* (New York: Basic Books, 1989). For a more recent book, see Eric Schlosser, *Command and Control: Nuclear Weapons, the Damascus Accident, and the Illusion of Safety* (New York: Penguin Books, 2014).

5. Jeane Kirkpatrick and others, *Final Report of the Federal Advisory Committee on Nuclear Failsafe and Risk Reduction* (Department of Defense, 1992).

6. Sidney Drell and others, *Science-Based Stockpile Stewardship,* JASON Report JSR-94-345 (McLean, Va.: MITRE Corporation, 1994).

7. Barack Obama, "Remarks by President Barack Obama in Prague as Delivered," *The White House,* April 5, 2009, https://obamawhitehouse.archives.gov/the-press-office/remarks-president-barack-obama-prague-delivered.

8. It is important to note that there was also resistance to nuclear disarmament in the United States. For a range of views, see, for example, George Perkovich and James M. Acton, eds., *Abolishing Nuclear Weapons: A Debate* (Washington, D.C.: Carnegie Endowment for International Peace, 2009).

9. Ashton Carter, "Communication Technologies and Vulnerabilities," in Carter, Steinbruner, and Zraket, *Managing Nuclear Operations*, pp. 217–81.

10. James M. Acton, "Escalation through Entanglement: How the Vulnerability of Command-and-Control Systems Raises the Risks of Inadvertent Nuclear Escalation," *International Security* 43, no. 1 (2018), pp. 56–99.

11. See William J. Perry and Tom Z. Collina, *The Button: The New Nuclear Arms Race and Presidential Power from Truman to Trump* (Dallas: BenBella Book, 2020); Fred Kaplan, *The Bomb: Presidents, Generals, and the Secret History of Nuclear War* (New York: Simon and Schuster, 2021).

CHAPTER 2

Basics of Deterrence and U.S. Nuclear Doctrine and Forces

Charles L. Glaser
Brian Radzinsky

This chapter provides a basic substantive foundation for understanding and engaging the chapters that follow. It begins with a review of deterrence theory as it applies to nuclear strategy. The following sections review core elements of the U.S. nuclear posture, focusing on its nuclear forces, basic deployment and alert practices, the core concepts underlying the command and control of nuclear forces, and U.S. nuclear doctrine and targeting. We expect that most of this material will be familiar to readers who have studied nuclear weapons extensively. The chapter is geared to readers who are newer to this subject.

Nuclear Deterrence Theory

A deterrent policy attempts to convince an adversary not to take an action by threatening a response to the adversary's action that would leave the adversary worse off than if it had not acted. Deterrence attempts to influence an adversary's intentions and decisions, not its capabilities. As an approach to influencing behavior, deterrence is not limited to military affairs. For example, economic sanctions and parking tickets can be threatened to influence behavior in other realms. States employed deterrence policies before the invention of nuclear weapons, but nuclear weapons increased the importance of deterrence and spurred tremendous advances in deterrence theory.[1]

Deterrence can operate via two basic mechanisms. A state can threaten to inflict costs that exceed the benefits of taking action; this is termed deterrence by punishment. In the nuclear realm, this would involve threats to destroy targets that the adversary values. Alternatively, a state can threaten to deny a state the benefits it is hoping to achieve by taking action; this is termed deterrence by denial.[2] For example, to deter a conventional attack, a nuclear power could threaten a nuclear attack against the adversary's conventional forces. Such a strategy would aim to convince the adversary that its attempt to invade would fail and therefore that it would not acquire the territory it desired. What makes this a deterrent strategy is that the threatened attacks on the adversary's military forces are meant to convince the adversary that defeat would be extremely likely and it is therefore not in its interest to attack. If deterrence fails, then defense—that is, defeat of the adversary in battle—becomes necessary. All else being equal, deterrence is more likely to succeed when the punishment a state threatens is larger and when the state's ability to deny success is greater. Because nuclear weapons, especially thermonuclear weapons, are uniquely capable of inflicting damage on an extremely large scale in a short amount of time, the threat of nuclear attack can be a highly effective deterrent.

Whether a state's deterrent threat is successful depends on its credibility—that is, the adversary's assessment of the probability that the state will carry out its threat. All else being equal, the more credible a threat, the more likely that deterrence will succeed.

Credibility depends on two factors: a state's capability to carry out its threat and its willingness to carry it out. A state's willingness to carry out a threat depends, in turn, on the costs and risks of carrying out the threat. Carrying out a threat can be risky when the adversary has the ability to retaliate. Therefore, another factor affecting the credibility of a threat is how much the side making the deterrent threat values the interest it is protecting. When a state's interests are relatively small, it may decide that the risks of retaliation are unwarranted; recognizing this, the adversary will doubt the state's credibility—that is, the adversary will conclude that the probability that the state will carry out its threat is relatively low. The riskier it is to carry out a deterrent threat, the more the credibility of the threat depends on the stakes.

For this reason, deterring nuclear attacks against the U.S. homeland is generally believed to be easier than deterring attacks against U.S. allies, that is, extending deterrence. Extended deterrence is more difficult because U.S. interests in protecting its homeland are greater than its interests in protecting its allies. Consequently, an adversary might doubt that the United States would escalate to nuclear attacks in response to a conventional attack on an ally but have little doubt that the United States would escalate to nuclear attacks in response to a massive conventional attack against the U.S. homeland that the United States was unable to defeat. For the same reason, it can also be more difficult to deter smaller attacks even against highly valued stakes. For instance, it may be more difficult for the United States to credibly threaten nuclear use in response to nuclear attack against the U.S. homeland that did not result in massive losses.

Establishing sufficiently credible nuclear threats, especially for extending deterrence, was among the most difficult challenges the United States faced during much of the Cold War. The Soviet Union was believed to be the conventionally stronger power in Europe, and the United States saw nuclear weapons as a way to overcome this disadvantage. However, once the Soviet Union acquired nuclear weapons and the ability to attack the United States, the risks of attacking the Soviet Union with nuclear weapons became truly enormous, potentially totally catastrophic. The United States, therefore, searched for ways to make its threats to escalate to nuclear war credible despite the possibility that doing so could end up destroying the United States itself. Much of the Cold War debate focused on the requirements for extending deterrence to Europe.[3]

The challenge continues today, but in a somewhat different form. On one hand, the conventional military balance between the United States and China or Russia is much less uneven, and the United States is planning a robust conventional defense of its allies in Asia and Europe. Yet there are still scenarios in which the United States might be confronted with nuclear escalation in a regional war against either China or Russia, or a smaller nuclear power such as North Korea. In one, an adversary escalates by launching a limited nuclear attack in response to U.S. and allied success at the conventional level. The Russian invasion of Ukraine raises a similar possibility—once Ukrainian forces greatly slowed the Russian campaign, analysts worried that Russian President Putin might launch a limited nuclear attack and explored a variety of nuclear, as well as conventional, responses available to the United States and its NATO allies. The United States would then have to consider how to respond to such escalation. In a different scenario, the United States and its allies are losing in a conventional conflict. The United States would then find itself in a position similar to its Cold War position. In the case of Russia and China, which can attack the United States with large numbers of nuclear weapons, these scenarios raise the question whether U.S. nuclear escalation would be sufficiently credible to deter attacks on U.S. allies in the first place.[4]

Deterrence theory identifies a variety of approaches for increasing the credibility of U.S. nuclear threats. First, the United States could try to reduce the damage an adversary can inflict in all-out retaliation. If sufficiently effective, this "damage-limitation capability" should increase the credibility of U.S. nuclear threats because an all-out nuclear war would be less costly for the United States. However, throughout much of the Cold War the United States was unable to acquire a significant damage-limitation capability.[5] Beginning in the middle to late 1960s, Soviet forces became too large and survivable to preemptively destroy; the Soviet Union had an assured destruction capability—the ability to inflict society-destroying levels of damage against the United States following a full-scale U.S. attack against Soviet forces. There is currently debate about whether China will soon acquire an assured destruction capability and whether the United States can deny China this capability.[6]

A second approach is to develop a range of nuclear weapons response options, sometimes referred to as limited nuclear options. The threat of a limited nuclear attack could be more credible than the threat of an all-out attack because a limited attack could be less destructive for the target and thereby create incentives for it to keep its own retaliation limited. This could increase the deterrer's willingness to launch an attack, which would, in turn, increase the credibility of its threat. For states concerned about civilian casualties, environmental effects, and so forth, a limited attack could also be easier to imagine than an all-out attack. Recognizing this, the adversary should find the state's threat of a limited nuclear attack to be more credible. It is important to note that the logic of limited nuclear options and commensurate restraint applies even when the state lacks the ability to limit damage. The logic of limited options requires the attacker to believe that a limited nuclear war might not escalate to an all-out nuclear war. Whether this is possible has been the source of much debate.[7]

Beginning in the 1960s, U.S. declaratory policy began to incorporate the logic of limited nuclear options and their prominence increased as the Cold War continued. The United States also built options into its war plans, although for decades the plans may not have been as limited and flexible as U.S. leaders envisioned, as discussed by Frank Miller in chapter 3 of this volume.[8]

One type of limited nuclear option would be to attack the adversary's conventional forces. This threat of U.S. nuclear use could be more credible because the United States would be relying on nuclear weapons to prevent a costly military defeat. If such attacks can also be kept sufficiently limited to encourage the adversary to keep its own response limited, then nuclear threats against conventional forces may be more credible. However, it is important to note that the target of a limited attack may not see attacks on military forces as less costly than attacks on civilians. U.S. declaratory policy has held that some regimes may place very high value on their military forces. Thus it is possible that destroying these forces, while preserving the regime's ability to retaliate with nuclear weapons, could therefore make major retaliation more rather than less likely.

A third approach for increasing the credibility of U.S. threats is to integrate nuclear weapons with U.S. and allied conventional forces, deploying them with a range of military units on the front lines, delegating the authority to use these weapons to local commanders, and so forth. This can not only create the impression that conventional and nuclear war are somehow linked but can also create incentives for the local commanders to use nuclear weapons earlier in the war, before the weapons are destroyed or their ability to receive launch orders from U.S. leaders is severed. Even if the U.S. president did not delegate authority for the use of these weapons in advance, the prospect of losing the ability to communicate with soldiers on the front lines would increase incentives to delegate authority, which would increase the probability of accidental or unauthorized use, creating what Thomas Schelling famously terms a "threat that leaves something to chance."[9] The adversary's recognition of this path to nuclear escalation could contribute to deterrence.

A state's ability to deter a nuclear attack depends on its forces' ability to survive an adversary's attack.[10] If the state's forces were vulnerable, and therefore would not be available for retaliation, then its nuclear deterrent threat would lack credibility. Deterrence does not require that forces be perfectly survivable. Rather, enough nuclear weapons must be expected to survive that the state's retaliatory attack could inflict unacceptable damage. A state's nuclear command and control must also be sufficiently survivable under a range of scenarios that the state can launch its weapons even when its nuclear command and control is stressed or under attack. During the Cold War, the United States devoted tremendous effort to ensuring the survivability of its forces and nuclear command and control, and some of the most serious

concerns about the adequacy of U.S. nuclear forces were over their survivability. After the Cold War ended, concerns about the survivability of U.S.
forces diminished. As noted in chapter 1, however, advances in technology
may further increase the difficulty of maintaining adequately survivability
nuclear forces.

During the Cold War, the United States' and the Soviet Union's abilities
to deploy survivable nuclear forces capable of inflicting extremely high levels
of retaliatory damage created a condition that came to be known as mutual
assured destruction (MAD). An assured destruction capability was defined
by Secretary of Defense McNamara as the ability to destroy 20–25 percent
of the Soviet population and 50 percent of its industrial capability in a retaliatory attack.[11] When both countries possessed this capability, they were in
a situation of mutual assured destruction. To rephrase some of the preceding
discussion, the challenge of deterrence in MAD is to make sufficiently credible threats, given the adversary's ability to inflict assured destruction levels of
damage in retaliation.

Although often referred to as a strategy—in which a country's only nuclear
attack option is to launch its entire force at an adversary's cities—MAD is a
condition of very high mutual vulnerability, not a strategy. In MAD, a country could have a variety of strategies, include ones that target an adversary's
forces and leadership, and provide numerous limited nuclear options.

The theory of the nuclear revolution is a set of arguments about how the
military and political logic of MAD differs from that of the prenuclear world.[12]
According to the theory, difference in force size no longer matters, because
larger forces do not enable a state to inflict significantly greater damage and
therefore do not provide deterrent or coercive advantages. More precisely, large
forces could inflict greater damage, but this difference would not be politically
significant because even the smaller forces would be able to destroy the adversary as a functioning and organized state. Similarly, states had virtually no
reason to target opposing nuclear forces because the forces that would survive
an attack would be able to inflict essentially the same amount of damage as the
opposing force could before the attack: a state could not significantly limit the
damage its adversary could inflict, so targeting forces would make no sense.[13]

In MAD, in a crisis or limited war, the outcome would depend on the balance of states' interests, not the balance of forces (since the states would have
the ability to inflict the same amount of damage). States could use threats to
escalate to increase the probability of all-out war. The state that cares more
should be willing to run larger risks and therefore should do better in the

bargaining that defines crises and some limited wars. A crisis would be a pure "competition in risk taking."[14]

Because states usually care more about their own territory than others' territory, MAD and this competition in risk taking would favor the political status quo. Wars and even intense crises would become rare. Because building survivable nuclear forces would cost the major power less than the forces capable of destroying them, arms races would be greatly moderated. The major powers would settle into a world in which they essentially accepted MAD instead of trying to escape. The nuclear revolution would tame both territorial aggression and arms competition.[15]

Neither the United States nor the Soviet Union ever acted according to this logic. The United States continued to target Soviet nuclear forces. It devoted great effort to improving the ability of U.S. forces to destroy Soviet forces and worried a great deal about the Soviet ability to destroy U.S. forces, even though the U.S. assured destruction capability was robust.[16] During the latter half of the Cold War, official descriptions of U.S. nuclear doctrine offered a variety of reasons for targeting Soviet forces, including that Soviet leaders believed that the ratio of forces influences bargaining power, that Soviet leaders placed great inherent value on their nuclear forces and therefore the United States needed to threaten them, and that credible limited nuclear options needed to be targeted against Soviet forces. Critics challenged all these arguments and offered arguments from organizational and bureaucratic politics to explain what they regarded as the illogic of U.S. nuclear policy.[17]

More recently, scholars have developed a different set of arguments that question the nuclear revolution. One strand holds that maintaining an assured destruction capability is more difficult than was widely believed during the Cold War and that the United States came closer to undermining the Soviet assured destruction capability than was known at the time.[18] A complementary strand argues that simply creating the possibility of undermining an adversary's assured destruction capability can provide bargaining advantages. Consequently, there are political advantages to targeting the adversary's forces even if a damage-limitation capability remains out of reach.[19] Arguments that technological advances are increasing states' abilities to target nuclear forces add yet another dimension to the challenges to the logic of the nuclear revolution: even if MAD was robust in the past, it may not be in the future.[20] Analysis and debate over the coming competition between retaliatory and damage-limitation capabilities, and the implications for nuclear strategy, will play out over the coming decades.

Basic Overview of U.S. Nuclear Forces and Their Survivability

ICBMs, SLBMs, and Aircraft

The United States is said to have a nuclear "triad" because it can deliver nuclear weapons using three different types of delivery systems operating in different physical domains: intercontinental ballistic missiles, submarines, and airplanes.

Intercontinental ballistic missiles (ICBMs) are based in the continental United States and arrive at their targets by flying through space on a largely predictable, ballistic flight path. The United States deploys 400 Minuteman III ICBMs; each currently carries one warhead, although they are capable of carrying up to three warheads.[21] The United States plans to replace the Minuteman III with the Ground-based Strategic Deterrent, a new ICBM that will be deployed in existing Minuteman silos beginning in 2029.[22] Although the Air Force bases that exert administrative control over the ICBM force are located in three states (Montana, North Dakota, and Wyoming), the missiles themselves are dispersed across large areas of rural Colorado, Montana, Nebraska, North Dakota, and Wyoming. Crews work in the missile-launch control centers at all times. The underground launch control center is a hardened facility in which ICBM crews supervise the roughly ten missiles under their command and monitor communications channels for orders from higher authority.

Submarine-launched ballistic missiles are deployed on nuclear ballistic submarines (SSBNs) and, like ICBMs, fly on a ballistic flight path. The United States' fourteen nuclear-armed ballistic missile submarines operate from two home ports—Naval Base Kitsap-Bangor in Washington state, and Naval Base Kings Bay in Georgia.[23] Each could originally carry up to twenty-four submarine-launched ballistic missiles. To comply with New START (the New Strategic Arms Reduction Treaty), each submarine has had four of its missile tubes converted, making them incapable of launching a missile, and so now carries a maximum of twenty missiles.[24] Nuclear ballistic submarines are equipped with the Trident D-5 missile, which can carry multiple warheads.[25] Submarine-launched ballistic missiles can be launched from patrol areas that span vast swathes of ocean. Unlike ICBMs, which are based in silos that are easily observable in commercial satellite imagery, U.S. nuclear-armed submarines operate stealthily in the ocean and are therefore considered the most survivable element of the U.S. nuclear triad.[26] The United States is developing a new nuclear-powered submarine, termed the *Columbia*-class, to replace the current generation *Ohio*-class SSBNs. The United States plans to build at least twelve *Columbia*-class boats.[27]

Finally, the United States can deploy nuclear weapons on aircraft, including long-range bomber aircraft—the B-52H and B-2A—and shorter-range fighter aircraft. The B-52H is certified only to deliver nuclear-armed air-launched cruise missiles—the AGM-86B. In the future, it will also deliver the Long-Range Stand Off (LRSO) air-launched cruise missile. The B-2, which is a stealth bomber—meaning that it is designed to be difficult to detect with radar—is certified to deliver nuclear gravity bombs, namely the B83 and variants of the B61 gravity bomb. A replacement stealth bomber (designated the B-21) is under development.[28] Because the B-52 can carry air-launched cruise missiles, which can fly over a thousand miles on their own, these bombers do not need to penetrate enemy air defenses.[29] U.S. nuclear bomber aircraft are based at three locations in the continental United States—Whiteman Air Force Base, in Missouri, is the home of the B-2A, while B-52Hs operate out of Minot Air Force Base, in North Dakota, and Barksdale Air Force Base, in Louisiana—but are periodically rotated to other bases in the United States. These aircraft also conduct conventional strike missions and therefore may be flown to locations abroad, although without nuclear weapons.[30] To carry out a round-trip strike mission on targets in Eurasia from the United States, bomber aircraft rely on in-flight refueling tankers based at various locations in the United States and elsewhere. The U.S. tanker fleet is undergoing a transition to the KC-46 *Pegasus*.[31]

The United States also maintains a fleet of F-15 *Strike Eagle* aircraft capable of delivering B61-3/4/10 nuclear bombs. Eventually, the B61-12 gravity bomb will replace earlier versions of the B61.[32] In addition, under the NATO "nuclear sharing" arrangement, several non-U.S. air forces are able to deliver U.S. nuclear weapons with dual-capable aircraft (DCA).[33] The United States also has the ability to forward-deploy DCA and nuclear weapons to other regions.[34] The president stipulates the quantities and locations of forward-deployed U.S. nuclear weapons in a classified Nuclear Weapons Deployment Authorization directive.[35] The authority to both deploy and employ these weapons rests with the president.

The present U.S. nuclear posture is significantly simpler than it was during the Cold War, when the United States had shorter-range missiles and artillery for use in land warfare and multiple kinds of nuclear weapons for naval warfare. Until 1991, the United States also deployed sea-launched nuclear cruise missiles; those weapons were formally retired following the 2010 Nuclear Posture Review.[36]

Ensuring the Survivability of U.S. Forces

U.S. nuclear forces are designed, in part, to ensure that the United States retains the ability to retaliate massively to any large-scale first strike on its nuclear forces and home territory. This is to convince any nuclear-armed adversary that it could not carry out a large-scale first strike that would significantly reduce the U.S. ability to inflict damage in retaliation.

The survivability of U.S. ICBMs depends heavily on the capabilities of the state that might attack them. If an adversary's nuclear forces are small compared with the size of the U.S. ICBM arsenal, U.S. ICBMs will be highly survivable simply because the number of U.S. targets is too large to be covered by the adversary's warheads. This is the case today with China; however, the U.S. government estimates that China is significantly expanding the size of its arsenal.[37] An adversary with larger nuclear forces, which are also highly accurate, poses a much larger threat to U.S. ICBMs. This is the case today with Russia, and it might soon be with China.[38]

There are several ways to increase the survivability of ICBMs. They can be deployed in hardened underground silos, which then requires an adversary to use more accurate or larger warheads (or both), as well as possibly more warheads, to destroy them with high probability. They can be made mobile and, thereby, harder to find and target, which then requires the adversary to barrage the entire area in which the missiles are deployed. They can be hidden in above-ground shelters or tunnels. And they can be launched on warning of an adversary attack, thereby leaving before enemy weapons arrive.[39]

The United States, Russia, and China deploy ICBMs in hardened underground silos. Unlike Russia and China, however, the U.S. does not deploy mobile land-based missiles.[40] Each U.S. ICBM is located several miles away from other missiles and from the underground command post that controls the missile (the Minuteman III launch control center).[41] These silos and launch control centers are hardened to withstand significant attacks. However, a large attack of highly accurate nuclear weapons could destroy a large percentage of Minuteman ICBM silos. This attack would likely require targeting two nuclear weapons on each missile silo and therefore require about 800 warheads. Only Russia currently has sufficiently accurate nuclear missiles and a sufficiently large number of strategic warheads to launch this type of attack.

Deterrence is another important, though indirect, contributor to ICBM survivability. An adversary may be technically capable of destroying ICBMs, but dissuaded from doing so if an attack is unlikely to translate into a military advantage. For instance, arms control agreements that limit the numbers of deployed warheads can raise the strategic and military costs of attacks on ICBMs. By capping the numbers of U.S.- and Russian-deployed intercontinental-range warheads, the 1991 Strategic Arms Reduction Treaty (START) and follow-on agreements created a situation in which attacks on ICBMs could require a significant number of the attacker's deployed warheads, especially if each ICBM is only equipped with one warhead, as is the U.S. Minuteman III missile. The attacker might be unwilling to pay this military price.

An adversary contemplating an attack on U.S. ICBMs may also be deterred by the greater political ramifications of a large-scale nuclear attack on the American heartland. Whereas an attack on a U.S. ballistic missile submarine would imperil a single vessel and its crew, an attack on U.S. ICBMs could spread fallout over much of the Midwest and, depending on the prevailing winds, could reach the densely populated mid-Atlantic states as well.[42] While U.S. ICBMs might not survive such an attack, the consequences would almost certainly alter the terms of debate over whether and how the United States would respond to such an attack.

One often-discussed approach to ICBM survivability is to launch on warning or launch under attack. Except for those undergoing maintenance, Minuteman III ICBMs are on twenty-four-hour alert. All Minuteman III missiles on alert in the U.S. arsenal are ready to launch promptly after receipt of a valid launch order. These weapons are said to be on "alert" because they can be launched on such notice. "Launch on warning" typically refers to the launch of nuclear weapons after indication has been received that an adversary has launched an attack. "Launch under attack" typically refers to a launch that takes place after indication has been received that nuclear weapons have denoted on U.S. soil.[43] In the 1970s and 1980s, launch on warning took on greater significance in the public debate on U.S. nuclear policy because the Soviet threat to the U.S. ICBM force was growing significantly. As the Minuteman force became more vulnerable to high-yield and increasingly accurate Soviet warheads, U.S. government and civil-society experts began debating whether a launch-on-warning policy was feasible and desirable.[44] Today, critics of ICBMs argue that the vulnerability of U.S. ICBMs increases the risk that a future president would prematurely launch ICBMs when confronted with tactical warning of an attack (whether real or mistaken).[45]

The actual role of launch under attack and launch on warning in U.S. policy is more complicated. The United States arguably had something resembling a policy of launch on (strategic) warning in the early days of the Cold War, when political and military leaders largely expected to launch nuclear-armed bombers at the Soviet Union once they could confirm that a Soviet attack on Europe was underway.[46] In the early 1960s, U.S. experts contemplated a launch-on-warning policy, but the United States was not able to detect when a Soviet attack against U.S. territory had begun.[47] It was only in the late 1970s that the United States had the capability to detect a Soviet attack in progress and had reason to worry that U.S. ICBMs were vulnerable to a Soviet first strike. This led Carter administration officials to call for the development of plans to launch ICBMs after an attack had been confirmed to be in progress, ideally by the detection of nuclear detonations on U.S. territory.[48]

However, the Carter administration also sought to ensure that the survivability of U.S. forces did not depend on this option.[49] In 1981 the Reagan administration affirmed this guidance, codifying that U.S. policy was not to rely on launch on warning to preserve a second-strike retaliatory capability.[50] Subsequent administrations have reaffirmed that U.S. policy is to ensure a second-strike capability through means other than launch on warning, such as through continuous submarine patrols.[51] In 2013 the Obama administration pledged to reexamine and further reduce the role of launch under attack in contingency-planning scenarios. However, the Obama administration committed to maintaining a launch-under-attack capability.[52] The president retains the option of launching ICBMs if an attack is confirmed based on data from multiple warning systems.[53]

There are two basic approaches for enabling SSBNs to survive: quieting— that is, decreasing the noise emitted by an SSBN to reduce the opponent's ability to find it with devices that collect underwater sounds; and bastion deployment—that is, operating SSBNs in an area that is relatively easy for the state to defend and in which it is relatively difficult for the opposing state to operate anti-submarine warfare forces.

U.S. SSBNs rely primarily on quieting to avoid detection by would-be attackers. Current and planned U.S. nuclear ballistic missile submarines employ a variety of technologies and operating practices to ensure that they are not detectable by sonar and other anti-submarine warfare tools. In port, SSBNs are dockside and visible to overhead imagery, and are thus vulnerable. SSBNs can also be vulnerable when they are underway from their ports to the open ocean. As a result, the United States employs a variety of methods to protect submarines in transit from port. Unlike the United States, during much of the Cold War the Soviet Union used, and Russia now uses, a bastion strategy.[54] China is reported to be considering a bastion strategy for its new and increasingly capable SSBN force.[55]

U.S. *Ohio*-class SSBNs operate on a roughly 224-day cycle, remaining out on patrol for about 77 days before returning for a 35-day maintenance period, after which a second crew undertakes a second patrol followed by another maintenance period.[56] A submarine patrol typically involves remaining submerged and undetected in open ocean for long periods of time, awaiting instructions from higher authority. Each boat has two crews, known as the blue and gold crews. During the maintenance cycle, the crew turns over, and the boat receives any needed repairs. In addition, each submarine undergoes an extensive period of refueling and overhaul—roughly every twenty years, in the case of the current-generation *Ohio*-class boats.[57]

Because some SSBNs are in port undergoing repair, only a fraction of the entire submarine fleet is at sea at any given moment. Of those, some are likely to be transiting to different patrol locations. The remaining boats (approximately four or five) are likely to be on station, meaning that they are in position to attack a particular adversary and can therefore execute a launch order promptly.[58] Although any U.S. ballistic missile submarine can launch its missiles after receiving a valid launch, some submarines' patrol routes may take the boats to locations from which they would be unable to strike a particular target. A submarine patrolling deep in the South Pacific would have a hard time striking Europe, for example. Because the Trident D-5 missile has a maximum range of approximately 4,000 nautical miles, the areas in which the boat could patrol while remaining in range of its targets are potentially quite large.[59]

The survivability of aircraft depends first on their ground basing and second on their ability to avoid detection and interception in flight. Unless protected by air defenses or hardened shelters, all aircraft are vulnerable to attack when on the ground. Thus ensuring the survival of aircraft from attack requires that they take off before they can be destroyed. During the Cold War, the United States ensured the survivability of its bomber aircraft by maintaining a portion at high readiness—that is, on "strip alert" on the ground.[60] This allowed for the aircraft to take off on short notice and find greater safety in the air over friendly or neutral territory. From 1960 to 1968, a portion of U.S. nuclear bombers also flew continuous airborne alerts, taking off with nuclear weapons and flying predetermined routes to await further orders. This practice was known as a positive control launch, in reference to the fact that the aircraft were instructed to wait in designated areas for a positive launch order from a higher authority. After the airborne alert ended in 1968, some Strategic Air Command (SAC) commanders retained the authority to order a positive control launch of aircraft on ground alert to protect against a potential short-notice attack.[61]

With the end of the Cold War, the United States ended its bomber ground alert in 1991.[62] On a day-to-day basis, U.S. bombers are now not armed with nuclear weapons. Rather, weapons are kept at secure storage sites. The low peacetime readiness of the bomber force requires the force to be generated—that is, have its alert status raised—before it can employ nuclear weapons. Nuclear weapons would then be moved out of storage and loaded onto bomber aircraft. Generating the bomber force requires a decision by the president, the secretary of defense, or a military commander with the authority to do so. Aircraft would then be loaded with nuclear weapons and may travel to preassigned staging areas. The process of loading nuclear weapons onto aircraft is likely to take some time and may be visible to satellites passing overhead.

Because the bomber force is not currently generated on a day-to-day basis, U.S. bombers are more vulnerable in peacetime than they were during the Cold War. In theory, a large surprise attack on the three bomber bases could destroy almost all of the U.S. nuclear-capable long-range aircraft. In a crisis, however, the United States could generate its bomber force to reduce the time between an order to attack and the start of the attack. The low readiness of U.S. bombers reflects the judgment of the U.S. leadership that a surprise attack on homeland bomber bases is much less likely than it was during the Cold War and that U.S. SSBNs and ICBMs provide a large survivable force even under the most challenging conditions.

Once airborne, aircraft are potentially vulnerable to attack by intercepting fighter aircraft and integrated air defenses. As a result, the United States has adopted stealth technology for some of its aircraft to increase the chances that these aircraft will avoid detection by air defense radar. The B-2 employs stealth technology, as does the F-35 fighter, which will receive nuclear certification by 2023. In contrast, the B-52 and U.S. fourth-generation fighters (the F-15 and F-16) are not stealthy. In its nuclear role, the B-52 is armed with air-launched cruise missiles that enable it to carry out nuclear strike missions from beyond the range of enemy air defenses.

Current-generation air-launched cruise missiles (ALCMs) rely on their small size and low-altitude flight capability to evade air defenses.[63] The United States has limited ability to defend targets against cruise missiles. The U.S.

Ground-based Midcourse Defense (GMD) is designed to engage targets in the midcourse phases of ballistic flight and therefore could not be used against cruise missiles flying at lower altitudes. However, other U.S. air and missile defense systems could defend localized targets against cruise missiles.[64] According to some reports, potential U.S. adversaries are pursuing the capability to defend against cruise missiles, including current-generation ALCMs.[65]

In addition to their individual ability to survive attack, the U.S. ICBMs and bombers influence each other's survivability because an attack against one of these legs of the triad would provide information that increased the survivability of the other. The flight time of an adversary's ICBM attack against U.S. ICBMs would provide warning that increased the time available to the United States for getting its bombers into the air. Conversely, if an adversary first attacked U.S. bombers with a short-warning attack from submarines near the U.S. coast, the United States would have time to launch its ICBMs after the confirmation of these attacks on U.S. soil. Thus it is important to analyze the survivability of these legs not only independent of each other but also jointly.

Finally, U.S. nuclear weapons storage sites based in the United States and Europe rely on a range of security measures, including hardening, to protect weapons from attempted destruction. Weapons Storage Areas (WSA) are facilities, like munitions storage igloos, in which weapons can be stored safely and securely. Weapons Storage Vaults (WSV) are incorporated into hardened aircraft shelters. The weapons themselves are stored underground, and the buried structure is covered with a hardened lid.[66] These facilities are also protected by extensive security measures. The locations of these facilities are not disclosed to the public, but their purported locations are widely discussed in the media. It is also likely that Russian military intelligence is aware of the locations of these sites. These facilities are therefore vulnerable to attack by Russia, especially by a nuclear or conventional weapons attack designed to destroy the vaults or their systems for raising nuclear bombs to ground level. Soviet military plans may have included attacks on these storage areas in the early stages of a major war in Europe.[67] Preemptive attacks on nuclear weapons storage sites may also feature in contemporary Russian military plans.

Nuclear Command and Control

To support the use (and nonuse) of its nuclear weapons, the United States, like all major nuclear powers, has developed an elaborate command-and-control system [68] In the broadest terms, a nuclear command-and-control system serves as the link between decisionmakers and those who execute those decisions. To issue effective threats, decisionmakers must be able to follow through on the threats they make, while also promising that they will act with restraint if the adversary chooses to be deterred. With reliable command and control, decisionmakers can be confident that the orders they give will be carried out and that allies and adversaries will know this. In addition to supporting the credibility of deterrent threats, a robust nuclear command-and-control system contributes to preventing accidental and inadvertent escalation, ensuring civilian control over nuclear weapons, and supporting the termination of hostilities, including nuclear hostilities.

In practice, a command-and-control system involves a series of formal hierarchical relationships between individuals and organizations; procedures guiding the behavior of these different components; and technologies that allow individuals and organizations to carry out these procedures efficiently and reliably. These basic elements are reflected in the requirements assigned to the U.S. nuclear command-and-control system, as described in Defense Department publications:

- attack detection, warning, and characterization: identifying an attack in progress, characterizing its likely impacts, and providing warning time to decisionmakers
- nuclear planning: supporting the development of nuclear response options
- decisionmaking: allowing for the presidential-level assessment, review, and consultation that occurs to decide on courses of action involving nuclear forces
- force direction: enabling the secure transmission of orders from the president and national authorities to relevant personnel
- force management: providing the capabilities to ascertain and direct the status, movement, and operations of nuclear forces[69]

The personnel involved in executing presidential orders range from the highest level, the president, to the personnel serving in command posts, ICBM control launch centers, submarines, and bomber aircraft. These personnel are supported by a mix of facilities and technologies, including warning systems, such as space- and land-based radars; communications systems, such as communications satellites, radio networks, and landlines; and a series of primary and secure alternate command posts, which are connected to the broader command-and-control system. Chapter 7 describes the U.S. nuclear command-and-control system and explains how it supports these functions.

Authority, Delegation, and the Always/Never Dilemma

Almost every country that has developed nuclear weapons has publicly declared that authority to use these weapons rests with the national leadership.[70] The United States is no exception. In the United States, the president has the sole authority to order the use of nuclear weapons. The trappings of this authority—special briefcases, heightened security, institutionalized lines of succession, exquisite communications—serve to highlight both the gravity associated with the decision to use nuclear weapons and the importance of ensuring that the president is able to give orders under a wide range of conditions.

At the same time, the challenges of operating nuclear arsenals under a range of situations—from peacetime to nuclear war—create incentives to delegate some degree of authority and control to others. One danger is that a surprise attack or attacks during an ongoing conflict could sever reliable communication between the president, top military officials, and military personnel responsible for launching nuclear attacks. In a system in which only the president could order the use of nuclear weapons, such an attack would cripple the U.S. ability to retaliate, potentially encouraging aggression. An adversary might intentionally exploit this weakness by attacking the U.S. president and the constitutionally delegated successors, hoping to decapitate the United States. Military requirements for rapid response also create some incentives to delegate authority. If targets need to be struck quickly, waiting for a decision from the president may take up valuable time. In a very different scenario, fighting in a conventional war could sever communication to field commanders, leaving them unable to use the nuclear weapons under their control. Delegating launch authority to political and military leaders, and even to nuclear operators, could reduce or even eliminate these command vulnerabilities.

But this "solution" could involve high costs. Most consequentially, delegation increases the probability that nuclear weapons will be used. A commander or operator with delegated authority may judge that the conditions warrant nuclear use when the president would have concluded otherwise. Another possibility is accidental or unintentional use. For instance, a nuclear weapons operator may misinterpret a garbled radio message as a use order when no such order was issued. Personnel operating in the fog of war might also misinterpret non-nuclear attacks or even an accidental detonation as the start of a nuclear attack and respond with nuclear attacks of their own. The more people have the physical ability to use nuclear weapons, the greater the risk that mishaps, misunderstandings, and mishandling of nuclear weapons could arise that culminate in a nuclear detonation. For national leaders, there might also be a psychological cost to giving up some of the solemn authority involved in decisions about nuclear use. Leaders may be instinctually reluctant to leave such important decisions to subordinates, whether junior military personnel or even relatively senior and trusted advisers.

This trade-off between ensuring that nuclear weapons will always function when ordered but also that they will never be used or explode when not ordered is sometimes termed the always/never dilemma, and it is central to understanding nuclear operations. Others capture this trade-off by distinguishing between positive and negative control.[71] Ideally, decisionmakers would prefer that any actions involving nuclear weapons always reflect leaders' preferences and never otherwise. The dilemma arises because various elements of the command-and-control system could be too inflexible or vulnerable to meet these two requirements simultaneously. This generates the requirement for delegation, which, in turn, places these two goals in tension.

During the Cold War, U.S. presidents conditionally delegated the authority to initiate nuclear use to military commanders. Declassified records confirm that Presidents Eisenhower, Kennedy, and Johnson authorized a series of standing orders granting select military commanders the authority to use nuclear weapons under certain conditions.[72]

There were two principal rationales for such orders. The first was the need to make credible the U.S. pledge to use tactical nuclear weapons to defend against a Soviet land attack on Europe. Although NATO policy was to defend against such an attack with conventional forces, the size and strength of the Soviet military made such a defense difficult. NATO forces might therefore be forced to use tactical nuclear weapons before the president could issue a use authorization to the U.S. general in charge. Adding to the challenge of rapidly communicating presidential orders was the fact that the U.S. nuclear command, control, and communications system was extremely vulnerable to surprise attack in the late 1950s and early 1960s. One influential assessment of the system undertaken in 1959–1960 expressed "little confidence [in the event of a Soviet surprise attack] . . . that the Presidential decision would be made and military execution orders be received by the combat elements of the strategic nuclear forces before the high command is disrupted."[73] Perhaps with the vulnerability of communications in mind, the Eisenhower orders stressed that retaliation for a Soviet attack could only be authorized by the president unless "immediate communications have become impossible between the president and responsible officials."[74]

The historical record also reveals that these decisions were by no means taken lightly. Eisenhower agonized over whether to pre-delegate authority, and he personally drafted the language that formed the basis for the orders that persisted into the Johnson administration. Eisenhower's advisers were also aware of the political and military risks of pre-delegation.[75] Kennedy administration officials echoed these concerns. Secretary McNamara was especially concerned with the U.S. ability to ensure command and control over tactical nuclear weapons in Europe.[76]

The Kennedy administration appears to have renewed the Eisenhower orders "almost verbatim," however. These orders were not reviewed again until 1968. President Johnson also seems to have grappled with the complexities and risks of pre-delegated authority. Asked about pre-delegation during a campaign rally in 1964, Johnson stated that he alone exercised control over nuclear use, prompting his national security adviser to explain that Johnson had, in fact, reauthorized the Eisenhower pre-delegation orders earlier that year.[77] When the Johnson administration reviewed the pre-delegation orders in 1968, all of the administration officials expressed discomfort with the risks of pre-delegation but judged that some contingency plans were necessary "in the event the President has been killed or cannot be found . . . to prevent a breakdown in the chain of command."[78] Johnson opted to make the orders more restrictive but did not abandon pre-delegation entirely.

Such concerns about decapitation—the potential for national leaders to lose contact with nuclear forces—are not unique to the United States. The United Kingdom has a long-standing policy of the prime minister issuing a "letter of last resort," which instructs the captains of U.K. ballistic missile submarines on what to do if it appears, based on certain conditions, as if the British government has been destroyed.[79] The Soviets built a semi-autonomous system to issue nuclear launch orders to achieve the same effect—ensuring retaliation despite decapitation.[80]

While working to ensure the ability to retaliate, the United States has also taken seriously the risks of unauthorized use. Beginning in the mid-1960s, for instance, the United States began strengthening the security of its Europe-based forces and adopting stronger barriers to accidental or unauthorized use.[81] By the 1980s, most U.S. nuclear forces, except submarine-launched ballistic missiles, appear to have been equipped with coded-use control devices.[82] Changes in alert posture and other operational practices also reflected a growing appreciation of the risks of accidents and unauthorized use. For instance, airborne alerts of B-52 aircraft ended in 1968 after a series of accidents involving nuclear weapons.[83]

Although improvements in communications and nuclear weapons technology have made it easier to safeguard weapons without significant barriers to responsiveness, the always/never dilemma continues to lurk in the background of decisions about U.S. nuclear posture. For other countries, especially less technologically sophisticated nuclear powers, such dilemmas may be even more acute.

U.S. Nuclear Doctrine and Targeting

The United States assigns a variety of different strategic purposes to its nuclear weapons. Most important, it relies on nuclear weapons for deterrence of a range of attacks and also the undermining of coercive threats. The United States also includes a role for damage limitation—reducing the costs the adversary can inflict in an all-out attack—that, in addition to being valuable on its own, could contribute to the effectiveness of the U.S. deterrence threats by increasing their credibility. Finally, the United States relies on nuclear weapons for assurance, providing its allies with confidence that the United States can provide them with a high level of security.[84]

In the broadest terms, U.S. nuclear weapons have long had three basic deterrence functions: to deter nuclear attacks on U.S. territory and U.S. military forces; to deter nuclear attacks against U.S. allies; and to deter major non-nuclear attacks on U.S. territory, forces, and allies. The United States retains a degree of ambiguity about what falls into the category of major non-nuclear attacks. In addition to major conventional attacks, the United States has kept open the possibility of using nuclear weapons in response to attacks involving chemical or biological weapons.[85] Major cyberattacks could also fall into this category. These roles have been made explicit in some cases, such as in the U.S. nuclear commitments to NATO, Japan, and South Korea. In addition, in the post–Cold War era, the United States has endeavored to limit the role of nuclear weapons in deterring non-nuclear attacks. The United States pledged in 2010 and again in 2018 that it "will not use or threaten to use nuclear weapons against non-nuclear weapons states that are party to the NPT and in compliance with their nuclear non-proliferation obligations." These pledges echo other so-called "negative security assurances" made in the post–Cold War era.[86]

U.S. nuclear forces serve different roles in peacetime, crisis, and wartime. U.S. nuclear forces (and dual-capable forces) may be called on to undertake operations to send signals to key allies as well as adversaries. These missions sometimes take place in peacetime and can involve bomber deployments to overseas bases as well as flights over allied territory or other key areas.[87] Signaling operations could also take the form of exercises, potentially undertaken in tandem with U.S. allies. The point of these operations is to demonstrate that the United States has the capability to operate in particular areas with particular forces.

Such demonstrations could also take place in crises, in which case the purpose would be to send costly signals that indicate the extent of the U.S. interests involved and of the risks the United States is willing to run. However, conducting such operations in crises also risks sending the wrong signal. For example, an adversary might mistakenly conclude that a U.S. attack was imminent and increase the alert status of its forces, which could inadvertently create incentives for the United States to attack.

At all stages and intensities of conflict, including in peacetime, U.S. nuclear forces are designed to deter surprise attacks, especially surprise attacks on U.S. nuclear forces.[88] During the Cold War era, the potential for a surprise nuclear attack was a frequent preoccupation of U.S. leaders and military planners. Today, this possibility seems more remote. However, some analysts continue to maintain that the ability to deter a "bolt out of the blue" attack is an important element of strategic stability.[89]

In crises, U.S. nuclear weapons are expected to contribute to deterring a major conventional war, as well as deterring adversaries from launching nuclear attacks and attempting nuclear coercion. To deter a conventional attack in Europe, especially during the Cold War but also today, the United States threatened to escalate a major conventional war to a nuclear war; its doctrine includes the possibility of using nuclear weapons first. Experts and policymakers have for decades debated the possibility of shifting to a policy of "no first use" or "sole use," which would rule out a role for nuclear weapons in deterring conventional war. Even if the United States adopted this change, an adversary likely could not be confident that the United States would not escalate, so its nuclear weapons would likely retain some of their ability to contribute to deterrence of conventional war. In addition, U.S. nuclear forces are also expected to deter adversaries from attempting to leverage their own nuclear forces for coercive advantage. U.S. adversaries could attempt nuclear coercion by nuclear saber rattling, staging nuclear exercises or weapons tests meant to highlight the possibility of nuclear use, or threatening to escalate directly to limited nuclear war. U.S. nuclear forces could contribute to deterring or offsetting these coercive attempts by responding or threatening to respond in kind.

If hostilities were to escalate to the level of major conventional war, U.S. nuclear forces would be expected to continue to deter adversary nuclear coercion, limited nuclear use, and larger-scale nuclear attacks. The United States attempts to deter limited nuclear use through the threat of limited or larger-scale nuclear retaliation, depending on the U.S. assessment of what kind of nuclear response would most likely prevent further escalation and contribute to war termination. Limited nuclear attacks could be performed by nuclear weapons deployed in the theater of conflict. For example, during the Cold War, the United States deployed thousands of nuclear weapons in Europe to deter a Soviet invasion. Some U.S. nuclear weapons remain in Europe today.[90] U.S. strategic nuclear forces—bombers or missiles—could also carry out limited strikes. U.S. nuclear weapons might also contribute to deterrence via a less deliberate threat, if adversaries appreciate that a conventional conflict could trigger an interactive process that neither side could fully control nor fully understand but that could escalate to nuclear war.[91]

The flexibility provided by limited nuclear options is a central pillar of U.S. nuclear strategy.[92] Since the Kennedy administration, U.S. presidents have sought a range of nuclear employment options so that they would not be forced into a choice of either ordering an all-out cataclysmic retaliatory nuclear attack or accepting that a nuclear attack would go unanswered. This interest in flexibility led to the development of a range of weapons types and the command-and-control capabilities to support more limited or discriminate nuclear operations.[93]

The United States has also developed limited nuclear options because different adversaries may be deterred by different kinds of threats. This has been an especially salient concern of U.S. strategists during the post–Cold War era with the rise of multiple nuclear-armed challengers, which has driven U.S. efforts to "tailor" deterrence to different adversaries.[94] Perhaps all decisionmakers can be deterred from launching a massive nuclear attack by the certainty that such action will result in a civilization-ending nuclear exchange. Below the purely existential level, however, there is likely to be some variation in what decisionmakers value and their tolerance for punishment. Some national leaders may be especially insensitive to large attacks on civilian population centers if they themselves can survive such attacks; whether or not this is actually the case, U.S. planning has taken this possibility into account. Individual leaders may also vary in their optimism about their ability to profit from aggression, necessitating that U.S. deterrent threats take different forms. The entire debate in the strategy literature about the merits of deterrence by denial compared with deterrence by punishment reflects the inherent difficulty of anticipating what will influence individuals in novel scenarios[95]—hence the U.S. desire to retain a range of nuclear employment options and the impetus to develop plans and capabilities that reflect the United States' best estimate of what will deter particular adversaries.

This emphasis on flexibility is an enduring theme in U.S. nuclear policy, although as Janne Nolan eloquently documents in a series of works, realizing this ambition has been a fraught process spanning many years.[96] Today, as discussed by Michael S. Elliott, in chapter 5 of this volume, adaptive planning is a core element of U.S. nuclear operational planning.

Most important in a major war, U.S. nuclear forces would attempt to deter large-scale nuclear attack. To accomplish this, the United States threatens to destroy targets that the adversary values most, which could include targets that would allow the adversary to enjoy the benefits of aggression in a postwar world, such as the instruments of political and military control.

What kinds of targets might be struck if the United States ordered an all-out retaliatory attack on an adversary? Although current U.S. war plans are highly classified, the United States has released some information about what might or might not be targeted in a U.S. nuclear strike campaign. In 2013 the Obama administration released the results of a review of U.S. nuclear employment options. Along with this announcement, the administration announced that it had directed military planners to ensure that nuclear employment plans comported with the international law of armed conflict, which requires that the use of force be necessary, proportionate, and discriminate. Nuclear strike plans were directed to "apply the principles of distinction and proportionality and seek to minimize collateral damage to civilian populations and civilian objects."[97] The guidance also added that the United States would not intentionally target civilian populations, purely civilian cultural and religious sites, and so forth. At the same time, the Obama administration's guidance required that the United States "maintain significant counterforce capabilities against potential adversaries."[98]

Previous reviews of U.S. nuclear targeting policy concluded that the United States should think about targeting in terms of affecting an adversary's escalation calculus at multiple stages of a conflict. Past studies concluded that the United States should have the ability to target hardened underground command and control sites, adversary nuclear weapons, and adversary nonnuclear military forces, including those that could be dispersed early in a conflict. Some of these targeting categories may persist in current U.S. plans.[99]

Of course, the exact targets that would be struck depend on U.S. assessments of which targets need to be destroyed to accomplish deterrence or wartime objectives. The composition of a U.S. nuclear employment campaign could also depend on the events leading up to the attack. For instance, it would not make much sense to strike adversary missile silos if those missiles had already been launched. It would also not make much sense to directly target adversary leadership protection sites if the United States still held out hope of negotiating a peace with the leaders in those bunkers. On the other hand, it might make sense to strike any remaining adversary nuclear weapons (even after an adversary strike), especially if adversary leaders placed high value on those weapons, if such an attack could reduce further damage to the United States, or if striking those targets would contribute to a favorable post-war balance of power.

Some Cold War–era nuclear war plans also included an additional category: major industrial centers and war-supporting economic and industrial targets.[100] It is unclear whether these types of targets are still included in U.S. war plans. On the one hand, major industrial sites might be a source of significant financial and military benefit for adversary leaders. On the other hand, they tend to be located near urban areas, may produce civilian goods, and may involve large numbers of civilians. It is possible that at least some war-supporting industrial targets remain in today's war plans. However, in the 1970s nuclear strategists and planners began to focus on a "victory-denial" approach, which emphasized targets that adversary leaders saw as valuable for prosecuting aggression and enjoying its benefits. Notably, in the late-1970s, with respect to the Soviet Union, U.S. officials questioned whether "threatening to impede [Soviet economic] recovery by destroying large amounts of Soviet population and industry is the most effective deterrent."[101]

Beyond deterrence, but also potentially complementing it, U.S. policy includes a role for damage limitation—reducing the damage an adversary can inflict in an all-out attack.[102] A damage-limitation attack attempts to destroy the adversary's weapons before they are launched and its nuclear command-and-control systems before launch orders can be communicated to its nuclear forces.[103] The United States might decide to launch such a damage-limitation attack because it had sufficiently credible warning that an adversary was planning to launch a large nuclear attack against the United States or an ally. It might also launch a damage-limitation attack once an adversary has launched a limited nuclear attack and was reserving other nuclear weapons for possible use later in the war.

A damage-limitation capability could enhance U.S. deterrent capabilities by increasing the credibility of U.S. threats to use nuclear weapons. Because the United States would suffer less damage than its adversary in an all-out war, the risks of taking escalatory actions, including employing limited nuclear options, are smaller, which should, in turn, increase the credibility of threats to take these actions. Closely related, a damage-limitation capability could provide a bargaining advantage when facing a more vulnerable nuclear adversary.

Damage limitation is a controversial role for U.S. nuclear weapons. First, analysts disagree about the benefits offered by a damage-limitation capability. Some analysts argue that damage limitation is primarily an insurance policy against deterrence failure, while others emphasize its value for enhancing deterrence. Second, analysts disagree about the feasibility of a damage-limitation capability against major nuclear powers—Russia and China—in politically relevant scenarios.[104] Damage limitation against smaller nuclear powers—for example, a resource-constrained country such as North Korea—is likely to be more feasible.[105] If infeasible, the pursuit of damage limitation would not provide strategic benefits but could fuel an arms race. Third, some analysts believe that a damage-limitation capability generates crisis instability, creating incentives for a country to launch a preemptive damage-limitation nuclear attack relatively early in severe crisis or war.[106]

Finally, U.S. policy holds that nuclear weapons play an important role in assuring U.S. allies that U.S. commitments and capabilities provide a high degree of security—which, in turn, reinforces their decisions to forgo nuclear weapons.[107] Thus, U.S. nuclear weapons play an important role in U.S. nonproliferation policy. However, among scholars there is disagreement about whether U.S. security guarantees are effective in preventing proliferation. Some experts argue that extended deterrence has contributed to U.S. efforts to prevent the spread of nuclear weapons.[108] Others argue that the historical record is more complex and that a nuclear commitment from an ally is not sufficient to inhibit an insecure state's pursuit of its own nuclear deterrent.[109] France, for instance, received a nuclear commitment from NATO but was skeptical that the United States would follow through on its deterrent threats.

The roles assigned to U.S. nuclear weapons could change in the future, either broadening or diminishing as the security environment and presidential priorities evolve. The 2018 Nuclear Posture Review, for instance, clarified the role of U.S. nuclear weapons by raising the possibility of nuclear retaliation in response to a cyberattack that resulted in massive economic damage, substantial social disruption, or significant loss of life.[110] At the same time, multiple presidential administrations have explored the feasibility of moving toward a no-first-use or sole-purpose policy.[111] As noted above, although U.S. doctrine is retaliatory in nature, current U.S. doctrine retains the possibility of using nuclear weapons first.[112] This is required to maintain the credibility of nuclear threats intended to deter non-nuclear strategic attacks. Consequently, the United States has refused to rule out the possibility of first use in extreme circumstances. Preservation of a first-use option reflects both concern about the range of potential scenarios in which the United States could benefit from the threat of first use to deter and also the belief of U.S. allies that a no-first-use doctrine would reflect a weakening of U.S. security commitments.[113]

The chapters that follow address in much greater depth many of the issues reviewed here. Some explore the political process through which U.S. nuclear doctrine has been made, others describe the mechanics of nuclear targeting and the operations and capability of the U.S. nuclear command-and-control system, and still others examine the role of nuclear operations in extended deterrence and arms control.

Notes

The views expressed here are the personal views of the authors and should not be attributed to their employers, the U.S. government, Lawrence Livermore National Laboratory, or its sponsors.

1. George H. Quester, *Deterrence before Hiroshima: The Airpower Background of Modern Strategy* (New York: John Wiley and Sons, 1966). Maybe the most important and influential work on nuclear deterrence is by Thomas C. Schelling, *Arms and Influence* (Yale University Press, 1966).

2. Glenn H. Snyder, *Deterrence and Defense: Toward a Theory of National Security* (Princeton University Press, 1961).

3. Robert Jervis, *The Illogic of American Nuclear Strategy* (Cornell University Press, 1985); Charles L. Glaser, *Analyzing Strategic Nuclear Policy* (Princeton University Press, 1990).

4. The two countries forces are, however, significantly different: Russia's force is much larger and most likely more survivable, which may influence U.S. options and in turn the credibility of its threats.

5. Recent scholarship, however, has questioned this widely accepted understanding of the infeasibility of significant damage limitation, as noted briefly in the text that follows.

6. Charles L. Glaser and Steve Fetter, "Should the United States Reject MAD? Damage Limitation and U.S. Nuclear Strategy toward China," *International Security* 41, no. 1 (2016), pp. 49–98; and Brendan Rittenhouse Green and others, "Correspondence: The Limits of Damage Limitation," *International Security* 42, no. 1 (2017), pp. 193–207.

7. See, for example, Desmond Ball, "Can Nuclear War Be Controlled?" *Adelphi Papers* 169 (London: International Institute for Strategic Studies, 1981), and Ashton B. Carter, "Assessing Command System Vulnerability," in *Managing Nuclear Operations,* edited by Ashton B. Carter, John D. Steinbruner, and Charles A. Zraket (Brookings, 1987): 555–610.

8. See also Janne Nolan, *Guardians of the Arsenal* (New York: Basic Books: 1989).

9. On delegation and command and control breakdowns, see Paul Bracken, *The Command and Control of Nuclear Weapons* (Yale University Press, 1983). On the manipulation of risk and threats that leave something to chance, see Thomas C. Schelling, *The Strategy of Conflict* (Harvard University Press, 1960): 202–3.

10. An early important study that makes this point is Albert Wohlstetter, "The Delicate Balance of Terror," *Foreign Affairs* 37, no. 2 (1959), pp. 211–34.

11. See "Draft Memorandum from Secretary of Defense McNamara to President Johnson," in *Foreign Relations of the United States, 1961–1963,* vol. 8, *National Security Policy,* edited by David W. Mabon (Government Printing Office, 1996), Document 152, https://history.state.gov/historicaldocuments/frus1961-63v08/d151.

12. Robert Jervis, *The Meaning of the Nuclear Revolution: Statecraft and the Prospect of Armageddon* (Cornell University Press, 1990).

13. For discussion of different ways to conceptualize damage limitation, see Glaser and Fetter, "Should the United States Reject MAD?," pp. 54–62.

14. Schelling, *Arms and Influence,* 91.

15. Of course, much depends on how states define their interests. States seeking to regain lost territory may be more willing to risk war. The competition in risk taking would therefore favor change rather than the status quo.

16. U.S. official statements on the risks associated with U.S. force vulnerability varied. For instance, Carter administration Secretary of Defense Harold Brown observed that an attack on U.S. ICBMs would limit U.S retaliatory options, particularly attacks against remaining Soviet nuclear forces, even if such an attack did

nor imperil U.S. assured destruction capability. See Harold Brown, *Department of Defense Annual Report, Fiscal Year 1980,* Historical Office, U.S. Department of Defense, https://history.defense.gov/Portals/70/Documents/annual_reports/1980_DoD_AR.pdf?ver=2014-06-24-150830-927.

17. For an overview of different rationales discussed inside the U.S. government for some of these capabilities, see Austin Long and Brendan Rittenhouse Green, "The Geopolitical Origins of U.S. Hard-Target Kill Counterforce Capabilities and MIRVs," in *The Lure and Pitfalls of MIRVs: From the First to the Second Nuclear Age,* edited by Michael Krepon, Travis Wheeler, and Shane Mason (Washington, DC: Henry L. Stimson Center, 2016). For criticism, see Jervis, *The Illogic of American Nuclear Strategy*; and Glaser, *Analyzing Strategic Nuclear Policy.* On the U.S. assessed need to target Soviet military forces, see Walter Slocombe, "The Countervailing Strategy," *International Security* 5, no. 4 (1981), pp. 18–27. Few official descriptions of U.S. policy emphasized the possibility that the Soviet Union saw advantages in relative superiority, but this view was prevalent among policymakers. See, for example, Paul H. Nitze, "Assuring Strategic Stability in an Era of Détente," *Foreign Affairs* 54, no. 2 (1976), pp. 207–32. For an exception, see the report of the "President's Commission on Strategic Forces," commonly known as the "Scowcroft Commission": "The overall military balance, including the nuclear balance, provides the backdrop for Soviet decisions about the manner in which they will advance their interests." Brent Scowcroft et al., *Report of the President's Commission on Strategic Forces,* April 1983, pp. 3–6.

18. Austin Long and Brendan Rittenhouse Green, "Stalking the Secure Second Strike: Intelligence, Counterforce, and Nuclear Strategy," *Journal of Security Studies* 38, nos. 1–2 (2015), pp. 38–73; and Brendan R. Green and Austin Long, "The MAD Who Wasn't There: Soviet Reactions to the Late Cold War Nuclear Balance," *Security Studies* 26, no. 4 (2017), pp. 606–41.

19. Brendan Rittenhouse Green, *The Revolution That Failed: Nuclear Competition, Arms Control, and the Cold War* (Cambridge University Press, 2020).

20. Keir A. Lieber and Daryl G. Press, "The New Era of Counterforce: Technological Change and the Future of Nuclear Deterrence," *International Security* 41, no. 4 (2017), pp. 9–49.

21. On the warhead loading of the Minuteman III missile, see Office of the Deputy Assistant Secretary of Defense for Nuclear Matters, *Nuclear Matters Handbook 2020, Revised* (Washington, DC: Department of Defense), p. 27, www.acq.osd.mil/ncbdp/nm//NMHB2020rev/docs/NMHB2020rev.pdf (subsequently referenced as *Nuclear Matters Handbook 2020*). Until 2005, the United States also deployed the Peacekeeper ICBM, which was deployed with ten warheads, in a number of former Minuteman silos (p. 27).

22. Office of the Secretary of Defense, *Nuclear Posture Review* (Department of Defense, February 2018), p. X, https://media.defense.gov/2018/Feb/02/2001872886/-1/-1/1/2018-NUCLEAR-POSTURE-REVIEW-FINAL-REPORT.PDF.

23. "Locations," About SSP, Navy Strategic Systems Programs, www.ssp.navy.mil/about/locations.html.

24. "Ballistic Missile Submarines," Submarine Force Pacific, U.S. Navy, www. csp.navy.mil/SUBPAC-Commands/Submarines/Ballistic-Missile-Submarines/.

25. The U.S. Navy has not disclosed how many warheads it deploys on Trident missiles, but some open-source estimates argue that each Trident D5 carries an average of four warheads. This calculation is based on the numbers of total deployed U.S. warheads commensurate with New START obligations. See Jacob Cohn, Adam Lemon, and Evan Braden Montgomery, *Assessing the Arsenals: Past, Present, and Future Capabilities* (Arlington, VA: Center for Strategic and Budgetary Assessments, 2019), 16n2, https://csbaonline.org/uploads/documents/Assessing_Web_FINAL. pdf.

26. FACTSHEET: "The Importance of the Nuclear Triad," U.S. Department of Defense, November 24, 2020, https://media.defense.gov/2020/Nov/24/2002541293/- 1/-1/1/FACTSHEET-THE-IMPORTANCE-OF-MODERNIZING-THE- NUCLEAR-TRIAD.PDF.

27. Office of the Secretary of Defense, *Nuclear Posture Review*.

28. Office of the Secretary of Defense, *Nuclear Posture Review*, p. 50.

29. Air Force Global Strike Command, "AGM-86 B/C/D Missiles," Fact Sheet, August 2019, www.af.mil/About-Us/Fact-Sheets/Display/Article/104612/ agm-86bcd-missiles/.

30. Office of the Deputy Assistant Secretary of Defense for Nuclear Matters. *Nuclear Matters Handbook 2020, Revised*, p. 28.

31. Office of the Deputy Assistant Secretary of Defense for Nuclear Matters, *Nuclear Matters Handbook 2020, Revised*, p. 29.

32. Office of the Deputy Assistant Secretary of Defense for Nuclear Matters, *Nuclear Matters Handbook 2020, Revised*, p. 29.

33. "NATO's Nuclear Deterrence Policy and Forces," NATO, May 11, 2021, www.nato.int/cps/en/natohq/topics_50068.htm

34. Office of the Deputy Assistant Secretary of Defense for Nuclear Matters, *Nuclear Matters Handbook 2020, Revised*, p. 30.

35. Office of the Deputy Assistant Secretary of Defense for Nuclear Matters, *Nuclear Matters Handbook 2020, Revised*, p. 41.

36. Office of the Secretary of Defense, *Nuclear Posture Review Report* (U.S. Department of Defense, April 2010), p. 26, https://dod.defense.gov/Portals/1/ features/defenseReviews/NPR/2010_Nuclear_Posture_Review_Report.pdf.

37. Office of the Secretary of Defense, *Military and Security Developments Involving the People's Republic of China 2021*(Washington, DC: U.S. Department of Defense, 2021), https://media.defense.gov/2021/Nov/03/2002885874/-1/-1/0/2021- CMPR-FINAL.PDF.

38. See, for instance, Dennis Evans and Jonathan Schwalbe, *Intercontinental Ballistic Missiles and Their Role in Future Nuclear Forces*, National Security Report (Baltimore, MD: Johns Hopkins University, Applied Physics Laboratory, 2017), www. jhuapl.edu/Content/documents/ICBMsNuclearForces.pdf

39. For an extensive Cold War study of options for increasing ICBM survivability, see Jonathan R. Medalia, *Assessing the Options for Preserving ICBM Survivability*,

Congressional Research Service Report 81-222 F (Washington, DC: Congressional Research Service, September 28, 1981). See also U.S. Office of Technology Assessment, *MX Missile Basing*, September 1981, https://ota.fas.org/reports/8116.pdf.

40. Office of the Secretary of Defense, *Nuclear Posture Review 2018* (Defense Department, February 2018), https://media.defense.gov/2018/Feb/02/2001872886/-1/-1/1/2018-NUCLEAR-POSTURE-REVIEW-FINAL-REPORT.PDF.

41. U.S. Air Force Nuclear Weapons Center, "Minuteman III (LGM-30G)," www.afnwc.af.mil/Weapon-Systems/Minuteman-III-LGM-30G.

42. William Daugherty, Barbara Levi, and Frank Von Hippel, "Casualties Due to the Blast, Heat, and Radioactive Fallout from Various Hypothetical Nuclear Attacks on the United States," in *The Medical Implications of Nuclear War*, edited by F. Solomon and R. Q. Marston (Washington, DC: National Academies Press, 1986), www.ncbi.nlm.nih.gov/books/NBK219165/#_ddd00095_.

43. However, the terms *launch on warning* and *launch under attack* are sometimes used interchangeably; see Steven Starr et al., "New Terminology to Help Prevent Accidental Nuclear War," *Bulletin of the Atomic Scientists,* September 29, 2015, https://thebulletin.org/2015/09/new-terminology-to-help-prevent-accidental-nuclear-war/. Indication that an adversary has decided to attack is typically referred to as strategic warning in U.S. military parlance. The indication that an attack is in progress is typically referred to as tactical warning.

44. See, for instance, John Steinbruner, "Launch Under Attack," *Scientific American* 250, no. 1 (1984), pp. 37–47; and Richard L. Garwin, "Launch Under Attack to Redress Minuteman Vulnerability?" *International Security* 4, no. 3 (1979/1980), pp. 117–39.

45. See, for instance, Ryan Snyder, "The Future of the ICBM Force: Should the Least Valuable Leg of the Triad Be Replaced?" *Arms Control Association Policy White Paper* (Washington, DC: Arms Control Association, March 2018), www.armscontrol.org/policy-white-papers/2018-03/future-icbm-force-should-least-valuable-leg-triad-replaced; and Bruce G. Blair, Jessica Sleight, and Emma Claire Foley, *The End of Nuclear Warfighting: Moving to a Deterrence-Only Posture* (Washington, DC: Global Zero, September 2018), www.globalzero.org/wp-content/uploads/2019/02/ANPR-Final.pdf.

46. See, for instance, David Alan Rosenberg, "The Origins of Overkill: Nuclear Weapons and American Strategy, 1945–1960," *International Security* 7, no. 4 (1983), p. 6.

47. Jerome Wiesner, "Warning and Defense in the Missile Age," June 3, 1959, Dwight D. Eisenhower Library, Anne Whitman File, Dwight D. Eisenhower Diaries, Box 42, Staff Notes June 1–15, 1959 (also available in National Security Archive published microfiche collection, U.S. Nuclear History: Nuclear Weapons and Politics in the Missile Era, 1955–68, Washington, DC, 1998, https://nsarchive2.gwu.edu/NSAEBB/NSAEBB43/doc2.pdf).

48. U.S. Department of Defense, *Nuclear Targeting Policy Review: Summary of Major Findings and Recommendations,* November 1978, Jimmy Carter Presidential Library, Zbigniew Brzezinski Collection, Subject File, Box 35, Presidential Directive

59, 9/78–4/79. Also available at National Security Archive, https://nsarchive.gwu.edu/dc.html?doc=6144730-National-Security-Archive-Doc-28-U-S-Department.

49. The Carter administration's overarching nuclear policy guidance, known as PD-59, emphasizes that U.S. forces should be survivable and resilient to a first strike and directs that U.S. forces be postured and planned in such a way that a substantial "Secure Reserve Force" would exist after U.S. and Soviet initial attacks. See "Nuclear Weapons Employment Policy," Presidential Directive/NSC-59, July 25, 1989 (declassified July 31, 2010), National Security Archive, https://nsarchive2.gwu.edu/nukevault/ebb390/docs/7-25-80%20PD%2059.pdf.

50. National Security Council, *National Security Decision Directive 13: Nuclear Weapons Employment Policy,* October 13, 1981, National Security Archive, https://nsarchive.gwu.edu/briefing-book/nuclear-vault/2019-06-11/launch-warning-nuclear-strategy-its-insider-critics.

51. "Clinton Issues New Guidelines on U.S. Nuclear Weapons Doctrine," *Arms Control Today,* November 1997, www.armscontrol.org/act/1997-11/news/clinton-issues-new-guidelines-us-nuclear-weapons-doctrine.

52. "Fact Sheet: Nuclear Weapons Employment Strategy of the United States," *The White House,* June 19, 2013, https://obamawhitehouse.archives.gov/the-press-office/2013/06/19/fact-sheet-nuclear-weapons-employment-strategy-united-states. See also "Testimony of Robert Scher, assistant secretary of defense for strategy, plans, and capabilities," *President Obama's Nuclear Deterrent Modernization Plans and Budgets: The Military Requirements:* Hearings before the House Subcommittee on Strategic Forces of the Committee on Armed Services, 114th Cong. (2nd sess.), www.govinfo.gov/content/pkg/CHRG-114hhrg20822/html/CHRG-114hhrg20822.htm. Scher noted, "The United States does not have a launch-on-warning policy. We instead retain the option for the President to launch intercontinental ballistic missiles (ICBMs) under attack, while also planning to ensure that we are not reliant on doing so. The difference between launch-on-warning and launch-under-attack is attack assessment. Launch-under-attack is not based solely on a single warning indicator; rather, an attack assessment considers data from multiple sensors and the apparent intent of the incoming attack in the context of the international situation."

53. U.S. Department of Defense, "The Importance of the Nuclear Triad," Fact Sheet, November 24, 2020, https://media.defense.gov/2020/Nov/24/2002541293/-1/-1/1/FACTSHEET-THE-IMPORTANCE-OF-MODERNIZING-THE-NUCLEAR-TRIAD.PDF.

54. See Michael Kofman, "The Role of Nuclear Forces in Russian Maritime Strategy," in *The Future of the Undersea Deterrent: A Global Survey,* edited by Rory Medcalf and others, (Canberra: Australian National Security College, 2020), pp. 32–34, https://nsc.crawford.anu.edu.au/sites/default/files/publication/nsc_crawford_anu_edu_au/2020-02/the_future_of_the_undersea_deterrent.pdf.

55. See Tong Zhao, *Tides of Change: China's Nuclear Ballistic Missile Submarines and Strategic Stability* (Beijing: Carnegie-Tsinghua Center for Global Policy, 2018), chap. 4, https://carnegietsinghua.org/2018/10/24/tides-of-change-china-s-nuclear-ballistic-missile-submarines-and-strategic-stability-pub-77490.

56. "Fleet Ballistic Missile Submarines—SSBN," U.S. Navy Fact Files, January 29, 2019, www.navy.mil/Resources/Fact-Files/Display-FactFiles/Article/2169580/fleet-ballistic-missile-submarines-ssbn/.

57. Congressional Budget Office, *Crew Rotation in the Navy: The Long-Term Effect on Forward Presence* (Washington, DC: Congressional Budget Office, 2007), pp. 3–4, https://apps.dtic.mil/dtic/tr/fulltext/u2/a473646.pdf. The length of each deterrent patrol is an operational decision. The nuclear power plants that provide electricity for U.S. submarines produce a nearly unlimited supply of energy. The constraint on patrol duration is therefore the needs of the crew for food. Fresh water and air are produced on board the boat. In 2014 the USS *Pennsylvania* set a record for the longest deterrent patrol by remaining at sea for 140 days. Ahron Arendes, "Pennsylvania Gold Sets New Record for Longest Ohio-Class SSBN Patrol," U.S. Pacific Fleet, June 14, 2014, www.cpf.navy.mil/news.aspx/030416.

58. Amy F. Woolf, *U.S. Strategic Nuclear Forces: Background, Development Issues* (Washington, DC: Congressional Research Service, December 10, 2020), p. 35, https://fas.org/sgp/crs/nuke/RL33640.pdf

59. U.S. Navy, "Trident II (D5) Missile," last updated September 22, 2021, www.navy.mil/Resources/Fact-Files/Display-FactFiles/Article/2169285/trident-ii-d5-missile/Top of Form.

60. "Strip alert" refers to an operating practice in which bomber aircraft are kept fueled and loaded with nuclear weapons near the runway. The U.S. Air Force's Strategic Air Command began this practice in 1958. Strategic Air Command set for itself a goal of having one-third of its bomber force loaded with nuclear weapons and ready to take off at all times. By 1961, 50 percent of the Strategic Air Command bomber fleet was on alert. John T. Bohn, *The Development of Strategic Air Command, 1946–1976* (Offutt Air Force Base: Office of the Historian, Strategic Air Command, 1976), p. 59.

61. Bohn, *The Development of Strategic Air Command*, p. 93; Leonard Wainstein and others, *The Evolution of U.S. Strategic Command, Control, and Warning: 1945—1972* (Arlington, VA: Institute for Defense Analyses, 1975), p. 176. See also Office of the Historian (Strategic Air Command), *Alert Operations and the Strategic Air Command: 1957–1991* (Government Printing Office, 1991).

62. Office of the Historian (Strategic Air Command), Alert Operations and the Strategic Air Command, 64.

63. U.S. Air Force, FACTSHEET: "AGM-86B/C/D Missiles," www.af.mil/About-Us/Fact-Sheets/Display/Article/104612/agm-86bcd-missiles/.

64. Congressional Budget Office, *National Cruise Missile Defense: Issues and Alternatives* (Washington, DC: CBO, 2021), www.cbo.gov/system/files/2021-02/56950-CMD.pdf.

65. See "S-500 Prometheus," CSIS Missile Threat Project, July 1, 2021, https://missilethreat.csis.org/defsys/s-500-prometheus/.

66. Office of the Deputy Assistant Secretary of Defense for Nuclear Matters, *Nuclear Matters Handbook 2020, Revised* (Washington, DC: Department of Defense), pp. 40 and 109, www.acq.osd.mil/ncbdp/nm//NMHB2020rev/docs/

NMHB2020rev.pdf. NATO refers to such systems as a weapons security and survivability system.

67. According to one Cold War CIA report: "The most important front targeting objective during both conventional and nuclear operations, as identified in classified [Soviet] military writings, is the complete destruction of NATO's land-based nuclear delivery capability immediately opposite Soviet forces." Directorate of Intelligence, *Soviet Planning for Front Operations in Central Europe* (Central Intelligence Agency, 1983 [Declassified 2015]), www.archives.gov/files/declassification/iscap/pdf/2012-090-doc1.pdf.

68. Other nuclear powers also have nuclear command-and-control systems. On Russian nuclear command and control, see Leonid Ryabikhin, "Russia's NC3 and Early Warning Systems," NAPSNet Special Reports, July 11, 2019, https://nautilus.org/napsnet/napsnet-special-reports/russias-nc3-and-early-warning-systems/; and Valery E. Yarynich, *C3: Nuclear Command, Control, and Cooperation* (Washington, DC: Center for Defense Information, 2003). On Chinese nuclear command and control, see Fiona Cunningham, "Nuclear Command, Control, and Communications Systems of the People's Republic of China," NAPSNet Special Reports, July 18, 2019, https://nautilus.org/napsnet/napsnet-special-reports/nuclear-command-control-and-communications-systems-of-the-peoples-republic-of-china/. On British nuclear command and control, see John Gower, "United Kingdom: Nuclear Weapon Command, Control, And Communications," NAPSNet Special Reports, September 12, 2019, https://nautilus.org/napsnet/napsnet-special-reports/united-kingdom-nuclear-weapon-command-control-and-communications/. On French nuclear command and control, see Benoît Pelopidas, "France: Nuclear Command, Control, and Communications," NAPSNet Special Reports, June 10, 2019, https://nautilus.org/napsnet/napsnet-special-reports/france-nuclear-command-control-and-communications/. On Indian nuclear command and control, see M. V. Ramana and Lauren J. Borja, "Command and Control of Nuclear Weapons in India," NAPSNet Special Reports, August 01, 2019, https://nautilus.org/napsnet/napsnet-special-reports/command-and-control-of-nuclear-weapons-in-india/. On Pakistani nuclear command and control, see Feroz Hassan Khan, "Nuclear Command, Control and Communications (NC3): The Case of Pakistan," NAPSNet Special Reports, September 26, 2019, https://nautilus.org/napsnet/napsnet-special-reports/nuclear-command-control-and-communications-nc3-the-case-of-pakistan/. Much less is known about the Israeli and North Korean command-and-control systems. On North Korea, see Myeongguk Cheon, "DPRK's NC3 System," NAPSNet Special Reports, June 06, 2019, https://nautilus.org/napsnet/napsnet-special-reports/dprks-nc3-system/. On Israel, see Avner Cohen, "Israel's NC3 Profile: Opaque Nuclear Governance," NAPSNet Special Reports, October 11, 2019, https://nautilus.org/napsnet/napsnet-special-reports/israels-nc3-profile-opaque-nuclear-governance/.

69. Office of the Deputy Assistant Secretary of Defense for Nuclear Matters, *Nuclear Matters Handbook 2020, Revised*, pp. 21 and 25.

70. Hans Born, Bates Gill, and Heiner Hänggi, *Governing the Bomb: Civilian Control and Democratic Accountability of Nuclear Weapons* (Oxford University Press, 2010).

71. Positive control involves making sure that nuclear weapons will be ordered to launch and that these orders will be carried out. Nuclear powers have strong incentives to ensure positive control. Measures that would have made it easier for U.S. forces in Europe to retaliate to Soviet aggression with nuclear weapons would have improved positive control. This requires developing a command-and-control apparatus that is reliable and responsive, allowing for the correct and, when necessary, rapid execution of orders. Measures to secure nuclear weapons from unauthorized and accidental use are forms of negative control.

72. On the Eisenhower administration's orders, see "Authorization for the Expenditure of Nuclear Weapons in Accordance with the Presidential Authorization Dated 22 May 1957" (declassified 1994), National Archives and Records Administration, https://nsarchive2.gwu.edu/NSAEBB/NSAEBB45/doc3.pdf. On the Johnson administration, see See "Notes of the President's Meeting with Secretary of Defense Clark Clifford et al., October 14, 1968" (partially declassified 2012 by the Interagency Security Classification Appeals Panel), National Security Archive, https://nsarchive2.gwu.edu/nukevault/ebb406/docs/Doc%205A%20Furtherance%20document%20Oct%201968.pdf. President Nixon was briefed on these plans soon after his inauguration. Garrett Graff, *Raven Rock* (New York: Simon and Schuster, 2017), p. 202.

73. Wainstein and others, *The Evolution of U.S. Strategic Command and Control and Warning*, p. 239.

74. "Authorization for the Expenditure of Nuclear Weapons in Accordance with the Presidential Authorization Dated 22 May 1957." Revised between January 28, 1959, and May 12, 1960, Dwight D. Eisenhower Library, Records of the White House Office of the Special Assistant for National Security Affairs, NSC Series, Subject Subseries, box 1, file "Atomic Weapons, Corresp. & Background for Pres. Approval & Instructions for Use of," https://nsarchive2.gwu.edu/NSAEBB/NSAEBB45/doc3.pdf.

75. "Memorandum of Conference with the President, June 27, 1958, 11:05 AM" (declassified April 4, 2001), National Security Archive, https://nsarchive2.gwu.edu/NSAEBB/NSAEBB45/doc1.pdf.

76. "Memorandum from Secretary of Defense McNamara to the Chairman of the Joint Chiefs of Staff (Lemnitzer)," in *Foreign Relations of the United States, 1961–1963*, vol. 8, *National Security Policy*, edited by David W. Mabon (Government Printing Office, 1996), Document 86 https://history.state.gov/historicaldocuments/frus1961-63v08/d86.

77. These orders empowered a specified set of very senior commanders to use nuclear weapons against military targets "without contacting the President if the necessary delay would make it impossible for them to prevent [an] imminent attack." "Memorandum from the President's Special Assistant for National Security Affairs (Bundy) to President Johnson," in *Foreign Relations of the United States, 1964–1968*, vol. 10, *National Security Policy*, edited by David S. Patterson (Government Printing Office, 2001), Document 54, https://history.state.gov/historicaldocuments/frus1964-68v10/d84. The similarity to the Eisenhower orders was noted in passing

by a Johnson administration official in a meeting to review the order. See "Notes of the President's Meeting with Secretary of Defense Clark Clifford et al."

78. "Notes of the President's Meeting with Secretary of Defense Clark Clifford et al."

79. John Gower, "United Kingdom: Nuclear Weapon Command, Control, and Communications," NAPSNet Special Reports, September 12, 2019, https://nautilus.org/napsnet/napsnet-special-reports/united-kingdom-nuclear-weapon-command-control-and-communications/.

80. On Soviet command and control, see Yarynich, *C3: Nuclear Command, Control, and Cooperation;* and Brendan R. Green and Austin Long, "The MAD Who Wasn't There: Soviet Reactions to the Late Cold War Nuclear Balance," *Security Studies* 26, no. 4 (2017), pp. 606–41.

81. National Security Action Memoranda: NSAM 40, Policy Directive Regarding NATO and the Atlantic Nations, JFKNSF-329-015, John F. Kennedy Presidential Library and Museum, April 1961, www.jfklibrary.org/asset-viewer/archives/JFKNSF/329/JFKNSF-329-015#folder_info; Mel Lyman, "Crimson Tide: They Got it All Wrong," *Comparative Strategy* 18, no. 4 (1999), pp. 309–12.

82. See, for instance, U.S. Department of Defense and U.S. Department of Energy, *Nuclear Weapons Surety: Annual Report to the President 1986*, www.esd.whs.mil/Portals/54/Documents/FOID/Reading%20Room/NCB/97-F-0685_Nuclear_Weapons_Surety_Report_1986.pdf.

83. Office of the Historian (Strategic Air Command), *Alert Operations and the Strategic Air Command: 1957–1991*, p. 24. See also Eric Schlosser, *Command and Control: Nuclear Weapons, the Damascus Incident, and the Illusion of Safety* (New York: Penguin Books, 2013), p. 325.

84. On the history of U.S. nuclear doctrine, see Lawrence Freedman and Jeffrey Michaels, *The Evolution of Nuclear Strategy*, 4th ed. (London: Palgrave Macmillan, 2019). See also Fred Kaplan, *The Bomb: Presidents, Generals, and the Secret History of Nuclear War* (New York: Simon and Schuster, 2020); and Scott D. Sagan, *Moving Targets: Nuclear Strategy and National Security* (Princeton University Press, 1990).

85. Office of the Secretary of Defense, Nuclear Posture Review 2018, p. 20. See also Office of the Secretary of Defense, *Nuclear Posture Review Report*, p. vii.

86. Office of the Secretary of Defense, *Nuclear Posture Review 2018,* p. 21. This "negative security assurance" has evolved over the years. In 1995 the Clinton administration pledged not to use nuclear weapons against any non-nuclear-weapons state party to the Nuclear Non-Proliferation Treaty except in the case of "an invasion or any other attack on the United States, its territories, its armed forces or other troops, its allies, or on a State toward which it has a security commitment, carried out or sustained by such a non-nuclear-weapon State in association or alliance with a nuclear-weapon State." See Kelsey Davenport, "Nuclear Declaratory Policy and Negative Security Assurances," *Arms Control Association Fact Sheet,* March 2018, www.arms-control.org/factsheets/declaratorypolicies. The *Nuclear Posture Review 2010* pledged that the United States "will not use or threaten to use nuclear weapons against non-nuclear weapons states that are party to the NPT [Nuclear Non-Proliferation Treaty]

and in compliance with their nuclear non-proliferation obligations." See Office of the Secretary of Defense, *Nuclear Posture Review Report* (Defense Department, April 2010), p. viii; and

87. The U.S. Air Force refers to these as assurance and deterrence missions. See, for example, Major Jeffrey M. Bishop, "Air Force B-2 Spirit Stealth Bombers Arrive in UK," *U.S. Air Forces in Europe and Air Forces Africa Public Affairs*, June 9, 2017, www.af.mil/News/Article-Display/Article/1209825/air-force-b-2-spirit-stealth-bombers-arrive-in-uk/.

88. Office of the Secretary of Defense, *Nuclear Posture Review 2018*, p. 21.

89. See Michael S. Gerson, "The Origins of Strategic Stability: The United States and the Threat of Surprise Attack," in *Strategic Stability: Contending Interpretations*, edited by Elbridge A. Colby and Michael S. Gerson (Carlisle, PA: Strategic Studies Institute, U.S. Army War College, 2013), pp. 1–47. See also C. Robert Kehler, "The U.S. Needs a New ICBM Now," *Information Series 444* (Fairfax, VA: National Institute for Public Policy, August 16, 2019), www.nipp.org/2019/08/16/kehler-c-robert-the-u-s-needs-a-new-icbm-now/.

90. The United States also once deployed nuclear weapons on bases in East Asia, although this is no longer the case. The United States deploys nuclear weapons in NATO territory for delivery by the dual-capable aircraft of NATO members. See "NATO's Nuclear Deterrence Policy and Forces," updated April 16, 2020, www.nato.int/cps/en/natohq/topics_50068.htm#:~:text=Dual%2Dcapable%20aircraft,DCA)%20capability%20to%20the%20Alliance.

91. On possible escalatory paths, see Barry R. Posen, *Inadvertent Escalation: Conventional War and Nuclear Risks* (Cornell University Press, 1992); and Caitlin Talmadge, "Would China Go Nuclear? Assessing the Risk of Chinese Nuclear Escalation in a Conventional War with the United States," *International Security* 41, no. 4 (2017), pp. 50–92.

92. This is in contrast to the first decades of the Cold War, when the United States could feasibly carry out only very large nuclear attacks.

93. See chap. 3, this volume.

94. See M. Elaine Bunn, "Can Deterrence Be Tailored?" *Strategic Forum* 225 (2007), pp. 1–8.

95. See Paul Huth and Bruce Russett, "Deterrence Failure and Crisis Escalation," *International Studies Quarterly* 32, no. 1 (1988), p. 42; and Michael J. Mazarr, "Understanding Deterrence," RAND Corporation, 2018, www.rand.org/pubs/perspectives/PE295.html.

96. Janne Nolan, *Guardians of the Arsenal: The Politics of Nuclear Strategy* (New York: Basic Books, 1989).

97. Scott D. Sagan and Allen S. Weiner, "The Rule of Law and the Role of Strategy in U.S. Nuclear Doctrine," *International Security* 45, no. 4 (2021), pp. 126–66.

98. U.S. Department of Defense, *Report on Nuclear Employment Strategy of the United States*, Specified in Section 491 of 10 U.S.C. (Washington, DC: Department of Defense, 2013). See also U.S. Department of Defense, *Report on Nuclear*

Employment Strategy of the United States 2020, Specified in Section 491(a) of Title 10 U.S.C., www.esd.whs.mil/Portals/54/Documents/FOID/Reading%20Room/NCB/21-F-0591_2020_Report_of_the_Nuclear_Employement_Strategy_of_the_United_States.pdf; Robert Soofer and Matthew R. Costlow, "An Introduction to the 2020 Report on the Nuclear Employment Strategy of the United States," National Institute of Public Policy, *Journal of Policy and Strategy* 1, no. 1 (2021), https://nipp.org/wp-content/uploads/2021/10/Analysis-1.1R.pdf.

99. Harold Brown, "Memorandum for the President: Nuclear Targeting Policy Review" (November 28, 1978, National Archives [DECLASSIFIED UNDER AUTHORITY OF THE INTERAGENCY SECURITY CLASSIFICATION APPEALS PANEL, E.O.13526, SECTION 5.3(b)(3), ISCAP APPEAL NO. 2011-064, document no. 39], www.archives.gov/files/declassification/iscap/pdf/2011-064-doc39.pdf.

100. History and Research Division, Strategic Air Command, *History of the Joint Strategic Target Planning Staff: Preparation of SIOP-63* (Offutt Air Force Base: U.S. Air Force Strategic Air Command, 1964) (declassified February 13, 2007), p. 15, https://nsarchive2.gwu.edu//nukevault/ebb236/SIOP-63.pdf.

101. U.S. Department of Defense, *Nuclear Targeting Policy Review: Summary of Major Findings and Recommendations*. Declassified by the Interagency Security Classification Appeals Panel October 24, 2013, Appeal Number 2011-002-doc1 (Office of the Secretary of Defense, 1978), p. iii, www.archives.gov/files/declassification/iscap/pdf/2011-064-doc39.pdf.

102. The 2018 *Nuclear Posture Review* noted that "if deterrence fails, the United States will strive to end any conflict at the lowest level of damage possible and on the best achievable terms for the United States, allies, and partners. U.S. nuclear policy for decades has consistently included this objective of limiting damage if deterrence fails." See Office of the Secretary of Defense, *Nuclear Posture Review 2018,* p. vii, https://media.defense.gov/2018/Feb/02/2001872886/-1/-1/1/2018-NUCLEAR-POSTURE-REVIEW-FINAL-REPORT.PDF.

103. Anti-submarine warfare forces could contribute to a state's damage-limitation capability, as could missile defense, by reducing the number of launched weapons that reach their targets.

104. On this debate during the Cold War, see Glaser, *Analyzing Strategic Nuclear Policy.* See also Long and Green, "Stalking the Secure Second Strike."

105. On the potential role of damage limitation in U.S. strategy toward North Korea, see Vince A. Manzo and John K. Warden, "Want to Avoid Nuclear War? Reject Mutual Vulnerability with North Korea," *War on the Rocks,* August 29, 2017, https://warontherocks.com/2017/08/want-to-avoid-nuclear-war-reject-mutual-vulnerability-with-north-korea/.

106. On crisis stability, see Schelling, *Strategy of Conflict*, pp. 207–54, and Schelling, *Arms and Influence,* pp. 221–48.

107. The U.S. role as a provider of security to non-nuclear-armed allies also provides the United States with leverage to dissuade these allies from pursuing nuclear

capabilities of their own. See Gene Gerzhoy, "Alliance Coercion and Nuclear Restraint: How the United States Thwarted West Germany's Nuclear Ambitions," *International Security* 39, no. 4 (2015), p. 91–129.

108. See Philipp C. Bleek and Eric B. Lorber, "Security Guarantees and Allied Nuclear Proliferation," *Journal of Conflict Resolution* 58, no. 3 (2014), pp. 429–54, www.jstor.org/stable/24545647; Susan J. Koch, "Extended Deterrence and the Future of the Nuclear Nonproliferation Treaty," *Comparative Strategy* 39, no. 3 (2020), www.tandfonline.com/doi/full/10.1080/01495933.2020.1740569. See also Jeffrey W. Knopf, *Security Assurances and Nuclear Nonproliferation* (Stanford University Press, 2012); and Francis J. Gavin, "Strategies of Inhibition: U.S. Grand Strategy, the Nuclear Revolution, and Nonproliferation," *International Security* 40, no. 1 (2015), pp. 9–46.

109. In a recent meta-analysis of the quantitative literature, Mark Bell finds that having a nuclear-armed ally has not had a statistically significant impact on the risk of nuclear proliferation. However, Bell's analysis finds no statistical relationship between almost any of the variables cited in the literature. Mark Bell, "Examining Explanations for Nuclear Proliferation," *International Studies Quarterly* 60, no. 3 (2016), 520–29. Individual case studies provide some evidence for the role of nuclear forces in assuring allies. See Matthew Fuhrmann and others, "Book Review Roundtable: The Future of Extended Deterrence," *Texas National Security Review,* February 28, 2018, https://tnsr.org/roundtable/book-review-roundtable-future-extended-deterrence/.

110. Office of the Secretary of Defense, *Nuclear Posture Review 2018,* p. 21.

111. *No-first-use* refers to a pledge to not be the first party in an armed conflict to use nuclear weapons. *Sole-purpose* refers to a statement of policy that the sole purpose of nuclear weapons is to deter nuclear attacks. See Anna Peczeli, "Best Options for the Nuclear Posture Review," *Strategic Studies Quarterly* 11, no. 3 (2017), pp. 73–94. The Obama administration engaged in a far-reaching study over whether to move toward a no-first-use or sole-purpose policy. See James N. Miller, "No to No First Use—for Now," *Bulletin of the Atomic Scientists* 76, 1 (2020), pp. 8–13, www.tandfonline.com/doi/abs/10.1080/00963402.2019.1701278; and Brad Roberts, "Debating Nuclear No-First-Use, Again," *Survival* 61, no. 3 (2019), pp. 39–56, www.tandfonline.com/doi/abs/10.1080/00396338.2019.1614788.

112. As Walter Slocombe observes in *Managing Nuclear Operations,* even during the Cold War, U.S. nuclear doctrine was (as it remains) retaliatory in character. Walter B. Slocombe, "Preplanned Operations," in Carter, Steinbruner and Zraket, *Managing Nuclear Operations,* pp. 121–41.

113. Miller, "No to No First Use—for Now."

CHAPTER 3

Establishing the Ground Rules for Civilian Oversight

Franklin C. Miller

As Henry Kissinger once noted, after World War II, the United States "added the atomic bomb to [its] arsenal without integrating its implications into [its] thinking."[1] Although some strategists, notably Bernard Brodie in his 1959 book *Strategy in the Missile Age*, recognized that the destructive power of nuclear weapons meant that war, as the world had known it before 1945, was forever altered, the United States military initially incorporated nuclear weapons into its war planning as if they were simply more powerful conventional weapons. During the initial years of the Cold War, the first U.S. nuclear weapons were carried by air force intercontinental bombers; their targets, in the event of war, were Soviet urban-industrial centers, both because these were easily locatable and because the air force's primary strategic role in World War II was the destruction of German and Japanese war-supporting industries. Once NATO had been formed, the target set was broadened to include invading Soviet forces. And when the Soviet Union developed its own nuclear weapons capability, the destruction of that capability also became a U.S. objective.[2]

The target set described above, however, was more the result of war planning than of deterrent planning; it was in many ways the outgrowth of executing a battle plan than had been proved in World War II rather than an attempt to demonstrate to the Soviet leadership that its own vital assets would be destroyed in the event they attacked the West. For many of the following decades, even as both the geopolitical situation and Soviet and U.S. capabilities changed in major ways, U.S. nuclear planning—with a few significant exceptions, noted below—remained almost exclusively under the purview of U.S. military authorities.

It is important for scholars to note that U.S. targeting plans after 1949 always included a mix of military, leadership, and industrial economic targets in the USSR. During the late 1960s and early 1970s, a fiction developed in popular and academic circles that there was an ongoing struggle in the Defense Department between those who favored counterforce targets (that is, military sites and leadership and command-and-control capabilities) and those who believed only in targeting countervalue assets (that is, industrial facilities and cities).[3] This fiction, or deceit, was promoted by former defense secretary Robert McNamara, who used the countervalue metric as an internal Pentagon weapon against air force ambitions to deploy larger numbers of its intercontinental ballistic missiles and bombers than he deemed necessary.[4] According to that popular fiction, the issue was that counterforce targets were of a war-fighting nature and should be eschewed, whereas countervalue targets represented a pure and stabilizing minimum deterrent.

In understanding U.S. nuclear deterrent strategy, two facts must be kept in mind. First, as has been noted, U.S. deterrent plans since 1949 had always featured a mix of target types and, except perhaps in the late 1940s and early 1950s—mostly as a smokescreen for a struggle between the air force and the navy for nuclear roles; there was never any serious consideration given to focusing exclusively either on counterforce or countervalue assets. Second, the lack of such consideration in more recent times reflected the fact that as American strategic deterrence theory became more refined and sophisticated in the late 1970s and early 1980s, thanks to the increased influence of civilian officials, it focused on morphing the nuclear retaliatory plans into deterrent plans, which held at risk what Soviet leaders were perceived to value. Those assets were nuclear and conventional military forces, the ability to command and control the Soviet Union, and the industrial potential to sustain war. Since deterrence is about influencing the potential enemy's leaders, the U.S. deterrent necessarily had to focus on those assets the Soviets believed most valuable.

This chapter discusses those occasions when the nuclear war-planning process was influenced in major ways by the intervention of senior civilian authorities. There were five periods when this occurred

The Early Years (1948–1959)

Initially, nuclear target planning was exclusively a military prerogative (although President Truman made clear that only he could authorize the use of a nuclear weapon—a precedent followed by presidents to this day).⁵ Each service essentially created and maintained nuclear strike plans for the nuclear-capable systems it operated (principally air force strategic bombers and tactical fighters and navy carrier-based strike aircraft). Those service- and combatant-commander strike plans were generally not shared or coordinated with those created by their counterparts in the other services. The tiny size and lack of political heft in the new Office of the Secretary of Defense (OSD) meant that the defense secretary's civilian advisers were not involved in the nuclear planning process: the secretary interacted directly with the Joint Chiefs of Staff when nuclear targeting issues arose and depended on them for information and assessments.

In the late 1950s, President Eisenhower grew uncomfortable with the mix of counterforce and countervalue targets in the nuclear war plans (he thought the emphasis of the plans was too heavily weighted toward military targets), and in November 1958 he directed the Joint Chiefs to conduct a study on whether an optimum mix of targets, including more industrial-economic ones, could be developed as an alternative to the existing plan. The Joint Chiefs and their respective staffs struggled over the course of the next several years to respond to this tasking; at the same time, they were also at odds with one another over whether an integrated target plan was needed to avoid the duplication and overlap caused by the existence of separate service and combatant plans. The navy, in particular, fought the idea of subordinating its targeting—and, by extension, its nuclear forces—to the air force. In early February 1960, the Joint Chiefs forwarded an optimum-mix targeting plan to President Eisenhower along with the compromise recommendation that the list become the basis of a national integrated strategic plan to be overseen by a newly created organization, the Joint Strategic Target Planning Staff (JSTPS).

The agency was to be co-located at the air force's Strategic Air Command headquarters in Omaha and would be headed by a Strategic Air commander. The navy's concerns were assuaged by the fact that the JSTPS lacked operational control over any forces and was not allowed to set warhead requirements for either service. The navy also obtained the right to have a vice admiral position established as the vice director of the new organization. Although Eisenhower (and several of the service chiefs) was reportedly uncomfortable with the large number of targets in the proposed plans, in August 1960 he approved the recommendations with respect both to the plan and to the creation of the JSTPS.[6] The resulting single integrated operational plan, dubbed SIOP 62, was completed in December 1960 and became active early in the Kennedy administration, in April 1961. The plan created a single all-out attack against counterforce and countervalue targets in Russia and China and was designed to be executed under a variety of conditions of warning and alert postures, including potentially in a first-strike attempt to limit damage to the United States and its allies by pre-emptively destroying Soviet nuclear forces.

The Kennedy-Johnson Years (1961–1968)

While the details of the SIOP were closely held, the Eisenhower administration's approach to deterrence was well known and well advertised.[7] Known as the massive retaliation strategy, it sought to offset Soviet conventional superiority by threatening, in response to a Soviet attack anywhere in the world, an immediate all-out nuclear strike against the Soviet homeland and Soviet forces, using U.S. tactical, theater, and strategic nuclear weapons. As Russian nuclear capability grew throughout the 1950s, first at the tactical and theater level and later in the decade in the emergence of the ability to strike the U.S. homeland, academics and strategists began to question whether the threat of an immediate massive strike against the Soviet Union was credible.[8] Senior figures in the incoming Kennedy administration shared this skepticism and came into office in January 1961 determined to introduce flexibility into the "single-option" SIOP.

With some significant input and guidance from Secretary McNamara, SIOP 62 was modified to create flexibility by providing somewhat graduated response options to various levels of Soviet attacks. Nevertheless, all of the U.S. options—attacks on Soviet nuclear threat targets (nuclear weapons systems, storage sites, nuclear command and control except at the national level, and nuclear weapons infrastructure sites), nuclear threat plus other military forces, and finally those military attacks combined with strikes at the urban-industrial infrastructure—were still fairly massive. In addition, in an attempt to allow for controlled escalation should deterrence fail, Secretary McNamara directed that the counternuclear and countermilitary options be built in such a manner that targets in urban areas could be withheld from attack should the president so direct.

To ensure that the Soviet leadership received this message, he announced the policy change in a major public speech in July 1962.[9] This message signaled the Soviet leadership that the United States would be capable of retaliating in a manner that avoided Soviet cities and therefore sought to induce the Soviets to build similar war plans, which, if deterrence were to fail and war were to come, would provide them the option of not attacking American cities. The United States overtly retained the capacity and the plans to strike at Soviet cities as an incentive for the Soviet leadership to abstain from hitting American ones. The new SIOP, labeled SIOP 63, also included a variety of options (called withholds) allowing the president to avoid striking various Soviet allies' homelands. The war plan embodied in SIOP 63 remained basically unchanged throughout the remainder of the Kennedy and Johnson administrations.

The Nixon-Ford Years (1969–1976)

National Security Council staff memorandums from 1969 indicate concern that the SIOP structure had again become insufficiently flexible to deter attack options that the Soviet Union might become capable of executing, and National Security Study Memorandum 64 issued in July 1969 initiated an interagency study on ways to deter limited Soviet nuclear attacks.[10] No major progress appears to have been made until February 1973, when Nixon's national security adviser, Henry Kissinger, signed National Security Study Memorandum 169 (known inside the nuclear community simply as NSSM 169) directing a review of U.S. nuclear policy, initiating what became the third major civilian intervention in the U.S. nuclear war-planning process.[11] The NSSM 169 process considered the growth in Soviet nuclear capabilities in three areas: the major expansion of its intercontinental ballistic missile force; the entry into service of the Yankee-class nuclear ballistic submarine, which provided the Soviet Union a truly survivable nuclear threat against the United States (thereby undercutting the underpinning of the pre-emptive damage-limiting counternuclear option that had existed in U.S. planning in one form or another since the late 1940s); and the growth in Soviet theater and tactical nuclear capabilities.

The results of the NSSM 169 study informed President Nixon's nuclear targeting policy directives contained in his January 1974 National Security

Decision Memorandum (NSDM) 242.[12] The memorandum mandated three major changes to the nuclear war plans:

- First, in addition to the existing major response options, it ordered that "plans should be developed for limited employment options . . . in which the level, scope and duration of violence . . . can be clearly and credibly communicated to the enemy."
- Second, it called for "maintenance of survivable strategic forces in reserve for protection and coercion during and after major nuclear conflict."[13]
- Third, it set as a principal goal the "destruction of the political, economic, and military resources critical to the enemy's postwar, influence, and ability to recover at an early time as a major power."

In his Nuclear Weapons Employment Policy (NUWEP) policy of 1974 (drafted by the OSD staff), Secretary of Defense James Schlesinger directed, in detail, through the Joint Chiefs chair, the JSTPS to implement these changes.[14] This policy order was historic as it was the first time that a defense secretary had issued detailed planning guidance for nuclear forces. Despite significant decisions made by the president and the secretary of defense about how the SIOP should be modified to strengthen deterrence, many of the provisions of NUWEP 74 never found their way into the war plan. Furthermore, the war planners' task at the JSTPS was complicated by the fact that neither NSDM 242 nor NUWEP 74 clearly defined which Soviet assets were deemed critical to postwar recovery; as a result, the planners were forced to devise a system allocating "points" to various factories, but sadly, without proper guidance, this was done in a fashion that lacked a coherent military rationale. Thus the targets held at risk by the plan as being of the highest priority turned out to be of no particular significance to the Soviet leadership's national security goals.

The Carter Administration (1977–1980)

As a result of the Carter administration's broad review of national security policy (Presidential Review Memorandum 10), the Defense Department was directed to examine whether U.S. nuclear deterrence policy as expressed in NSDM 242 and NUWEP 74 was best designed to deter Soviet aggression. The resulting study, the Nuclear Targeting Policy Review, almost two years in the making and led by elements of the OSD, concluded that the Soviet political and military leadership were seriously preparing to fight and win a nuclear war. Given this conclusion, the study team decided that NSDM 242's focus on denying the Soviet Union the ability to be the first nation to recover from a massive nuclear exchange was a distinctly America-centric, mirror-image projection—not the Soviet point of view; following on from this, they believed that the NSDM 242 emphasis on retaliating against targets critical to industrial and military reconstitution was misguided. Instead, the team recommended focusing on holding at risk those assets the Soviet leadership deemed most valuable: its nuclear and conventional military forces, its own ability to command and control the Soviet Union, and its war-supporting industrial (for example, military end-item) production.

In the words of then Secretary of Defense Harold Brown, the overall goal was to make Soviet victory in a nuclear war, as seen through Soviet eyes, as improbable as possible.[15] Secretary Brown accepted the conclusions of the Nuclear Targeting Policy Review,[16] as did President Carter's national security adviser, Zbigniew Brzezinski. The result of this collaboration was Presidential Decision (PD) 59, which reoriented U.S. targeting priorities to focus on assets the Soviet leadership believed essential to fighting and winning a nuclear war.[17] Among its other changes, PD 59 stated that the United States required nuclear and conventional capabilities such that any adversary "contemplating aggression . . . would recognize that no plausible outcome would represent a victory or any plausible definition of victory." PD 59 also mandated that the U.S. response to Soviet nuclear attack should be such that the adversary "would not achieve his war aims and would suffer costs that are unacceptable." It focused U.S. targeting on Soviet nuclear forces and their military command-and-control facilities, other military forces, and war-supporting industry.

Provisions for striking the Soviet political control system were also included. Overall, this represented a clear rejection of the NSDM 242's emphasis on recovery targets. PD 59 reaffirmed the guidance mandating urban-area avoidance options in the counternuclear and countermilitary attacks. Other requirements included the following: "While it will remain our policy not to rely on launching nuclear weapons on warning that an attack has begun, appropriate pre-planning . . . will be undertaken to provide the President the option of so launching."[18] In addition, "The forces designated for the [nuclear] reserve should be the most survivable and enduring" and should be capable of being withheld "if necessary for a prolonged period."

These policy requirements were included in Harold Brown's NUWEP 80 directive to the JSTPS through the Joint Chiefs.[19] As was the case with Schlesinger's NUWEP 74, much of the NUWEP 80 was not reflected in the war plans, although this was unknown to Brown and his senior staff and was undiscovered until the mid-1980s.

Reagan and George H. W. Bush (1981–1992)

Members of Ronald Reagan's National Security Council staff rewrote PD 59, and President Reagan issued it as a new presidential directive, National Security Decision Directive (NSDD) 13, in October 1981.[20] Despite some media frenzy owing to incendiary political language (which was not in any way actionable) contained in the document, NSDD 13 did not alter PD 59's formulation of U.S. deterrence or targeting policy in any significant way. It reaffirmed the need to deny enemy war aims, to provide limited options, and to designate forces to be withheld from major attack options to be highly survivable. It also reaffirmed the policy of having, but not relying on, a launch-under-attack option. Following on from McNamara's city-avoidance option and subsequent reiterations by his successors, NSDD 13 included the following direction: "Methods of attack on specific targets should be chosen to limit collateral damage consistent with effective accomplishment of the attack objective. Where appropriate, overall plans should include the option of withholds to limit such collateral damage." Secretary of Defense Caspar Weinberger signed a NUWEP in 1982 to implement NSDD 13.

Since the early years of the nuclear age, OSD staff had been effectively excluded from overseeing the implementation of nuclear war plans, even though, beginning with NUWEP 74 and carrying on through NUWEPs 80 and 82, that staff had the responsibility for drafting the secretary of defense's policy guidance on which the plans were to be based. Essentially, the Joint Staff and the JSTPS refused to grant OSD staff access to the actual nuclear war plans in any level of detail. (Much of this stemmed from the strongly felt attitude in the military community that civilians had intruded overly into war planning during the Vietnam war—with disastrous results.) Therefore OSD staff, which wrote the guidance but lacked the bureaucratic clout to challenge the JSTPS and the Joint Staff, was unable to determine whether the guidance was reflected in the plans, and so the policy initiatives called for in NSDM 242, PD 59, and NSDD 13 (through 1984) and their associated NUWEPs did not truly go into effect.

All of this began to change in 1985, when the responsibility for nuclear targeting policy in OSD was shifted to the staff of the assistant secretary of defense for international security policy (hereafter referenced simply as ISP).[21]

Already tasked with responsibility for nuclear deterrence declaratory policy, policy input to strategic modernization programs, overseeing U.S. interaction with the United Kingdom on nuclear deterrence matters, and other aspects of nuclear policy but not targeting policy, the ISP team was quite familiar with the requirements set forth in the various NUWEPs signed by the respective secretaries of defense. They saw the president's and the secretary of defense's belief that they had nuclear options—that, in reality, did not exist—as a real danger to U.S. national security. ISP had acquired new staff who had previously worked on targeting issues on the navy staff, and the office was able to access war plan details obtained from an obscure data analysis office in the OSD (which the JSTPS used to validate its methodology) that had been reassigned to ISP in an unnoticed reorganization. With these new assets, the team discovered that in five key areas, areas specifically called out in the presidential and secretarial guidance documents, the war plans did not comply with national policy.

First, the plans lacked limited options for the use of nuclear weapons "in which the level, scope and duration of violence . . . [could] be clearly and credibly communicated to the enemy." Instead, they contained several large options in which all three legs of the nuclear triad were employed. These options would have been unrecognizable as "limited" to Soviet warning systems; in addition, the size and the eighteen-hour duration of the attacks would have suggested that the United States had initiated a major nuclear war.

Second, the instruction to provide a presidential withhold for selected urban areas had been interpreted in such a way that "urban area" was defined as that part of a city where 95 percent of the population resided, thereby opening up most of the city center (dominated by government buildings rather than residences) to attack.

Third, to avoid bureaucratic and interservice schisms, elements of all three triad legs were included in the reserve force. This occurred at a time when one of the main concerns of the U.S. national security establishment was the vulnerability of the Minuteman III land-based missile to Soviet attack.

Fourth, the SIOP covered many of the targets inside the Warsaw Pact, which were also assigned to NATO strike aircraft. This meant that NATO pilots were tasked to risk their lives, aircraft, and weapons to attack targets that would have already been destroyed by U.S. intercontinental and submarine-launched ballistic missiles.

Finally, despite explicit guidance to the contrary, the plan was heavily reliant on launch under attack.

Like its predecessors, the ISP team tried to engage the J-3 (operations) and J-5 (policy) organizations within the Joint Staff, as well as the director of the Joint Staff and also the JSTPS, to bring the plans into compliance with the policy, but the effort met with stone walls. Accordingly, the staff then took the unprecedented step of addressing each issue in serial fashion to Secretary Weinberger, making clear to him that guidance signed out by his boss (and close friend) Ronald Reagan was, in essence, being ignored.[22] In response to each of the five cases, the secretary wrote explicit directions to modify the plans to accurately reflect presidential policy, directions that the OSD staff monitored through its data analysis shop to ensure proper implementation. Thereafter, the Joint Staff and the JSTPS, unwilling to receive additional corrective memos from the secretary of defense, agreed to work with the ISP within agreed limits.[23] While none of these changes introduced new policy, they were significant in that they represented the first time the OSD was able to gain access to war plans (albeit at the aggregated or "options" level rather than at the individual target level) and to have them modified to reflect accurately the policy mandated by the secretary of defense.[24]

The SIOP Review of 1989–1991

The arrival of Dick Cheney in 1989 as George H. W. Bush's secretary of defense created additional major changes. Under Defense Secretaries Caspar Weinberger (1981–1987) and Frank Carlucci (1987–1988), ISP had forced its way to accessing the SIOP options structure and the types of targets each contained but was restricted by the Joint Staff and the JSTPS from examining or analyzing specific or individual targets. Secretary Cheney was familiar with the work already being performed by the OSD and the ISP. When, early in his tenure, he was presented his initial briefings on the SIOP by the commander of Strategic Air Command, he had concerns about many of the targeting packages. He turned to the ISP to help him understand the issues he had raised. After study, ISP reported back that while problems in the construction of the major- and limited-attack options had been resolved, the selection of targets and allocation of U.S. weapons against them inside the attack options—and indeed the war-planning process itself—were significantly flawed. ISP's analysis demonstrated that some targets were being struck by an inordinately large number of weapons; that some of the most highly accurate U.S. weapons (designed and acquired to use against hard targets) were being used against war-supporting industrial (soft) targets; and that some target sets were left uncovered owing to poor understanding of the intent of the plan. As a result, the secretary, with the full backing of the chairman of the Joint Chiefs of Staff, General Colin Powell, ordered a close-hold, full-scale, top-to-bottom review of both the SIOP and the JSTPS planning process; the review was to be led by ISP and was to include representatives from the Joint Staff and the JSTPS. There were to be no restrictions on the data or internal JSTPS documents to be shared with the review team. All books and documents were to be made accessible. Cheney required that he and Powell receive periodic update briefings.

Officially known as the Strategic Nuclear Targeting Review, the effort quickly became known as the SIOP Review. Part 1 of the review involved a scrub of the entire target base. Some targets were found to be entirely notional—presumed to exist but not found by analysts. Other target sets were only partially covered. For example, one set of targets involved rail lines that would be used by the Soviet Union to rapidly shift ground forces and their heavy equipment from eastern to western Russia. Since these lines were only partially attacked, rail and road networks that had not been targeted would still have been available for the Red Army's use. On the other hand, some target sets were overcovered: for example, the attack on tank production began at the iron ore mines.[25]

Finally, the team discovered that data processing had triumphed over military analysis: many military targets—airfields, for one—had been divided into "critical elements." For example, runways, petroleum storage, ammunition bunkers, and control towers were each treated as singular targets, without consideration of their location in relative proximity to one another. The team recommended major changes to the target base and to the way it would be prepared in the future; Cheney, with Powell's concurrence, approved all the recommendations.

Part 2 of the review took the newly revised target base and examined how weapons were applied to each valid target. In every case, the same two questions were addressed: Does the target need to be hit by a missile or a bomb (that is, is it time sensitive)? Does it need to be hit by two weapons or one (that is, is its destruction so critical that a second weapon needs to be applied to ensure its destruction if the first one fails to arrive)? Those recommendations were also provided to Secretary Cheney and General Powell and, again, were approved.

While not a goal of the review, the process also resulted in a significant reduction in the numbers of weapons needed to carry out the SIOP. In early

1989, General John T. Chain, head of Strategic Air Command, had told Congress, "I need 10,000 [nuclear] weapons because I have 10,000 targets." When the SIOP review wrapped up in the spring of 1991, the number of weapons needed had been cut by somewhat over 40 percent, to 5,888. Without intending to, or even being aware of the details of that late 1950s controversy, the review team had addressed the concerns of President Eisenhower and some of his Joint Chiefs about overkill by rationalizing the target base.

The last major reform that emerged from the SIOP review also hearkened back to a problem created in the Eisenhower administration. As noted earlier, when the JSTPS was being created to build an integrated strategic nuclear war plan, the Joint Chiefs could not agree on whether it would be authorized to levy warhead requirements binding on the various services. The Navy, in particular, refused to agree to a construct in which an air force–dominated organization would decide how many nuclear warheads the Navy might deploy. As a result, the responsibility for procuring nuclear weapons systems remained with the individual services; the services, in turn, provided the strategic weapons they deployed to the JSTPS, where all of them were included in the SIOP. As a result, no single individual or entity in the U.S. government was in charge of determining how many nuclear warheads were needed to satisfy national requirements.

This somewhat stunning fact was placed directly before Cheney and Powell in one of their update briefings when they asked the vice admiral overseeing the day-to-day activities of the JSTPS whether the 4,900 limit on ballistic missile warheads then being negotiated in the Strategic Arms Reduction Treaty (START) was adequate to meet U.S. targeting needs; the officer replied honestly and factually that he could not answer that question because there was no agreed requirement for the number of missile warheads. Based on this, the OSD and the Joint Staffs recommended separately to Cheney and Powell that the JSTPS be converted into a new four-star U.S. Strategic Command, one of whose responsibilities would be to set national requirements for nuclear forces. Cheney and Powell concurred, and in 1992 the JSTPS was disestablished, and U.S. Strategic Command was inaugurated in its place shortly afterwards, in 1992.[26]

The methodology and teamwork created by the SIOP review was employed to make one additional major intervention in the nuclear war plans in late 1991. It was increasingly clear after the abortive August 1991 coup against Soviet president Gorbachev by Soviet hardliners that the Soviet Union might break apart. At Secretary Cheney's direction, the review team reassembled to assess what U.S. deterrent requirements might be if that dissolution were to occur. The team conducted a mini SIOP review of the targets in those four Soviet republics (Russia, Belarus, Ukraine, and Kazakhstan) where Soviet strategic nuclear weapons were based. The team concluded ultimately that an additional 2,000 or so warheads might become unnecessary if the United States had to hold at risk only the four nuclear successor states to the Soviet Union.[27]

ISP recommended to Cheney that the United States might use the significant warhead surplus discovered in the original review, augmented by the findings of this new work, to propose a new arms reduction agreement with Russia, trading large reductions in both sides' strategic nuclear weapons for the elimination of intercontinental ballistic missiles carrying multiple independent-reentry vehicles. (These weapons were frequently viewed as sources of strategic instability because a single warhead could destroy between three and ten warheads on a missile it was attacking, thereby producing "a favorable exchange ratio.") Cheney supported the idea, as did his cabinet colleagues and, more important, President Bush. This proposal became the basis for the START II treaty, signed by George H. W. Bush and Russian president Boris Yeltsin in January 1993; sadly, the treaty never entered into force because missile defense politics in both Moscow and Washington became insurmountable obstacles.

Conclusions and Lessons Learned

The fundamental issue this chapter addresses is whether the president of the United States and the secretary of defense are satisfied with the deterrent options they have to manage crises and whether any changes they have called for in those options have, in fact, been put in place. Nothing could be more dangerous than a president trying to manage a crisis with a nuclear-armed adversary assuming—and basing decisionmaking on—options that do not exist. Since the history of nuclear planning from 1948 to 1992 demonstrates that this disconnect occurred on multiple occasions, the question that must be asked is why and how this happened.

Culture clearly played an important part. The generals and admirals who designed and fought in the winning campaigns against Germany and Japan in World War II were military men. They were not used to, and certainly not receptive to, civilian interference in their planning—a wholly American tradition that goes back at least as far as Lincoln's problems with his generals in the Civil War. This distrust was heightened by the entry of the Robert McNamara's "whiz kids," the team of young senior civilian analysts he brought into the Pentagon at the beginning of the Kennedy administration. The whiz kids' influence throughout the Defense Department—from choices between competing force structures and the numbers of tanks, planes, and ships that were required, to intervening in the redesign of SIOP 62—was deeply resented by the military. This resentment was stoked further by what was seen to be intrusive civilian influence in directing the war in Vietnam. Thus the military leadership in the Pentagon was predisposed to view civilian attempts to become involved in war plan preparation, particularly nuclear war planning, as an unnecessary, unwanted, and illegitimate intrusion on military prerogatives. That attitude prevailed well into the 1980s. Janne Nolan, in *Guardians of the Arsenal*, captures its spirit exactly in an interview she had with Lieutenant General Jack Merritt, who was at the time the director of the Joint Staff:

> The details of weapons employment are beyond the competence of all but a handful of individuals . . . and the military does not extend a warm welcome to persons who express an interest. As General Jack Merritt . . . put it: "You start talking about targeting or strategic command and control to the JCS [Joint Chiefs of Staff] and, baby, that's the family jewels. Anyone outside the military who tried this, the Chiefs told them to jump in the lake."[28]

Eventually, this attitude could not be overcome by reason but only with brute force. What had been lacking until 1985 was a very senior and influential OSD official (in this case, the assistant secretary of defense for international security policy, Richard Perle) who understood the dangerous disconnect between presidential assumptions and actual plans and a secretary of defense who believed absolutely that guidance signed by his close friend, the president of the United States, had to be followed. Presented with the five separate cases of serious mismatch between guidance and plan, Weinberger was true to form. None of this would have begun if the ISP staff had not agitated to take over the mission and if they had not found ways to ferret out information proving their case beyond a shadow of any doubt, but credit must also go to the senior leaders who supported them. Cheney's deep understanding of the issues, his keen ability to detect explanations that did not hold water, and his personal ties to the ISP staff prompted him to take decisive action to change the culture.

Another factor that contributed to the civilian-military dispute was the lack of any meaningful dialogue between the Washington-based policy community (both civilian and military) and the JSTPS war planners in Omaha. General Curtis LeMay, the legendary second commander of Strategic Air Command, moved his headquarters from Washington to Omaha in 1948 to reduce the Pentagon's influence. He succeeded beyond his wildest dreams. Much of the failure to implement the policies in NSDM 242/NUWEP 74, PD 59/NUWEP 80, and NSDD 13/NUWEP 82 was directly attributable to JSTPS planners' failure to understand (or seek to understand) the intent of those documents. The institutional pressure on the JSTPS to avoid creating interservice issues was also significant. It was thought better to include all three legs of the triad in every limited option and in the Secure Reserve Force rather than to optimize the plans as civilian policymakers had required; following the presidential guidance intent would have created immediate disputes between the navy and the air force, whereas not following the guidance was relatively cost free as long as the OSD remained without influence. To be fair, while some midlevel and even senior policymakers did try (but failed) to challenge the system, many considered the promulgation of the guidance documents as the end of their mandate and moved on to other things. Fundamentally, policy, however well crafted, is meaningless if not implemented.

A final contributing factor was that, in essence, no one was in charge. The late 1950s compromise that created the SIOP and the JSTPS ensured that no general or flag officer was charged with the responsibility of determining how many weapons were required. With an abundance of new warheads being assigned annually to the JSTPS, there was no perceived need or requirement for a rigorous review internal to the organization of target identification and weapon allocation. And whereas there were no rewards for recommending that targets be dropped from consideration, finding new targets was deemed a sign of success.

The forced tripartite OSD–Joint Staff–JSTPS collaboration of the SIOP review demonstrated to all concerned, Secretary Cheney and Chairman Powell in particular, but also to a wide swath of senior officials in all three organizations, that a collegial dialogue involving policymakers and target planners was hugely beneficial. The collaborative post–SIOP review work related to the breakup of the Soviet Union reconfirmed the validity of the model. Following from this work, an institutionalized trilateral pattern of dialogue and coordination marked the nuclear planning process throughout the ensuing eight years of the Clinton administration. That this cooperation continues to the present day is demonstrated in chapter 6 in this book, written by General Robert Kehler. It can only be sustained in the future, however, if two conditions are met: First, senior officials in the OSD, the Joint Staff, and at Strategic Command must continue to recognize its importance and require their subordinates to do the same. Second, the civilian officials seeking to modify targeting policy in the future must do so only because they believe changes are necessary to enhance deterrence; seeking changes to modify weapons requirements to fulfill political desires to reduce U.S. weapons will undo the trust and confidence that binds the three organizations together.

Notes

1. Henry Kissinger, *Nuclear Weapons and Foreign Policy* (New York: Anchor Books, 1958).

2. David Allen Rosenberg, "The Origins of Overkill," *International Security* 7, no. 4 (1983), pp. 3–71.

3. McNamara had created a metric dubbed "assured destruction," which specified that a major U.S. response to an all-out Soviet nuclear attack that would kill 25 to 35 percent of the Soviet population and destroy two-thirds of Soviet industry would be a sufficient deterrent. This was the so-called countervalue "pure" deterrent option. In reality, however, the United States, while it targeted urban areas, did not specifically seek to create or maximize civilian deaths. Assured destruction, while an effective bureaucratic weapon, was never incorporated into the war plan. (I am indebted to Fred Kaplan for confirming this point.)

4. While McNamara ceased speaking publicly or testifying about counterforce targeting after 1964, he was aware of and supportive of this part of U.S. policy throughout his tenure. Franklin C. Miller, "Tailoring U.S. Strategic Deterrent Effects on Russia," in *Tailored Deterrence: Influencing States and Groups of Concern,* Barry Schneider, and Patrick Ellis, editors (Montgomery, AL: USAF Counterproliferation Center, Maxwell Air Force Base, 2011), pp. 45–46.

5. For primary source materials on this era, see especially *The Creation of SIOP-62: More Evidence on the Origins of Overkill* (National Security Archive Electronic Briefing Book No. 130), https://nsarchive2.gwu.edu/NSAEBB/NSAEBB130/index.htm.

6. Ibid., especially document 23.

7. For insights into targeting deliberations in the early Kennedy years, see "History of the Joint Strategic Targeting Staff, Preparation of SIOP 63," https://nsarchive2.gwu.edu/nukevault/ebb285/sidebar/SIOP-63_history.pdf.

8. While little recognized, the Massive Retaliation policy had been modified in November 1957. General Lauris Norstad, the NATO Supreme Allied Commander

Europe, announced in a speech that in the event of a Soviet attack in Europe, the initial NATO response would be a major strike by tactical and theater-based nuclear weapons. If this failed to halt the Soviet offensive, a follow-on strike would be executed by U.S. strategic forces. It is unclear whether this change was initiated by political authorities (i.e., President Eisenhower or Secretary of Defense McElroy), or by Norstad himself. David N. Schwartz, *NATO's Nuclear Dilemmas* (Brookings Institution Press, 1983), p. 58. Also cited in Miller, "Tailoring US Strategic Deterrent Effects on Russia," p. 56.

9. Robert S. McNamara, Commencement Address, University of Michigan, Ann Arbor, July 9, 1962 (known as the "No Cities" speech), www.atomicarchive.com/resources/documents/deterrence/no-cities-speech.html.

10. *The Nixon Administration, the SIOP, and the Search for Limited Nuclear Options, 1969–1974,* National Security Archive Electronic Briefing Book 173, https://nsarchive2.gwu.edu/NSAEBB/NSAEBB173/.

11. National Security Study Memorandum 169, https://irp.fas.org/offdocs/nssm-nixon/nssm_169.pdf.

12. *The Nixon Administration, the SIOP, and the Search for Limited Nuclear Options, 1969–1974.*

13. Previously, there was no provision for U.S. strategic forces to be withheld in reserve from the execution of the largest SIOP option.

14. In promulgating NSDM 242 and NUWEP 74, the Nixon administration created a template that has been used by every successive administration to provide civilian guidance to military authorities on new nuclear war planning: a presidential document is first provided, followed by an expanded document issued by the secretary of defense.

15. Secretary of Defense, Memorandum to the President, Subject: Nuclear Targeting Policy Review, 28 November 1978, www.archives.gov/files/declassification/iscap/pdf/2011-064-doc39.pdf. The document contains a summary of the policy review's conclusions.

16. Secretary of Defense, Memorandum to the President.

17. "Jimmy Carter's Controversial Nuclear Targeting Directive PD-59," Declassified National Security Archive Electronic Briefing Book 390, https://nsarchive2.gwu.edu/nukevault/ebb390/, Document 12.

18. "Jimmy Carter's Controversial Nuclear Targeting Directive PD-59," Document 12. The intent of this particular element of guidance was not to establish a launch on warning capability (which had existed since NSDM 242/NUWEP 74) but rather to require that, should a president elect not to launch on warning, sufficient forces and credible retaliatory options would still exist.

19. Department of Defense, "Policy Guidance for the Employment of Nuclear Weapons (NUWEP)," October 1980, https://nsarchive2.gwu.edu/nukevault/ebb390/docs/10-24-80%20nuclear%20weapons%20employment%20policy.pdf.

20. "National Security Decision Document 13," October 1981, https://fas.org/irp/offdocs/nsdd/nsdd-13.pdf.

21. The author led ISP's efforts during the Reagan and George H. W. Bush administrations.

22. For a fuller description of the bureaucratic battle between the OSD and the ISP, on the one hand, and the Joint Staff and the JSTPS, on the other, and of the reforms that were ultimately accomplished in the Reagan and George H. W. Bush years, see George Lee Butler's autobiography, *Uncommon Cause* (Outskirts Press, 2016), vol. 2, chap. 23. Another version may be found in Fred Kaplan, *The Bomb* (Simon and Schuster, 2020).

23. The appointment of Admiral Bill Crowe as chair of the Joint Chiefs of Staff also helped: earlier in his career, Crowe had served in the OSD, and unlike many of his staff, he understood the proper role of civilian oversight; additionally, he was on excellent personal and professional terms with senior ISP officials.

24. Eventually, all these changes were consolidated and published as part of NUWEP 87.

25. Kaplan, *The Bomb,* pp. 184–85.

26. The Joint Staff recommendation emerged from a broader review of the Combatant Command structure carried out by Lieutenant General Lee Butler; the OSD recommendation came solely from the work carried out in the SIOP review. An unanticipated effect of this change was that Strategic Air Command was also disestablished, owing to some ill-conceived Air Force decisions. Its component parts—the intercontinental ballistic missile force and the bomber and tanker forces—were assigned to other air force major commands, and air force focus and emphasis on the nuclear deterrent mission withered, causing significant harm. After the unauthorized movement of nuclear-armed cruise missiles in 2007, Secretary of Defense Gates created a review panel chaired by former defense secretary James Schlesinger. The panel recommended reconsolidating most of the air force's nuclear capabilities into a single four-star nuclear deterrence command. Several months later, air force secretary Mike Donley created Air Force Global Strike Command, headed by a three-star general. While it was not precisely the organization envisioned by the Schlesinger panel, the command unit essentially met this need. More recently, in 2015, the commander of the Air Force Global Strike Command was elevated to the status of four-star general.

27. The vast majority of the targets were in Russia. After the breakup of the Soviet Union, and following negotiations with the United States, Ukraine, Kazakhstan, and Belarus returned their nuclear weapons to Russia.

28. Janne Nolan, *Guardians of the Arsenal* (New York: Basic Books, 1989), p. 249.

CHAPTER 4

Civil-Military Relations in Nuclear War Planning

James N. Miller

This chapter offers my perspective on civil-military relations relating to nuclear war planning, based on my experience during the first five years of the Obama administration. I served as principal deputy under secretary of defense for policy from 2009 to 2012 and as under secretary of defense for policy from 2012 until 2014. The chapter focuses on how three key questions were answered during my period in government service, from 2009 to 2014: What nuclear force structure should the United States retain under the New START (Strategic Arms Reduction Treaty) with Russia? Should nuclear declaratory policy be changed, and in particular, should the United States adopt a no-first-use policy? How should guidance for the employment of nuclear weapons be adjusted to account for geopolitical shifts, to provide better options and more decision time to the president, and to set parameters for any deeper reductions below the levels of the New START? Answering these questions involved many formal interagency and Department of Defense meetings that included both senior civilians (the president and the secretary of defense and their staffs) and senior military officers (the Joint Chiefs of Staff and the commander of U.S. Strategic Command and their staffs) as well as important informal conversations.

Establishing Acceptable Limits for New START Negotiations

On April 7, 2009, less than three months after taking office, President Obama gave a major speech in Prague outlining a far-reaching agenda for nonproliferation and arms control and calling for the long-term elimination of all nuclear weapons. Six months later, Obama received the Nobel Peace Prize, based mainly on his "vision of and work for a world without nuclear weapons."[1]

Given Obama's Prague agenda and the international acclaim it received, one might have expected a White House–directed examination of nuclear targeting to be a top priority at the outset of his administration. Instead, the president agreed with Defense Secretary Robert Gates's recommendation to defer such a review and to use the prior administration's targeting guidance as the basis for determining minimally acceptable U.S. nuclear force levels for the purpose of New START negotiations. Soon after the new administration took office, these negotiations commenced—with some urgency, given the treaty's pending expiration on December 5, 2009. This approach had two main benefits.

First, there was consensus in the administration and broader national security community that getting a new strategic arms treaty in place should be an urgent priority. Using the previous administration's guidance allowed a much accelerated Defense Department review of how deep reductions in warheads and delivery systems could go, in turn allowing New START negotiations to be pursued (and as it turned out, concluded) much sooner.

Second, basing the New START review on George W. Bush's presidential guidance and more detailed guidance from the secretary of defense (signed out by the carried-over secretary, Robert Gates) avoided the risk that some senators would oppose New START ratification on the grounds that the pro-abolition Obama administration may have reverse engineered targeting guidance to allow deep reductions.

The decision to rely on the past administration's targeting guidance was not made without due diligence. Based on a quick review of nuclear planning guidance and the nuclear war plans in April 2009, it was clear that any plausible reductions in deployed U.S. strategic warheads would result in U.S. force levels well above the requirements to meet the guidance inherited from the Bush administration. Because of Russia's increased reliance on nuclear weapons, it also seemed highly likely that Russia's bottom-line number for strategic nuclear weapons would be well above any number proposed by the United States.

In early 2009, President Obama directed that U.S. nuclear force levels under any new treaty should be determined as part of the Department of Defense-led Nuclear Posture Review (NPR), which began early in the administration. Of note, civilians in the Office of the Secretary of Defense (OSD) co-led the NPR with the Joint Staff and reported key findings and recommendations to a deputies-level interagency group chaired by the deputy national security adviser (and including me as well as the vice chairman of the Joint Chiefs of Staff). These seemingly small procedural steps ensured that OSD and National Security Council (NSC) civilians, along with senior uniformed officers from U.S. Strategic Command and Joint Staff, would have a formal role in considering acceptable nuclear force levels as the New START was negotiated.

Civilians involved in the process of determining "how much is enough" for the United States under a potential new treaty knew that they needed to avoid pressuring senior military officers to change their best military advice. If civilians' respect for, and desire for, unbiased military advice had not been enough (as, in my view, it was), it was clear to all that the strong support of General Kevin Chilton, commander of the U.S. Strategic Command, and the Joint Chiefs of Staff could be vital to getting Senate consent to ratifying the treaty. Attempting to pressure senior military officers was not only professionally and ethically improper but also could backfire if senior military officers were asked during the Senate's consideration of the treaty whether they had been pressured by civilians.

The Joint Chiefs of Staff held a number of meetings in "the Tank" to receive the views of General Chilton and the service chiefs and to formulate their best military advice regarding acceptable levels of U.S. strategic nuclear forces under a New START. The joint chiefs also provided their best military advice regarding issues such as how many on-site inspections were needed. Notably, the joint chiefs invited me, as Secretary Gates's senior civilian responsible for New START and for the NPR, to several of these sessions, including to give a presentation on the NPR's analysis of alternative strategic force structures (various mixes of land-based intercontinental ballistic missiles, submarine-launched ballistic missiles, and heavy bombers). This continued civilian-military discourse in formal meetings, as well as frequent informal meetings and phone calls, helped move along the process of getting General Chilton's and the joint chiefs' best military advice on New START limitations.

After considering recommendations from General Chilton and the service chiefs, along with analysis from the ongoing NPR, the joint chiefs of

Staff made unanimous recommendations for minimum strategic nuclear force levels under the New START negotiations that represented significant reductions from then-current levels.

Of note, the chiefs recommended that the United States ensure the treaty's limits on delivery systems be kept high enough to allow maintaining a robust triad, including a substantial land-based leg composed of single-warhead intercontinental ballistic missiles. The rationale for this recommendation, as later articulated in the 2010 NPR report, was to bolster strategic stability by requiring an adversary to spend at least one warhead (more likely two) to destroy one U.S. intercontinental ballistic missile warhead. Thus the Joint Chiefs of Staffs' recommendations regarding the New START went beyond the requirements of nuclear war fighting to a consideration of maintaining strategic stability with China and Russia.

After receiving the joint chiefs' recommendations along with an endorsement from his civilian staff, Secretary Gates forwarded the chiefs' recommendations, with his endorsement and additional comments, to the president.

During much of 2009 when the New START negotiations were underway, senior NSC staffer Gary Samore ably led scores of secure video teleconference meetings between a small interagency group and the New START negotiating team (led by Rose Gottemoeller, the assistant secretary and later under secretary of state, and including senior OSD and Joint Staff representation). The Department of Defense was represented in these meetings by the Joint Staff's director for strategy, policy, and plans, vice admiral (and later admiral and vice chairman of the Joint Chiefs of Staff) James (Sandy) Winnefeld, and me. Notably, within this small interagency group, civilians felt unencumbered in questioning the rationale behind Defense's "best military advice," and both vice admiral Winnefeld and I freely offered our views on U.S. negotiating strategy.[2]

Civil-military teamwork—and some overlap in roles—was also essential in the endgame of New START negotiations, when joint chiefs chairman admiral Mike Mullen was instrumental in closing the deal. Admiral Mullen twice led interagency trips to Moscow that included senior OSD, Joint Staff, State Department, and NSC representatives, where he worked with Russia's chief of the general staff General Nikolai Makarov to help resolve New START limits and technical provisions relating to verification.[3]

Advocates of Samuel Huntington's model of civil-military relations, in which civilians give only broad guidance to military leaders and military leaders refrain from commenting on issues of strategy and policy, probably would be appalled by civil-military relations as outlined here: a senior OSD civilian engaging freely in the joint chiefs' discussion of nuclear targeting requirements; a senior Joint Staff official offering advice on treaty negotiating strategy; and the nation's senior military officer traveling twice to Moscow to help close a diplomatic deal. However, one must ask, would it really have been better for the nation if the joint chiefs had not availed themselves of insights from analysis of alternative nuclear force structure because they came from a senior civilian? If the NSC and State Department had not listened to sensible advice on negotiating strategy because it came from a senior military officer? If the Chairman of the Joint Chiefs had demurred on helping the New START get completed because treaty negotiation was not in his job description? Of course not.

Some might perceive the strategy to defer a review of nuclear policy and targeting in order to accelerate negotiations and bolster ratification prospects for the New START, and to accept the recommendations of the U.S. Strategic Commander and the Joint Chiefs of Staff in setting negotiating guidance for treaty limits on warheads and delivery systems, as an abdication of civilian oversight of military nuclear planning. However, a major review of nuclear policy, and then nuclear targeting guidance, was indeed conducted, in the NPR and in a subsequent in-depth strategic-requirements review.

In any event, the Obama administration decision to delay an in-depth targeting review produced the desired outcome. The New START treaty was signed in April 2010. The Senate gave its consent to ratification that December. And the treaty entered into force in February 2011.

Declaratory Policy in the Nuclear Posture Review: "No for Now" to No First Use

In spring 2009, President Obama signed out guidance for the congressionally mandated NPR, which mandated that the review be consistent with, and indeed seek to implement, the priorities outlined in his April 2009 speech in Prague. Consistent with Prague, one of the five pillars of the NPR was to reduce the role of nuclear weapons in U.S. strategy.[4] A central question within this pillar was whether the United States should adopt a no-first-use declaratory and employment policy—and if not, whether other changes would be appropriate. Discussion and debate on this issue continued within the Department of Defense and in the NSC process, in parallel with the New START negotiations, through 2009.

Since the atomic bombings of Hiroshima and Nagasaki in August 1945 and the subsequent end of World War II, U.S. presidents had held open the possibility of using nuclear weapons not only in response to a nuclear attack but also if needed to defeat a major non-nuclear attack or in response to the use of chemical or biological weapons (the development, deployment, and use of which the United States has foresworn). Indeed, the threat of nuclear first use was central to U.S. strategy for deterring a Soviet attack on U.S. allies in Europe throughout the Cold War.

Two decades after the end of the Cold War, and at a time when the United States was spending more on defense than the rest of the world combined, it was reasonable for President Obama to ask that the NPR consider whether the United States should still threaten the first use of nuclear weapons. This question had, of course, arisen before, and indeed the case for a no-first-use stance was eloquently made nearly twenty-five years earlier by former national security adviser McGeorge Bundy:

> Decade by decade, our reliance on the threat to go first is becoming more dangerous. Politically, the threat is divisive for the people of all the countries concerned, because so many of us know that in reality a deliberate decision to begin the "nuclear exchange'"—as experts so bloodlessly describe it—would put at hideous risk the whole society in whose defense a leader made that choice. Technically, the danger is rising because the interlocking capabilities on both sides are developing in such a way that it will be only too natural for commanders, in a time of sufficiently intensified crisis, to demand that they be authorized to "'go first'" lest their forces be destroyed.[5]

Over the preceding decades, the three main arguments against shifting to a no-first-use policy had remained consistent. First, nuclear weapons remain useful for deterring great-power wars, which had resulted in the deaths of tens of millions of people in the twentieth century before the advent of nuclear weapons. Second, the United States needs to rely on nuclear weapons to deter chemical and biological weapon use, given that it has foresworn such weapons. Third, U.S. allies and partners need to rely on the U.S. "nuclear umbrella"; if allies and partners believe that reliance has been pulled back, they may well pursue nuclear weapons of their own.

In a series of formal and informal meetings in late 2009 and early 2010, senior members of the Obama national security team weighed all these arguments, and others, in assessing the pros and cons of shifting to a no-first-use declaratory policy. Of particular concern was the threat of biological weapons. Since the collapse of the Soviet Union, there had been credible reports—including from Russians—that the Russian government maintained a covert biological weapons program.[6] Moreover, many believed that North Korea was also pursuing biological weapons, potentially including smallpox and anthrax.[7] Estimates suggested that a biological weapon could kill millions or tens of millions of civilians, raising two key questions for policymakers: First, if an adversary were to kill millions of Americans through biological attack, would a nuclear response be on the table? Second, if so, would it not make sense to make clear that this was the case, to enhance deterrence of such a biological attack?

After extensive discussions with NSC deputies, as well as a small group meeting in the Oval Office in which I responded to a range of thoughtful and probing questions from President Obama, the president approved a statement that was supported by Secretary Gates and the Joint Chiefs of Staff:

> There remains a narrow range of contingencies in which U.S. nuclear weapons may still play a role in deterring a conventional or CBW [chemical and biological weapons] attack against the United States or its allies and partners. The United States is therefore not prepared at the present time to adopt a universal policy that deterring nuclear attack is the sole purpose of nuclear weapons, but will work to establish conditions under which such a policy could be safely adopted.[8]

President Obama had committed in his April 2009 Prague speech to reducing the role of nuclear weapons in U.S. policy,[9] and the 2010 NPR described how this commitment would be met:

> "The United States will continue to strengthen conventional capabilities and reduce the role of nuclear weapons in deterring non-nuclear attacks, with the objective of making deterrence of nuclear attack on the United States or our allies and partners the sole purpose of U.S. nuclear weapons.
>
> The United States would only consider the use of nuclear weapons in extreme circumstances to defend the vital interests of the United States or its allies and partners.
>
> The United States will not use or threaten to use nuclear weapons against non-nuclear weapons states that are party to the NPT [Nuclear Non-Proliferation Treaty] and in compliance with their nuclear nonproliferation obligations."[10]

There can be no debate regarding civilian oversight of U.S. nuclear declaratory policy in the early Obama administration: After hearing from both civilian and military advisors, President Obama made the final decisions, including the rejection (for the time, at least) of a no-first-use policy and approval of the specific language quoted above for the 2010 NPR. It is difficult to sort out the relative impacts of senior Defense Department civilian versus military leaders in informing the president's decision, because all of the senior officials involved from the department (including Secretary Gates and me, on the civilian side, and the Joint Chiefs of Staff and U.S. Strategic Commander, on the military side) believed that shifting to a no-first-use declaratory policy was (as of 2010, at least) not in the national security interests of the United States and that the language cited above was (depending on the individual) between marginally acceptable and highly desirable (the latter being my view).[11]

Modifying Guidance for Nuclear Employment

After the New START treaty was ratified in February 2011, attention turned to a presidentially directed review of nuclear employment guidance and nuclear war planning, variously called a strategic requirements review and a Nuclear Posture Review follow-on analysis. This study had two main aims. The first was to align employment guidance (the president's, the defense secretary's, and the joint chiefs chairman's increasingly detailed direction to the U.S. Strategic Commander regarding objectives to be pursued and constraints to be followed in the nuclear war plans) and the plans themselves with the realities of a changed and changing security environment, including increased risks of nuclear proliferation (from North Korea and Iran, in particular) and the need to sustain strategic stability with Russia and China. This presidential guidance started a process that would result in revised war plans and targeting, as well as changes to the decisionmaking process in crisis or conflict (for example, how options would be presented to the president and who would be involved in time-urgent consultations).[12]

The second aim of the study was to provide a new bottom line regarding how deep U.S. reductions could go below New START's limits of 1,550 accountable nuclear warheads.[13] The two aims of the study raised immediate questions for some observers in Congress: Would deliberations of how to best protect U.S. national interests by sustaining robust nuclear deterrence lead the study and pull along, as a by-product, a new and (presumably but not necessarily) reduced demand function for nuclear weapons? Or, as some in Congress feared, would a quest for lower numbers be in front, with any analysis of U.S. nuclear targeting requirements being reverse engineered?

In fact, the review was strategy driven, focused on protecting U.S. national interests, and grounded in realistic assessments of America's adversaries and their nuclear capabilities. There was no attempt to work backward from a desire for reduced numbers to inappropriately revised guidance. Written direction provided by President Obama called for a straight-up review. The small interagency group that conducted the review was dominated by like-minded people who were committed to playing it straight and who had strong support from their bosses (including the national security adviser, the secretary of defense, and the joint chiefs chairman). And if these factors had not been enough, all participants already knew precisely what the Department of Defense had already provided as the lowest militarily acceptable number of U.S. strategic nuclear warheads for the New START negotiations, based on the prior administration's nuclear targeting guidance (as described earlier in this chapter), and that there was substantial room for reductions below New START's 1,550 accountable weapons, even if the guidance did not change at all.[14]

In addition to starting more than two years into the president's first term, the Obama guidance and targeting review broke from past practice in two ways. First, the review process, like the Obama administration's NPR, was led by the Defense Department but involved senior interagency participation from the Departments of State and Energy and the intelligence community and was coordinated by the NSC staff. The signal from having NSC chair the meetings was clear: this is the president's review. And there was a sound rationale for including a senior representative from each of the other agencies: the review was intended to set the bounds of any future strategic arms control negotiations (State Department), define the size of the nuclear stockpile needed to hedge against geopolitical and technical risk (Energy Department), and, of course, to assess what was required to deter the leaders of several key nuclear-capable states (intelligence community).

Second, the review process started with . . . reviews. Brad Roberts, the deputy assistant secretary of defense, and his team led a structured review of past administrations' presidential and departmental guidance, highlighting significant changes that had occurred while noting the many areas of strong continuity over decades—including (for the edification of any participants who might have favored a "minimum deterrence" strategy) a prohibition on deliberately targeting civilians.

General Robert Kehler, commander of the U.S. Strategic Command, and his senior civilian aide Greg Weaver then led a detailed review for the small group of then-current nuclear targeting. This review highlighted about a dozen areas where current targeting practices complied with current (Bush administration) guidance, but the resulting targeting seemed to make little sense. These areas were the result not of stupid guidance or rogue actions by STRATCOM but of the use of a long linear process (that is, a one-way street) from presidential guidance to secretary of defense guidance to joint chiefs chairman's guidance to deliberate war plans and, finally, to targeting implementation. At each stage of the process, more detailed guidance was provided, and the potential for unintended effects increased owing to a range of factors, including interaction with other targeting choices and specific thresholds for damage expectancy. To their credit, the STRATCOM targeteers at the end of the daisy chain had carefully documented many of these problematic areas.

It is important to recognize the unique factors that allowed this first-of-its-kind interagency review of guidance and targeting practices to lead off with a highly substantive review and follow a strategy-driven analytical process. First, the Defense Department team was deeply knowledgeable and unconcerned about risks to "turf" in sharing sensitive information. For example, deputy assistant secretary Brad Roberts and Michael Elliott, the Joint Staff deputy director for strategic stability, were both deeply knowledgeable and steeped in interagency discussions; moreover, Roberts had helped backstop New START negotiations, and Elliott had been part of the negotiating team. STRATCOM commander Robert Kehler's analytical bent and depth of knowledge (including a prior stint as deputy STRATCOM commander), combined with long-serving STRATCOM civilian Greg Weaver's penchant for connecting the dots from deterrence theory to targeting, provided the necessary grist for the mill. Perhaps even more important than Kehler's and Weaver's knowledge and analytical bent was their willingness to fully share detailed information regarding nuclear targeting and give an unflinching assessment of areas they viewed as problematic. Contrary to the early experiences related by Frank Miller in chapter 3, Kehler and Weaver accepted the legitimacy of civilian oversight of nuclear war planning, saw the review process more as an opportunity than as a threat, and wanted to make the process as well informed as possible.

Second, senior members of the OSD team who formulated the review process had been immersed in nuclear issues for decades; they had tracked the trials and tribulations, and many of the specific changes, from prior reviews (including those led by Frank Miller, described in chapter 3). Owing partly to having overseen the Defense Department's deep dive on Bush administration guidance and targeting requirements during the NPR process and partly to involvement in past reviews in and out of government, they had taken a page from past successful internal Defense Department reviews and had strong ideas coming into the review regarding what may have to be changed to bring guidance and targeting practice into alignment with the president's policy objectives, the changing security environment, and common sense.[15]

Third, in preparation for the review, most members of the group had done recent "deep dives" on nuclear issues. This included gaining insights into nuclear command and control by flying on the Advanced Airborne Command Post (a specially outfitted Boeing E-4 aircraft, colloquially referred to as the Doomsday plane) and participating in highly illuminating exercises both in the air and during a full day hosted by General Kehler at Strategic Command. These efforts built knowledge and reinforced collegiality—and highlighted a number of issues regarding nuclear decisionmaking in crisis that were addressed in the review.

Finally, as an unplanned benefit of the review's delay, most of the civilian and military participants in the small group had built strong trust relationships over the preceding two years, in large measure by working closely together on New START (often on a daily basis when negotiations were underway), the NPR (involving more than a dozen deputy-level meetings in which many had participated), and a range of other issues since the start of the administration.[16] Having trust relationships allowed information (including highly classified intelligence and war plans) to be shared without concerns that it would be leaked or misused and, more important, facilitated an open discussion of not just the "what" of strategic guidance and targeting, but also the "why," including a frank consideration of the uncertainties associated with how much weaponry is enough to deter future adversaries' national leaders across a range of unlikely but plausible scenarios.

In most of the dozen or so cases of nuclear targeting oddities (or, in several cases, absurdities) highlighted by General Kehler, following the inherited guidance of a decade earlier had resulted in unnecessary redundancy, which in the event of war could cause unnecessary additional civilian casualties and perhaps raise risks of unintended escalation from limited to all-out war. A few cases cut in the other direction: following legacy guidance had resulted in a failure to target a particular type of asset that might reasonably be valued by adversary senior leaders or to hedge by withholding certain types of reserve weapons. Thus the review resulted in areas of addition as well as subtraction of targeting requirements.

Reviewing these dozen or so cases of guidance gone amok not only provided insights into appropriate targeting changes but also led to a discussion regarding the nature of effective guidance and oversight. The current secretary of defense's (and even more so the chairman's) nuclear guidance was lengthy and highly prescriptive. My experience in drafting guidance for conventional war plans and leading civilian review of plans, in support of the secretary of defense and under secretary of defense for policy, suggested an alternative model in which the guidance is concise and the war plan review is iterative and in-depth. My colleagues in uniform agreed, and at Defense's urging, the interagency group agreed to recommend to President Obama and Secretary Panetta that guidance from the president and the secretary of defense be at a much higher level and less detailed, while the review of war plans including targeting practices would be iterative and as detailed as needed.[17]

This presidentially mandated review process was conducted painstakingly, with questions arising from discussion in the White House Situation Room often taken back to STRATCOM staff (and often OSD and Joint Staff as well) for further analysis. As a result, the study took more than a year, rather than the originally directed ninety days, to complete.[18]

In addition to highlighting areas of current targeting practice worthy of review, STRATCOM staff reviewed potential major changes to guidance and reported on their implications for targeting, in terms of overall numbers, preferred type of weapons system, timing considerations, and implications for the size of the reserve force to deter escalation and coercion by other nuclear powers. By the time the review process ended in 2012, the participants not only had drafted new guidance but also had a detailed understanding of its implications for strategic nuclear weapons requirements. Nevertheless, all recognized that this review was the beginning, not the end, of a process that would conclude with revised war plans, updated targeting, and a continued iterative process of refinement.

The review spent considerable time on the potential use of U.S. nuclear weapons in the context of a regional conflict in which the President did not face a time-pressured "launch under attack" decision whether or not to direct the employment of ICBMs against the adversary, but instead would have time to consult with senior advisors regarding the pros and cons of various options. Although "adaptive planning" or "crisis action planning" was

envisioned in such a scenario, preplanned options would provide the starting point for consideration, and so these options deserved thoughtful consideration, engagement with the regional combatant commanders and their
staffs (who had little or no nuclear expertise), and a deliberate assessment of
escalation dynamics through focused intelligence assessments, wargaming,
exercises, and analysis.

The question of whether any reductions might be taken unilaterally, or
only if negotiated with Russia, was a point of discussion within the group.
The study considered both cases, one where Russia stayed at New START
levels and a second where Russia reduced to the same levels as the United
States. Because the Obama-approved 2010 NPR had noted the importance of
sustaining "rough parity" with Russia, and owing to the reality that Congress
quite likely would (and later did through legislation) block any U.S. reductions substantially below Russian force levels, the unilateralist perspective
was never really in play. Moreover, most members of the review team believed
it important to take account of the interests of many allies that the United
States retain its commitment to a second-to-none posture; this message had
come through loud and clear during the extensive international consultations conducted in 2009–2010 as part of the Nuclear Posture Review. The
president made the final call, for follow-on negotiations rather than unilateral reductions, with strong support from his secretaries of state, defense,
and energy.[19]

When the review process concluded in early 2012, discussion turned to a
rollout plan (how to brief Congress, what to say publicly) as well as next steps
in nuclear planning and in arms control. Now a downside of the delay hit: it
was the early stages of a re-election campaign.

The classified revision of war plans and targeting could move forward, but
what about any proposals to the Russians for deeper reductions below New
START levels? Would the Russians negotiate in good faith in the final year
of Obama's term, or did it make sense to wait until the election was decided
to attempt any arms control initiative? The issue was complicated further by
the reality that the Russians would seek limitations on U.S. missile defenses
as part of any such negotiations. Whatever one thought about the strategic
sensibility of negotiated limitations on U.S. missile defenses (there were differences of view within the Obama administration), such limitations were not
politically viable for the United States; however, the Russians would certainly
insist that missile defense be included in any discussion of reducing below
New START levels, resulting in domestic political headaches. The timing

answer became clear to all on March 26, 2012, when President Obama was caught on a "hot mike" telling Russian prime minister Medvedev that he would have "much more flexibility" after the presidential election.[20]

Thus it was more than four years after President Obama took office, and indeed more than two years after the start of the nuclear targeting review study, that selective results of the "ninety-day review" were made public in June 2013, simultaneously through three venues: a major presidential speech in Berlin, a White House fact sheet, and a report to Congress.

The numerical bottom line, of course, got the most attention. President Obama disclosed it in Berlin in June 2013, noting that with the agreement "we can ensure the security of America and our allies, and maintain a strong and credible strategic deterrent, while reducing our deployed strategic nuclear weapons by up to one-third."[21]

Although some White House and State Department staff had wanted to retain the option for the United States to make such reductions unilaterally, Secretary of Defense Panetta (along with his civilian and military advisers) and Secretary of State Clinton strongly opposed such a move. President Obama made his decision public in June 2013, announcing in Berlin that "I intend to seek negotiated cuts with Russia to move beyond Cold War nuclear postures."[22]

The White House fact sheet and congressional report provided additional details. In a bow to the president's obligation to ensure U.S. security with a credible and capable nuclear deterrent, the fact sheet led by affirming that "the United States will maintain a credible deterrent, capable of convincing any potential adversary that the adverse consequences of attacking the United States or our allies and partners far outweigh any potential benefit they may seek to gain through an attack."[23]

The guidance also directed the Defense and Energy Departments to take "an alternative approach to hedging against technical or geopolitical risk, which will lead to more effective management of the nuclear weapons stockpile."[24] A robust nondeployed hedge of nuclear warheads was to be maintained, but in essence the guidance stipulated that the United States would not retain more warheads than could plausibly or reasonably be deployed, as had sometimes been the case. (The ninety-day review process had included a deep dive into this question.)

This change opened up the possibility of long-term cost savings for the Department of Energy, since it would have to retain fewer weapons in the nonalert strategic stockpile (these long-term savings would be offset somewhat by near-term added costs of warhead dismantlement). This new guidance also allowed the administration to determine how many nondeployed strategic warheads were needed—and therefore to assess how many total warheads would be needed if the United States and Russia were to pursue negotiations covering nonstrategic and nondeployed warheads as well as deployed strategic warheads.

The review had bad news for anyone hoping to see the United States adopt a minimum deterrence strategy and good news for those who supported the long-standing U.S. approach to focus on militarily relevant targets: the fact sheet and congressional report noted that the new guidance "requires the United States to maintain significant counterforce capabilities against potential adversaries. The new guidance does not rely on a 'counter-value' or 'minimum deterrence' strategy."[25] It is important to understand that *counterforce* does not mean focused only on the other side's nuclear forces. Counterforce targeting may include the planning of attacks on non-nuclear forces and war-supporting infrastructure; it specifically means that civilian populations are not to be targeted. Indeed, U.S. policy has long held that, consistent with international law, noncombatant casualties must be minimized.

The new guidance made clear that the United States would continue to abide by the law of armed conflict, noting that "plans will, for example, apply the principles of distinction and proportionality and seek to minimize collateral damage to civilian populations and civilian objects. The United States will not intentionally target civilian populations or civilian objects."[26]

The Obama review included a range of additional directions to the Department of Defense, particularly focused on reducing reliance on nuclear weapons. Only time would tell whether this guidance would result in major change, modest change, or none at all:

First, the department was directed to "strengthen non-nuclear capabilities and reduce the role of nuclear weapons in deterring non-nuclear attacks." Such changes were intended to meet three objectives: sustain or bolster extended deterrence and assurance of allies; raise the threshold for nuclear use (that is, reduce the role of nuclear weapons); and spur the development of new non-nuclear capabilities that at some future date might make a no-first-use policy (also know as "sole purpose") strategically wise.

Second, the department was directed to "reduce the role of launch under attack in contingency planning, recognizing that the potential for a surprise, disarming nuclear attack is exceedingly remote. While the United States will retain a launch under attack capability, [the Defense Department] will focus planning on the more likely 21st century contingencies."[27] This language was intended to improve planning for deterrence in the context of a regional conflict and to shift a nuclear command-and-control system that had long focused predominant attention on the least likely of the low likelihood scenarios for nuclear war—a "bolt out of the blue" attack on U.S. strategic forces—to focus more on the potential escalation of regional conflicts. How well did the Obama review perform in adjusting guidance, war plans, and targeting practice to meet the demands of a changing world? For one, the review succeeded in identifying a dozen or so areas where current targeting should change, to bolster deterrence, promote strategic stability, and reduce the risks of inadvertent escalation from limited nuclear use to all-out nuclear war.

The Obama review also clearly met its goal to establish parameters for any follow-on negotiations below New START levels. The stipulation of "up to one-third reductions" signaled potential negotiated cuts in accountable warheads, and the review on stockpile hedging (though details remain classified) opened the door to substantial reductions in nondeployed nuclear weapons as well.

Perhaps most important, the review demonstrated and further directed a new approach to nuclear war planning guidance and review that involved in-depth civilian oversight from the Office of the Secretary of Defense (and the Joint Staff), with periodic updates to the NSC staff. If sustained over time—including over future administrations—this approach had the potential to help lock in serious civilian oversight (as long as serious civilians are in the right positions) and to build an ongoing discourse between the military and civilians responsible for guiding plans relating to this awesome capability.

One of the subtleties of civil-military relations is that active-duty military officers often play a key role in supporting civilian oversight of the military; for example, as New START was being negotiated in 2009, the office of the under secretary for policy had about 140 senior officers on its staff, most of whom were colonels or navy captains (along with about 450 government civilians). It is somewhat less common for civilians to occupy impactful senior roles in military organizations, but this was very much the case in New START preparations in the Defense Department. Mike Elliott served as the Joint Staff's representative to the New START negotiations and then as adviser to the Chairman of the Joint Chiefs of Staff on New START, and he had served previously as a trusted adviser in U.S. Strategic Command.

Greg Weaver served as the deputy director for strategy, plans, and policy to the U.S. Strategic Command's General Chilton. Both Elliott and Weaver were civilians, and both played important roles in defining the best military advice regarding New START's limits. (Elliott also served for a time as a key member of the New START negotiating team, representing the Joint Staff and taking the lead in negotiating one of the toughest issues, telemetry. Weaver would serve later in the office of the under secretary for policy, as principal director for nuclear and missile defense policy, and then yet later in the Joint Staff, as deputy director for strategic plans and policy.)

The importance of ongoing review and adjustment of nuclear planning—including a serious discourse involving knowledgeable civilians and military personnel—have been evident in the history since results from the Obama administration's nuclear targeting review were announced in June 2013. Less than a year later, in February 2014, Russia annexed Crimea and invaded Ukraine. This action ended any lingering hopes of a reset in U.S.-Russian relations and, in combination with Russia's violation of the Intermediate-Range Nuclear Forces Treaty, killed any hopes of a new arms control agreement in the near term. Equally important, these actions and an aggressive nuclear modernization program by Russia and (albeit a very different one) by China, as well as a multiyear campaign of nuclear and missile tests by North Korea, are indicators that the ongoing adaptation of nuclear guidance, plans, and targeting—with a healthy dose of continuity to avoid emboldening adversaries and frightening allies—is essential today and likely to be so for as long as nuclear weapons exist. And this process must—as the Obama review did—involve not only civilians requesting the advice of senior military officers but an in-depth substantive review by civilians working in support of the president and the secretary of defense.

Reflections on Civil-Military Relations

As Frank Miller describes in chapter 3, until the mid-1980s, despite drafting nuclear weapons employment guidance for the secretary's signature, staff serving in the office of the secretary of defense "had been effectively excluded from overseeing the implementation of the nuclear war plans." A sustained campaign, starting in 1985, with strong support from the secretary of defense, was needed to get civilians "read into" the nuclear war plans, and Frank Miller's chapter tells the story of how extensively in-depth civilian reviews impacted nuclear war plans. Some on Capitol Hill appeared to take notice of the ongoing struggle, as Congress mandated in the Goldwater-Nichols Act of 1986 that the under secretary of defense for policy (and, by extension, the under secretary's designated staff) would assist the secretary in reviewing war plans.[28] Thus by the time President Obama took office in January 2009, OSD review of nuclear (and conventional) war plans had been established practice for two and a half decades. This does not mean that all military personnel welcomed this civilian role or that all civilians with this weighty responsibility fulfilled the role with equal skill. Having the civilian review role defined in statute did mean, however, that the basic principle did not need to be relitigated with every new administration or turnover of personnel. However, the authority and responsibility to review war plans is only a starting point; it still mattered tremendously that the civilians involved in this process fulfilled their role with determination and thoughtfulness.

Samuel Huntington's seminal work on civil-military relations advocates what Huntington calls the "objective" model of civil-military relations. In this model, the job of civilians is to provide clear strategic objectives and then get out of the way, leaving it to the military professionals to plan and conduct war fighting.[29] This neat division of labor remains the preeminent conception of "appropriate" civil-military relations to many civilians and military professionals and indeed is the basis for the multilayered top-down process for nuclear (and conventional) war planning: high-level presidential guidance informs more detailed but still high-level secretary of defense guidance, which informs much more detailed guidance from the Chairman of the Joint Chiefs of Staff, which, finally, guides the development of the relevant nuclear operational plans (once known as the single integrated operational plan). This applied version of Huntington's objective model of civil-military relations is a reasonable starting point for war planning, but relying on it alone would have three serious pitfalls.

First, there is a risk that guidance may not be followed by military planners and operators. Chapter 3 explains how extensively this was the case when civilians first pried their way into reviewing nuclear war plans in the mid-1980s.[30] "Fire and forget" civilian guidance is a poor idea. Indeed, a sustained discourse between civilians and military overseers on the Joint Staff as well as military planners in U.S. Strategic Command (and other combatant commands) is essential not just to ensure compliance with civilian guidance but also to advance learning that, in turn, produces both better guidance and better plans.

Second, sometimes when seemingly sensible civilian guidance is followed to the letter, military planners may discover in building the war plan or in conducting detail targeting analysis that the guidance is unachievable or that following the guidance would result in a waste of military assets (in the nuclear arena, "overkill") or damaging secondary effects, or both. One case that has potential to combine both is attacks on suspected adversary chemical and biological weapons and missile delivery systems, which could take up an inordinate share of military forces with little diminution of possibly hidden, mobile, or deep underground adversary weapons of mass destruction and delivery systems; result in serious collateral damage to neighboring allies and partners; produce disproportionate civilian damage that could undermine U.S. and international support for the war; and lead the adversary to escalate early in the conflict. By no means do these potential second-order effects mean that it is always a bad idea to target adversary weapons of mass destruction. However, it means that the benefits and risks should be weighed in war plan review (and operations)—and that presidential and secretary of defense decision points regarding targeting weapons of mass destruction need to be built into war plans. Some targets might be preapproved, other targets might require certain conditions to be met, and yet other targets might explicitly require approval of the defense secretary or the president in the event of a conflict. This idea of building high-level civilian decision points into war plans to avoid undesired escalation and to weigh secondary effects is directly contrary to Huntington's concept of "objective" (hands-off) civilian control.

Third, if we accept that war is the continuation of policy by other means, as Carl von Clausewitz argued, then a sustained discourse between civilians providing guidance (and overseeing at least the broad contours and critical escalation points of operations) and the military professionals implementing this guidance (and conducting operations) is critical to ensuring that policy goals can be achieved. This requires that civilians listen to, as well as speak to, military planners. And it requires that military planners accept that civilians will ask probing questions to understand the basis for officers' best military judgment. In my experience with the Obama administration's nuclear review processes, senior civilian officials and military officers showed respect for each other's experience and judgment but did not show deference to the other's specific conclusions. Instead, a robust dialogue, and sometimes intense debate, ensued. Civilian officials questioned senior military officers' judgments regarding military matters, and uniformed officers felt free to offer their critique and advice on matters ranging from the hierarchy of U.S.

national interests to details of negotiating strategy. In my view, such dialogue is essential to providing the president with the necessary depth and breadth of knowledge—and the sense of alternative views—to make well-informed decisions to protect and defend U.S. national interests.

Notes

1. Barack Obama, "How We Can Make Our Vision of a World Without Nuclear Weapons a Reality," *Washington Post*, March 30, 2016.

2. Michael McFaul, senior NSC adviser to President Obama on Russia at the time and later the U.S. ambassador to Moscow, humorously but fairly captured the dynamic between Gottemoeller's negotiating team in Geneva and the interagency "backstopping" team: "We in Washington were the conservative naysayers, always pulling back on the reins of our creative Geneva team. I [McFaul] may have been the worst offender, though my Pentagon colleagues did their share of saying *nyet* as well." Michael McFaul, *From Cold War to Hot Peace: An American Ambassador in Putin's Russia*" (Boston: Houghton, Mifflin, Newcourt, 2018), p. 140.

3. Other senior officials played central roles in bringing New START to fruition, including President Obama (who engaged Russian president Dmitry Medvedev to resolve a number of issues) and National Security Advisor Jim Jones (who repeatedly engaged Medvedev's foreign policy adviser, Sergei Pridhodko, and twice led senior interagency teams to Moscow). For further details, see the "New START," in McFaul, *From Cold War to Hot Peace*, pp. 139–57.

4. The five pillars of the 2010 NPR were as follows: preventing nuclear terrorism and nuclear proliferation; reducing the role of U.S. nuclear weapons; maintaining strategic deterrence and stability at reduced nuclear force levels; strengthening regional deterrence and assuring U.S. allies and partners; and sustaining a safe, secure, and effective nuclear arsenal. See Office of the Secretary of Defense, *Nuclear Posture Review 2010* (Defense Department, April 2010), https://dod.defense.gov/Portals/1/features/defenseReviews/NPR/2010_Nuclear_Posture_Review_Report.pdf.

5. McGeorge Bundy, "No First Use," *New York Times*, July 20, 1986, p. 23, www.nytimes.com/1986/07/20/opinion/no-first-use.html.

6. A report published by the National Defense University in 2018 notes that "there is great cause for concern that well-resourced secret Russian institutes with access to modern microbiology techniques will provide the basis for the Putin administration to establish a third-generation BW [biological weapons] program." Raymond Zilinskas, *The Soviet Biological Weapons Program and Its Legacy in Today's Russia*, Center for the Study of Weapons of Mass Destruction, Occasional Paper 11, July 2016, p. 46, https://inss.ndu.edu/Portals/68/Documents/occasional/cswmd/CSWMD_OccasionalPaper-11.pdf?ver=2016-07-18-144946-743. See also Ken Alibeck and Stephen Handelman, *Biohazard: The Chilling True Story of the Largest Covert Biological Weapons Program in the World, Told from Inside by the Man Who Ran It* (New York: Random House, 1999).

7. The RAND Corporation's Bruce W. Bennett testified that "the exact nature of the North Korean biological weapon threat is not known, but a variety of serious biological weapons agents may have been developed by North Korea, and North Korea is also reported to have experimented on political prisoners with some of these agents." "The Challenge of North Korean Biological Weapons," testimony presented before the Committee on Armed Services Subcommittee on Intelligence, Emerging Threats, and Capabilities, U.S. House of Representatives, October 11, 2013, p. 15, www.rand.org/pubs/testimonies/CT401.html.

8. Office of the Secretary of Defense, *Nuclear Posture Review Report 2010*, p. viii, https://dod.defense.gov/Portals/1/features/defenseReviews/NPR/2010_Nuclear_Posture_Review_Report.pdf. As the group entered the Oval Office, I was responding to probing questions from the president regarding U.S. declaratory and employment policy.

9. See "Remarks by President Barack Obama in Prague as Delivered," April 5, 2009, White House, Office of the Press Secretary, https://obamawhitehouse.archives.gov/the-press-office/remarks-president-barack-obama-prague-delivered.

10. Office of the Secretary of Defense, *Nuclear Posture Review Report 2010*, p. ix.

11. As of the writing of this chapter, the author's views remain unchanged. See James N. Miller, "No to No First Use—for Now," *Bulletin of the Atomic Scientists*, January 2020, https://thebulletin.org/premium/2020-01/no-to-no-first-use-for-now/.

12. The revision of presidential guidance drives updates to the more detailed secretary of defense guidance (Nuclear Weapons Employment Planning, or NUWEP), in turn driving changes to the yet more detailed Chairman of the Joint Chiefs' guidance (the nuclear annex to the Joint Strategic Capabilities Plan), in turn driving change to the "deliberate" (preplanned) nuclear employment plans, in turn driving changes in actual targeting practice.

13. Because nuclear-capable bombers count as one warhead under New START, no matter how many weapons they actually carried, both the United States and Russia could deploy many hundreds of weapons beyond the nominal New START limit of 1,550 deployed strategic weapons.

14. It was theoretically possible that the small group could end up recommending a net increase in U.S. nuclear weapons required for deterrence and stability. However, given what participants knew going into the review based on the Nuclear Posture Review analysis to set minimum numbers for New START and General Kehler's initial comments that highlighted significant areas of "overkill," this result was understood as unlikely in the extreme. (If this result had occurred, one can imagine a very surprised President Obama asking how "reducing the role of nuclear weapons"—a key Obama objective articulated as one of the five pillars of the 2010 Nuclear Posture Review—resulted in needing more not fewer nuclear weapons).

15. Roberts had played a leading role in the development of the report of the congressional Commission on the U.S. Strategic Posture, the so-called Perry-Schlesinger commission, on which, before becoming principal deputy under secretary, I also served. While a senior staffer on the House Armed Services Committee in 1991, I had been one of two congressional staff ever "read into" the Strategic Command war

plans, and I remained current over the years. Both Roberts and I had completed a deep immersion during the Nuclear Posture Review process, which Roberts led and I oversaw for the Department of Defense.

16. For example, Vice Chairman of the Joint Chiefs Admiral Winnefeld and I had worked closely together from the outset of the administration on New START, missile defense, and other issues. There were similarly close working relations between Roberts, Joint Staff Lead Rear Admiral Phil Davidson and his J-5 deputy, Mike Elliott, and strategic command J-5 deputy director, civilian Greg Weaver—and their teams. Christine Wormuth, the NSC senior director for defense, and Natalie Quillian, NSC director, led the review for the White House; both were on detail from the office of the under secretary of defense for policy, where Wormuth had served as principal deputy assistant secretary and Quillian as my civilian special assistant. Tom D'Agostino, administrator of the National Nuclear Security Administration, Ellen Tauscher, a state department under secretary, and State Department senior adviser Robert Einhorn also participated actively in this small group review process; all had worked closely with the OSD and Joint Staff teams on New START negotiations and the Nuclear Posture Review.

17. For example, in the 1990s, while I was deputy assistant secretary, my office had responsibility for writing secretary of defense guidance for conventional war plans and leading the civilian review process; as deputy under secretary, I oversaw this former office and, for a number of the war plans, served as senior civilian approval authority in lieu of the secretary of defense. Admiral Winnefeld similarly had been involved in war plan development (as commander of the U.S. Northern Command) and review (as Joint Staff director for strategy and policy) in previous jobs and continued in a substantive oversight role as vice chairman.

18. National Security Advisor Tom Donilon announced the review was underway in a speech at the Carnegie Endowment for International Peace in March 2011. Although the results were not announced until June 2013, the vast majority of analytical work including draft guidance was completed by early summer 2012.

19. The question of unilateral cuts re-emerged in the last year of President Obama's second term, a topic beyond the scope of this chapter.

20. J. David Goodman, "Microphone Catches a Candid Obama," *New York Times*, March 26, 2012, www.nytimes.com/2012/03/27/us/politics/obama-caught-on-microphone-telling-medvedev-of-flexibility.html.

21. The White House, Office of the Press Secretary, "Fact Sheet: Nuclear Weapons Employment Strategy of the United States," June 19, 2013.

22. The White House Office of the Press Secretary, "Remarks by President Obama at the Brandenburg Gate—Berlin, Germany," https://obamawhitehouse.archives.gov/the-press-office/2013/06/19/remarks-president-obama-brandenburg-gate-berlin-germany. Emphasis added.

23. The White House Office of the Press Secretary, "Remarks by President Obama at the Brandenburg Gate.

24. The White House Office of the Press Secretary, "Fact Sheet: Nuclear Weapons Employment Strategy of the United States," https://obamawhitehouse.archives.

gov/the-press-office/2013/06/19/fact-sheet-nuclear-weapons-employment-strategy-united-states. Additional details are provided in a report to Congress, "Report on Nuclear Employment Strategy of the United States, Specified in Section 451 of 10 U.S.C.," https://fas.org/wp-content/uploads/2013/06/NukeEmploymentGuidance_DODbrief061213.pdf.

25. Report on Nuclear Employment Strategy of the United States, Specified in Section 451 of 10 U.S.C.," p. 4.

26. Report on Nuclear Employment Strategy of the United States, Specified in Section 451 of 10 U.S.C.," p. 4.

27. The White House, "Fact Sheet: Nuclear Weapons Employment Strategy of the United States."

28. The Goldwater-Nichols Act stipulates that "the Under Secretary [of Defense] shall assist the Secretary of Defense—(A) in preparing written policy guidance for the preparation and review of contingency plans; and (B) in reviewing such plans." Public Law 99-433, "Goldwater-Nichols Department of Defense Reorganization Act of 1986," 99th Congress, October 1, 1986, www.govinfo.gov/content/pkg/STATUTE-100/pdf/STATUTE-100-Pg992.pdf.

29. Samuel P. Huntington, *Man, the State, and War* (Columbia University Press, 1956)

30. I had some analogous experiences during my service in the Pentagon, starting in 1997 when I took responsibility for the office that drafted the secretary of defense's guidance for conventional war fighting. The Joint Staff took the secretary's relatively concise contingency planning guidance as the starting point and drafted much more detailed implementing guidance, known as the Joint Strategic Capabilities Plan (JSCP), for the combatant commands to follow in developing their war plans. When in 1997 I was sworn in as deputy assistant secretary responsible for war plan guidance and review, it seemed a natural question to ask whether the Joint Staff's JSCP differed in any material ways from the secretary's guidance. After some initial back-and-forth owing to Joint Staff reluctance to share "its" guidance to combatant commanders with civilians, two OSD staff members were allowed to review the JSCP. Although most of the secretary's guidance had been implemented faithfully, the chair's guidance omitted some secretarial guidance, while also adding text that meaningfully altered secretarial guidance. As it turned out, most deviations from the secretary's guidance were caused by error or oversight, but some were intentional. Among the intentional changes, in my view the majority were made for good reasons: for example, an updated intelligence assessment of the adversary's likely concept of operations or its military capabilities. Indeed, after the JSCP review took place, several deviations resulted in out-of-cycle updates to the secretary's guidance (and, it should be noted, the JSCP was revised to redress other errors of omission or commission).

CHAPTER 5

Turning Presidential Guidance into Nuclear Operational Plans

Michael S. Elliott

Peace is our profession.

—United States Strategic Command

The general who wins the battle makes many calculations
in his temple before the battle is fought. The general
who loses makes but few calculations beforehand.

—Sun Tzu

Although statements of policy relating to the purpose of nuclear weapons
have varied over the years, one central theme has endured(the purpose
of nuclear weapons is to deter attacks, particularly nuclear attacks, against the
United States, its friends, or its allies and, should deterrence fail, to terminate
the conflict on terms favorable to the United States.)Deterrence hinges on
a combination of demonstrated capability and will—the ability to impose
unacceptable costs on an adversary and deny it success, as well as the will to
do so, if necessary.

Yet the exact circumstances under which a president might face a decision
to use nuclear weapons are difficult to anticipate. A president could be faced
with the challenge of responding to a rapid change in the threat posed to
the United States, its friends, or its allies, necessitating a swift response. Or
a president could be confronted with the possibility that a conventional conflict could escalate to nuclear use. A potential nuclear attack on the United
States, its friends, or its allies could be massive and unbearable, or it could

95

be more limited. How should the United States respond in these scenarios? What would be the consequences of nonuse of nuclear weapons? What elements of its arsenal should it attempt to bring to bear, and how should it do so? What targets should be held at risk? How much opposition would U.S. and allied forces face in carrying out nuclear operations?

The president of the United States periodically issues nuclear employment guidance that conveys administration policy with respect to the strategic aims of nuclear operations. This guidance may also stipulate constraints and restraints on particular actions undertaken in the course of these operations. But presidential guidance will almost certainly not contain the detailed information necessary for the Department of Defense and the U.S. military to carry out nuclear operations in support of the president's orders in a real-world contingency.

Therefore the Department of Defense, in peacetime, develops deliberate plans for employment of nuclear weapons. The department must be prepared to deal with a wide range of potential threats—some existential and some that do not threaten the existence of the United States, its friends, or its allies but could nonetheless cause significant damage to U.S. and allied territory, people, and forces around the world.

Because each potential adversary has unique capabilities and national interests, the Defense Department develops a detailed understanding of the specific capabilities of each potential adversary and when and how these capabilities might be used against U.S. vital interests. While each scenario will vary with the capability of each potential adversary, the department must be prepared to respond to the most challenging scenario on any given day, unless and until such time as the United States is confident that a no-notice or short-notice major attack with nuclear weapons from an adversary is no longer possible. The department must be prepared with some plans to respond on short notice, meaning within minutes or hours, depending on the scope of an adversary's attack.

Since not all scenarios require a short-notice response, planners must also prepare plans to respond to other challenging but foreseeable enemy attack scenarios. Indeed, the very act of planning for the potential use of nuclear weapons builds a better understanding of the issues involved in a wide range of scenarios. As a result, planning improves the Department of Defense's ability to respond even in nuanced, seemingly hard-to-plan situations.

Nuclear planning also provides a number of other benefits. First, the exercise of planning is invaluable for better understanding those "unplannable" circumstances, because the planning process itself provides opportunities for interaction with the policy community as planners work through hypothetical circumstances. Second, nuclear operational planning also provides an opportunity for intense interaction between planners and civilian leadership. While interacting with planners, civilian leaders may articulate appropriate planning restraints and constraints to cover a variety of circumstances. In addition, they may also respond to the planning process by adjusting policy, as a full understanding of the implications of an emergent plan become apparent. This is the most challenging and crucial part of the process. This dialogue is most effective when the process leads to more effective policy, improved plans, and a comprehensive understanding of the implications of each potential scenario and its associated response options. Exercises and war games employed during this interaction often reveal shortcomings and subsequent adjustments to existing plans. Finally, these discrete benefits of planning together contribute to deterrence by conveying to allies and adversaries alike that the United States government is prepared to address a wide spectrum of contingencies with the full range of capabilities at its disposal.

Terminology and Outline

The term *plan* covers a wide range of subjects, including intelligence collection plans, concept plans, operational plans with associated time-phased force deployment plans, logistics support plans, and force deployment plans, among others. What planners once called the single integrated operational plan (SIOP) is now best thought of as a family of plans designed to address a wider range of contingencies from a more diverse set of potential adversaries. Although each of these different plans is essential to effective military operations, nuclear force employment planners face overarching challenges, particularly since the end of World War II.

From Plan to Plans:
Evolving Threats, Forces, and Organizations

The United States' nuclear arsenal went through a major transformation in the years following World War II. High-altitude bombardment with a small number of gravity bombs gave way to a Cold War peak of thousands of warheads delivered by bombers, fighters, cruise missiles, and both land-based and sea-launched ballistic missiles, as well as the use of tactical nuclear weapons from land and sea. Plans for the use of these weapons increased in complexity from the limited sorties of World War II through the SIOP and more recent operational plans. This process was shaped by the complex interaction of changing adversary capabilities, evolving knowledge, improvements to command and control, and changing conceptions of deterrence. The development of these plans became increasingly centralized, first within the military services and then, most recently, within an integrated U.S. Strategic Command (STRATCOM) working closely with civilian officials. A brief review of the changes that unfolded during the Cold War will help highlight the evolution.

Origins of Nuclear Operational Planning

The first U.S. nuclear forces had their origin in the strategic bombers (light, medium, and heavy) of the U.S. Army Air Corps, which were assigned to multiple commands around the globe throughout the course of World War II. The first two operationally available nuclear bombs were slated for delivery by the 509th Composite Group—a unique flying organization composed of B-29 Superfortress bombers as well as C-47 Skytrain and C-54 Skymaster transports. The 509th Composite Group was given the task of planning for movement, staging, and ultimately employment of the first two bombs.[1]

During World War II, planning air operations of far-flung army Air Corps units were managed at the theater level, based on priorities set at the national level. Within each theater of operations, plans were developed at the wing and group levels.(In other words, planning for non-nuclear strategic bombing was globally decentralized.)Plans reflected the context of a particular geographic theater of operations as interpreted by wing- and group-level staff officers. This nascent union—between a military organization with established practices and traditions and a revolutionary technology that created unique requirements—would have a lasting impact on nuclear planning for much of the Cold War.

Otherwise, the essential elements of planning the nuclear strikes on Japan were completed somewhat as they would be today. Primary and alternate targets were selected by intelligence specialists with political and military objectives in mind, just as they would be for a conventional bombing strike. From an aircrew perspective, it was a straightforward mission, with one bomb for one target and some additional special instructions related to the effects of the bomb and post-strike procedures. But key information about nuclear weapons was heavily classified and compartmented, and very few people within government had knowledge of the nascent policy or plans. Fat Man and Little Boy were essentially developmental weapons pushed into operational service to end what had been a bloody four-year war. While scientists and engineers had some idea of the awesome power they were about to unleash, the operators had little understanding of nuclear effects. The result was that these unique operational capabilities and requirements were imposed summarily on the World War II planning apparatus.[2]

Postwar Evolution of Forces and Organizations

Immediately after World War II, top political and military leaders were faced with the simultaneous challenges of military demobilization, reconstruction of Europe and Japan, and an increasingly aggressive Soviet Union. To square this circle, strategic bomber forces were consolidated in a new command within the U.S. Army Air Forces in March 1946—thus was born Strategic Air Command (SAC). While this was a crucial step in aligning and focusing U.S. military power on the challenge posed by the Soviet Union, the most significant changes would occur later, after almost two years of planning, discussion, and passage of the National Security Act of 1947.

The act consolidated the War and Navy Departments under a new National Military Establishment (later the Department of Defense) headed by a secretary of defense. It also created the National Security Council, the Central Intelligence Agency, and the Joint Chiefs of Staff, including a newly minted Chairman of the Joint Chiefs of Staff, who would become the nation's senior military officer. These changes were intended to help manage interservice competition and provide a structure through which key decisions related to, among other things, nuclear policy, strategy, acquisition, organization, and plans could be made by a single secretary of defense. The act would also set the stage for establishing the essential command-and-control mechanisms needed to manage a large and complex nuclear enterprise and to employ its forces at the direction of the president.[3]

The National Security Act also established an independent U.S. Air Force as a separate branch of service under the Department of the Air Force.[4] Among its many responsibilities, the air force would lead planning for bombing campaigns, modeled after strategic campaigns of World War II, to destroy the Soviet Union's means of waging war, should a war begin. Strategic Air Command became an air force major command.

In the decade following World War II, the strategic bombers of SAC were the only forces capable of waging a strategic campaign against the Soviet

Union. The command led the steady technological transformation of strategic forces beginning in the late 1940s from the B-36 and B-50 to the piston-jet hybrid B-36. Because it "owned" all the existing and emerging aircraft capable of delivering nuclear weapons, and because President Eisenhower thwarted navy ambitions to develop its own forces for the strategic bombing mission, the air staff was the center of strategic nuclear campaign planning, albeit under direction from the Joint Chiefs of Staff.[5] Strategic Air Command would not assume direct responsibility for planning until 1951.[6]

Early air force plans evolved from the air campaign planning experience of World War II, which presumed an offensive campaign would take place after a period of mobilization.[7] In such campaigns, a strategic bombing blitz would be only one element of a broader offensive effort, aimed at destroying critical military infrastructure and stocks, such as fuel depots. The first post-war plans for an air offensive on the Soviet Union assumed no atomic bombs would be used, since only a handful were in the U.S. stockpile in the years after the war. The first offensive strategic bombing plan involving the use of atomic weapons was EARSHOT JUNIOR—a supplement to a broader conventional air offensive.[8] In 1947 Joint Staff planners directed the development of plan BROILER, which assumed the use of nuclear weapons. The following year, the Joint Chiefs of Staff adopted an updated plan, HALFMOON, which included a strategic atomic offensive in its first phase.[9] Through 1950, however, the U.S. stockpile of nuclear weapons was sufficiently small and delivery systems were insufficiently accurate to permit their use against purely military targets, such as troops or transit hubs.[10] What this meant, in practice, was that only large-area targets such as industrial complexes could be engaged in the early days of nuclear planning.

By 1953, however, SAC's offensive capacity had grown significantly to more than 1,500 aircraft, including twenty-eight aerial refueling squadrons. The nuclear weapons stockpile began growing exponentially after an expansion of plutonium and uranium production and warhead production capabilities. Ultimately, the development of multiple independently targeted reentry vehicle technology, which expanded warhead delivery capability for intercontinental ballistic missiles (ICBMs) and submarine-launched ballistic missiles (SLBMs), in combination with significant improvements in accuracy across all delivery systems, led to an improved capability to engage geographically distributed military targets, including those of a hardened nature.

Simultaneously with the rapid evolution of the strategic and tactical forces, the air force was working diligently to develop missile technology and in 1959 expanded its strategic role with the emergence of the Atlas D inter-continental ballistic missile. Strategic Air Command's receptivity to ICBMs was also helped by the development of megaton-yield thermonuclear weap-ons, which increased confidence that relatively low-accuracy ICBMs would destroy their assigned targets.

The U.S. Navy was also building on the lessons of the emergent technolo-gies of World War II to develop naval nuclear propulsion, missile technology, and, in conjunction with the National Laboratories, more compact nuclear warheads to fit their missiles. In December 1959, the USS *George Washington* (SSBN-598), a nuclear-powered submarine armed with the Polaris SLBM, gave the navy a new role in the strategic nuclear mission. While SAC was fully prepared to incorporate the newly operational Atlas ICBMs, the emer-gence of the ballistic missile submarines armed with Polaris missiles intro-duced new frictions into planning, particularly with respect to coordination. (Unless SAC and navy plans were reconciled, the possibility existed that forces from both services could strike the same targets twice, or even put the other's forces at risk.)

Around the same time, the air force and the navy were equipping their land-based and carrier-based fighter aircraft with offensive nuclear bombs as well as warheads designed for airborne and seaborne defensive systems. The U.S. Army was also fielding a wide range of nuclear warheads, including artillery shells and short-range ballistic missiles. In principle, these weapons could fill a number of requirements. For one, they could offset U.S. conven-tional weakness in theaters for which a U.S. nuclear response with its "stra-tegic" forces would be inappropriate or undesirable, although some civilian leaders questioned the operational rationale for some of these systems.[11]

Within SAC, planning for strategic operations was evolving as each new generation of more capable bombers and bombs became available. However, plans for employing the wide variety of tactical and battlefield nuclear weap-ons available to commanders in Europe, the Atlantic, and the Pacific were developed independently of SAC. This quickly compounded the coordina-tion problem created by independent navy strategic forces: targets of strategic importance to SAC might also be of operational importance to theater com-manders, once again creating the possibility of overkill or fratricide.[12]

With this and ongoing planning friction with the theater commanders in mind, the air force proposed a new approach to the strategic planning and execution problem, which was to consolidate all strategic forces, includ-ing the Polaris missile submarines, under a new unified command: the U.S.

Strategic Command. Not surprisingly, the army and navy disagreed with this approach: a unified command, they thought, would dilute the bureaucratic influence of the relatively smaller army and navy forces.[13]

In the absence of support for a unified command, the framework of a coordination board was created to reduce overlaps within the various plans. Unfortunately, this framework would prove incapable of producing efficiently coordinated plans.[14]

The Challenge of Synchronizing Plans

In August 1960, Secretary of Defense Thomas Gates, recognizing the clear need to synchronize planning for nuclear weapon employment, presented a proposal to President Eisenhower that he hoped would resolve the interservice debate over the future approach to planning for nuclear operations. The crux of the problem was coordinating the independent planning activities of air force and navy planners.[15]

Secretary Gates's proposal would create a new position of Director of Strategic Target Planning at SAC headquarters in Omaha. This officer would serve in a dual-hatted capacity as the SAC Commander in Chief and would be given the authority to develop a National Strategic Target List and a SIOP. Gates believed the arrival in service of ballistic missiles, particularly the Polaris missile, had placed an urgent need for an integrated planning system to replace the then-current practice of developing independent command plans from common joint targeting guidance with periodic coordinating conferences. Gates went on to argue that this approach would result in improved efficiency by eliminating duplication of targets in the independent plans of the services.[16]

Despite strong resistance from the chief of naval operations, Admiral Arleigh Burke, President Eisenhower agreed with Gates's proposal and approved preparation of an initial set of plans, although the Chairman of the Joint Chiefs was required to review the completed plans and make a recommendation as to whether the proposed process should remain in place.[17]

The new Joint Strategic Target Planning Staff (JSTPS), led by General Thomas Power, commenced work on the first National Strategic Target List and SIOP in the final weeks of 1960. In its original incarnation, JSTPS clearly favored SAC in terms of manpower, with 219 SAC personnel, who also retained their SAC staff jobs, serving alongside twenty-nine navy personnel, ten army personnel, three marines, and an additional eight non-SAC air force officers. Although the JSTPS would be led by a SAC general, the vice director would be a navy three-star admiral. This was not insignificant, because the vice director would maintain the highest degree of day-to-day interaction with the planning staff. The first plan produced by the JSTPS contained 2,600 installations and 1,050 desired ground zeros in the National Strategic Target List, with 3,500 strategic nuclear weapons available.[18]

One key aspect of this new planning approach was that SAC and navy forces would be committed to the plan while remaining under the operational command of their respective services rather than of the Director of Strategic Target Planning. Strategic Air Command was a "specified command"—a U.S. military command with a unique and continuing mission composed of forces from a single military department, the U.S. Air Force. It was also an air force major command, meaning it was responsible for developing and providing combat-ready air force personnel for the nuclear deterrence mission. This divided command structure for planning and executive nuclear operations created different levels of integration of plans, force development, and plan execution between the air force and the navy. In the air force, the same person serving as DJSP was tasked to develop a plan (the SIOP) for combat-ready air forces to be provided by him in his capacity as commander of the air force major command. These planned forces would then conduct operations under his authority as SAC Commander in Chief—the specified commander. Conversely, navy ballistic-missile submarine forces and related submarine support forces were equipped, maintained, trained, and operated by the commanders of submarine forces Atlantic and Pacific, but these commanders played no role in the development of the SIOP, other than to formally commit their forces.

(While this arrangement solved the issue of planning coherence and efficiency, it did not address the issue of unity of command of the strategic forces.) Unity of command requires that an individual or organization take direction (orders) from only one commander. Unity of command should, in principle, ensure full synchronization of all elements of a military operation by avoiding issuance of conflicting or poorly timed orders from multiple commanders.

The Cold War Peak Years

The technical evolution of bombers continued unabated through the 1960s, from the B-47 and B-52 to the supersonic B-58s. Each of these bombers was designed to fly great distances, with support from airborne refueling tankers, at very high altitudes to avoid enemy fighters, which posed the principal threat to bombers throughout the 1950s. However, the advent of

surface to air missiles forced SAC and the JSTPS to change their approach
to bombing by developing new low-altitude penetration tactics and plans to
avoid flight within the lethal envelope of those missiles or the detection range
of fighters. Neither the B-47 nor the B-58 were suited to low-altitude penetration tactics. The B-52 was adapted with improved electronics (including
a terrain avoidance radar and radar altimeter), strengthened structures, and
a shorter vertical stabilizer to reduce weight and meet the evolving mission
requirement for low-altitude flight.[19]

Bomber crews in the 1970s were trained extensively for low-altitude all-
weather tactics, flying the B-52 and FB-111 to avoid the sophisticated and
steadily growing integrated air defense system of the Soviet Union and the
non-Soviet Warsaw Pact. However, advancements in surface-to-air missile
technology and radar-guided anti-aircraft artillery in the late 1980s ultimately
drove bombers away from the ground again. The response to this increasingly
deadly operating environment was the emergence of standoff weapons such
as air-launched cruise missiles (ALCM) and the advanced cruise missile, both
launched from the B-52. Another response was the pursuit of stealth technology, which emerged with deployment of the B-2.

The air force made equally giant leaps in technology through the evolution of Atlas, Titan, Minuteman I, II, and III, and Peacekeeper ICBM systems. Throughout this process, the air force also worked closely with the
National Laboratories to ensure that appropriate warheads were available for
the growing ICBM force. As each new ICBM variant was delivered, plans
were enhanced by systems of increasing range, payload potential, and accuracy, which, in turn, improved the probability of achieving planning objectives against the growing Soviet threat.

While improvements in the range and payload potential of ballistic missiles provided a rapidly improving capability to planners, improvements in
the accuracy of ICBM guidance systems made a profound difference in strategy and plans. Circular error probable is a measure of the expected accuracy
of a weapon, generally based on analysis of test shots. In nonexpert terms,
circular error probable represents the radius of a circle around the intended
target within which half of the warheads shot would land (in this case, carried by a specific type of ballistic missile).

Early ballistic missiles could reach a target area more than 6,000 kilometers from their launch point; those missiles carried only a single nuclear warhead, with a circular error probable measured in kilometers, not meters. This
meant only a very large warhead, which could inflict damage over an area

measured in square kilometers, could be expected to strike a relatively large target at intercontinental range. While these systems were suited for plans designed to attack an adversary's industrial capacity, they were not capable of striking smaller military targets with the needed precision.

Improvements in ballistic missile guidance systems from kilometers to hundreds and then tens of meters changed the potential role of the ballistic missile. Given the combination of substantial yield and precision in the hundreds of meters, the ballistic missile became suitable for attacks on hardened military targets such as submarine bases, bomber bases, and even enemy ICBM silos. Continually improving accuracy of ballistic missiles made them capable "hard-target killers." This improved accuracy, coupled with the advent of payloads containing multiple independently targeted reentry vehicles, provided planners with the capability to develop plans to counter the enemy's military forces.

The evolution of strategic nuclear weapons was dramatic. From the relatively low-yield beginnings of Fat Man and Little Boy, the National Laboratories and the military services teamed to develop more advanced gravity bombs with larger yields, as well as new standoff weapons, including the AGM-28 Hound Dog, the AGM-69A short-range attack missile, the AGM-86A air-launched cruise missile, and the AGM-129A advanced cruise missile. Concomitant with improvements in nuclear weapons and their delivery systems, advances in navigational aids and computer technologies produced substantial improvements in the circular error probable of air-delivered weapons sufficient to hold most hardened targets at risk.

The day-to-day readiness of nuclear-capable bomber forces evolved over the seventy-five years following the end of World War II as the forces of the Soviet Union evolved and the risk to the bomber force increased. When the risk of a Soviet preemptive strike became a real, if not probable, prospect, a portion (initially one-third) of the SAC bomber and tanker force was postured near the runway for immediate launch, a posture called "alert," in 1957. Within three more years, SAC was training for and proficient in airborne alert, wherein a portion of the bomber and tanker force could constantly remain airborne for twenty-four hours, ready to perform a strike mission as a deterrent against Soviet attack.[20] Strategic Air Command assumed airborne alert, known as Operation Chrome Dome, in 1960 and maintained a portion of its bomber and tanker force in this posture as a deterrent until 1968. Realizing it was not enough to have bombers and tankers on alert, SAC developed and executed another new concept to maintain a continuously operating airborne command post, with a general officer on board, to ensure the president's orders could be executed.

Throughout the Cold War years, the U.S. Navy was hardly standing still. Following commissioning of USS *George Washington*, over the ensuing three decades the navy would lead the world in developing and deploying fifty-nine nuclear-powered ballistic missile submarines (SSBNs), most recently with deployment of the last Ohio Class SSBN, the USS *Louisiana*, in September 1997, and the missiles they carried (initially sixteen and ultimately twenty-four launch tubes) with sequential development of the Polaris, Poseidon, Trident I, and Trident II ballistic missile systems. Significant improvements in SLBM accuracy were sufficiently dramatic to make the Trident II missile a true hard-target killer. Throughout the lifetime of the ballistic missile submarine, the navy demonstrated an ability to always maintain a substantial percentage of the force at sea, through use of rigorous SSBN maintenance and sustainment programs and, operationally, by maintaining and rotating two combat-ready crews for each SSBN. This highly capable and robust ballistic missile submarine force has served as a powerful deterrent by ensuring a devastating response to any potential attack.

Each new class of ballistic missile provided increased range (from about 1,400 nautical miles for the Polaris A-1 to greater than 7,500 nautical miles for Trident II) and payload potential, which increased flexibility for SSBN operational patrols and greater flexibility for nuclear operational planners. One of the dividends of increased missile range was the ability of the SSBN to operate in a larger patrol area and therefore become more difficult to locate by antisubmarine forces. This, coupled with a vastly improved propulsion system, makes the U.S. fleet ballistic missile submarine the most survivable leg of what is called the triad.

Consolidation of Nuclear Forces under United States Strategic Command

The end of the Cold War triggered massive changes in the geopolitical environment. The Department of Defense was a highly interested and somewhat surprised observer of the precipitous chain of events, lasting from June 1989 through December 1991, that culminated in the end of the Cold War. Undoubtedly one of the most interested observers was General Jack Chain, the Commander in Chief of SAC and director of the Joint Strategic Target Planning Staff.

At first, the Department of Defense response to these changes was adaptive and evolutionary. General Chain was about to deliver a new SIOP, the product of an eighteen-month development cycle, when Poland elected a non-Soviet-aligned government in the summer of 1989. At that time, Soviet conventional and nonstrategic nuclear forces and significant elements of the Soviet integrated air defense system were still dispersed throughout the non-Soviet member nations of the Warsaw Pact (Bulgaria, Czechoslovakia, East Germany, Hungary, Poland, and Romania).

Over the next thirty months, Germany would reunify and join NATO. Warsaw Pact member nations would withdraw from the pact, one after another. The Baltic states would achieve independence. Finally, in December 1991, the Soviet Union would dissolve, leaving the now independent states of Belarus, Kazakhstan, and Ukraine with deployed Russian nuclear weapons on their territory.

In 1990, amid these rapid geopolitical shifts, General Chain and the JSTPS monitored the changing intelligence picture of Europe and adapted the active SIOP as new guidance emerged from the Pentagon. General Chain was simultaneously leading development of a new SIOP, which would become effective in the fall of 1990. This SIOP would incorporate guidance reflecting each major shift in the geopolitical landscape. Despite these efforts to adapt, it was becoming clear that the magnitude of changes would necessitate a more dramatic response. (The ultimate response was shaped by several other factors.)

First, the Department of Defense was still adjusting to the implications of the Goldwater-Nichols Act of 1986, which instituted major changes to the military chain of command and the relationship between the individual military services. Second, some of the regional combatant commanders were ready to declare the Cold War over and reap a peace dividend by divesting their nuclear forces and their associated planning staffs.[21] Third, progress in arms control, driven, in part, by the internal struggles of the Soviet Union, suggested to some an accelerating reduction in the threat.

As NATO and the regional commands sought to reduce their nuclear planning activities, there was also a growing understanding throughout the Department of Defense that the emerging multipolar world order and the subsequent shifts in the security environment confronting the United States would require a new focus on regional conflict—a challenge for which SAC was not designed. Together, these factors pointed toward a more centralized approach to nuclear planning and a concentration of expertise, both of which could be better served by transformation of the existing organizational structure.

It was in this context that Lieutenant General George Lee Butler, the director of plans and policy (J-5) on the Joint Staff, and General Colin Powell, Chairman of the Joint Chiefs of Staff, were discussing what the future might look like, given the unfolding events in Europe, the Strategic Arms Reduction Treaty, the evolving threat, and the requirements of Goldwater-Nichols. Throughout the last half of 1990 and first half of 1991, General Powell led a debate among the Joint Chiefs on how best to adapt the roles and responsibilities described in the Unified Command Plan.[22]

In January 1991, while the Unified Command Plan debate continued in the Pentagon, General Butler assumed duties as SAC Commander in Chief and Director of Strategic Target Planning. While SIOP planning was well underway when General Butler took charge of planning, two significant events were also already in motion. First, strategic arms reduction treaty negotiations had been completed, and the treaty would be signed on July 31, 1991. While not yet ratified, provisional implementation would begin the process of reducing strategic offensive arms to not more than 6,000 such weapons for each party. Second, a major review of nuclear weapon employment policy was underway. Those shaping the new policy were well aware of the implications of the disintegration of the Warsaw Pact, the dissolution of the Soviet Union, and the impact of the Strategic Arms Reduction Treaty. The presidential nuclear policy document in effect at the time was National Security Decision Directive 13, signed by President Reagan in October 1981. Although Department of Defense policy, based on National Security Decision Directive 13, was adapted to the rapidly changing events in Europe, the first post–Cold War planning guidance, titled Policy Guidance for Nuclear Weapons Employment Planning and known as NUWEP 92, would guide General Butler as he led planning for what would become SIOP 92.[23]

In Washington, General Powell suggested that the Joint Chiefs examine the idea of creating a unified command, specifically a strategic command, to assume responsibility for all nuclear forces and the planning associated with those forces. Under the proposed Joint Staff plan, Strategic Air Command would be disestablished, and its forces would be distributed to other air force major functional commands; and the Joint Strategic Target Planning Staff would be disestablished and its planning functions incorporated in the new unified command. Finally, command of U.S. strategic nuclear forces, including U.S. land-based ballistic missiles, ballistic missile submarines, and nuclear-capable heavy bombers, would reside with the new combatant commander.[Strategic Command would become a true joint command with representation of air force, navy, marine, and army staff.[24])

General Butler, now in Omaha, was a strong proponent of and a willing partner in adjusting air force management of the legacy forces of Strategic Air Command. The air force had long advocated the unified-command approach to nuclear force management, and the navy, under the leadership of Admiral Frank Kelso, accepted this new approach, with the important caveats that 35 percent of the command staff would be navy billets and that command would rotate between the air force and the navy. General Butler assumed responsibility, through the JSTPS, to submit an implementation plan that would activate STRATCOM on June 1, 1992, with full transition in six months. With the Joint Chiefs in agreement and an implementation plan approved by General Powell, President Bush signed the new Unified Command Plan on April 7, 1992.[25] Once the change had been codified, General Butler led execution of the transition: STRATCOM was born, and the new SIOP 92 was completed and took effect, on June 1, 1992. Although STRATCOM has experienced substantial evolutions in the breadth and nature of its global mission over the past three decades, it is focused today on its mission of nuclear deterrence in a global threat environment that has evolved dramatically in the twenty-first century.

Although the challenges facing planners were considerable in the early years and grew and shifted constantly during the peak years of the Cold War, the plans successfully evolved to meet the challenges. What was unique to the early years was the degree of oversight to which the plans were exposed. While the Joint Chiefs exercised an important role in evaluating the plans, it was only in the final years of the Cold War that civilian oversight became an important reality in reviewing and approving nuclear operational plans. Given the extraordinary new challenges facing planners in the twenty-first century, the level, intensity, and importance of the oversight process cannot be overstated.

Challenges Facing Planners Today

Planners must operate within the policy and guidance statements presented to the Department of Defense by national authorities. Guidance related to nuclear weapons posture and policy flows from the president of the United States in the form of policy decision directives. Based on the president's policy direction, the secretary of defense issues more detailed policy guidance and objectives for deployment and employment of nuclear weapons. The Chairman of the Joint Chiefs of Staff subsequently publishes military directives to implement the defense secretary's guidance. These policy and guidance documents detail the relevant political context for nuclear operations and outline desired policy objectives. Guidance statements are not necessarily restricted to the nuclear domain. For instance, they may provide context and guidance on ways to achieve the overall deterrence of threats to U.S. interests. Nuclear weapons would then be only one element of a broader strategic toolkit.

One of the age-old debates of the civil-military relationship is the tension related to the appropriate level of detail in issuing planning guidance. The concept of civilian control of the military is well understood throughout our government. Having said that, military leaders expect to be given specific policy objectives and will always seek a great degree of latitude in how best to achieve the policy. Tension arises when policymakers stray too far into the military arena or when the military pushes too far into the policy arena. Put simply, it is not the job of policymakers to pick targets or tell the experts how to operate the equipment. Conversely, it is an absolute obligation of the military to ensure that the policy community is fully apprised of how its policy will be implemented and the implications of each plan. The habitual relationships developed among key leaders of each administration during development of policy and subsequent plan review activities are key to this outcome.

Consider this hypothetical example of a policy and guidance statement: Country X, a nuclear-armed state possessing intermediate-range ballistic missiles, seeks to expand its regional influence by undermining the government structures of its neighbor, country Y. Country X has initiated a campaign of misinformation and staged confrontational protests and acts of terrorism designed to elicit an aggressive and potentially ill-advised response from the government of country Y. The United States seeks to support country Y, a key regional partner, through economic aid, military assistance, and advanced humanitarian crowd-control training for its national police force. The guidance offered might be as follows: "It shall be U.S. policy to deter country X from covert or overt military attacks on country Y or on U.S. assets and interests in the region. Should country X become increasingly aggressive in seeking to destabilize country Y, including through the use of military force, the U.S. Department of Defense shall limit damage to country Y and to U.S. assets and interests in the region and other regional allies, while reestablishing deterrence of country X."

There could be a number of ways through which U.S. forces could achieve these aims. The United States could threaten to destroy some tangible asset valued by country X's leadership if it attacks country Y or threatens U.S. interests. But which assets should be held at risk, and how should they be destroyed? The first challenge, which pertains most directly to the relevant combatant commander, is to enumerate specific outcomes (end states) that reflect the objectives laid out in the guidance. The combatant commander might specify a set of military end states as follows: "Country X is deterred from attacking country Y and U.S. regional assets, interests, and allies. Should deterrence fail, country Y and U.S. territory, its forces, and its allies are defended against attacks. Throughout hostilities, country X is deterred from employing ballistic missiles or nuclear weapons. Subsequent deterrence of country X is reestablished by reducing its ability to project force within the region."

The challenge facing planners working in support of the combatant commander is then to develop specific military objectives, tailored to the military capabilities of the adversary, that are designed collectively to achieve specified end states. An additional challenge confronting American nuclear operational planners is to resolve an inherent tension between achieving political and military objectives and the legal and implicit moral requirement to limit collateral damage in the area of conflict. All U.S. military operations, including nuclear operations, must abide by applicable treaties and domestic laws regarding the conduct of military operations, the use of force, and the laws of armed conflict. Planners must resolve these tensions within the bounds of those political, physical, and practical areas that fall under military control.

One way they might accomplish this is to plan to cut lines of communication between country X senior military leadership and deployed military forces by destroying key military communications facilities or disrupting local civil communications facilities in the vicinity of political-military leadership centers. Another option would be to plan to reduce country X's ability to project force by destroying key elements of its integrated air defense system, destroying rail and highway bridges to prevent flow of military forces and material, destroying key military commodities such as ammunition or fuel depots, or damaging or disrupting key military facilities such as airfields or port facilities through which military forces might flow.

Each of the potential target classes described above is clearly of military significance but could result in significant collateral damage if not planned properly. Because many military facilities are located in close proximity to population centers, planners must examine carefully the resources at their disposal and the characteristics of the specific targets to develop specific objectives that meet both legal and operational requirements.

The means of achieving each military objective is generally left to the combatant commander leading the planning effort. However, policymakers may limit this freedom of action by placing restraints (prohibitions on action) and constraints (required actions) on the combatant commander.

An example of a restraint might be, "Planners shall not strike targets within a specified distance of a noncombatant nation's border." In contrast, an example of a constraint might be, "Planners shall destroy all ballistic missile launch facilities within two hours."

While the norm would be for policymakers to outline any restraints and constraints at the beginning of the planning process, it is entirely possible that the oversight and review process could lead policymakers to add or delete restraints and constraints when a more detailed understanding of the draft plans become apparent. Active participation of policymakers in planning is therefore an important way to minimize the gap between how planners respond to guidance and the expectations that decisionmakers believe they have conveyed through formal guidance.

An important requirement for plans developed in the final years of the Cold War, and now a hallmark for planning in the twenty-first century, is (the desire to have a wide range of tailored responses available to address a much wider range of potential adversaries and circumstances.)Creating this wider range of options begins with establishing carefully tailored policies, restraints, constraints, and military objectives; the plans will be fundamentally flawed if the inputs are not realistic and precisely stated.

Planning for Nuclear Operations

The decades-long evolution of U.S. policy, forces, and plans did not happen in a vacuum; it was brought about in the context of both American and Soviet development of nuclear weapons, intercontinental ballistic missiles, and nuclear-powered submarines carrying submarine-launched ballistic missiles by potential adversaries. Initially, Soviet bomber and missile forces lacked sufficient range, precision, and numbers to pose a meaningful strategic threat to U.S. forces. However, new generations of Soviet missiles and a substantial growth in the size of Soviet forces gave the Soviet Union the capability to attempt a nuclear first strike, which posed a meaningful strategic threat to the United States. Over the past seventy years, nuclear operational planners were required to adapt not only to changes in the worldwide threat situation and the enemy order of battle but equally to evolutionary planning guidelines of increasing scope and new delivery systems, warheads, and military tactics. In a continuing evolution from a planning environment of navigation charts, plotters, dividers, handheld navigation computers, and sharp pencils, the modern world of planning for nuclear operations draws on sophisticated computing systems designed to interface graphically with planners and transmit data digitally to the weapon systems they support.

Approach Development

Mission Analysis

In developing an operational plan, planners must first evaluate all written guidance issued by the president, secretary of defense, and Chairman of the Joint Chiefs of Staff, described earlier, as it relates to planning for each specific contingency, to gain a full understanding of the planning task before them. While the commander of the U.S. Strategic Command is the principal combatant commander responsible for planning for potential nuclear operations, collaboration is essential among STRATCOM, the combatant commander for the area of responsibility in which the contingency might occur, supporting combatant commanders, such as the U.S. Transportation Command, and the directors of the relevant combat support agencies, such as the Defense Threat Reduction Agency.

Mission analysis is led by the STRATCOM Director for Plans and Policy (J-5) with support from the staffs of appropriate regional combatant command, service components, combat support agencies, and the Defense Intelligence Agency. The specific activities of mission analysis activities may vary with the scope of each mission; figure 5-1 lists key activities germane to nuclear operational planning.

When the staff completes its initial mission analysis, the J-5 will brief that analysis to the STRATCOM commander. Following this briefing, the commander will adjust the planning guidance and direct the STRATCOM J-5 to present an initial briefing to key staff elements within the Defense Department, principally the Office of the Secretary of Defense staff and the Joint Staff, to begin the horizontal integration and approval process.

FIGURE 5-1. Mission Analysis Activities

- Analyze higher headquarters guidance
  - Presidential
  - Secretary of Defense
  - Chairman, Joint Chiefs of Staff
- Review commander's initial planning guidance
- Determine known facts and develop planning assumptions
- Determine and analyze operational limitations
- Determine specified, implied, and essential tasks
- Develop mission statement
- Identify forces available for planning
- Develop risk assessment
- Develop mission success criteria

Source: Joint Planning, Joint Chiefs of Staff, June 16, 2017, PG V-21.

Course of Action Development

Following mission analysis and presentation of a mission analysis briefing in the Pentagon, the planning staff will begin the process of developing potential courses of action. A course of action is a potential way (solution, method) to accomplish the assigned mission. The staff develops courses of action to provide unique options to the commander, all oriented on accomplishing the military end state. A good course of action accomplishes the mission within the commander's guidance, provides flexibility to meet unforeseen events during execution, and positions the joint force for future operations.[26]

One unique feature of the development of a course of action for strategic nuclear operations is the need to plan for a wide range of potential responses for each potential situation, since the timing, nature, scope, and duration of an adversary's attack could vary dramatically. For this reason, STRATCOM planners develop multiple options for both a day-to-day force condition and a full-force generation condition. This is designed to offer the president the widest range of options, to be measured in both the timing and weight of any U.S. response. Following development, each course of action is analyzed along five conditions:

- *Adequacy:* Would the course of action accomplish the mission within the parameters of higher headquarters and commander's guidance?

- *Feasibility:* Would the course of action accomplish the mission within the established time space, and resource limitations?
- *Acceptability:* Would the consequences of execution of the course of action balance risk with the probability of mission success?
- *Distinguishability:* A key requirement of nuclear operational planning is to ensure U.S. intentions, as to scope of an attack, are distinguishable to the adversary. Does the course of action offer meaningfully different scope, consequences of execution, risk, or probability of success?
- *Completeness:* Does the course of action answer the questions who, what, where, when, how, and why?[27]

FIGURE 5-2. Course of Action Development

- Objectives
- Key tasks and purpose
- Forces and capabilities required, to include anticipated supporting forces and actions
- Integrated timeline
- Task organization
- Operational concept
- Communication synchronization
- Risk
- Required decisions and decision timeline (e.g., mobilization, DEPORD)
- Deployment concepts
- Main and supporting efforts

Note: DEPORD is a deployment order JP 5-0, Joint Planning, Joint Chiefs of Staff, June 16, 2017, PG V-21.
Source: Joint Planning, Joint Chiefs of Staff, June 16, 2017, PG V-21.

When the staff has completed its course-of-action analysis, the J-5 again briefs the results to the STRATCOM commander. Following this briefing, the commander approves or modifies the course of action and directs the STRATCOM J-5 to brief it to key staff elements within the Defense Department in order to further facilitate the horizontal integration and approval process. Based on feedback from these key staff elements, the courses of action are refined further. The result of the extensive mission analysis and refined course-of-action development and analysis provides the basis for the commander's estimate, with an associated mission statement developed by

FIGURE 5-3. Planning Guidance Drives the Planning Process

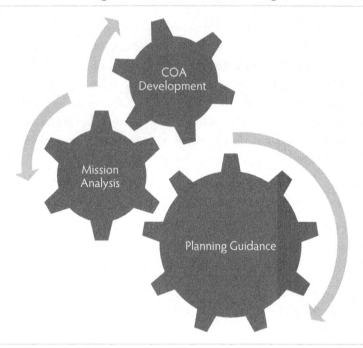

Source: Author.

the STRATCOM commander. The commander's estimate is delivered to principals in the Pentagon in briefing format, in which alternative courses of action are provided in a concise statement that defines who, what, when, where, why, and how the course of action will be implemented.[28] This briefing provides an opportunity for senior leadership in the Pentagon to review and shape the final stages of planning and, when the plan has been approved, provides the STRATCOM commander with sufficient guidance to continue full execution-level planning.

Oversight, Review, and Approval

Perhaps the most critical element of deliberate planning for employment of nuclear weapons is the oversight mechanism employed within the executive branch, to provide the Office of the Secretary of Defense staff with an opportunity to verify that policy direction is being properly implemented. Bearing in mind the extreme sensitivity of U.S. nuclear weapon employment policy and the plans generated from that policy, nuclear operational plans have always been afforded the highest level of protection by the Defense Department, dating back to the heavily compartmented plans of the 509th Composite Group of World War II.[29]

Although oversight and approval of nuclear operational plans has always been a key part of the process, policymakers in the Office of the Secretary of Defense became concerned in the 1980s that insufficient detail was being provided to the policy staff. To resolve this concern, the secretary of defense, following a comprehensive target review, ordered a greater degree of accessibility to nuclear plans for key members of the Office of the Secretary of Defense staff.

To this end, but with protection of policy and plans in mind, only a select list of policymakers and military advisers from key organizations within the department are given access to the plans as part of the review process. This includes staff from the Office of the Under Secretary of Defense for Policy, the Office of the Under Secretary of Defense for Intelligence and Security, the Joint Staff, and relevant combatant commanders.

The review process constitutes a series of in-progress briefings by the STRATCOM J-5 at key stages of the planning process. Plan review is intended to build consensus and approval of the plan at ever increasing levels of seniority in the Pentagon. Although I describe this process in three discrete steps, the number and frequency of the briefings will vary with the scope and difficulty of the mission.

The first in-progress review will typically cover the mission analysis, including early assessments of intelligence uncertainties, and provide an opportunity for staff dialogue related to challenges and risks identified during the mission analysis. The second in-progress review will typically cover preliminary course-of-action development and analysis, intelligence requirements, and risk. During these reviews, each organization is afforded an opportunity to discuss and debate issues identified in the planning process. At the final in-progress review, the STRATCOM commander presents a comprehensive briefing of the mission and proposed courses of action for the plan that defines who, what, when, where, why, and how each course of action would be implemented. This briefing also includes an assessment of the probable success, risk, and consequences of execution. Ultimately, the secretary of defense or a designated representative is the approval authority for each plan. On approval of the plan, detailed operational-level planning is completed and transmitted to operational forces.

Execution-Level Planning for Nuclear Operations

One of the unique and demanding features of nuclear operational plans is the requirement that these plans be available for immediate execution. This is so because the United States cannot predict whether or when a conflict might begin, and the consequences of not being fully prepared could be catastrophic, if not existential. The implication is that for planning before execution, unlike virtually every other operational plan, no further time is available. This requires careful evaluation of every imaginable variable associated with responding to a no-notice or short-notice attack. Although the planning process is not perfectly linear, as depicted in figure 5-4, the steps illustrated represent the essential tasks that are completed for each employment option created by U.S. Strategic Command.

One unfortunate misconception related to the act of preplanning nuclear operations and maintaining the readiness for an immediate response is that the nuclear forces of the United States are in a hair-trigger posture that could lead to a catastrophic miscalculation. In fact, the exact opposite is true—careful assessment, planning, and preparation provide decisionmakers with increased awareness and expand the available decision time in a rapidly unfolding situation and thereby facilitate the latest possible execution decision.

Targeting-Related Intelligence

Targeting is central to nuclear planning. The term *target* is used by professionals and laypeople alike, but in the case of war planning, more appropriate terminology would include the terms *installation* and *facility*.[30] Although *target* is never inappropriate, the more precise terms are used throughout this discussion.

Adequate intelligence is the lifeblood of the planning process. History is replete with military operations that failed, in part or as a whole, because of faulty intelligence data or assessments—for example, the attack on Pearl Harbor and the invasion of the Bay of Pigs. These major intelligence failures are the quintessential proof of the old saying, "Garbage in, garbage out." Conversely, military successes, such as the Battle of Midway and the Cuban Missile Crisis, would not have been achieved without timely, coherent intelligence analyses.

Collection of intelligence for nuclear planning is driven, over the long-term, by the Strategic Support Plan, which is developed and managed by the STRATCOM Director for Intelligence (J-2). Collection, processing, and distribution of

FIGURE 5-4. Essential Planning Activities for Nuclear Operational Plans

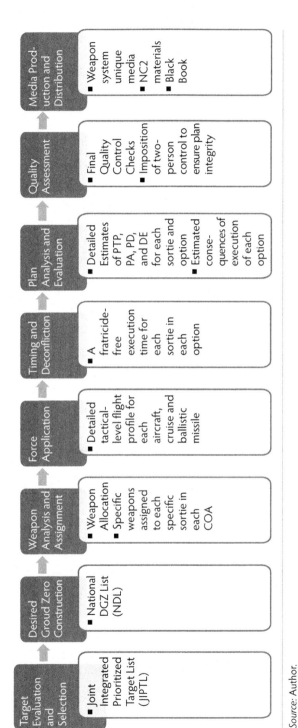

Target Evaluation and Selection	Desired Groud Zero Construction	Weapon Analysis and Assignment	Force Application	Timing and Deconfliction	Plan Analysis and Evaluation	Quality Assessment	Media Prod- uction and Distribution
▪ Joint Integrated Prioritized Target List (JIPTL)	▪ National DGZ List (NDL)	▪ Weapon Allocation ▪ Specific weapons assigned to each specific sortie in each COA	▪ Detailed tactical- level flight profile for each aircraft, cruise and ballistic missile	▪ A fratricide- free execution time for each sortie in each option	▪ Detailed Estimates of PTP, PA, PD, and DE for each sortie and option ▪ Estimated conse- quences of execution of each option	▪ Final Quality Control Checks ▪ Imposition of two- person control to ensure plan integrity	▪ Weapon system unique media ▪ NC2 materials ▪ Black Book

Source: Author.

specific guidance-driven intelligence requirements is managed by the Defense Intelligence Agency, drawing on the full breadth of intelligence agencies of the United States and, where possible, its allies. The resultant information related to worldwide facilities of potential planning interest is stored and maintained by the agency in the Defense Department's modernized integrated database.[31]

Target Evaluation and Selection

When planners in Omaha have identified specific military objectives and approved courses of action have been selected, targeting analysts, to achieve specific political objectives, employ various analytical techniques to nominate specific facilities for consideration by the Joint Targeting Coordination Board.[32] The board comprises functional experts from across the intelligence community, operational planners from each service component, and the joint combatant command appropriate for the specific mission.

The analytical techniques employed might include detailed examination of specified systems, functional analysis, key nodes within networks, capacity analysis, and relational dependencies of various militarily significant capabilities. Targeting analysts will identify key installations related to an adversary's capability to wage war and key facilities within each installation. Each agency or command represented in the Joint Targeting Coordination Board may nominate target systems or specific targets during the analysis phase.

The targeting analyst generally seeks to achieve the specified military objectives and present strike planners with the means of achieving the military objective with a minimal use of force and collateral damage. When the Joint Targeting Coordination Board has reviewed the nominated targets and the targets have been approved by the STRATCOM J-5, the resultant targeting information, called the Joint Integrated Prioritized Targeting List, is added to the modernized integrated database, if it is not already in the system.

Desired Ground Zero Construction

The one area that differs most significantly from targeting with conventional weapons is identification of the specific aim point required to achieve a specified level of damage from a nuclear weapon detonation. A desired ground zero (DGZ) is the subpoint above, on, or below the surface of the earth at which a nuclear weapon is detonated to achieve a specified level of damage on one or more facilities.

In conventional targeting an aim point represents the precise point of impact or center of impact of multiple weapons to achieve the intended objective and level of destruction.[33] In this day of precision-guided muni-tions, this is almost always a precise point of impact for a single weapon.

Unlike conventional weapons, even the smallest nuclear weapon produces destructive effects over a relatively wide radius. Because this radius is large, it is conceivable that a single weapon could be employed to destroy a single large facility or multiple facilities within a single installation or that the aim point could be offset from the facility to avoid collateral damage to other facilities in the area. Conversely, a large target complex, such as an airfield, might require multiple warheads to achieve the specified objective. The aim point for a nuclear weapon is the desired ground zero.

Damage criteria established for nuclear targeting reflects engineering-level analysis, derived from more than four decades of nuclear weapon testing, of the physical effects of a nuclear blast against a wide range of structures (for example, aircraft runway, hangers, bunkers, bridges, electrical substations, fac-tories) and systems (for example, aircraft, armored vehicles, air defense radars).

Damage levels, characterized as moderate or severe, are described in terms of the response of each structure or system to the effects of dynamic pres-sure (blast), overpressure (crush), and cratering. For each potential facility class, there exists a catalogued description of what moderate or severe damage would look like and, typically, a time factor of how long it would take to return the facility to operation (if ever).

When planners are assessing the relative effectiveness of different weapons against a specific facility, one of the measures used is probability of damage. Probability of damage is the probability of achieving a specified level of damage to a specific facility with a specific weapon type.

In the early days of targeting with nuclear weapons delivered by heavy bombers, the DGZ might have been the geographic center of the facility of interest, such as the center of a bomber airfield, the center of a large mili-tary industrial complex, or perhaps the central span of a rail bridge. In those early years following World War II, the potential targets for nuclear weapons numbered in the dozens and would be struck over a period of many weeks or months. The targeting process was a matter of bombing principles and precise navigation by highly trained aircrews. However, as the number of nuclear weapons grew and the scope of potential plans expanded, a more automated approach to aimpoint development became essential.

Today, STRATCOM employs an automated planning tool to develop DGZs for nuclear plans.[34] This system develops aimpoints by initially using a generic nuclear weapon (build weapon) to determine the geographic location where the weapon must be detonated to achieve the desired level of damage to a single facility. The tool then produces alternative DGZs for each weapon in the inventory, thereby providing maximum flexibility to planners. At times, multiple facilities may be located in a relatively small geographic area. In such a case, the system will identify the geographic point at which the build weapon must be detonated to achieve the specified probability of damage against the multiple facilities.

Weapon Analysis and Assignment

When the family of DGZs is complete, a weapon must be selected to attack the DGZ. In a perfect world, planners would have an unrestrained ability to pick a weapon tailored specifically to the DGZ. In reality, planners must analyze the stated military objectives, the threat environment, priority, and time sensitivity of each DGZ and the estimated probability of damage that would be achieved by individual nuclear weapon types; based on these criteria, they make a reasoned choice.

Planners must consider factors such as the range capability of individual weapon systems; the density of air and missile defenses, or both, in the vicinity of each DGZ; the available approach aspects to each DGZ; and, in the case of multiple independently targeted reentry vehicle ballistic missiles, the ability to footprint the reentry vehicles on each missile.[35]

Planners may also be restrained by policy. For example, policy could prohibit flight over noncombatant airspace, by aircraft or ballistic missiles. Depending on the target location, such a restraint could limit weapon assignment options dramatically, even to the point of sacrificing full achievement of the desired level of damage to a target.

From this analysis, planners allocate a weapon system type to cover each DGZ in a specific plan. At this point of the planning process, a shift from generic weapon systems to specific aircraft or missile sorties takes place when the weapon system assignments and DGZs are turned over to the force application planners.

Force Application (Strike Planning)

As recently as 1990, bomber and tanker planners relied on paper charts, rulers, and colored pencils, aided by ponderous (relatively speaking) mainframe computers, to develop routes of flight for bombers, tankers, and cruise missiles. Only in the past twenty-five years has the technology evolved sufficiently to facilitate rapid planning in the challenging multipolar environment of the twenty-first century. The technology now exists to rapidly develop targets and aimpoints; detailed bomber, tanker, and cruise missile routes of flight; and ballistic missile flight profiles. This is now done in a small fraction of the eighteen months the process required as recently as 1995.

Force application is the process of developing, from coherent operational-level plans, a detailed and fully executable tactical-level plan for each weapon allocated in each specific option (target package). This means a detailed flight profile from the authorized launch patrol area of each SSBN and its load of SLBMs; the launch facility of each ICBM; or a detailed route of flight from the specified takeoff base to the intended target or cruise missile launch point and subsequently to the preplanned post-strike landing base for each heavy bomber and mated tanker.

A significant difference between conventional and nuclear strike planning is that nuclear operational plans are centrally developed and distributed to the operational units for potential execution. There are multiple reasons for centralized planning of nuclear operations. Among them is the critical need for close interaction between policymakers, senior military leadership, and the operational command; ensuring absolute secrecy of the plans; and the unique skills and tools required to build effective nuclear plans.

Force application seeks to produce the highest probability to penetrate (PTP) defenses for each weapon to its intended target. PTP considers the impact of ballistic missile defenses or integrated air defense systems and, when multiplied by the weapon system reliability of each weapon, produces an expression of the probability of arrival of a weapon to its target. These measures are only relative measures of quality, one potential sortie variation to another, rather than an absolute projection of these probabilities.

In the U.S. operational concept, ICBMs are launched from a specific hardened launch facility, with presurveyed launch coordinates, and are guided by a precisely ground-aligned inertial navigation system. Conversely, U.S. SLBMs are housed in launch tubes in nuclear-powered ballistic missile submarines patrolling at sea in a known but large patrol area and launched from a point determined only in the last few seconds before launch of the missile. Submarine-launched ballistic missiles are launched based on positional data provided by an inertial navigation system, which are updated by various external means. To help compensate for potential positional variance at launch, SLBMs also derive updated position data in flight, including a system of star sightings (stellar inertial) to avoid depending on the global positioning system.

The missile graphic planning system is used to develop precise ballistic missile flight profiles for both ICBMs and SLBMs.[36] While the specific characteristics of each ballistic missile system, including the number and type of warheads and the speed and angle of reentry, will vary for each missile system, the most significant difference between the systems is the variance in launch location and its subsequent effect on the approach aspect to any particular target.[37]

In the early postwar years, long-range heavy bombers remained the principal weapon delivery system. Their mission was to launch from airfields within range of enemy targets and drop nuclear gravity bombs from high altitude in a campaign that could last months. Force employment planning for bombers is, at its essence, an exercise in navigation over great distances to reach the launch point for standoff weapons, such as cruise missiles, or the initial point of a bombing run to drop bombs. From the world of charts, plotters, the navigation whiz-wheel, and star charts to computer graphic–aided planning with precise digital terrain elevation data and precision inertial navigation systems, planning for bombers has evolved since the end of World War II in response to changes in aircraft technology, threats, and planning tools.[38]

As the rapidly changing nuclear weapon inventory changes in both character and quantity, the nature and scope of plans also changes. From a few dozen weapons in the early postwar years to tens of thousands of weapons in the 1980s, planning tools and the plans they produced became more complex and time consuming. Although early sorties were based on high-altitude navigation and bombing, in the 1980s planning became an exercise in high-altitude navigation to a preplanned low-altitude penetration point, through enemy air defenses, followed by a fuel-conserving high-altitude egress.

As long-range ALCMs entered the inventory in the early 1980s, planners focused first on understanding threat radar coverage and identifying areas for unimpeded cruise missile launch streams. An important requirement for ALCM planning is precise digital terrain elevation data, since the ALCM navigation system relies on terrain comparison maps. A terrain comparison map is a digital image of a terrain stored in the flight computer. The radar image taken in flight is compared with the stored image, and the ALCM's inertial navigation system position is then updated. Penetration of integrated air defenses at low altitude requires planners to take full advantage of terrain to mask the bomber's route of flight to the target, while navigating with the aid of navigation radar and inertial navigation systems. Over the years, B-52s could employ both standoff cruise missile launch points and penetration of enemy integrated air defense systems.

Timing and Deconfliction

When a nuclear weapon detonates, it releases sufficient radiation (X-ray, neutron, gamma) and blast effects to damage or destroy other weapons that are airborne within the weapons-effects radii of the first weapons. This phenomenon is referred to as fratricide.

Timing and deconfliction is the process of adjusting the arrival time of one or more nuclear weapons in a dense target area to avoid fratricide. Precisely how a weapon might be damaged depends on the altitude environment at the moment of detonation, whether it be high altitude, near surface, or surface burst. The deconfliction process is achieved by adjusting planned arrival times of each weapon to its target or adjusting the approach aspect of a weapon to its target to avoid the weapon-effects radii of the earlier arriving weapons.

Theoretically, plans could include any combination of strategic and nonstrategic systems or could be developed solely around any one of the systems available to planners. Historically, when extremely large and complex plans were developed by the JSTPS, timing and deconfliction of relevant NATO sorties was also performed by planners in Omaha. Given the potential complexity of nuclear operational plans today, timing and deconfliction is performed by the Plans and Policy Directorate of STRATCOM, in Omaha, as part of both the deliberate and adaptive planning processes, for both strategic and nonstrategic systems that may be included in a unique plan.

Plans Analyses and Evaluation

When each discrete plan (option or strike package) is complete, planners analyze the plan to assess the probability of success of achieving the stated objective of the plan. Analysts consider both objective and subjective measures to draw conclusions as to the relative, not absolute, value of each plan. If the projected probability of success is low, planners will attempt to modify the plan to improve the probability of success or, in some cases, will conclude that another approach is required.

In the nuclear planning world, one expression of success is damage expectancy. Damage expectancy (DE) is the product of the probability of arrival (PA) of a single weapon to its target and the probability of damage (PD) of that weapon to its target (DE = PA × PD).[39]

The mean damage expectancy for all weapon-target combinations in the plan is the overall damage expectancy for the particular option. A statistician would probably emphasize that while the average damage expectancy for a large option may fairly represent the damage across the target set, it may mask the importance of low damage against individual high-value targets within the set. What that means is that damage expectancy is only one of many factors used to evaluate the potential utility of a plan.

While the formula is simple, determination of the underlying data is a complex problem spanning multiple organizations. For example, the air force and the navy estimate prelaunch survivability based on facts or assumptions related to each individual sortie (for example, whether an SSBN is at sea and therefore survivable from an attack, the hardness of each ICBM launch facility, or silo, and whether a bomber sortie is generated and ready for immediate launch when an attack begins) and the character of a potential enemy attack (for example, the number and type of weapons employed).

The air force and the navy also provide STRATCOM planners with computed weapon system reliability for each delivery vehicle type, whether it be an ICBM, SLBM, bomber, or cruise missile. In addition, the National Laboratories compute reliability factors for each warhead type employed in the plan. The product of these reliability factors produces an overall reliability factor for each weapon in a plan. Mathematically, weapon system reliability is a product of carrier reliability, release system reliability, and warhead reliability.

While the mathematics and science of nuclear weapons effects were well understood from years of testing and experimentation, the tools employed by planners to evaluate plans have evolved over decades from hand calculations and slide rules to graphically aided models fed by engineering and intelligence databases. These tools include the extended air defense simulation, which is used to model engagements of aircraft and ballistic missiles with enemy integrated air defense systems. The simulation produces a value of probability to penetrate based on detailed intelligence data and characteristics of friendly systems. It is important to emphasize that the probability to penetrate produced by this model is a measure of relative performance of each individual sortie, not a representation of what will happen in an engagement.

Quality Assessment and Two-Person Control

Given the undeniable importance of accuracy and the efficacy of data developed during the nuclear planning process, STRATCOM embeds quality and accuracy checks throughout the process. While some quality checks are embedded in the software system, the final checks are performed by highly skilled planners, drawn from the ranks of experienced ICBM, SSBN, bomber, and tanker operators. Furthermore, to ensure the integrity of the database,

STRATCOM operates under a two-person rule when moving new or modified data into the approved final database. This policy serves the dual purpose of guarding against human error in the files management process and against unauthorized access to the databases.

Media Production and Distribution

The old saying, the job is not finished until the paperwork is done, applies equally to planning for nuclear operations despite the fact that very little paper changes hands in the process. When final approval of plans is achieved, weapon system–unique electronic media is produced for each leg of the triad and distributed through highly secure means to each operational location and worldwide command and control facilities.

Command-and-Control Planning

Although both command and nuclear command and control are discussed elsewhere in this volume, it is important to understand how the planning process and tools facilitate command and control of specific plans on order of the president. A key feature of the planning system is the ability of planners to draw data from the database, develop operational plans based on those data, and then return the detailed sortie-level data to the database. During this process, the system embeds precise sortie-level details, including launch and recovery information, flight profile of the sortie, weapon-to-target assignment information, and the option descriptor for each sortie and its mated weapons. It is in this stage that the detailed execution instructions required for nuclear command and control are embedded in the sortie data files and ultimately made available to each command-and-control element.

Following final review and approval of each plan, the data file containing detailed information related to each option is promulgated to each operational unit and made accessible to all nuclear command-and-control elements through the nuclear planning and execution system. Detailed information for each potential option, including the sortie descriptor, weapons, and targets, is provided in the database.

Maintaining Plans

Traditionally, changes in U.S. forces or intelligence information were incorporated in the single integrated operational plan through quarterly updates to the databases and subsequent adjustments to each effected SIOP sortie. The quarterly maintenance process was essentially a microcosm of the full eighteen-month development process. When more significant changes occurred, usually driven by changes in policy, those changes were incorporated in an annual revision of the plan.

Imagine for a moment the task facing planners in the early 1990s, as the United States fielded the B-1, the B-2, the advanced cruise missile, the Ohio-class ballistic missile submarine, and the Trident II missile while retiring the FB-111 and a substantial portion of the B-52 fleet, the short-range attack missile, Trident I, and the Minuteman II and Peacekeeper ballistic missiles.[40] This, while the Warsaw Pact was falling apart and the Soviet Union was collapsing, which, in turn, led to all Russian nuclear weapons being removed from the three remaining Warsaw Pact states, Kazakhstan, Belarus, and Ukraine. Changes to the underlying forces and target base became so frequent that planners began to execute monthly maintenance, and later "near real-time" maintenance, of the SIOP. Today, although the frequency of changes in nuclear operational plans is less, the importance of maintaining the currency and integrity of these plans is undiminished.

Although it may be that none of these plans will be executed, the very act of planning for the potential use of a nuclear weapon builds a better understanding of the issues involved for each potential scenario and, as a result, improve the president's ability to manage the crisis.

Concluding Thoughts

Throughout the history of nuclear weapons there has been a strongly held belief by some that the United States should lead a global effort to abolish these powerful weapons. In fact, in his 1984 State of the Union address, Ronald Reagan said, "A nuclear war cannot be won and must never be fought." President Reagan went on to say, in reference to the Soviet Union, "The only value in our two nations possessing nuclear weapons is to make sure they will never be used. But then would it not be better to do away with them entirely?"

Despite the strongly held conviction of President Reagan and each of his successors to date, nuclear weapons still exist. The number of nuclear weapon states has grown. And other states of grave concern continue to pursue a nuclear weapon capability.

This means that as long as nuclear weapons exist, the United States must bear the burden of maintaining a nuclear capability and posture sufficient to deter any adversary from employing nuclear weapons against the United

States, its friends, or its allies. Meticulous planning is the foundation of a military posture designed to maintain the peace. Furthermore, maintenance of a robust nuclear enterprise is not a simple or inexpensive task, but it is an absolutely necessary task. When compared with conventional weapons, nuclear weapons are special. It takes specialized training to employ nuclear weapon systems. It takes both specialized training and years of experience to plan nuclear operations. It takes many years of specialized training and experience to lead those who constitute our nuclear weapons enterprise, and only the very best are selected to do so. When dealing with nuclear weapons, policy, plans, and operations, there can be no mistakes: the closely held, deliberate, and rigorous processes described herein are essential to the future well-being of U.S. national security.

In this context, a major task facing the Defense Department is to remain focused on preserving the tools and expertise necessary to manage the nuclear weapons enterprise for the foreseeable future. It is an essential need to nurture each new generation of operators, planners, strategists, and policymakers in the unique skills and knowledge of nuclear weapons to maintain a strong deterrent posture as long as nuclear weapons exist.

Notes

1. "History of the 509th Composite Group, Activation to 15 Aug 1945," Air Force Historical Research Agency, August 15,1945, p. 1.

2. "History of the 509th Composite Group, Activation to 15 Aug 1945," p. 64.

3. National Security Act of 1947, Pub. L. No. 253, 61 Stat. 495 (1947). The act has been amended many times; the current version is codified at 50 U.S.G sec. 3001 et. seq.

4. National Security Act of 1947.

5. Phillip S. Meilinger, *Bomber: The Formation and Early Years of Strategic Air Command* (Montgomery, AL: Maxwell Air Force Base, Air University Press, 2012): 154.

6. David Alan Rosenberg, "The Origins of Overkill: Nuclear Weapons and American Strategy, 1945–1960," *International Security* 7, no. 5 (1983), p. 18.

7. Walton S. Moody, *Building a Strategic Air Force* (Montgomery, AL: Maxwell Air Force Base, Air Force History and Museums Program, 1995), p. 138.

8. Moody, *Building a Strategic Air Force,* p. 148.

9. Moody, *Building a Strategic Air Force,* p. 199.

10. Rosenberg, *The Origins of Overkill,* p. 16.

11. For an example of this logic, see John Foster Dulles, "Policy for Security and Peace," *Foreign Affairs* 32, no. 3 (1954), pp. 358–60. On civilian leaders questioning the procurement of these systems, see "Memorandum from Secretary

Defense McNamara to the Chairman of the Joint Chiefs of Staff (Lemnitzer)," *Foreign Relations of the United States, 1961–1963*, vol. 8, *National Security Policy*, edited by David W. Mabon and David S. Patterson (Government Printing Office, 1996), Document 86.

12. *Fratricide* refers to the destruction of one's forces by other elements of one's forces.

13. James T. Pratt III, *Strategic Target Planning and the JSTPS* (Carlisle, PA: U.S. Army War College, March 1988), p. 5.

14. Pratt, *Strategic Target Planning and the JSTPS*, p. 3.

15. Rosenberg, *The Origins of Overkill*, p. 4.

16. Rosenberg, *The Origins of Overkill*, p. 4.

17. Rosenberg, *The Origins of Overkill*, p. 5.

18. Rosenberg, *The Origins of Overkill*, p. 5.

19. Malcolm J. Abzug and E. Eugene Larrabee, *Airplane Stability and Control: A History of the Technologies That Made Aviation Possible* (Cambridge University Press, 2005), pp. 104–105.

20. *Strategic Air Command and the Alert Program: A Brief History* (Bellevue, NE: Offutt Air Force Base: Office of the Historian, Strategic Air Command, April 1988).

21. Gregory S. Gilmour, *From Sac to STRATCOM: The Origins of Unified Command over Nuclear Forces* (Monterey, CA: Naval Post Graduate School, June 1993), p. 50.

22. Gilmour, *From Sac to STRATCOM*, p. 50.

23. Gilmour, *From Sac to STRATCOM*, p. 50.

24. Edward J. Drea and others, *History of the Unified Command Plan, 1946–2012* (Washington, D.C.: Joint History Office, Office of the Chairman of the Joint Chiefs of Staff, 2013), p. 64.

25. Drea and others, *History of the Unified Command Plan*.

26. Joint Chiefs of Staff, *Joint Publication 5-0*, June 16, 2017, p. V-20.

27. Joint Chiefs of Staff, *Joint Publication 5-0*, June 16, 2017, p. V-28.

28. Joint Chiefs of Staff, *Joint Publication 5-0*, June 16, 2017, p. GL-6.

29. During the era of the SIOP, this information was classified as SIOP—Extremely Sensitive Information (SIOP-ESI). Post-SIOP, much of this information is protected as Nuclear Command and Control Extremely Sensitive Information (NC2-ESI). See "Safeguarding Nuclear Command and Control Command Extremely Sensitive Information," OPNAV Instruction 5511.35M, January 13, 2016, www.secnav. navy.mil/doni/Directives/05000%20General%20Management%20Security%20 and%20Safety%20Services/05-500%20Security%20Services/5511.35M.pdf.

30. "Installation: a grouping of facilities located in the same vicinity, which support particular functions," U.S. Air Force, *U.S. Air Force Intelligence Targeting Guide*, Air Force Pamphlet 14-210 (Washington, D.C.: United States Department of the Air Force, February 1, 1998), p. 120. "Facility: a real property entity consisting of one or more of the following: a building, a structure, a utility system, pavement, and underlying land. These measurable geophysical parameters define the real property. In the context of entity-level target development, a facility provides a function that

contributes to a target system's capability" (Joint Staff, *Target Development Standards* CJCSI 3370.01B), p. D-4.

31. Joint Staff, *Joint Targeting School Student Guide* (Dam Neck, VA: Joint Targeting School, March 1, 2017), p. 216.

32. The Joint Targeting Coordination Board is a group formed by the joint force commander to accomplish broad targeting oversight functions that may include but are not limited to coordinating targeting information, providing targeting guidance and priorities, and refining the joint integrated prioritized target list. The board is normally made up of representatives from the joint force staff, all components, and if required, component subordinate units. (Joint Publication 3-60, GL-6).

33. This aimpoint for conventional weapons is the desired mean point of impact (DMPI), defined as "the planned point whose coordinates are the arithmetic means of the coordinates of the separate points of impact of a finite number of projectiles fired or released at the same aiming point under a given set of conditions." U.S. Air Force, *U.S. Air Force Intelligence Targeting Guide,* p. 115.

34. This system is part of the Integrated Strategic Planning and Analysis Network and is called the National Designated Ground Zero List Integrated Development System, known by the acronym NIDS.

35. The footprint of a missile with multiple independently targeted warheads is the largest geographic area within which a single booster and post-boost vehicle can deposit its warheads. Because the device carrying the warheads on top of a single missile is limited in the amount of fuel it can carry, there is a finite distance that the device (the post-boost vehicle) can travel to disperse its warheads while flying above the earth. The footprint approximates the shape of the area that a single post-boost vehicle can transport its warheads. See Lynn Etheridge Davis and Warner R. Schilling, "All You Ever Wanted to Know about MIRV and ICBM Calculations but Were Not Cleared to Ask," Journal of Conflict Resolution 17, no. 2 (1973), p. 221, and A. B. Barbeau, *Strategic Offensive Weapons Employment in the Period about 1975,* Weapons Systems Evaluation Group Report 148 (Alexandria, VA: Institute for Defense Analyses, August 1969), p. 97.

36. The missile graphic planning system (MGPS) calculates a ballistic flight path from each missile launch location or area to a point in space from which the reentry vehicles are released to impact the target location(s), accounting for the rotation of the earth at the specific latitude of the target. The MGPS algorithms evaluate all aspects of the flight path to ensure no missile operating parameters are exceeded, including reentry speed and angle. The system is capable of examining the relationship of the target and obstacles in the missile flight path to avoid hitting (clipping) an obstruction. It also provides the first opportunity to deconflict the arrival of each weapon in order to avoid fratricide. When planners, using the MGPS, have developed all the ballistic missile sorties in the plan, each sortie is examined in a rigorous quality control process before electronic media are produced and ultimately distributed to each operational unit.

37. In the case of SLBM sorties, MGPS executes an algorithm to ensure the missile flight path is achievable from the entire preplanned patrol area of the SSBN.

This provides the ballistic missile submarine commander the flexibility to patrol throughout the patrol area to achieve the highest level of prelaunch survivability for the SSBN.

38. The air vehicle planning system (APS VI) is used for planning for bombers loaded with either gravity bombs or cruise missiles, air refueling tanker support, and the detailed route of flight for each cruise missile. The system provides the ability to visualize the complete route of flight with overlays of terrain and air defenses. In recent evolutions, APS is capable of optimizing routes for low observable (stealth) aircraft during selection of a route of flight through an integrated air defense system. For issues on route planning for both cruise missiles and low observable aircraft, see Myron Hura and Gary McLeod, *Route Planning Issues for Low Observable Aircraft and Cruise Missiles: Implications for the Intelligence Community* (Santa Monica, CA: RAND, 1993).

39. The probablility of arrival of each weapon is the product of prelaunch survivability, probability to penetrate enemy defenses, and weapon system reliability. The probability of damage for a given weapon-target combination is a function of the physical characteristics of the target, the weapon, and location of the weapon detonation.

40. The short-range attack missile is a hypersonic missile capable of both semi-ballistic flight and terrain-following flight profiles. The missile was carried by both the B-52 and FB-111.

CHAPTER 6

Commanding Nuclear Forces

General C. Robert Kehler, U.S.A.F. (ret.)

The wartime employment of Little Boy and Fat Man at Hiroshima and Nagasaki in August of 1945 changed the notion of warfare between major powers. Once they had been used to win a war, nuclear weapons soon became the most important tools to prevent a war. One result was the birth of what many have called the great paradox of the nuclear age: to prevent the use of nuclear weapons, the United States has to be prepared to use them. For the first time in U.S. history, the nation called on its armed forces to "wage deterrence" in open-ended cold war.[1]

In practice, waging deterrence presents commanders of nuclear forces with a host of enduring challenges. Perhaps the most difficult of these is the leadership challenge arising from the psychological tension between the endless imperative to deter and the constant readiness to strike. Strategic Air Command (SAC), the nuclear war-fighting command of Cold War fame, captured this apparent contradiction perfectly in its accurate (if ironic) motto, "Peace Is Our Profession." Its successor, U.S. Strategic Command (STRATCOM), adopted the same motto.

Deterrence credibility depends on the readiness of the forces to execute their combat missions; yet performing those missions represents failure of the primary deterrence objective. In essence, serving in the nuclear deterrent forces of the United States is the mental and emotional equivalent of playing on an elite, world-class sports team that prepares with great intensity every day for a game it hopes never to play and indeed seeks to prevent—a situation that places extraordinary demands on the men and women who lead and carry out our most foundational national security responsibility. Unlike a sports team, victory in the nuclear forces is defined as the absence of the ultimate contest. It takes exceptional leaders and people with unyielding mental and emotional discipline, clarity of purpose, and professional commitment to consistently meet the rigors of duty in such an environment.

Nuclear commanders have faced psychological and motivational challenges since the early days of the Cold War with the Soviet Union; but in many respects the Cold War was relatively straightforward when compared with the present. Commanders of that era operated in a completely different global security environment than today's nuclear commanders. I experienced that difference while serving in and commanding nuclear units during and after the Cold War. Most of the concepts, capabilities, and operational procedures developed for nuclear forces during the Cold War were tailored (often invented) for a single adversary who posed an unambiguous and immediate existential threat to our homeland and to our allies and partners overseas. The belief that a crisis or conflict could erupt suddenly and escalate quickly created a singular sense of urgency. None of us had to work hard either to convince the people we led of their importance or to motivate them to maintain their combat readiness. Nuclear crewmembers knew why they were needed, and despite debates at the margins regarding nuclear weapons in Congress, the media, and among academicians, a clear sense of purpose and elite esprit de corps formed the basis of their abiding commitment to the deterrence mission. For them, the reality of the threat and global importance of their mission justified the hard work, tedium, and rigid discipline they endured to carry it out.

This clear sense of purpose and importance began to erode as the Soviet Union and the Warsaw Pact dissolved and the Cold War faded into the background. Although Russia, and increasingly China, still deployed significant nuclear forces that could threaten the United States and our regional allies with massive destruction, nuclear crewmembers inevitably began to question the continued relevance of their mission to the new security challenges facing the United States. The urgent nuclear threat had seemingly receded along with the end of the Cold War. Under a series of presidential initiatives, bombers and associated aerial refueling tankers were released from their day-to-day nuclear commitment and reassigned to tactical and airlift commands as SAC deactivated. Nuclear testing was ended, force structure was dramatically reduced, equipment aged, and planned modernization was either deferred or eliminated. In parallel, policymakers across administrations sent conflicting signals regarding the continued importance, value, and relevance of the nuclear deterrent to U.S. national security. These questions were magnified as arms reductions (a few suggested complete elimination), nuclear terrorism, and nonproliferation took the place of deterrence at the top of the policy agenda; nuclear matters were subordinated within policy and planning staffs, and the enduring importance of nuclear weapons in U.S. national security strategy was played down. After the terror attacks of September 11, 2001, the United States deferred long-overdue nuclear force modernization for an additional decade as the all-consuming war on violent extremists dominated U.S. national security priorities.

(All these measures were understandable in light of a changed global security environment with new threats and challenges. However, taken together they created within the nuclear community a widely perceived mismatch between U.S. declaratory policy, which continued to emphasize the foundational importance of nuclear deterrence, and the intellectual and financial investment being made to sustain the people and capabilities on which deterrence is predicated.)

Between 2007 and 2013 a series of disturbing incidents and lapses in discipline reminded policymakers and commanders that they could not take for granted the men and women who perform the nuclear deterrence mission. Inertia had carried us forward from the end of the Cold War, but that inertia was reaching its end. Investigations led by former secretary of defense James R. Schlesinger, former SAC commander and air force chief of staff General Larry D. Welch, and former Navy Fleet Forces commander Admiral John C. Harvey concluded that U.S. nuclear forces were still meeting mission demands but critically important margins in sustainment resources and capability were eroding.[2] Their reports cited a number of causes, but prominent among them were "lack of interest and attention" throughout the Department of Defense, including at very high levels, and "significant disconnects . . . between what the Defense Department and Service leadership expected and what the leaders did to empower the forces to meet those expectations."[3] Investigations also confirmed a general decline in nuclear expertise and experience and a diminished nuclear culture that contributed to low morale and substandard behavior in the units.

While senior commanders and civilian leaders never lost overall confidence in the nuclear forces, it was obvious that major organizational changes, reforms, and improvements were needed to address these shortcomings. But the broader message was clear: to sustain a credible and effective nuclear deterrent, the warriors at the tip of the nuclear spear must have unequivocal and unambiguous clarity, commitment, and support from the chain of command that demands their efforts. This is an ageless leadership principle that we ignore again at great peril to the nation.

To wage deterrence successfully, commanders and leaders must contend with the unique psychological, operational, and cultural factors that make nuclear duty distinct within the profession of arms. To be sure, U.S. conventional forces play a vital deterrent role, and tens of thousands of our military men and women have been injured or have sacrificed their lives in contingencies and high-intensity conventional conflicts since the beginning of the nuclear age. But nuclear forces underwrite our freedom with a sustained readiness commitment that began in the late 1940s and extends indefinitely into the future. The demands associated with that commitment are relentless, standards are strict, and the civilization-ending potential of failure is unthinkable.

What follows is an overview of the challenges that characterize nuclear duty for the men and women who serve and those charged with leading them. Although much of the day-to-day responsibility for leading nuclear forces rests on the shoulders of the commander of STRATCOM and its immediate subordinate commands, elected officials, civilian appointees, and senior military leaders also play critical roles creating an environment conducive to principled and effective leadership of the nuclear forces. This chapter provides my personal perspective, as a former STRATCOM commander, regarding how to understand and contend with the challenges and responsibilities of nuclear duty. The chapter also describes the distinct roles played by the STRATCOM commander: as a leader of nuclear operators, as an expert in the art and strategy of nuclear deterrence, and as an adviser to the secretary of defense and president of the United States.

The Human Dimension of Nuclear Operations

Although policy, plans, and hardware typically dominate the conversation, the men and women who operate our nuclear forces and maintain, secure, and support the nuclear mission form the most important component of the U.S. nuclear deterrent. Absent their dedication and professional performance, policies and plans are empty words, and weapon systems not a credible threat. In general, three challenges characterize duty involving one of the three legs of the nuclear triad of land-based intercontinental ballistic missiles (ICBMs), nuclear ballistic missile submarines (SSBNs), and nuclear-armed long-range bombers. To a lesser extent, the same challenges also characterize duty with dual-capable fighter aircraft (DCA) deployed overseas in support of allies. The first challenge is that nuclear duty provides little of the psychological benefit that accrues to personnel in other areas of the military profession. The second is that nuclear duty involves a significant amount of abstraction: forces can only simulate the full range of actions and conditions they would likely encounter in a nuclear war. The third is that duty involving the most destructive weapons known to humanity raises unique ethical and legal challenges for commanders and operators alike. Commanders must consider all three as they guide, motivate, and inspire the people who make deterrence possible.

The Thanklessness of Nuclear Duty

Duty involving nuclear weapons is unlike any other military duty. By its nature, nuclear duty is virtually invisible, and its value is easily overlooked. It is performed quietly (in actual silence, in the case of ballistic missile submarines), often conducted in remote areas, wrapped in tight security, and carried out with little of the public recognition or glamour associated with most other military assignments. Success in nuclear deterrence is unlike success in conventional battle. The only direct evidence that nuclear deterrence is working is the absence of major conflict among the great powers and the continuation of daily life for the United States and our allies. The tangible indicators of military victory—control over territory, the defeat of the adversary's forces—do not exist when waging deterrence. Perpetual readiness does not provide nuclear personnel with the cognitive satisfaction from completing a mission that can offset its psychological demands. The nuclear deterrence mission is never complete.

The unique responsibilities of safeguarding nuclear weapons impose additional obligations on nuclear personnel. The enormous destructive power of these weapons and the potential consequences of their combat use serves as the constant backdrop for daily operational activities and imposes an absolute intolerance for errors. Nuclear weapons are handled with the utmost care and precision, performance and accountability standards are high and unrelenting, and failure is unacceptable (either in handling weapons or in daily deterrence operations). No one should underestimate the extraordinary physical and emotional demands this environment places on what are often our newest and most junior-ranking military members serving in their first duty assignments. Commanders expect them to demonstrate a level of professionalism, focus, and tolerance for intrusive oversight and direct supervision that is unlike any other area of service. They typically exceed all expectations.

Unique Pressures Faced by Nuclear Crewmembers

Nuclear crewmembers often perform their duty in a simulation world. Because nuclear weapons are involved, crewmembers can only practice the full range of their combat mission responsibilities in simulators. As a result, the character and tempo of most day-to-day nuclear operations in the "real world" are markedly different from the wartime mission procedures they practice in simulations. Real-world nuclear duty is characterized by training, tests, drills, exercises, evaluations, and inspections that approximate the wartime strike mission only to a limited extent (for example, all ICBM crewmembers "launch missiles" hundreds of times in simulators, but most will never test fire even one live missile; similar examples exist in the case of SSBNs and nuclear bombers). By contrast, in virtually every other operational discipline, military members perform most, if not all, aspects of their combat missions in a real world of sophisticated live-fire ranges, realistic exercises where they operate the same live systems and weapons they would use in combat, and actual deployments and contingencies. Of course, no nuclear crewmember wants to do in the real world what they practice in simulators; but it takes a great deal of mental maturity and discipline to consistently accord to daily real-world nuclear operations the required levels of attention to detail and flawless execution they must demonstrate in the world of simulations.

The degree to which nuclear duty creates other unique operational and psychological pressures on operators varies across the nuclear forces. It is difficult to compare human factors across bombers, SSBNs, ICBMs, and DCA since each is substantially distinct in composition, operational characteristics, psychological stresses, and personnel selection and development. Nevertheless, the most important distinction may be between the operators of ICBMs and the rest of the nuclear force.

While highly dedicated to the nuclear deterrence mission, those performing duty in B-52s, B-2s, and SSBNs naturally develop a broad range of skills associated with the routine operation of aircraft and submarines and their use in conventional as well as nuclear roles. These technical and tactical skills provide variety and create career opportunities beyond those generally available to the missile operators serving in the ICBM fields. Similarly, the relatively small number of fighter pilots committed to the theater nuclear deterrence mission can and do serve in other flying and related assignments, just as bomber crews can serve in conventional aircraft and SSBN crews can serve aboard attack submarines and other assignments.

Most air crews and sailors in the nuclear forces will most likely not spend their entire careers (perhaps not even the bulk of their nuclear duty time) focused exclusively on nuclear deterrence. Those assigned to long-range bombers and DCA will fly their platforms regularly to maintain conventional as well as nuclear proficiency and deploy to overseas locations, and they may be called on to drop live conventional ordnance in actual combat situations. In fact, since bombers are no longer routinely loaded with nuclear weapons, bomber commanders have to be vigilant to ensure crews retain nuclear focus and proficiency as conventional bomber task force operations have become the norm. Submariners have duty cycles that allow them to alternate between periods of readiness, recovery, and preparation for their next deterrence patrol. At sea, SSBN crews perform the highly intricate ballet of sailing their complex ships in the open ocean, the prerequisite to their deterrence mission. The unique mixture of nuclear weapons, nuclear propulsion, conventional as well as nuclear tactical concerns, and a harsh operating environment characterize the diverse demands of SSBN service. These realities in no way diminish the importance of the men and women who fly and sail nuclear platforms or call into question their commitment to the nuclear deterrence mission. But the professional development opportunities associated with their routine activities help relieve the tedium of nuclear duty, validate their career pathways, and provide them a reassuring sense of their contribution and operational value to the broader joint force and national security.

In contrast, the ICBM force is the only portion of the nuclear triad with a constant, forcewide readiness commitment and singular focus on the nuclear deterrence mission. In my experience, it is the least understood of all the nuclear forces. Owing to its relatively small size and niche position within the air force, few senior military or civilian leaders have had any direct experience in the ICBM force; most have had little exposure to it. ICBM units are constantly deployed (to use a conventional force analogy), drive over extensive distances in the course of their duties, and must contend with extreme weather conditions. While missile operations crews monitor status and are always ready to respond to presidential command, daily field operations are dominated by far-flung security and maintenance activities that are necessary to protect the warheads and facilities and sustain the combat readiness of the weapon system. In other words, what other units would call support activities are actually the daily operations at ICBM units. This is almost the complete opposite experience of other combat-ready U.S. military units, for whom the combat mission, not maintenance and security, drives daily focus and tempo. Career pathways are also far more limited for the small number of missile operators and maintainers, and it is tempting for them to view ICBM duty as a dead-end career. These real factors create unique issues within the ICBM force that commanders must address with creative leadership, positive motivation, and sound judgment.

The Importance of Human Reliability and Standards

Regardless of duty assignment, commanders across the force play the central role in validating and certifying the fitness of each person to perform nuclear duties. The United States entrusts duties involving nuclear weapons only to its military members (and certain civilians in the Department of Energy) who demonstrate the highest degree of reliability. Reliability is initially validated through meticulous medical, psychological, security, performance, and disciplinary screening and culminates with personal interviews between the member and commander. Commanders take in all the information and, if satisfied, certify the individual for nuclear duty. But that is just the beginning.

Once certified for nuclear duty, service members, from the lowest ranks to the STRATCOM commander, bear responsibility for monitoring their own as well as their fellow members' continued fitness for duty and are obligated to come forward with any potential or actual reliability concerns. Commanders oversee a nonpunitive Personnel Reliability Program that brings medical, personnel, and other specialists together on a recurring basis or as issues occur, to ensure continued reliability. As certifying officials, commanders have authority to temporarily remove individuals from nuclear duty until concerns are resolved or to permanently remove them if they are not.

In my view, the Personnel Reliability Program is the single most important program that underpins the trust and confidence of senior military and civilian leaders in the people who perform duty with nuclear weapons. Although the program is conceptually simple, it is administratively complex, with layers of bureaucratic rules and paperwork. Commanders must be vigilant to make certain that the program remains an effective tool to ensure human reliability and to make certain that its purpose is not lost in administrative demands. Ultimately, the reliability of the people who have access to nuclear weapons is determined by commanders who work together with frontline leaders and other experts to certify, monitor, and continuously validate their performance and behavior, not by inspectors scanning reams of paperwork for administrative compliance.

While all military members are expected to meet high personal and professional standards, those in nuclear operations are constantly evaluated to the highest and most stringent. Some have questioned the need for enforcement of high individual professional standards when literally all activities involving nuclear weapons are performed by teams. However, individual standards form the basis of the two-person concept, a bedrock principle of nuclear surety. The two-person rule dictates that all activities in the nuclear sphere be conducted in the presence of at least two authorized persons. This requires that all members have the same basic level of professional competence, enabling each person on a team to immediately detect and prevent an incorrect, inadvertent, or unauthorized act and enabling the team to act in agreement to employ the weapons in combat, if so ordered. In practice, that fundamental requirement translates into a minimum acceptable level of individual professional competence that is necessarily extremely high. There can be no weak links in the nuclear surety chain. This places responsibility on commanders to ensure that professional standards are relevant, sensibly enforced, and directly related to combat readiness. Commanders must clearly describe the linkage among human reliability, professional standards, combat readiness, and deterrence so the men and women performing the mission understand and accept the relevance of each piece to their daily duties.

Nuclear Duty and Ethics

The extraordinary demands of nuclear duty go beyond adherence to the highest standards of performance and discipline. Given the awesome destructive power of the weapons, the men and women who perform nuclear duty must also consider the unique moral and legal dimensions of the weapons the nation places in their care. For deterrence to be credible, military members must be confident in the moral and legal legitimacy of the weapons themselves and their use. They must also trust that the chain of command will address and resolve any moral or legal constraints before ordering their combat use. Commanders and senior civilian leaders, for their part, must be confident in the readiness of the forces to execute their mission if ordered and trust that those orders will be carried out as directed.

Morality and legality are two separate but intertwined concepts. Commanders presume that military members in today's all-volunteer force have resolved any personal ethical concerns regarding warfare and military service before joining the ranks. The moral perspectives of these volunteers are shaped by many sources and factors outside the military, and core military values, training, and professional education add to that foundation. Those assigned to duties involving the possible employment of nuclear weapons are given an opportunity to ponder the ethical implications of their use during initial orientation and again as commanders evaluate their reliability and certify them for those duties. Individuals either resolve any lingering personal concerns or are obliged to voice them, either during initial Personnel Reliability Program screening or later, as they perform their duties. As a crewmember and commander, I observed that a firm moral foundation was a common trait among those assigned to nuclear duty.

The legality of employing nuclear weapons is addressed differently. Military members are bound by the Uniform Code of Military Justice to follow lawful orders issued by an appropriate command authority. They are equally bound to question (and ultimately refuse) "clearly illegal orders" or orders that do not come from such authority.[4] Members are trained on these basic principles and are expected to know and apply the laws of armed conflict appropriately and fulfill their legal obligations regardless of rank or position in the command chain. Members are also trained on topics such as authority to act and rules of engagement that help establish and refine the circumstances and boundaries for their actions. None of this training encourages our service members to needlessly "screen the orders of superiors for questionable points of legality": military members are reminded that orders are presumed to be legal "absent specific knowledge to the contrary" and that the threshold for questioning and determining that an order is manifestly illegal is intentionally high.[5] Nevertheless, the basic message remains clear: U.S. military members do not blindly follow orders regardless of the source of the orders or the characteristics of the weapons.

Trust and confidence are not abstract concepts in the nuclear crew force. While crews constantly drill on processes and procedures that allow them to verify with certainty that nuclear control orders are authentic and have come from an appropriate command authority (the president of the United States, in the case of nuclear weapons), in the confines of a submarine, a missile-launch control center, or a bomber in flight, it is almost impossible to apply the tests of necessity, distinction, and proportionality that would allow them to personally verify the legality of such orders. While they are well schooled in their wartime procedures, in many cases nuclear crews will not know the specifics of either the situation or the target they are being ordered to strike. Nuclear crews must trust the chain of command and have confidence that commanders and policymakers are acting in the nation's interests, that they have met their responsibilities to enforce legal constraints, resolve any questions, and confirm the legality of any orders before such orders are transmitted to the forces. Such trust, confidence, and clarity of command authority up and down the command chain produces an environment that provides room for questions but not for corrosive doubts that could lead to confusion, hesitation, or inaction at the most critical moments.

Commanders at all levels play a direct role in affirming the moral and legal legitimacy of nuclear weaponry and in establishing trust and confidence in the command chain. U.S. policy has clearly and consistently confirmed the legality and morality of using nuclear weapons to defend vital national interests, provided such use is compatible with fundamental U.S. principles and values and compliant with the law. Character-based leadership visibly demonstrates commitment to those principles and core values. Finally, legitimacy requires constant reinforcement of basic ethical principles associated with military service and open discussion of issues concerning nuclear weapons and their use. Commanders must discuss these subjects and ensure that "members . . . under their command are, commensurate with their duties, aware of their duties under the law of war."[6]

This is critical business for commanders. Technical capabilities are important, but deterrence credibility ultimately depends on human factors. Absent legitimacy, trust, and confidence, the credibility of our deterrent could be called into question by adversaries, who may perceive a lack of U.S. national resolve to use nuclear weapons; by U.S. citizens and political leaders, who may no longer support the deterrent force; by our military members, who may question the motivations and intentions of their leaders; and by our allies, who may feel compelled to seek their own security arrangements.

The Advisory Responsibilities of Nuclear Commanders

The STRATCOM commander serves as a military adviser and expert to the secretary of defense and the president. The commander also provides military advice and expertise to the Joint Chiefs of Staff, its chair, and Congress. The STRATCOM commander frequently engages with other senior civilian and military leaders while carrying out command responsibilities in a variety of areas, from developing plans and options to nuclear decisionmaking.

The Dynamics of Twenty-first Century Deterrence

Deterrence is about human beings, what they value and what they believe. Credible deterrence exists when an adversary believes it cannot achieve its objectives and will suffer unacceptable consequences if it tries. It is based on demonstrated capability and unambiguous national resolve, both of which must be understood by and in some way communicated to an adversary. Adversaries may not know exactly when or how the United States might use nuclear weapons in a given situation, but they can never be allowed to doubt that the United States would do so in extreme circumstances where vital national interests are at stake.[7]

The twenty-first century has brought complex security problems and new dynamics that challenge commanders and test the credibility of the U.S. nuclear deterrent in new ways. While nuclear weapons remain foundational to our security strategy and those of our allies, deterrence and extended-deterrence policy and doctrine must now account for a wide variety of potential adversaries with differing motivations and objectives and posing different strategic threats. The United States no longer faces a single potential nuclear adversary or enjoys a single alliance or ally. Technologies and threats are advancing at an unprecedented rate, and surprise at the tactical or operational level can quickly produce decisive strategic results. The nuclear club has grown, and in the present environment, unlike the Cold War period, "there is no requirement that escalating crises must involve a major power to go nuclear."[8] While either Russia or China can unleash large-scale nuclear attacks against the United States, both have also developed sophisticated employment doctrines that include the potential use (first use, in Russia's case) of low-yield weapons in regional conflict situations. North Korea presents a host of unknowns, and the possibility of third-party nuclear use (for example, India versus Pakistan) and proliferation create additional risks and concerns.

Another significant change has occurred since the end of the Cold War. Nuclear weapons no longer pose the sole credible strategic threat to the United States and its allies. While a large-scale nuclear attack of any kind remains the worst-case scenario, adversaries and potential adversaries see the ability to threaten targets in the United States and allied homelands with conventional, cyber, and the limited use of nuclear weapons as a means to change the strategic situation in their favor. For the first time since the beginning of the nuclear age, adversaries such as Russia and China can realistically attack important facilities and critical infrastructure in the United States and allied homelands with long-range conventional (including hypersonic) weapons without having to cross the nuclear threshold. They can also attack targets with cyber weapons without having to cross the kinetic threshold. Other potential adversaries are increasingly able to do the same with long-range ballistic missiles, cruise missiles, drones, cyber weapons, and terror-type weapons that are available and affordable. Adversaries are also threatening the United States in and through the strategically important and militarily critical area of space. Such threats against homeland and infrastructure are intended to coerce U.S. policymakers and commanders as they weigh the potential risks and costs of continued engagement or intervention in support of its national interests, its allies, and its partners around the globe.

The new asymmetric strategies and capabilities presented by our adversaries demand a significant change in U.S. deterrence calculations, plans, and operations. While the familiar overarching deterrence principles remain sound, how commanders apply those principles and array strategic capabilities in support of deterrence and assurance objectives must match contemporary security realities. The United States cannot rely on a one-size-fits-all approach to deterrence or planning based on our Cold War experience with the Soviet Union.[9] Even planning against contemporary Russia and China should not be based solely on that previous experience. The only common feature among today's nuclear armed adversaries is they are nuclear armed. As General Larry D. Welch has said, "The deterrence calculus did not change abruptly with the demise of the Soviet Union. Instead, the scope of deterrence considerations and needs expanded."[10]

Nuclear weapons remain fundamental to our national security, but today's deterrence strategies and plans must integrate all elements of military and national power together to maintain credibility and be effectively used in conflict. We must adopt a dynamic and adversary-specific approach that accounts for uncertainty, identifies potential risks, and includes hedges and strategic options that can be rapidly adapted when the inevitable surprises occur.[11] Commanders must apply the full range of nuclear, conventional, defensive, space, and cyberspace capabilities to today's complex deterrence problems.

In essence, commanders and planners must apply the lessons of twenty-first century warfare to the needs of twenty-first century deterrence. Such an approach requires clear guidance, predictive and frequently updated intelligence, ready forces, and a responsive planning process that provide the president flexible nuclear and non-nuclear options. It also requires deep knowledge of individual adversaries, their values and decisionmaking processes, and their risk tolerance. Acquiring that knowledge while addressing the often unique collection and analysis requirements to support current and future U.S. weapon systems imposes unprecedented demands on the intelligence community.

The Nuclear Planning Process

As a former SAC commander once said, it is in the nuclear commands (primarily STRATCOM today) that the weapons, delivery systems, plans, and people come together to form the war-fighting instrument that figures into the deterrence equation.[12] The effectiveness of that war-fighting instrument is critically dependent on the viability of the contingency plans produced by STRATCOM. To meet today's more dynamic deterrence requirements, the nuclear planning process now follows the same interactive, objective-based process used for conventional military operations. This approach is characterized by an ongoing dialogue between senior civilians (responsible for policy, strategic guidance, and insight) and senior military commanders and the Joint Chiefs of Staff (responsible for plans, operations, and advice). It stands in stark contrast to the relatively inflexible, military-dominated planning cycles of the Single Integrated Operational Plan of the Cold War, which produced a collection of static options that were maintained and updated as adversary capabilities and targets changed.

The nuclear planning process begins when the president issues a directive stating the broad objectives the military must achieve with nuclear weapons if deterrence fails. The secretary of defense adds essential depth and clarifying guidance. Acting on the secretary of defense's behalf, the under secretary of defense for policy develops overarching strategy, planning scenarios, and specific planning objectives and, for most nuclear policy matters, serves as the important link between the Defense Department and the broader interagency community and National Security Council staff. The chair of the Joint Chiefs of Staff provides a final military perspective, and the STRATCOM commander applies judgment and experience to translate policy and guidance into contingency plans and actions. The Joint Strategic Target Planning Staff of the Cold War era is long gone, and today's STRATCOM develops plans and options within general guidance from above that is far less prescriptive than the voluminous and highly detailed guidance of those earlier days. In my experience, less detailed guidance has allowed STRATCOM to broaden its focus from target planning to interactive option development with policymakers, a positive change that helps align plans to policymakers' intent.

The planning process is well understood and straightforward. Deliberate planning includes mission analysis, intelligence assessment, course-of-action and option development, and modeling. The result is an adversary-specific plan containing a range of options (nuclear, non-nuclear, or a combination) designed to achieve wartime objectives and immediately available for use by the president. Crisis planning follows a similar (though much faster) process; the output is an option specifically matched to the demands of an emerging situation. The STRATCOM planning team includes a variety of operational, technical, and legal experts from within the staff, backed by service component commands, outside agencies, and analysts from across government. The team routinely interacts with their counterparts in the office of the under secretary of defense for policy, the Joint Staff, defense agencies, intelligence community, and other combatant commands.

Commander Involvement in Planning

The STRATCOM commander is personally involved in all phases of the planning effort from policy and guidance development to target selection. The commander also provides an important senior military perspective to planners and civilian policymakers as they collectively apply the art of war to nuclear plans. Although the planning process is straightforward, in my experience four important areas typically took (and deserved) much of my attention: political-military interaction, planning assumptions, legal constraints, and integration with other combatant commands. The first three areas have been on commanders' agendas for many years (although the nature of the political-military interaction regarding nuclear planning has improved significantly); the fourth has been expanding in scope over the past decade or more. All four areas are critically important to the success of the planning process, and all require deep interaction between the STRATCOM commander and civilian and military leaders, planners, and legal and other experts.

Political-Military Interaction

The first and most important area for commander involvement comes at what the military commonly calls the political-military intersection. As with all U.S. war-fighting commands, the chain of command runs from the president through the secretary of defense to the STRATCOM commander. The chair of the Joint Chiefs of Staff serves as the senior military adviser to the president and transmits orders from the president to the war-fighting commands. But other senior civilian and military leaders also play important roles in nuclear policy development, oversight, planning, and execution. Years of experience in twenty-first century conventional contingency operations around the globe have convinced U.S. military commanders and senior policymakers that personal relationships and trust are critical to success at this high level of interaction.[13] The STRATCOM commander bears much of the responsibility for building and fostering such relationships and trust regarding nuclear planning and operational matters.

During my time as STRATCOM commander, I was privileged to serve with senior political appointees, civilian authorities, and military leaders who shared that view of the importance of relationships and trust. As the commander responsible for almost all nuclear planning, my perspective and advice were sought as policy, strategy, and guidance were developed, and my voice was influential in shaping all three. In return, I made sure the responsible senior policymakers had insight into our nuclear plans and operational procedures. While we did not always agree, the result was a collaborative approach to nuclear planning that linked national policy and objectives to plans and enhanced the ability of civilians and military leaders alike to fulfill their complementary responsibilities. I benefited from the insights and perspective provided by Secretaries of Defense Robert Gates, Leon Panetta, and Charles Hagel; Joint Chiefs chairs Admiral Michael Mullen and General Martin Dempsey; Joint Chiefs vice chairs General James Cartwright and Admiral James Winnefeld; Under Secretary of Defense for Policy James N. Miller; military service chiefs, fellow combatant commanders, and many others. I welcomed this open approach and found it far more productive than the often-contentious exchanges between military and civilian leaders I observed while participating as a Pentagon staff officer in the Strategic Nuclear Targeting Review some twenty years earlier.

Planning Assumptions

The STRATCOM commander helps shape and validate the assumptions the planners must make to meet U.S. policymakers' long-standing desire for flexible options that can limit damage, control escalation, and restore deterrence if a nuclear exchange occurs.[14] Meeting this desire is a particularly important (and difficult) challenge in nuclear planning since, despite years of study and theoretical speculation, other than the one-sided use of two crude weapons seventy-five years ago during World War II, no one has ever experienced the reality of a modern nuclear war. Deterrence has kept it so, and the resulting uncertainties and risks associated with nuclear war continue to help keep the nuclear threshold high. However, as a practical matter, when crafting nuclear options, planners are forced to make calculated assumptions regarding adversary perceptions and behavior based on a certain amount of ambiguity (created in part by deliberate adversary deception). This is an area where the depth of U.S. intelligence assessments and the mutual understanding developed by the United States and the Soviet Union over the course of interactions during the Cold War (including important military-to-military contact) continues to inform our judgment, reduce risks, and contribute to stability. It is also where a lack of direct contact, familiarity, or experience with contemporary Russia, China, and other nuclear-armed adversaries presents significant and potentially risky knowledge gaps that could lead to instability, misunderstanding, or miscalculation in a crisis.

Senior commanders deal constantly with ambiguity and risk. Knowledge of the adversary is never perfect, and risks, especially those associated with the use of nuclear weapons, can never be completely eliminated. Today's global international security environment is not a repeat of the Cold War, and planners must base assumptions on current intelligence assessments and adjust as additional information becomes available. Commanders and policymakers must state intelligence collection requirements clearly and demand high-priority collection and analyses that help minimize the assumptions that have to be made between nuclear theory and reality. Such demands must be matched by strong advocacy for the significant resources needed to meet them and continued encouragement to restore routine military contact, especially with Russia and China.

Legal Constraints

Historically, commanders at STRATCOM and its predecessors SAC and the Joint Strategic Target Planning Staff have been deeply involved with the application of legal constraints to target selection and option development. The United States long ago rejected the intentional targeting of civilian populations with nuclear weapons. Today's guidance to "adhere to the law of armed conflict and the Uniform Code of Military Justice" and "minimize civilian damage to the extent possible consistent with achieving objectives" is explicit and mirrors similar language that has existed in U.S. policy and guidance for decades.[15] Nuclear options and orders are no different in this regard from those for any other weapon. The basic legal principles of military necessity, distinction, and proportionality apply to nuclear weapons just as they do to every other weapon. Legal constraints are implemented rigorously at every step in the planning process via a combination of target selection and weapon application techniques, and legal advisers are a permanent presence in planning and decisionmaking. Today, planners and legal advisers have additional challenges to address the legal implications of conventional and cyber weapons, as those weapons are increasingly included in strategic plans.

One crucial point for commander involvement relates to what the scholars Scott Sagan and Allan Weiner describe as the bridge between legal constraints and the application of strategic calculations to nuclear plans and operations.[16] This is where civilian policymakers and legal advisers play key roles in helping commanders apply judgment to the balance between the two. Over the past two decades, planners have faced increasing internal and external pressure to refine (to make more restrictive, according to some advocates) how the laws of armed conflict are applied to nuclear operations. As a commander, I fully embraced U.S. policy to apply legal principles to nuclear plans and welcomed the clarity that came with the academic and policy debates on those principles. But I was concerned that increasingly restrictive constraints and legal interpretations appropriate to conventional war may not be achievable (or desirable, if carried to extremes) when applied to nuclear weapons and their unavoidable collateral effects. The risk associated with those collateral effects is a major factor that contributes to deterrence; caution is needed to ensure that reducing or eliminating that risk does not make an enemy's decision to initiate conventional war (a potential trigger for escalation to nuclear use) or, ultimately, to cross the nuclear threshold less consequential and deterrence less effective. Michael Walzer has addressed the moral dimension of this persistent nuclear dilemma by telling us that nuclear weapons "are simply not encompassable within the familiar moral world."[17] The same may be true for nuclear weapons and aspects of the familiar legal world of conventional war.

When it comes to nuclear weapons, Sagan and Weiner remind us that "legal logic and strategic calculations are intricately intertwined."[18] In my experience it is possible to strike an appropriate balance between legal constraints and strategic objectives in nuclear plans and operations, but striking that balance requires leaders to make choices based on their experience, judgment, and a clear understanding of legal and policy principles. The STRATCOM commander must highlight where such judgment has been applied during planning so that policymakers can offer their perspective and make informed choices regarding plans and options.

Plan Integration

The fourth and newest area for commander engagement is the integration of plans and capabilities across the combatant commands. In the twenty-first century, maintaining credible strategic deterrence requires nuclear plans to be integrated with other global and regional plans and all elements of U.S. power to form integrated campaigns. No other weapon produces the same deterrent effect as nuclear weapons, whose deterrent value cannot be added on or presumed as a crisis or conflict unfolds. Rather, nuclear weapons must be deliberately integrated with other forces and weapons during the planning process so they can be used effectively both to enhance deterrence (and thereby avoid a crisis or conflict) and to prevent or limit escalation if conflict erupts. Integrated planning also enhances our ability (and strengthens the policy goal) to substitute conventional and non-kinetic weapons (for example, cyber weapons) against some targets that once could only be held at risk by nuclear weapons.

While conventional and non-kinetic weapons cannot replace nuclear weapons in scope, scale, or deterrent effect, they are becoming increasingly relevant at the strategic level of conflict. When called for, conventional and non-kinetic options might best be provided by forces already present in a theater of operations or from other commands with unique global capabilities, such as the U.S. Cyber Command or U.S. Space Command. An integrated campaign plan provides the flexibility for either STRATCOM or others to offer these capabilities and options to the president, thereby further enhancing deterrence by complicating enemy calculations of success. Integrated planning does not make nuclear weapons more usable or a nuclear war more likely, as some assert. Rather, considering nuclear weapons and leveraging their singular deterrent effects at every phase from peacetime to extreme circumstances improves deterrence effectiveness and makes their combat use less likely.

A final consideration has occupied the STRATCOM commanders' time for the last decade or more. Deterrence is based on combat readiness, and combat readiness is based on viable contingency plans and ready forces. But highly classified wartime contingency plans alone do not visibly demonstrate that readiness. As former STRATCOM commander General Kevin P. Chilton has noted, "Effectively influencing a competitor's decision calculus requires continuous, proactive activities conducted in the form of deterrence campaigns tailored to specific competitors."[19] An integrated deterrence campaign plan is required to methodically and carefully orchestrate all the visible activities and public messages that together demonstrate U.S. resolve, assure allies, and influence adversaries. Conducted as a campaign, activities such as periodically deploying nuclear-capable bombers overseas, SSBN port visits, test flights of ICBM or submarine-launched ballistic missiles, friendly competitions between units, and uploading weapons in a large-scale exercise have become the primary weapons for waging deterrence—with images and words tailored to the specific adversary serving as the bullets.

The plans prepared by the STRATCOM commander and staff are successively reviewed and approved by the military and civilian chain of command and ultimately presented to the president by the secretary of defense. At every step, the plans are reviewed collaboratively by senior civilian and military leaders to ensure they achieve national objectives, comply with national policy, and meet the standards of the law. Assessing the potential direct and indirect casualties from nuclear options is an essential part of this civilian review of the revised plans and of any options that might be provided to the president in extreme circumstances. The president can be confident that any nuclear option presented has been structured to meet national objectives and prepared in full compliance with moral principles and legal constraints.

Nuclear Force Capabilities and Operations

The United States uses its nuclear weapons every day to deter conflict, assure allies, prevent coercion, and hedge against uncertainty, and it does so without desiring to ever employ them in combat. The capabilities represented in those forces have been defined both by tangible factors (for example, the objectives the president directs the military to achieve if deterrence fails and the threats those forces would have to overcome) and intangible factors (for example, deterrence and stability considerations, rough parity with other nuclear powers, hedging against geopolitical uncertainty and technical failure). Since the early 1960s, U.S. strategic deterrence strategy has rested on the familiar nuclear triad. Each triad leg continues to contribute a primary benefit to the whole. Submarines at sea are the most survivable, bombers are the most flexible, and ICBMs are the most responsive. As a group of former STRATCOM commanders noted in 2017, "The combined capabilities of the triad provide the President with the mixture of systems and weapons necessary to hold an adversary's most valuable targets at risk, with the credibility of an assured response if needed—the essence of deterrence."[20]

Hedging and Signaling Strategies

The mixture of systems, weapons, and readiness levels inherent in the triad provides leaders with options to hedge against unforeseen technical failures or geopolitical change. Depending on the nature of the issue and the timelines involved, commanders can recommend a number of adjustments to the force and its configuration, including adjusting targeting plans either within or across triad legs, returning bombers to nuclear alert status, uploading submarine-launched ballistic missiles and ICBMs with additional weapons from the national stockpile, or a combination of the three. Each of these alternatives produces results on a different time scale, each carries unique political considerations (for example, uploading additional weapons onto submarine-launched ballistic missiles and ICBMs may carry arms control treaty implications), and each presents varying degrees of visibility to an adversary.

Hedging strategy presumes a robust nuclear industrial base that can sustain a safe, secure, effective stockpile and provide the full range of support from life extension programs through longer-term development and deployment of new weapons if ever needed. Shortly after I took command of STRATCOM, I visited the key Department of Energy facilities for a first-hand look at their condition and to personally show my support for the people and the modernization programs needed to keep our weapons viable. Along with other members of the joint Departments of Defense and Energy's Nuclear Weapons Council, I supported a strategy that allowed a smaller overall stockpile provided the United States modernized the national laboratory and industrial facilities and retained the design and engineering skills needed to produce new weapons. I also supported retaining the capability to test nuclear weapons if compelling safety factors, technical concerns, or other considerations made it necessary. Without a modern industrial base and a stockpile strategy that preserves the skills to test or produce weapons, our hedging strategy is ineffective, and our deterrent could literally rust away. Commanders must advocate strongly for the nuclear industrial base to prevent that from happening.

Nuclear forces are also the ultimate tools for signaling national concern, intent, or resolve. Adversaries watch our nuclear forces carefully for any indication of change or unusual activity. We observe similar activities among our potential adversaries; our allies watch both parties. Commanders and senior policymakers can recommend a range of signaling options to the secretary of defense and the president for consideration in a variety of scenarios. Such options may include bringing forces to a condition of readiness (force generation), positioning people and forces to reduce their reaction time (posture changes), and dispersing forces to alternate locations. Such powerful signals can enhance deterrence and prevent escalation of a crisis or conflict by forcing adversary leaders to consider the increased risks and potential consequences of their actions before they act. Of course, the United States always has the option to send an equally powerful signal of restraint by leaving nuclear forces in their normal day-to-day configuration.

While these hedging and signaling strategies remain conceptually sound, today's nuclear force size and configuration and the reduced capability and capacity of the industrial base require us to reconsider and tailor these traditional approaches, just as we have reconsidered and tailored our traditional deterrence strategies and plans. Today's nuclear triad is far smaller and, on a day-to-day basis, is configured differently than it was during the Cold War. Since the end of the Cold War, the numbers of deployed U.S. and Russian strategic weapons have been reduced dramatically, to about 10 percent of Cold War highs. U.S. theater nuclear forces have also been reduced to a small number of dual-capable fighter aircraft deployed in support of NATO. Heavy bombers have not been loaded and poised to take off with nuclear weapons since 1992, when those bombers and supporting tankers were released for use by commanders on conventional tasks. In essence, the United States now relies on a nuclear dyad of ICBMs and at-sea SSBNs and a small force of forward-deployed DCA and weapons to meet daily deterrence and assurance requirements. The United States retains the classic nuclear triad with all its benefits but only generates it for a short time during exercises or in the event the president has ordered the bombers returned to nuclear alert in response to a national need or world events.

Today's Triad

Each triad leg has taken on additional responsibilities in today's dyad configuration, with bombers assuming a dual nuclear-conventional role similar to the classic forward-based DCA force. In fact, dual-capable long-range bombers and bomber task forces have become two of the most credible and effective signaling and extended deterrence tools in the nation's deterrence tool kit. Short of nuclear generation, long-range bombers can be loaded with conventional munitions and deployed for combat operations in conjunction with theater forces or as a conventional alternative (or complement) to nuclear operations. Bombers also provide flexibility and serve as an immediate shock absorber that can be quickly uploaded with nuclear weapons in response to a variety of time-critical operational or hedging needs. Commanders must consider that bombers and tankers recommitted to day-to-day nuclear alert would not be available to project conventional military power (an essential role to counter adversaries deploying anti-access strategies). They would also not be available to provide conventional options intended to reduce the role of nuclear weapons and strengthen strategic deterrence below the nuclear threshold.

Day to day, the United States maintains most of its ICBMs and an at-sea portion of the SSBN fleet on alert and ready to respond to presidential command.[21] As the most survivable leg of the triad, the SSBN fleet is assigned the bulk of the operationally deployed U.S. weapons (to include a small number of low-yield weapons). Mobilizing the remainder of the available SSBN fleet and dispatching it to sea would be a dramatic signal of U.S. concern and resolve. As a disincentive to a first strike by Russia, U.S. ICBMs now carry single warheads. Since almost all ICBMs are constantly in a high readiness condition, force generation does not provide much in the way of visible signals. However, ICBMs remain the most immediately retargetable and responsive portion of the force, and since the advent of the ICBM-SSBN dyad configuration, they have taken on additional responsibilities as the daily hedge against unforeseen technical problems in the SSBN fleet and as an enabler for other operational needs, such as adjusting at-sea operations when needed for major submarine maintenance or modernization. Both triad legs play a complementary role in responding to geopolitical change, but neither can be uploaded quickly with additional weapons from the stockpile and, without planned improvements in the industrial base and a stockpile strategy that preserves the skills to produce weapons, new weapons may not be available for years, if at all.

Today's triad also plays a more important role than it did during the Cold War in reassuring our allies and partners of our extended nuclear guarantee. While the so-called central strategic systems in the triad provided the ultimate nuclear umbrella during the Cold War, the tactical nuclear weapons that were forward deployed in both the European and Pacific theaters provided the most visible assurance of U.S. extended deterrence security guarantees. Today, with a much more limited nuclear posture in Europe and no forward-deployed nuclear weapons in South Korea, allies and partners have asked for additional assurance. Here again, the routine global operations and frequent overseas presence of long-range B-2 and B-52 bombers and the resumption of SSBN overseas port visits play highly visible and, therefore, crucial roles in sustaining the credibility of that guarantee, reinforced by clear declaratory policy and personal interaction between senior U.S. and allied military and civilian leaders. I was pleased during my years of service to host and visit a number of our allies to deliver such reassurance in person.

The Nuclear Decision Process

To release nuclear weapons, crews must have an explicit order from the president of the United States. While all U.S. military forces operate under strict civilian control, the commander in chief retains sole authority to order the combat employment of U.S. nuclear weapons; that authority is not delegated down the chain of command. That was not always the case. Faced with the possibility of a surprise Soviet nuclear attack that resulted in the president's death or isolation from command of the nuclear forces, early in the Cold War President Eisenhower elected to delegate to certain military commanders the authority to temporarily use nuclear weapons in emergency contingencies.[22] Such authorities were narrowed and eventually revoked completely as time passed, discomfort with delegation grew among policymakers and military leaders, and the Cold War waned. As STRATCOM commander, I had the authority to improve the readiness and survivability posture of nuclear forces in response to a sudden increase in the threat or warning of an actual attack (to include ordering any alert aircraft to take off and proceed to airborne holding points to await instructions), but I had no authority to order the employment of the weapons themselves.

The Nuclear Command-and-Control System

The president's ability to exercise authority and direction over the nuclear forces while maintaining positive control over weapon employment is ensured by the people, processes, and capabilities that make up the Nuclear Command and Control System (NCCS). The system has been designed and built to address the demands of what Peter Feaver and Kenneth Geers have called the "trilemma" facing U.S. policymakers in the nuclear age: nuclear weapons must always be available for use; nuclear weapons must never be used accidentally or without authorization; nuclear weapons must have the highest level of civilian control.[23] Fundamentally, the system must meet the information and decisionmaking needs of the president and other senior civilian and military leaders in a wide variety of highly stressing contingencies (to include a less likely but still possible surprise nuclear attack), and it must do so with high confidence.

Satisfying these demands has resulted in a system designed with resilience, redundancy, and survivability to ensure that an adversary cannot hope, under any conditions, to neutralize our deterrent by successfully disconnecting the president and other civilian and military leaders from one another or from the nuclear forces. But the NCCS that was originally fielded to meet Cold War needs must evolve to remain viable. Decisionmakers are accustomed to consuming and sharing information in a manner and with the quality and speed widely available in commercial applications, features that must also be available in the NCCS. Today's NCCS must also function in the face of new threats, such as cyber or long-range conventional weapons that could arrive quickly and may very well be employed to make attribution or intent difficult to discern. Adding to the concern, space is now a contested domain, and satellites critical to the NCCS are potentially at risk.

It is conceivable that a future strategic attack on the United States could begin through cyberspace or by means of hypersonic conventional weapons as opposed to nuclear-tipped ballistic missiles. Regardless of the attack method, commanders and leaders must remain confident that the NCCS will function despite enemy attempts to disrupt communications or to sow doubt and confusion by manipulating or denying access to critical data. These new threats present significant technology and procedural challenges as well as an urgent need for improved resilience across the NCCS. Without the necessary investments and improvements, the NCCS will become the Achilles' heel of the nuclear deterrent.

A Human-Controlled Process

The U.S. approach to nuclear decisionmaking is characterized by three primary attributes. First and most important, given the risks and consequences of any decision to use nuclear weapons and the severe time constraints posed by some extreme situations, the United States has concentrated authority to command employment of those weapons in the hands of the nation's highest elected official (that is, the president or constitutional successor, in extremis). Command authority is clear and unambiguous, and assured connectivity to the president is a must. Second, both the NCCS and the weapons themselves are controlled by human beings; no mission-critical action or decision happens automatically. As is true across our military missions, we have placed our confidence in well-trained, competent people supported by specially certified sensors and systems. Third, all activities associated with nuclear weapons are surrounded by mutually reinforcing layers of safeguards and oversight.

While ultimate authority rests with the president, the nuclear decision process is carefully orchestrated and includes assessment, review, and consultation between the president and key civilian and military advisers, followed by preparation and transmission of any presidential decision through an order that goes directly to the forces.[24] The process can respond to time-critical scenarios as well as those allowing more decision time. Once the forces validate and authenticate the order, to ensure it has come from the president, they will implement it without fail.

The decision to use nuclear weapons is not an all-or-nothing choice. Successive administrations have directed the military to prepare a range of graduated options intended to provide decision flexibility and improve the likelihood of limiting damage, controlling escalation, and restoring deterrence at the lowest possible level of conflict if an exchange occurs. Options are clearly defined in scope and duration, and the president retains the ability to terminate nuclear operations if deemed necessary at any time. Preplanned options can be supplemented with adaptive options to meet the exigencies of an ongoing crisis or conflict, and conventional and nonkinetic options are increasingly available to add more flexibility and choices below the nuclear threshold.

The Time Factor

Time is always an important factor in the decision equation. During the Cold War and into the early post–Cold War era, the nuclear decision process was dominated by a sense of urgency created by the threat of a worst-case massive surprise nuclear attack from the Soviet Union that could potentially disrupt our command and control and destroy a significant portion of our retaliatory forces (especially ICBMs) before the United States could respond. This situation raised concerns in some circles that so-called use-or-lose time pressures could lead decisionmakers to inadvertently trigger nuclear war based on false alarms or miscalculations. But tremendous geopolitical and other changes have occurred over the past several decades, and the decision process is no longer dominated by that one overriding concern.

Today's long-term great-power competition between the United States and Russia and China is different from the global ideological conflict of the Cold War, changing the context for nuclear decisionmaking. Although Russia's invasion of Ukraine has created its own escalation dangers, to date the United States and Russia continue to avoid a direct military confrontation where an incident could quickly escalate into general war. While the rapid pace of Chinese military advances may eventually indicate otherwise, China does not yet possess the nuclear force capabilities to attempt a disarming nuclear first strike against the United States; nor does any other potential nuclear adversary. In addition, the United States has expended much time and effort to mitigate use-or-lose pressures by reducing both the incentive for a surprise first-strike and the impact such an attack would have on our leaders and forces. For example, the United States has assigned roughly two-thirds of its operationally deployed warheads to survivable SSBNs and downloaded ICBMs to a single warhead (thereby increasing the warhead price an enemy must pay to attack them). Arms control agreements (currently New START with Russia) have further reduced first-strike incentives by progressively limiting the number of operationally deployed warheads available to both sides. The United States has also deployed more-effective warning systems, planned for a wider variety of response options, and taken steps to improve connectivity between the president, key leaders, and nuclear forces under all conditions of stress.

Today, the NCCS must accommodate the far more complex hybrid scenarios (nuclear, conventional, non-kinetic) that are possible and plausible in the twenty-first century. A time-urgent, massive surprise nuclear attack may be the least likely; a regional contingency that is going badly for an adversary may be the most likely stimulus for nuclear use. Nevertheless, Russia is still capable of mounting a massive surprise nuclear attack at any time with catastrophic consequences and, as we have seen, its leaders are quick to threaten to use nuclear force. China appears to be on an aggressive pathway to deploy such a capability as well. I believe such an attack remains only a remote possibility today, at least in part, because the United States continues to effectively deter it with the capability to respond promptly—even while under attack. The nation must continue to deter such an attack as long as any adversary has the capability to carry it out.

Increasing decision time and reducing the potential for miscalculation are desirable objectives, but from a commander's perspective I continue to believe that the controversial steps of removing responsive nuclear-strike capability from the U.S. deterrent force (that is, "de-alerting") or revising current U.S. declaratory policy in favor of sole-use or no-first-use policies, as some suggest, would make us less secure, would embolden or even incentivize adversaries to act aggressively, would alarm allies who rely on the U.S. nuclear guarantee, and would be unwise. De-alerting is a particularly dangerous, unverifiable, and destabilizing move that would increase an adversary's incentive to strike first in a crisis or conflict before U.S. weapons could be returned to combat readiness. In addition, any attempt by the United States to enhance deterrence at such a crucial time by returning de-alerted systems to alert status could be misunderstood by an adversary as a precursor to a U.S. attack and trigger the very nuclear use we are trying to deter. We cannot remove time from the decision equation; however, we can continue to reduce the impact of surprise, disruption, and delayed response by knowing more about our adversaries, by fielding a modern and ready deterrent force that presents them with unacceptable choices, and by increasing U.S. decisionmakers' awareness and confidence with highly resilient warning, command, control, and communications systems.

Nuclear Decisions

As it was during the Cold War, the nuclear decision process is again a topic of debate among U.S. policymakers. Recently, several members of Congress and former senior government officials have challenged the sole authority presidents claim regarding the use of nuclear weapons that was largely derived based on Cold War circumstances. This challenge is framed around two related but distinct issues: the constitutional limits of presidential authority to use military force (specifically, nuclear weapons) absent congressional consultation or authorization and the absence of a two-person safeguard at the top of the command chain. Some participants in this debate (to include the Speaker of the U.S. House of Representatives) have publicly worried that unlimited authority and lack of a two-person safeguard introduces the potential for a president to issue illegitimate or illegal nuclear employment orders. Several lawmakers have proposed limiting a president's authority to use nuclear weapons through legislation that would require congressional preapproval in certain scenarios. Others would add a requirement for confirmation from a second executive branch civilian official, such as the vice president or the secretary of defense, or perhaps a legislative branch official, such as the Speaker of the House, as a two-person safeguard before a presidential order to use nuclear weapons could be issued.

The legal and procedural implications of these matters are profound, and their impact is unknown on the credibility of nuclear deterrence. These are complex issues that can be resolved only by the civilian executive and legislative branches of our government working together, informed and strengthened by the advice provided by senior military leaders. While historically such debates have helped to strengthen deterrence, I remain mindful of the caution posed by General Russell E. Dougherty, who commanded SAC in the mid-1970s: "Nuclear debates . . . should not be passed along to operational commanders as dilemmas or conundrums; they need to be resolved by policymakers who offer practicable guidance."[25] His caution is still valid. An open-ended debate that presents an unresolved dilemma about the fundamental legitimacy or legality of presidential authorities and orders will be exploited by our adversaries and can shake the trust and confidence we carefully foster in the forces—an unacceptable situation for the nation and allies who rely on our security guarantees.

It is the prerogative of our national political leaders to define the limits of presidential authority to use force and adjust the nuclear decision process to meet the nation's needs, and the military will willingly comply. Policymakers can debate the limits of presidential war powers and decide whether the commander in chief must consult or get approval from Congress before ordering the employment of nuclear weapons. While I would urge Congress to proceed with caution on this issue, I am most concerned about the ramifications of changes to the decision process itself.

Given the need for absolute command clarity and timely action when nuclear weapons are involved, adding a second executive or legislative branch official as a check on the authority of a commander in chief introduces unnecessary complexity and layers to the decision process that could create confusion and cause delay—or worse, paralysis—in critical situations. Of equal importance, such an addition may not provide the reassuring two-person safeguard some seek, particularly if the second person is a like-minded official or a presidential appointee serving in an acting capacity and unconfirmed by the Senate. Policymakers and legal experts would have to determine whether dividing a president's command authority between two or more officials is legal or constitutional; regardless, as a commander I would not recommend what is seemingly a divided command arrangement at any level of command, let alone at the level of the commander in chief, where orders to use nuclear weapons must originate and simplicity and clarity are paramount.

Safeguards do exist at the top of the nuclear command chain. As the commander of U.S. Strategic Command, I shared the responsibility with the secretary of defense, the chair of the Joint Chiefs of Staff, combatant commanders, and other senior military and civilian leaders to raise any potential policy and legal issues on behalf of the men and women in the nuclear operating forces. It was our duty to pose hard questions, voice any concerns or objections directly to the president, and ensure that issues were resolved before a final decision was made. I personally participated in hundreds of tests, evaluations, and nuclear decision exercises over my career. In every case, the commanders, advisers, and other essential military and civilian professionals involved in the decision process acted in concert to ensure that any decision to use nuclear weapons met the most stringent legal and necessity standards before any orders would be transmitted to the forces. All understood their responsibilities, and all were prepared to provide the president with the information and advice needed to reach a legal decision appropriate to the circumstances.

The chain of command is not a debating society, and the members involved in the nuclear decision process are not poised to refuse orders. It is exceedingly unlikely that an issue arising in the decision process would become an unresolvable dispute or, at the extreme, would result in the military refusing a presidential order. Nevertheless, the military members assigned to duty in the NCCS serve as a de facto final safeguard in the decision process. Every U.S. military member is duty bound to question and, if necessary, "refuse to comply with clearly illegal orders"—to include nuclear employment orders coming directly from any president.[26] No change in the nuclear decision process would relieve each individual of that obligation. Every military member is trained to the same standard, and I am confident all would carry out their duty; but the military does not bear this nuclear safeguard responsibility alone.

Existing constitutional checks and balances (including the Twenty-fifth Amendment) are available to provide the means for appropriate elected and appointed civilian officials to proactively circumscribe the limits of presidential authority and, if ever necessary, declare "that the President is unable to discharge the powers and duties of his office."[27] Those civilian officials have a crucial constitutional obligation the military does not (and should not) have when matters involve the authorities, duties, and responsibilities of the commander in chief. Experience would suggest that we cannot predict the circumstances and manner in which our civilian officials would carry out these responsibilities, and the threshold for invoking constitutional safeguards will always be high. Commanders and senior military leaders must take every opportunity to help our civilian officials understand the nuclear decision process and advise them regarding the potential effect their words and actions have on the trust and confidence our military men and women must place in the chain of command.

During my time in command, I believed that the nuclear decision process struck an appropriate balance between deterrence and safeguards while retaining positive civilian control over the use of the weapons. I was fully confident that, if ever needed, any nuclear order transmitted to the operating forces would be necessary, consistent with U.S. policy, and fully compliant with the law. I was equally confident that the human-controlled decision process would come to a stop and no orders would be issued if legitimate legal questions arose, especially if the situation did not obviously meet the threshold described in policy for the United States to consider the use of nuclear weapons. I remain fully confident today.

No adversary should believe the United States would remain impotent in extreme circumstances where vital national interests are at stake. Senior military leaders and policymakers must act together to keep it that way; and all must embrace their unique and crucial responsibilities regarding nuclear weapons and their use. Of all the enduring challenges associated with waging deterrence, this is the most consequential.

Conclusion

Nuclear commanders will continue to face unique leadership challenges as the United States wages deterrence in the twenty-first century. Meeting those challenges requires principled military and civilian leaders who understand the relentless operational and psychological demands that characterize duty at the tip of the nuclear spear and who can guide, motivate, and inspire our young military members to sustain their unwavering commitment to the deterrence mission. Nuclear weapons have prevented nuclear use and major conventional war since 1945 and will continue to do so as long as the United States' nuclear forces remain credible and the men and women who perform the mission receive the unequivocal support of the nation that demands their efforts. Establishing and sustaining their trust and confidence in the chain of command is the most important requirement of all.

Notes

1. For a more complete description of this concept, see Kevin Chilton and Greg Weaver, "Waging Deterrence in the Twenty-First Century," *Strategic Studies Quarterly* 3, no. 1 (2009), pp. 31–42.

2. U.S. Department of Defense, "Independent Review of the Department of Defense Nuclear Enterprise," June 2, 2014, p. ii.

3. U.S. Department of Defense, "Report of the Secretary of Defense Task Force on DoD Nuclear Weapons Management, Phase II: Review of the DoD Nuclear

Mission," December 2008, p. iii; U.S. Department of Defense, "Independent Review of the Department of Defense Nuclear Enterprise," June 2, 2014, p. 1.

4. U.S. Department of Defense, *Department of Defense Law of War Manual June 2015 (Updated December 2016)* (Office of General Counsel, December 13, 2016), p. 1048.

5. U.S. Department of Defense, *Department of Defense Law of War Manual*, p. 1049.

6. U.S. Department of Defense, *Department of Defense Law of War Manual*, p. 1052.

7. Office of the Secretary of Defense, *Nuclear Posture Review 2018* (Defense Department, February 2018), p. 21.

8. Paul Bracken, *The Second Nuclear Age* (New York: Times Books, Henry Holt, 2012), p. 11.

9. Office of the Secretary of Defense, *Nuclear Posture Review 2018*, p. vii.

10. Keith B. Payne, "Redefining 'Stability' for the New Post–Cold War Era," *National Institute for Public Policy Occasional Paper* 1, no. 1 (2021), p. v.

11. Andrew F. Krepinevich, *7 Deadly Scenarios* (New York: Bantam Dell, 2009), p. 12.

12. Russell E. Dougherty, "The Psychological Climate of Nuclear Command," in *Managing Nuclear Operations*, edited by Ashton B. Carter, John D. Steinbruner, and Charles A. Zrakat (Brookings, 1987), p. 417.

13. U.S. Department of Defense, *Insights and Nest Practices: Joint Operations*, 5th ed. (November 2017), p. 1.

14. Office of the Secretary of Defense, *Nuclear Posture Review 2018*, p. 23.

15. Office of the Secretary of Defense, *Nuclear Posture Review 2018*, p. 23.

16. Scott D. Sagan and Allen S. Weiner, "The Rule of Law and the Role of Strategy in U.S. Nuclear Doctrine," *International Security*, 45, no. 4 (Spring 2021), pp. 126–66.

17. Michael Walzer, *Just and Unjust Wars*, 4th ed. (New York: Basic Books, 2006), p. 282.

18. Sagan and Weiner, "The Rule of Law and the Role of Strategy in U.S. Nuclear Doctrine," p. 160.

19. Chilton and Weaver, "Waging Deterrence in the Twenty-First Century," p. 34.

20. General C. Robert Kehler and others, "The U. S. Nuclear Triad Needs an Upgrade," Open letter, *The Wall Street Journal*, January 23, 2017, p. A17.

21. Office of the Secretary of Defense, *Nuclear Posture Review 2018*, p. 22.

22. William Burr, ed., "First Declassification of Eisenhower's Instructions to Commanders Predelegating Nuclear Weapons Use, 1959–1960," *National Security Electronic Archive Briefing Book 45, May 18, 2001* (National Security Archive, George Washington University, June 3, 2020), nsarchive2.gwu.edu/NSAEVV/NSAEBB45/index.html.

23. Peter Feaver and Kenneth Geers, "When the Urgency of Time and Circumstances Clearly Does Not Permit . . . : Pre-delegation in Nuclear and Cyber

Scenarios," in *Understanding Cyber Conflict: Fourteen Analogies,* edited by George Perkovich and Ariel E. Levite (Georgetown University Press, 2017), p. 212.

24. Deputy Assistant Secretary of Defense for Nuclear Matters, *Nuclear Matters Handbook, 2016* (Defense Department, 2016), p. 80.

25. Dougherty, "The Psychological Climate of Nuclear Command," p. 417.

26. U.S. Department of Defense, *Department of Defense Law of War Manual,* p. 1048.

27. U.S. Const. amendment XXV, § 4.

CHAPTER 7

Command and Control of U.S. Nuclear Forces

John R. Harvey
John K. Warden

The nuclear command-and-control (NC2) system of the United States is the critical link between U.S. nuclear forces and the sole executive authority of the president to execute those forces. It supports nuclear crisis decisionmaking by the president, wherever located, by enabling the discovery, integration, and provision of accurate, tailored information, ensuring the means for the president to consult with key advisers, and providing assured capabilities to, when necessary, execute nuclear strikes or terminate nuclear operations. The system also provides the president with means to convey deterrence signals by adjusting force posture or redeploying forces. The NC2 system must function in peacetime, crisis, and conflict—during and after an adversary nuclear attack, and under all conditions of warning and force alert posture—while allowing for graceful degradation of capabilities in plausible threat environments. The resilience of the NC2 system and the perception of its resilience by U.S. adversaries and allies are critical components of deterrence, assurance, and strategic stability.

Today's NC2 system was developed and fielded during the Cold War and was designed to meet security needs at the time. In the current security environment, the likely pathways to major conventional conflict and nuclear escalation are far different. In consequence, the NC2 information and decisionmaking support needs of the president are more varied and extensive.

Efforts are underway to modernize the legacy NC2 system, including replacing the so-called "thin line" architecture and developing a future NC2 concept and associated architecture to address the challenges of modern conflict, but the years-long process is in its early stages.

The Enduring Importance of Nuclear Command and Control

The U.S. nuclear command-and-control system reflects the unique role of nuclear weapons in national security strategy, but it also is the product of the security environment in which it was meant to function. Designed primarily to deter what was considered the most stressing scenario—a large-scale Soviet first strike aimed at destroying or disabling U.S. nuclear forces or command and control—the system has the capability to detect an incoming attack, assess it, achieve a presidential decision to retaliate, and swiftly execute that decision within a matter of minutes, including the option to launch nuclear forces before they could be destroyed on the ground. Understanding and having observed this U.S. defense capacity, no Soviet leader could have believed that devastating retaliation could be avoided, which in itself deterred a disarming strike in the first place.

Even as the likelihood of an attempted disarming first strike has receded, the NC2 system remains critical. With all elements of its nuclear posture, the United States has to balance its goals of enhancing deterrence and assurance, maintaining flexible options to achieve U.S. objectives should deterrence fail, and reducing the likelihood of miscalculation or inadvertent nuclear employment. The NC2 system is designed with this balance in mind; it is meant to ensure that U.S. nuclear forces will be employed if and when the president so orders (positive control) but not in any other circumstances (negative control).[1]

The U.S. NC2 system has prioritized reducing the likelihood of miscalculation or inadvertent nuclear employment. Because of the destructive power of nuclear weapons, U.S nuclear forces and operations are subject to negative control measures that far exceed other military capabilities. A combination of technologies and procedures are used to significantly reduce the likelihood of accidental or unauthorized employment. In addition, political control of nuclear weapons employment is kept under tight centralized control of the president.[2] These measures make it more challenging for the NC2 system to enable the president to exercise positive control, if necessary.

The United States maintains nuclear forces to communicate to potential adversaries that they could be used in extreme circumstances and, as a result, that aggression against it or its allies and partners would result in intolerable costs and unacceptable risks. Each element of the U.S. nuclear posture—survivable ballistic-missile submarines (SSBNs) at sea, intercontinental ballistic missiles (ICBMs) postured for prompt launch, and bombers and dual-capable aircraft capable of signaling and flexible strike options—is meant to enhance deterrence and assurance and maintain the ability to achieve U.S. objectives should deterrence fail. Doubt about U.S. capabilities would increase the likelihood of both adversary aggression and nuclear escalation during a conflict. Allies who may come to doubt the credibility of U.S. security guarantees may act counter to U.S. nonproliferation goals in seeking their own nuclear forces.

Nuclear command and control is a necessary component of three important attributes of the U.S. nuclear posture. First, the NC2 system helps to ensure survivable forces. While each leg of the U.S. nuclear triad complements strengths in the other two legs, SSBNs, in particular, provide a survivable second-strike capability, so that even after enduring a counterforce strike, an ensuing U.S. response would impose unacceptable damage. The United States maintains a handful of its fourteen Trident SSBNs continuously at sea. Some number of those are on day-to-day alert and able to launch missiles within minutes of receiving an execution order. The remainder of at-sea SSBNs are on modified alert and may require some transit time, of hours to days, to reach designated launch areas. Today, SSBNs at sea cannot be easily located by an enemy, so there is no urgency to launch missiles in fear of their destruction. In-port SSBNs being readied for sea patrols are vulnerable to attack, but during times of rising tensions they could be ordered to sea, an order that would take a few days to carry out.[3]

In the past, one or two SSBNs were in long-term overhaul and not able to be rapidly dispersed. With the Ohio-class SSBNs nearing end of life, refueling overhauls are on hiatus until Columbia-class SSBNs enter the force in the 2030s. U.S. SSBNs at sea ensure that even in an intense crisis or escalating conflict, an adversary is likely to think twice when contemplating a disarming first strike against the United States. The NC2 system facilitates survivability by ensuring that SSBNs at sea can communicate with higher authority and receive launch orders without revealing themselves to an adversary. In addition, the system itself must also be survivable and enduring in the face of a number of plausible attacks in order to minimize an adversary's incentive to target the president, or key NC2 links and nodes, to either slow or prevent U.S. nuclear retaliation.

Second, the NC2 system facilitates promptness. There are extreme circumstances under which a president may perceive an urgent need to use nuclear weapons to achieve a critical objective: among others, the need to reestablish deterrence after an adversary conducts limited nuclear strikes and before subsequent attacks occur; to strike adversary nuclear forces before they are employed—for example, if the president learned that an adversary attack had been ordered and was in process but missiles had not yet been launched; or, following an enemy launch, to employ U.S. nuclear forces before they, or associated NC2, are destroyed or incapacitated.[4] In each of these constrained time windows, the NC2 system must enable the president to understand the situation, consult with advisers, choose among acceptable employment options, and execute forces in time to achieve U.S. objectives.

Of the elements of the nuclear triad, ICBMs provide the most prompt strike option. About 400 U.S. single-warhead Minuteman III ICBMs operate from locations in the western United States—Malmstrom Air Force Base in Montana, Minot Air Force Base in North Dakota, and F.E. Warren Air Force Base in Wyoming. The missiles are deployed in fixed, hardened launch facilities (silos) scattered over vast regions in the vicinity of these bases. Most are on alert and could be launched within minutes of receiving an execution order. During peacetime, U.S. ICBMs are not directly targeted on potential enemy installations or forces; if a launch occurred by accident, missiles would fly into the ocean. At the same time, when a valid launch order is received, retargeting can occur within minutes.

Fixed ICBMs are considered potentially vulnerable to a large first-strike by Russia's highly accurate ICBMs armed with multiple independently targeted reentry vehicles (MIRVs), which have a flight time to U.S. targets of roughly thirty minutes. The United States retains the option to launch its ICBMs before the arrival and detonation of Russian warheads. Whether any president would ever execute a rapid launch in even this dire circumstance is unknowable. That said, U.S. prompt launch capability is planned for, and exercised, so that no potential adversary poised to strike U.S. ICBMs could ever be certain that a president would not execute the plan.

Third, the NC2 system enables flexibility. With its strategic bombers, dual-capable aircraft, and, potentially, a future nuclear sea-launched cruise missile, the United States has a flexible force that can be postured to send deterrence messages or employed to conduct limited nuclear strikes. U.S.

nuclear-assigned strategic bombers (B-2s and B-52s) are deployed from two locations in the United States—Minot Air Force Base and Whiteman Air Force Base in Kansas. During the Cold War and until 1991, several bombers at dozens of bases were kept on day-to-day alert with nuclear bombs loaded, ready to take off within several minutes. Today, bombers do not stand at alert on runways ready to takeoff within minutes; it would take substantially more time to bring the force to full alert. Once on alert, bombers with uploaded bombs could be dispersed to airfields across the United States to increase the likelihood of their survival if threatened by short-warning attack. Finally, bomber operations, including forward deployments and associated NC2, provide the president an important means to adjust force posture in ways that visibly signal to an adversary that a crisis is taking on a more serious nuclear dimension.

Together, these three attributes of U.S. forces, facilitated by NC2, complicate an adversary's planning, reducing the likelihood that it will employ nuclear weapons against the United States or one of its allies. A posture that maintains survivability, promptness, and flexibility also ensures that, if deterrence fails, the president has options to achieve U.S. objectives at the lowest level of damage possible.

Basic Elements of Today's NC2 Architecture

Today's NC2 system is a legacy of the Cold War. It is fundamentally the same system that was in place during the 1970s and was described by former secretary of defense Ash Carter more than thirty-five years ago in his seminal article in *Scientific American*.[5] There has been some upgrading and modernization of components, but the basic architecture remains in essence as it was and is characterized by information technologies and electronics that range from modern-day to 1960s vintage. Portions of the system are dedicated to the nuclear mission. Other portions are multiple-use applications employed during general-purpose military operations.

The NC2 system serves four functions: to provide clear, unambiguous, and timely detection and characterization of an attack; in the event of an attack, to establish a conference among the president and senior advisers to convey critical information needed to assess the attack and determine a timely response; to communicate an authenticated presidential decision in the form of an emergency-action message to nuclear forces, taking into account force survivability; and to provide enduring control of surviving forces. In support of these activities, as a fifth NC2 function, U.S. Strategic Command, in coordination with the secretary of defense and the Joint Staff, develops preplanned strike options and provides capabilities for rapid, adaptive planning to address unforeseen contingencies. Figure 7-1 illustrates specific NC2 functions.

Fielding and modernizing NC2 systems relies on a discipline grounded in certain key principles. First, only the president can authorize use of U.S. nuclear weapons.[6] Even under the enormous stress of a nuclear crisis, the NC2 system, through a combination of technologies and procedures, must ensure that nuclear forces are employed only when the president so orders and not in any other circumstance. This has enormous implications for NC2, discussed more fully in the next section.

Second, to avoid mischaracterizing an attack, two distinct physical means for launch detection are used for attack assessment.[7] This so-called dual phenomenology is achieved from infrared sensors on launch detection satellites and subsequent detection in flight by early-warning radars. Attack assessment and decisionmaking conference procedures have also been modified over the

FIGURE 7-1. NC2 Functions Supporting Presidential Nuclear Crisis Management

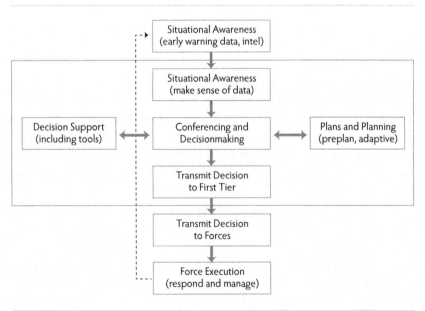

Source: Author.

years to further reduce the likelihood of a false warning leading to nuclear employment.[8]

Third, the NC2 system seeks to provide two survivable, physically distinct, and, where possible, two-way communications links between presidential authority and forces. In the case of bombers en route to targets, two-way communications provide means for their recall before a strike or for damage assessment after a strike.

An NC2 "thin line," defined as that part of the architecture that must function after the electromagnetic pulse effects from precursor high-altitude nuclear detonations, is maintained to detect incoming ballistic missiles, survive large-scale nuclear strikes against key nodes, and perform even in a postattack environment where the electromagnetic pulse has damaged terrestrial links and nuclear scintillation effects have disrupted airborne and satellite communications.[9] To ensure thin-line connectivity in harsh threat environments, careful attention is paid to harden critical subsystems and communications links to electromagnetic pulse and other nuclear effects.

Acquisition oversight for the sustainment and modernization of major pieces of the architecture is split between the individual services (air force, navy, and army) and the Defense Information Systems Agency. Their integration into a complex system of systems, supported with adequate funding, has been a challenge for decades. Both the Obama and Trump Nuclear Posture Reviews called attention to shortfalls in NC2 funding and governance, and significant progress has been made in redressing these problems. In 2018 Defense Secretary James Mattis placed the commander of Strategic Command in charge of overseeing the health of the NC2 enterprise.[10]

The basic elements of today's NC2 architecture include launch detection satellites, early-warning radars, attack assessment, command centers, and communications.

Launch Detection Satellites

Within minutes of a ballistic missile launch, whether a large or small attack, satellites in geosynchronous and high-polar orbits would detect the hot infrared signal generated during the boost phase of a ballistic missile trajectory. Today, components of the space-based infrared system (SBIRS)—consisting of four geosynchronous satellites (illustrated in figure 7-2) and two sensor packages in polar orbit to provide 24/7 coverage of the earth's surface—has nearly replaced the older Defense Support Program satellites that provided launch detection for decades. The next-generation overhead persistent infrared (OPIR) satellites

FIGURE 7-2. Space-Based Infrared System Satellite

Source: U.S. Air Force Space Command

are in development to replace the SBIRS. In addition to coverage provided by satellites in high-earth orbit, the new system will also field a proliferated constellation of cheaper, smaller satellites operating in low-earth orbit to enhance detection and, presumably, to provide some redundant capability to hedge against loss of one or more high-earth-orbit satellites from attack.

Early-Warning Radars

Large, ground-based, phased-array early-warning radars would provide independent confirmation of a ballistic missile attack targeting the United States. Three radars (located at Thule, Greenland; Fylingdales, U.K.; and Shemya Island, in the Aleutians) detect launches in midcourse, about ten to twenty minutes after launch. The PAVE PAWS radars located at air force stations in Cape Cod, Massachusetts; Beale, California [figure 7-3]; and Clear, Alaska, as well as the large phased array radar located at Cavalier, North Dakota, detect strategic ballistic missiles in the latter stages of their trajectories.

FIGURE 7-3. PAVE PAWS Radar Facility at Beale Air Force Base

Source: Command: Modern Operations / Modern Air Naval Operations database. http://cmano-db.com/facility/569/.

Attack Assessment

Facilities located in or near NORAD headquarters at Peterson Air Force Base in Colorado Springs, and elsewhere in the United States for backup, would collect launch detection satellite and early warning radar data and integrate the data with other relevant intelligence on the launches, and then use this information to assess the nature and scope of the attack. The process consists of four steps: surveillance of ballistic missile and other events through a variety of sensors; correlation of surveillance data with other intelligence and open-source information; assessment of the validity of warning information; and assessment of the severity of the threat to the United States or an ally.[11]

Command Centers

A network of command centers provides venues to establish a conference among the president and key presidential advisers to consider nuclear employment options and the means to communicate execution decisions to forces.[12] A president, therefore, whether in residence at the White House, at a trip site, at an alternate location, or in transit, must have 24/7 connectivity with senior advisers for just such a circumstance. As an example, if a large-scale attack on the United States were confirmed, the National Military Command Center (NMCC) in the Pentagon would establish a conference call over survivable communications among the president in the White House Situation Room, the Chairman the of Joint Chiefs of Staff at the NMCC, the commanders of Strategic Command and NORAD (located, respectively, at Offutt Air Force Base in Omaha and Peterson Air Force Base in Colorado Springs), and others, as determined by the president. If the president or the president's advisers were dispersed, or if Washington were to come under attack, a conference could be established through air-mobile command posts—the E-4B National Airborne Operations Center (NAOC) and E-6B Take Charge and Move Out (TACAMO) aircraft (figures 7-4 and 7-5)

FIGURE 7-4. E-4B National Airborne Operations Center

Source: U.S. Air Force

FIGURE 7-5. E-6B TACAMO Aircraft

Source: U.S. Navy

that can communicate with the president and key advisers wherever they are located. In addition, a road-mobile command post—the Mobile Consolidated Control Center—includes vehicles and associated equipment that provide a limited set of command-and-control capabilities during and following a nuclear conflict.

Communications

Communications in support of nuclear operations, including conferencing, force execution, and war termination, consist of a variety of satellite, airborne, and landline links across the radio frequency spectrum.[13] These range from those used in peacetime, day-to-day work environments (for example, cell phone, computer networks, secure Wi-Fi, e-mail, high-frequency [HF] radio) to links purposely fielded to operate in hostile nuclear environments characterized by multiple nuclear detonations, including at high altitudes, producing intense electromagnetic pulse fields that disrupt most unhardened communications links. Survivable, antijam communications resilient to electromagnetic pulse and ionospheric disruption are provided by MILSTAR satellites in geosynchronous orbit operating in ultrahigh frequency (UHF) and extremely high frequency (EHF) bands. Today, MILSTAR is being replaced with modern and more capable advanced EHF (AEHF) satellites that provide, among other things, much higher quality voice communications in severe jamming and nuclear-scintillation environments. Communication with submarines operating at depth is provided by links operating in the low frequency (LF) and very-low frequency (VLF) bands. The navy maintains in the United States, and at a few overseas locations adjacent to submarine patrol areas, several ground-based, send-only VLF transmitters as part of its Fleet Broadcast System. In addition, the primary mission of the navy's E-6B TACAMO aircraft is LF and VLF communications with undersea submarines. When transmitting, these aircraft fly in tight circles so that a trailing wire antenna several thousand feet long can be oriented vertically for optimal reception at these frequencies (figure 7-6).

High-bandwidth communications available today from the commercial sector offer high-quality voice, video, and data transfer rates in benign environments. Senior officials prefer phone systems and computer networks with such capabilities and would most likely rely on them, when available, in the early stages of a nuclear conflict. In hostile environments, as unhardened commercial systems are lost, a seamless transition to hardened systems is

FIGURE 7-6. TACAMO Communications Operations

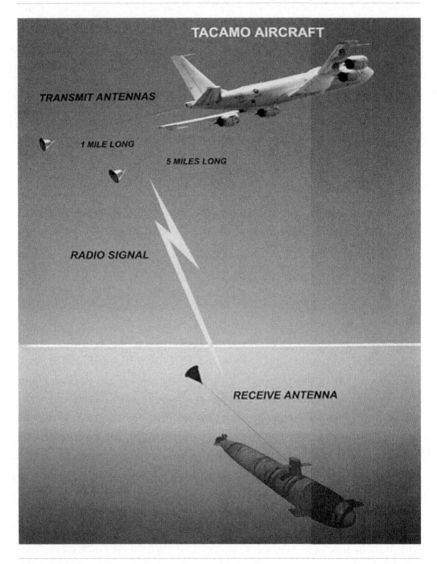

Source: U.S. Navy Museum

essential to ensure uninterrupted connectivity as a conflict evolves. Just as important, senior officials must learn—through exercises—to function with the much lower bandwidth that is inevitable with hardened communications. Figure 7-7 identifies the basic elements of the strategic NC2 architecture and conveys its complexity.

FIGURE 7-7. Representative NC2 System Connectivity

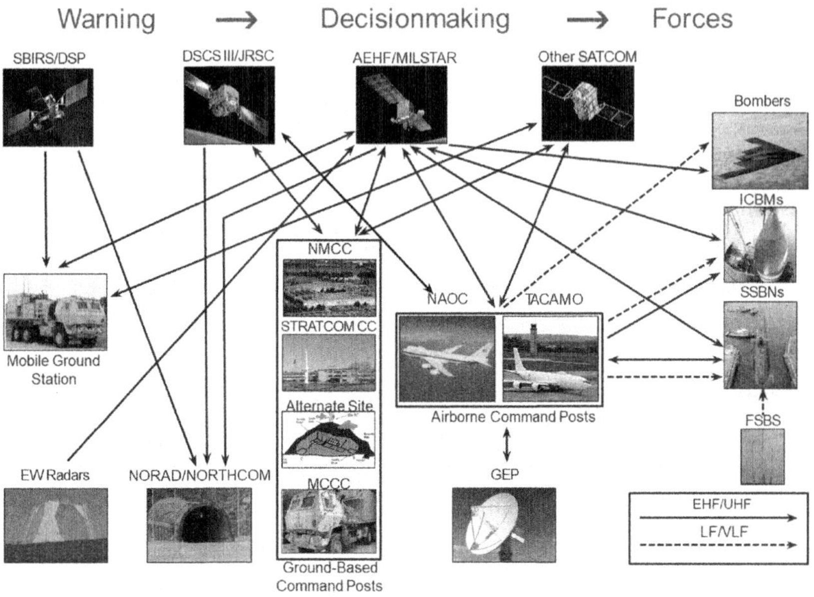

Source: Author.

National Leadership Command Capability

The National Leadership Command Capability (NLCC) comprises the capabilities within the office of the president for crisis management generally, capabilities that include crisis communications, conferencing, and planning and decision support. Whether for a nuclear strike, a catastrophic weather event, a flu epidemic, or a cyberattack on the electrical grid, the White House team must combine a host of information sources, boil the information down to essentials, tailor it for consumption by the president, set up contact with key advisers, and provide decision support. Particularly in scenarios where a president does not face a highly constrained time window to employ U.S. nuclear weapons, broader information-gathering and decision-support elements in the U.S. government are likely to play a larger role in nuclear decisionmaking. The box in figure 7-1 highlights the nuclear crisis management piece involving the NLCC.

In a nuclear crisis, depending on the time urgency of response, a president will seek a broad set of information on global political developments and the status of U.S. and adversary forces, including intelligence on an adversary's alerting of nuclear forces, corroborating information from allies and partners, attack assessment derived from early-warning data, and reports on damage assessment. In the midst of a conventional conflict, for example, a president would want to know any indications of impending nuclear employment by the adversary. After limited first nuclear use by an adversary, a president would most likely seek a rapid postattack assessment before deciding how to respond. This information would be provided by the intelligence community, from open sources, from combatant commands, and from U.S. allies and partners. When and if a decision is made to respond with nuclear weapons, the president would communicate that decision to a "first tier" (see figure 7-1), which, depending on circumstances, could be the secretary of defense, the Strategic Command commander, the colonel on duty in the National Military Command Center, or the flag officer flying airborne alert on an E-6B TACAMO command-and-control aircraft.

The NLCC, while generally operated, maintained, and modernized with Defense Department resources, is owned and managed by the White House, optimized to meet the needs of the president across a range of crisis contingencies. This fact has complicated efforts to achieve a seamless interface with other pieces of the NC2 system, particularly regarding crisis communications. Today, senior-leader communications consist of a hodgepodge of separate links for communicating unclassified, secret, and top-secret information, provided and maintained by different sponsors and interconnected in an ad hoc network that has been built up over decades. With a lot of continuous attention, the system works well, but there are serious questions about whether this is the best way to maintain secure, reliable, cyber-resilient senior-leader communications over time.

NC2 for Nonstrategic Nuclear Forces

The NC2 system must also facilitate command and control of nonstrategic nuclear forces. During the Cold War, the United States had thousands of nuclear weapons of all types in Europe to support NATO's defense against Soviet invasion. A variety of nuclear forces in Europe were fully integrated into allied defense planning and kept under the operational control of the Supreme Allied Commander Europe. In a conflict, the commander had the ability to send a request to the president for nuclear employment at a particular time and place to achieve a defined operational objective or ask for broader authorization to employ nuclear weapons in Europe.[14]

Today, U.S. and NATO nonstrategic nuclear forces consist only of B-61 gravity bombs that can be carried by U.S. F-15E strike aircraft and allied dual-capable aircraft; these forces maintain operational readiness levels far lower than those common during the Cold War. NATO does not have pre-planned nuclear employment options, nor has it made necessary investments to increase survivability of its nuclear forces and command and control. While NATO does have a long-established nuclear consultation, planning, and decisionmaking system that could, in a conflict, be used to approve a nuclear strike, coming to a consensus decision among thirty allies on an operationally relevant timeline would be challenging.[15] All NATO nonstrategic nuclear weapons remain under U.S. custody until the president authorizes their employment. Once uploaded by U.S. personnel, they would be delivered to their targets by U.S. or allied dual-capable aircraft. The 2018 Nuclear Posture Review highlights the need to "ensure the NATO NC2 system is modernized to enable appropriate consultations and effective nuclear operations, improve its survivability, resilience, and flexibility in the most stressful threat environments."[16]

The United States also has extended deterrence commitments to other allies, including Japan, South Korea, and Australia. It consults regularly with these allies on nuclear issues but does not have nuclear burden-sharing arrangements as it does with NATO. This may change in the future and, if so, new NC2 capabilities and consultative processes would be required.

Launch Execution and the Positive and Negative Control of Nuclear Weapons

The mechanisms for seeking presidential authorization to employ U.S. nuclear forces, and their subsequent execution, are intimately connected with the objective of assuring the positive and negative control of those forces. The goal is to significantly reduce the risk of accidental or unauthorized launch and ensure the proper launch of nuclear weapons if and when the president issues a lawful order. The balance between positive and negative control is a delicate one because rigorous negative control increases the challenge of assured execution once an employment decision is made. Because of their enormous destructive power, U.S. nuclear weapons, associated forces, and operations are subject to negative control measures that far exceed those imposed on other military capabilities.

If a situation arises for which U.S. nuclear employment is a potential option, a conference is initiated with the president, wherever located, and key presidential advisers to review options.[17] If judged necessary, the president, with help from the president's military assistant, communicates a nuclear force execution decision to the National Military Command Center or, if need be, to an alternate surviving command post. A set of procedures exists to authenticate that any decision received by the command center has indeed been issued by the president.

Command center staff would generate an emergency-action message—a sequence of thirty or so alphanumeric characters that are correlated with a specific execution option contained in code books at launch units, which include ICBM launch control centers, bomber bases, and SSBNs at sea. The message is transmitted through a variety of communications links, a certain subset of which are highly survivable to hostile nuclear environments. It provides both the specific attack option for execution and the unlock codes for the weapon systems. Under the two-person rule, the emergency-action message is authenticated by multiple officers and, if validated, executed.[18]

Bombers on alert can be dispersed to increase their survivability to preemptive strike and can be recalled at any time before weapons release; means for receiving and processing emergency-action messages and unlocking weapons are resident in bomber cockpits. For submarine-launched ballistic missiles, the emergency-action message contains the combination to unlock an onboard safe containing launch keys. Many in the crew participate in the launch sequence, not just the commanding officer, introducing additional safeguards against unauthorized launch. Launch control centers that each control ten Minuteman III ICBMs require two people with separate keys to execute a launch, as illustrated in figure 7-8. "Votes" from two of five physically separate launch control centers are required before a squadron of fifty ICBMs can be launched.[19] Logistics, storage, maintenance, and physical security of nuclear warheads across all three legs of the triad are also subject to the two-person rule.

Employment of U.S. nuclear forces is by no means automatic but requires a person "in the loop" at all levels. The men and women who secure, maintain, and operate nuclear forces, and those in the operational nuclear chain of command, are subject to a rigorous personal reliability program administrated at the base level that involves monitoring all aspects of an individual's financial, domestic, physical, and psychological health.[20]

In summary, only the president can authorize nuclear release, and there is a complex process with multiple safeguards and redundant links to ensure both positive and negative control of nuclear weapons. U.S. nuclear forces

FIGURE 7-8. Two-Person Control Applied to ICBM Launch

Source: Senior Airman Jason Wiese (U.S. Air Force)

can be launched quickly, if necessary, but only with informed presidential authorization.

Providing Increased Presidential Decision Time

Earlier discussion on the alert level of U.S. nuclear forces, and the way a decision to execute those forces is reached and carried out, provides context for understanding the time pressure facing a president in a nuclear crisis and possible means to mitigate it. In this regard, no president has ever welcomed a choice either to either launch ICBMs quickly, before enemy warheads arrive on the missile fields, or to wait and lose them. President Obama's nuclear employment policy issued in 2013 called attention, with the Cold War's end, to a "significantly diminished probability of a disarming surprise nuclear attack."[21] It directed examination of options to reduce the role of ICBM launch under attack in U.S. planning. At the same time, because the risk could not be eliminated, he directed retention of that option, and the 2018 Nuclear Posture Review affirmed that decision.

One objective of NC2 is to increase the time that the president has to make decisions on nuclear weapons employment.[22] In a narrow decision window, there is limited time to gather information and evaluate courses of action, which increases the likelihood of miscalculation. With limited time to verify an attack assessment, a president may order a nuclear strike on false warning or without fully understanding adversary intent. A worst-case scenario would be a U.S. assessment that a massive Russian counterforce attack is underway that persuades the president to launch U.S. ICBMs on warning, when in fact there is no real threat. In another scenario, a president faced with a narrow time window for employment of nuclear weapons might be uncomfortable with the intelligence or options presented. As a result, a president might choose not to issue an employment order when doing so would have best advanced U.S. interests.

U.S. nuclear posture, including the NC2 system, is designed to reduce the likelihood that the pressure to quickly decide to employ nuclear weapons leads to unsatisfactory outcomes. Three mechanisms can relieve time pressures in decisionmaking: reducing the number of situations in which prompt employment of nuclear weapons would be required to achieve U.S. objectives; increasing the time available for information gathering and deliberation; and improving the ability to make the most efficient use of time available within constrained time windows.[23]

On the first point, reducing time pressures on the president for a rapid launch decision is often cast solely in the context of providing increased decision time. But that is only a part of the answer; another part involves reducing an enemy's incentive to mount nuclear attacks and the imperative for a time-urgent U.S. response if warning of an attack is provided. There are three factors today that mitigate the risk of a short-warning attack on Minuteman III ICBMs. First, maintaining demonstrably credible capabilities to launch U.S. ICBMs within minutes after receiving tactical warning of enemy launch is a key mechanism for deterring such attack; no enemy leader planning a precise attack on U.S. ICBMs could ever count on their assured destruction on the ground. Second, the evolution to single-warhead U.S. ICBMs under New START makes this force a much less attractive target than it was when the missiles carried three or ten warheads. Third, under New START, an increasing fraction of total strategic warheads are deployed at sea on survivable SSBNs. These forces provide the president with a viable choice not to make a rapid decision but rather to ride out an attack—or, in the case of uncertain warning, to wait for definitive confirmation of adversary nuclear strikes—while still retaining capabilities to achieve critical targeting objectives.[24]

Because ICBM vulnerability is a driver for rapid launch, another solution would be to field survivable ICBMs. In the 1970s and 1980s, when Russia's large, accurate, highly MIRVed ICBMs posed a considerable threat, significant resources and debate were devoted to establishing a politically viable, technically achievable, and cost-effective solution for ICBM survivability. Options involving deceptive basing, mobility, and increased hardness were examined. All failed, but not necessarily for technical reasons. Issues involving public interface and cost were seen as more pressing. Nearly three decades have passed, and there is little interest in exploring survivable basing within the ongoing program to replace the Minuteman III ICBM, but neither has the option been foreclosed.

Second, the United States can increase the time available for information gathering and deliberation. This starts with increasing the survivability of the decisionmaker. The Cold War scenario that most stressed a president's decision time and NC2 was not a surprise attack of Soviet ICBMs, which at least provided thirty minutes warning. Rather, it was the zero (or very short) warning decapitation strike on Washington from a low-flying, nuclear-armed, sea-launched cruise missile launched from a quiet Soviet submarine patrolling just off the Atlantic coast, coupled with a follow-on attack on U.S. ICBMs. Flight times for sea-launched cruise missiles were short, and there was little or no capability then to detect launch or to characterize the flight as threatening, including finding the signal in the noisy background of commercial air traffic in the region. If a close-in submarine were detected, certain steps could be taken to make forces, national leadership, and associated NC2 more survivable and resilient, but the United States never adequately solved this problem. Today, the decapitation threat posed by a Russian submarine carrying sea-launched cruise missiles remains. Additional threats could be posed by undetected or difficult to characterize launches of air-launched cruise missiles or future deployments of intercontinental-range ground-launched cruise missiles or hypersonic glide vehicles, all of which are part of Russia's ongoing nuclear modernization. In the future, other adversaries are likely to acquire capabilities for such short-warning attack.

Managing such risks can increase decision time by facilitating survival of the president or a lawful successor.[25] The United States maintains and exercises capabilities to evacuate the president rapidly from Washington, D.C.,

a primary target in a counterforce strike. Having awareness that a submarine carrying a cruise-missile is patrolling in coastal waters and the ability to
detect and characterize threatening flight trajectories from cruise missile or
other hypersonic glide vehicle threats would provide time to take such action.
Work on technologies to advance such capabilities is underway but requires
renewed attention. Detection of close-in, quiet submarines can be advanced
by restoring some capabilities that were allowed to wither away with the
end of the Cold War (for example, robust undersea sonar networks) and by
funding robust science and technology to improve U.S. undersea detection
capabilities going forward. For cruise missiles, the United States previously
deployed a prototype system, called Joint Land Attack Cruise Missile Defense
Elevated Netted Sensor System, in which a tethered aerostat located near
Aberdeen, Maryland was fielded with an advanced, sideways-looking radar
to detect and track cruise missiles threatening Washington. This program
ended following political outcry when the tethering cable came undone and
was dragged by the aerostat through Pennsylvania farmland, causing minor
damage. This was unfortunate; the system was a prudent, affordable program
providing initial capability to address a real threat.

In other scenarios, the president's decision time can be extended by
improved warning and timely situation assessment. The NC2 system, and
associated intelligence capabilities, could focus increased attention on indications and warning that the adversary is headed down a path toward nuclear
use, but before actual launch. Such information could facilitate a head start
on any required adaptive planning. After adversary nuclear employment,
presidential decisionmaking would be enhanced with fast, accurate reports
on damage assessment. Improved information flow in these areas, depending
on specific circumstances, would provide a president greater time to deliberate about courses of action.

A third mechanism for relieving time pressure is improving the ability of the president to make adequately informed decisions even in narrow
time windows. Perhaps the most important factor in this regard is the key
advisers and decision tools that a president would rely on to gain situational awareness and choose between various courses of action. If prepared
and effectively supported, presidential advisers can better serve in guiding a
president through an extremely fast-paced decision process.[26] Technology is
important as well. When the president is not collocated with key advisers,
effective remote conferencing capabilities, supported by reliable, secure, and

survivable communications links, will facilitate short-notice decision conferences addressing the evolving situation and the pros and cons of various courses of action.

Emerging Vision for Modern Conflict and Its Implications for NC2

During the Cold War, the most likely scenario for nuclear war involved escalation of a conventional conflict. Most believed that the initial stages of conventional war in Europe or Asia, and potentially even limited regional nuclear use, would leave the U.S. homeland relatively unscathed. Escalation to nuclear attacks on the United States would, therefore, evolve with fully alert nuclear forces and an NC2 system undegraded from strikes during the conventional or limited nuclear phase. In addition, while it was assessed to be a lower-probability scenario, the United States nonetheless viewed an attempted surprise disarming nuclear attack by the Soviet Union, potentially without strategic warning, as possible, if not plausible. As a result, U.S. forces were postured for resilience to that threat by keeping ICBMs launch ready, several SSBNs at sea at all times, and a portion of the bomber force on alert.

It is still important to ensure NC2 performance toward today's equivalent of Cold War threats. But the United States now faces a much more dynamic security environment, featuring multiple potential sources of conflict with peer competitors and with the emergence of nuclear-armed regional states. This environment poses more varied and complex conflict scenarios that will stress NC2 in different ways than traditional Cold War threats.

Four developments are driving these considerations, one political and three military-technical. First, Russia under Vladimir Putin is undermining the post–Cold War security order while also increasing the salience in Russian doctrine of potential limited first use of nuclear weapons in regional conflict. This is reflected in military exercises and ongoing modernization programs for nonstrategic nuclear weapons.[27] Russia's leaders may well believe that such limited use could achieve key political-military objectives short of escalation to global nuclear war. It is also possible that other potential nuclear-armed adversaries may share this view. Second, U.S. competitors, in particular Russia and China, are increasing capabilities for kinetic and non-kinetic attack on U.S. satellite systems.[28] Third, Russia and China are improving their capabilities for precision global conventional strike that can hold at risk key NC2 nodes, including radars, ground stations, command posts, and aircraft.[29] Fourth, and what may be most stressing for NC2, there is an increasing cyber threat to critical NC2 assets, including satellite systems.[30]

The transition from conventional to nuclear conflict could evolve much differently than that anticipated during the Cold War, in ways the legacy NC2 system is ill suited to address. The conventional model for escalation—a step-by-step progression from peacetime to crisis to regional then global conventional conflict to nuclear use—may no longer be valid. Rather, escalation to a large-scale nuclear strike may involve a set of discrete actions that blend together in unexpected ways:

- peacetime cyber surveillance and offensive cyber operations
- unattributed hybrid operations in run-up to crisis
- information operations in run-up and during crisis
- covert sabotage of critical installations
- cyber or kinetic attack on space assets, including NC2 space assets
- regional conventional conflict
- precision global conventional strikes on strategic targets
- limited, regional nuclear use involving few casualties
- limited, regional nuclear use on ground targets with moderate casualties

Consider a regional conflict that escalates to a global conventional phase in which U.S. nuclear forces and NC2 are degraded initially by cyber and antisatellite attacks and later by long-range precision conventional strikes. An attack on an AEHF satellite to degrade tactical communications in a conventional conflict would also degrade nuclear communications provided by that same satellite. Escalation to limited nuclear could feature use of nuclear weapons to produce high-altitude electromagnetic pulse but few immediate casualties on the ground, along with more widespread non-nuclear attacks on general purpose command and control assets. Escalation to a large nuclear attack with multiple detonations on U.S. territory—the Cold War scenario—could thus begin with severely degraded NC2.

To deal with such scenarios, the United States needs an NC2 system that can survive sustained conventional attacks and the ability to plan and conduct nuclear strikes in coordination with ongoing conventional operations. Nuclear forces might be called on to restore deterrence after an adversary had already conducted a nuclear attack or to destroy a portion of an adversary's nuclear forces before they could be employed. Legacy NC2 was optimized for rapid, large-scale execution of what some call the Cold War's multiple-choice test: Which of a few major preplanned strike options should the president choose? The required information and communications bandwidth were modest. In the future, more complex conflicts, where nuclear use initially may be quite limited, a president, in making decisions, would seek a much broader set of consultations with senior advisers, allies, and possibly adversaries—more of an essay test—requiring more robust two-way communications pathways. Figure 7-9 illustrates how anticipated information needs for managing a nuclear crisis could differ between a canonical bolt-out-of-the-blue Cold War scenario and one more closely associated with modern conflict.

FIGURE 7-9. In a Nuclear Crisis, What Will a President Want to Know?

Cold War Bolt-out-of-the-Blue massive strike
- What is the attack's origin or scope in terms of numbers, impact, and locations?
- Do I stay in Washington or evacuate?
- If I "ride it out," what are the implications for forces, NC2, and anticipated damage to the enemy?
- Which of four retaliatory strike options do you recommend?

"Modern" Conflict in the Twenty-first Century Involving Limited Nuclear Use
- Is Washington under attack?
- Is the attack accidental, or unauthorized, or authorized by a foreign power?
- How urgent is a decision needed?
- How is the conventional fight going?
- What is the readiness state of U.S. nuclear forces, NC2 and defenses?
- Have missile defenses shot down part or all of the threat?
- Before warhead arrival: What is the anticipated damage from the strike?
- After warhead arrival: What is the actual poststrike, post-ballistic missile defense engagement damage assessment?
- Who will be advising me on a response? Right now, to whom am I talking?
- What are the options to respond? Nuclear only? Conventional? Cyber?
- If I respond with nuclear weapons, how many innocent casualties?
- What are other impacts (e.g., regarding allies, nonproliferation)
- What is the perpetrator doing or saying about the strike? What are U.S. allies doing or saying?
- When do I execute plans for continuity of government? What is the status of emergency response?
- How do you know the information you are providing is accurate? How do I get more information?
- What do I need to tell the American people and when?

Fixing the Legacy System While Evolving to Next Gen NC2

There are two priorities for NC2 modernization.[31] First, the United States must fix the legacy NC2 system to address the modern equivalent of the Cold War scenarios for which it was designed. It is investing to sustain and modernize the NC2 "thin line," including alerted air and ground-mobile command centers, early-warning satellites and radars, and communications satellites as well as other links to surviving forces. Activities underway on the "thin line" and other elements of the legacy NC2 system include the following:

- Survivable satellite communications: Complete the transition from Mil-Star to AEHF satellites; explore advanced concepts for and approaches to global NC2 communications.
- Survivable communications to forces: Implement an LF communications link for the B-2 bomber; field much-delayed EHF terminals for delivery platforms and fixed and mobile command posts; complete Minuteman III communications upgrades.
- Early-warning system modernization: Complete transition to SBIRS; continue development of the next-generation OPIRs, both high- and low-earth-orbit components, to replace the SBIRS; complete the program to upgrade land-based radars, including Thule, Fylingdales, Clear, and PAVE PAWS radars based in the United States.
- Improve conferencing capabilities for the president (day-to-day and stressed environments).
- Strengthen connectivity with the president in certain transportation modes.
- Harden critical communications links to the effects of electromagnetic pulse.
- Recapitalize airborne command-post capabilities (E-4 NAOC and dual-mission E-6B TACAMO).
- Continue the cyber vulnerability assessment of U.S. nuclear forces and NC2.

The second modernization priority is to develop a concept and associated architecture for an NC2 system to address twenty-first century conflict and then field it. As reported, Russia and China are developing sophisticated counterspace, cyberspace, and long-range conventional strike capabilities that can potentially corrupt, disrupt, or even destroy satellites that support U.S. NC2. They are also pursuing sophisticated offensive cyber warfare capabilities that could threaten secure communications pathways and be used to disrupt other elements of NC2. Adversaries have developed or are developing numerous and capable long-range conventional strike systems that can hold at risk key NC2 nodes, including radars, ground stations, command posts, and aircraft.

Efforts to generate a "next-generation NC2" systems architecture responsive to these threats are underway, supported by studies carried out by the Defense Science Board, the Strategic Command's NC2 Enterprise Center, the Strategic Commander's Strategic Advisory Group, and others. In contemplating a systems architecture, several important issues must be addressed, decisions made, and associated challenges faced.

The Cyber Threat to NC2

The cyber vulnerability of U.S. nuclear forces and NC2 was not a major concern in the 1980s and earlier, when major pieces of the system were developed and fielded. It is today. Because NC2 and the forces it supports are extensive and dispersed, there are numerous, complex attack vectors into the system that are well understood by only a few experts. Approaches to their mitigation are, in some cases, counterintuitive. Exacerbating the problem, both offensive and defensive cyber activities tend to be highly classified; cyber offense experts, cleared at the highest levels, often are prevented from sharing ideas with their cyber defense colleagues, also highly cleared but not in the same security compartments. Consider four contrary views often heard on NC2 cyber resilience:

- Air gapping, 1970s analog information technology with vintage operating systems, and distributed systems acquisition, all help to ensure cyber resilience.
- Sophisticated adversaries understand the U.S. complex system at least as well as, if not better than, U.S. operators and are probably already "inside" the system, exploiting it today.
- The problem is so pervasive that the United States, Russia, and others should de-alert nuclear forces to avoid inadvertent launch caused by a third-party hack of launch control systems.
- The situation is so uncertain that one cannot really know.

A troubling situation for sure. Because of the rapid change in offensive and defensive cyber capabilities, uncertainty will continue; ensuring that NC2 remains secure will be an ongoing challenge. Despite air gapping and vintage information technology, the United States cannot be assured that today's legacy system is cyber resilient, given possible insider threats, among other things. More broadly, cyber penetration of NC2 raises two concerns: the ability of hackers to prevent an authorized nuclear response to an actual strike and the ability of hackers to instigate an inadvertent launch of forces absent a real threat.[32] On the former, an adversary could, in theory, cause early-warning systems to miss or mischaracterize an attack; disrupt the links that support presidential conferencing; alter or block a force execution emergency-action message; disrupt missile launch control systems, causing a delivery platform to malfunction; or cause nuclear warheads to dud on arrival. On the latter, an enemy hack could, in theory, cause early-warning systems to report a launch when none occurs, bypass launch control safeguards, or alter or block a war termination message.

While such attacks are theoretically possible, existing NC2 provides various means to mitigate the risk:

- strong negative control of nuclear systems, including rigorous and elaborate launch control safeguards with multiple redundancies complement cyber resilience;
- dispersed acquisition responsibility for various pieces of the system that complicates integrated across-the-board attacks;
- "human in the loop," not automatic, operations that provide means to flag and respond to otherwise anomalous behavior of the system; and
- personnel reliability programs for those who secure, operate, and maintain nuclear forces, helping to mitigate insider threats.

How can the United States ensure NC2 cyber resilience in the future? Most important, the culture of "Tell me what I need to buy for cyber resilience, so I can be done with it" must be replaced with a culture of "This problem will be persistent, day in and day out, for the life of the system; I must assume the adversary will gain access, and my job is to be aware of the full scope of such activity and devise ways to safely operate around it." This means continuous cyber surveillance of the system with high-quality operators, tearing down the offense-defense channels of communication, and establishing a permanent cyber offense "red team" to challenge defenders. Well-trained military officers who take a two-year rotational assignment at Cyber Command focusing on threats to NC2 are necessary but not sufficient. In addition, computer scientists at the doctoral level, who today command high salaries in Silicon Valley and elsewhere, must be enticed to spend the better part of a career gaining a deep understanding of, and the attack vectors into, a very complex system. One should assume U.S. adversaries have those people at the same level of expertise working to exploit the U.S. NC2 system. As a complementary approach to hedge cyber risks, consideration could be given to a bare-bones, stand-alone, covert NC2 capability that would remain totally offline and surface only in an emergency. Such an approach, of course, has serious downsides but is worth considering.

Modern Early Warning

Early warning will become increasingly challenging as Russia and China deploy nuclear- and conventional-armed hypersonic cruise missiles and hypersonic boost-glide vehicles that are far more difficult to track, characterize, and intercept than ballistic missiles. A collection of warning satellites and radars optimized to detect and track ballistic missiles may struggle with highly maneuverable hypersonic systems. Certain key U.S. assets, including those that support NC2, may be more vulnerable to attack. At a minimum, there is likely to be increased uncertainty about adversary intent when strategic launches are detected. U.S. modernization of early-warning systems to detect and characterize attacks rapidly, therefore, must account for a full complement of adversary means for strategic strike. Toward this end, next-generation OPIR high-earth-orbit satellites, slated to replace SBIRS, will be supplemented with a low-earth-orbit constellation that would improve detection and tracking of modern threats. This constellation will also provide the added benefit of making the overall system more difficult to attack and hence more resilient.

A Future for Satellite Communications

Today's NC2 satellite communication architecture is based on a very few large, expensive, multipurpose high-earth-orbit satellites that are vulnerable to direct attack or disruption of their data links by jamming or other means. A debate is underway about whether to continue with this approach or evolve to a "proliferated" low-earth-orbit constellation of many smaller, cheaper satellites. Such a constellation could be designed for rapid replenishment to restore lost functionally should a portion of the system come under anti-satellite attack. Given the emerging vulnerabilities of satellite systems, other options must also be considered:

- Develop the ability to stand up long-range airborne communications relay networks on short notice. This could be used to restore NC2 communications to regions covered by a lost AEHF satellite.

- Develop proliferated HF communications for use in stressed environments. High-frequency technology has traditionally been assessed as nonsurvivable owing to potential loss or delay of signal in a major nuclear exchange from radiation environments involving blackout and scintillation. Software-defined radio technology, however, could facilitate cost-effective proliferated HF links with multiple pathways that could avoid local ionospheric disturbances. As a result, in limited-use scenarios, HF may offer promise as a backup or replacement for satellite communications.

- Continue to increase the resilience of its space architecture by improving active and passive defense of satellite systems. This would help to ensure that satellite communications are available for NC2 in the midst of a high-end conflict.

Critically, some hard choices on the way ahead for global NC2 communications must occur before a conceptual systems architecture can be developed.

Survivability of NC2 Aircraft

The United States has long valued the inherent survivability of ballistic missile submarines at sea. It has spent wisely to stay on top of any technological developments that could conceivably put those assets at risk. Regarding aircraft, once aloft and outside integrated air defense zones, NC2 aircraft were generally thought to be survivable for an extended period. The United States should rethink this as it moves to replace aging aircraft. Specifically, Air Force One, NAOC, and E-6B aircraft may become more vulnerable to detection and targeting than they have been in the past. Advanced sensors with faster processing will improve the ability of adversaries to exploit electronic communications or other unique electronic signatures to locate, track, and target mobile platforms.[33] Going forward, effective NC2 will require robust communications links that enable management and direction of forces consistent with operational concepts that maximize survivability of mobile platforms.

NLCC Modernization

Future demands on presidential nuclear-crisis management will call for much-improved conferencing capabilities among senior leaders, supported by high-quality voice, video, and data communications resilient to stressed nuclear environments and adversary exploitation. Such capabilities must be available whether the president is in the White House, on the move, at a trip location, or at an undisclosed site. Given possible complex conflict scenarios characterized by conventional operations with allies and partners, combined offense and defense, and response to limited nuclear use, a president may wish to securely consult with a broader set of actors, including foreign leaders from allied, partner, and potentially adversary countries. These presidential needs, among others, will drive the approach to a modern NLCC architecture. A basic concept for such an approach, reflecting a modular, hierarchical, layered architecture based loosely on the open-system interconnection model used in the design of information technology networks, is illustrated in figure 7-10.[34]

Each horizontal box represents a function involved in the generation, movement, processing, and refinement of information supporting presidential crisis management. Each layer would take on a specific job and then pass its data up to the next layer. Overarching this process would be two additional functions, represented by the vertical blocks in figure 7-10. Overall management of enterprise and associated network operations would provide

FIGURE 7-10. Conceptual Architecture for National Leadership Command Capability (NLCC)

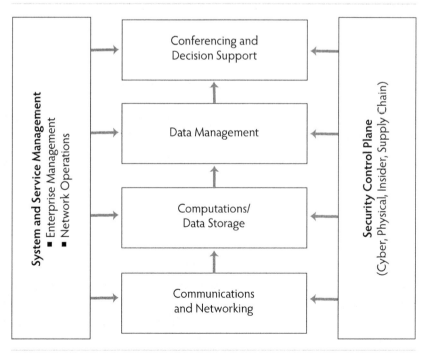

Source: Author.

for seamless transitions between multiple communications links, automatic switching, access to various information sources, and the ability to authenticate as well as rapidly add or remove individuals from conferences. Of utmost importance, a security "control plane" would oversee all aspects of enterprise integrity and resilience in the face of daunting cyber and physical security challenges. Highly skilled career personnel employing state-of-the-art tools would provide round-the-clock cyber situational awareness and facilitate effective operations when the system is under active surveillance or attack. A cyber offense red team would continuously challenge them by seeking chinks in the system's armor. Based on lessons learned to date, it is essential that a modern NLCC architecture have unity of design and integration and that system acquisition be overseen by a single authority. Finally, central to all NLCC modernization activities are efforts to acquire a broad understanding of the specific information, consultative, and communications needs of the president.

Implications for Adaptive Planning

Modern conflict will also drive changes to support more flexible adaptive planning and force execution. Responding to limited nuclear first use against U.S. forces or allies could require development of a new strike option tailored to the specific scenario at hand, upload of targeting coordinates to weapons systems computers, execution by one or more U.S. nuclear delivery systems, and reporting back on damage assessment. The process of situation assessment, course of action development and evaluation, and execution will all have to occur within a constrained time window, in coordination with key allies and partners, and in a way that is fully aligned with ongoing conventional military operations. This exceeds capabilities and processes in place today and will drive a much closer integration of mission planning with NC2.

Managing Overlap between Nuclear and General Purpose Command and Control

A key decision for future NC2 is the degree to which it will be integrated with conventional command and control. Traditionally, nuclear and conventional command and control have been kept mostly separate, relying on different software and hardware. Yet even in the legacy system, there is substantial overlap—large, multipurpose satellites, for example, host separate communications systems supporting nuclear and conventional operations.

Going forward, the United States will most likely continue to maintain some separation but may decide to integrate more aspects of NC2 with emerging concepts of joint, all-domain command and control. The benefits of a more integrated system could include lower cost, greater resilience through a more diverse set of communications paths, and the ability to rely on software that can be quickly updated and adapted for cyber protection. On the other hand, intermingling nuclear and conventional command and control offers adversaries a larger cyberattack surface. More important, U.S. adversaries may view a dual-use satellite providing tactical communications supporting conventional operations as a legitimate target. As modernization proceeds, the degree to which NC2 missions can and should be disentangled from other non-nuclear missions, at affordable cost, should be a factor in systems acquisition decisions.[35] Whatever decisions are made by the United States regarding the degree of overlap, associated risks will need to be managed.

Notes

1. Peter D. Feaver, "Command and Control in Emerging Nuclear Nations," *International Security* 17, no. 3 (1992–1993), pp. 160–87.

2. Walter B. Slocombe, *Democratic Civilian Control of Nuclear Weapons*, Policy Paper 12 (Geneva: Geneva Centre for the Democratic Control of Armed Forces, April 2006).

3. Boats in port are not launch capable.

4. William A. Chambers and others, *Presidential Decision Time Regarding Nuclear Weapons Employment: An Assessment and Options* (Alexandria, VA: Institute for Defense Analyses, June 2019), pp. 7–15.

5. Ashton B. Carter, "The Command and Control of Nuclear War," *Scientific American* 252, no. 1 (1985), p. 32–39.

6. In the past, presidents have predelegated a narrow set of nuclear-use decisions to subordinate commanders. For part of the Cold War, nuclear weapons were fielded with anti-aircraft missiles and air defense fighters under the North American Air Defense Command (NORAD). President Eisenhower pre-authorized the NORAD commander to employ nuclear weapons for defensive purposes, for example, in blunting a Soviet bomber attack. U.S. air defense units no longer are fielded with nuclear weapons, and related authorities have been revoked. There is nothing, however, to prevent a president from delegating certain nuclear-use decisions in the future. See Peter J. Roman, "Ike's Hair Trigger: U.S. Nuclear Predelegation, 1953–1960," *Security Studies* 7, no. 4 (1998), pp. 121–65. Related documents can be found in William

Burr (ed.), "First Declassification of Eisenhower's Instructions to Commanders Pre-delegating Nuclear Weapons Use, 1959–1960, National Security Archives, May 18, 2001, https://nsarchive2.gwu.edu/NSAEBB/NSAEBB45/printindex.html.

7. Office of the Deputy Assistant Secretary of Defense for Nuclear Matters, *Nuclear Matters Handbook 2020* (Department of Defense, 2020), p. 25.

8. Chambers and others, *Presidential Decision Time Regarding Nuclear Weapons Employment*, pp. 26–27.

9. Office of the Deputy Assistant Secretary of Defense for Nuclear Matters, *Nuclear Matters Handbook 2020*, pp. 25–27.

10. Office of the Deputy Assistant Secretary of Defense for Nuclear Matters, *Nuclear Matters Handbook 2020*, p. 28.

11. Office of the Deputy Assistant Secretary of Defense for Nuclear Matters, *Nuclear Matters Handbook 2020*, pp. 24–25; Chambers and others, *Presidential Decision Time Regarding Nuclear Weapons Employment*, pp. 20–22; Robert D. Critchlow, *Nuclear Command and Control: Current Program and Issues* (Washington, D.C.: Congressional Research Service, May 3, 2006), pp. 3–5.

12. Office of the Deputy Assistant Secretary of Defense for Nuclear Matters, *Nuclear Matters Handbook 2020*, pp. 22–25.

13. Office of the Deputy Assistant Secretary of Defense for Nuclear Matters, *Nuclear Matters Handbook 2020*, p. 25.

14. Major Michael W. Cannon, *Battlefield Nuclear Weapons and Tactical Gridlock in Europe* (Fort Leavenworth, KS: School of Advanced Military Studies, U.S. Army Command and General Staff College, November 17, 1988).

15. Shaun R. Gregory, *Nuclear Command and Control in NATO: Nuclear Weapons Operations and the Strategy of Flexible Response* (New York: St. Martin's Press, 1996).

16. Office of the Secretary of Defense, *Nuclear Posture Review 2018* (Department of Defense, February 2018), p. 36.

17. Office of the Deputy Assistant Secretary of Defense for Nuclear Matters, *Nuclear Matters Handbook 2020*, p. 18.

18. "How a U.S. Nuclear Strike Actually Works," Bloomberg Quick Take Originals, YouTube channel (video), February 1, 2018, www.youtube.com/watch?v=leiI2DVCF1A.

19. "Launching Missiles," National Museum of the United States Air Force, May 27, 2015. See also, "This Is the Process the U.S. Uses to Authorize a Nuclear Strike," CNBC (video), August 18 2017, www.cnbc.com/2017/08/18/this-is-the-process-the-us-uses-to-authorize-a-nuclear-strike.html.

20. Office of the Deputy Assistant Secretary of Defense for Nuclear Matters, *Nuclear Matters Handbook 2020*, p. 22.

21. "The Nuclear Weapons Employment Strategy of the United States," The White House, June 19, 2013, https://obamawhitehouse.archives.gov/the-press-office/2013/06/19/fact-sheet-nuclear-weapons-employment-strategy-united-states.

22. Chambers and others, *Presidential Decision Time Regarding Nuclear Weapons Employment*.

23. Chambers and others, *Presidential Decision Time Regarding Nuclear Weapons Employment.*

24. Pressure on a president to retaliate promptly to limited nuclear strikes by a nonpeer adversary can be alleviated somewhat with capable ballistic missile defenses. Defenses provide additional time to assess the degree to which they succeed in blunting the attack before a decision is needed on the specifics of U.S. retaliation.

25. The Presidential Succession Act lays out the line of succession if a president is killed. See "Vacancy in Offices of Both President and Vice President; Officers Eligible to Act," 3 U.S. Code § 19 (2006). This, coupled with activities to provide for continuity of government and operations in crises, helps to ensure there is always a legitimate command authority for nuclear forces. See Walter Slocombe, "Preplanned Operations," in *Managing Nuclear Operations,* edited by Ashton B. Carter, John D. Steinbruner, and Charles A. Zraket (Brookings, 1987), pp. 132–33; and U.S. Department of Homeland Security, "Federal Continuity Directive 1: Federal Executive Branch National Continuity Program and Requirements" (January 17, 2017).

26. Many advisers to the president are often underprepared for their role in nuclear employment decisionmaking. See Chambers and others, *Presidential Decision Time Regarding Nuclear Weapons Employment,* pp. 27–28, 39–40.

27. Office of the Secretary of Defense, *Nuclear Posture Review 2018*; Dave Johnson, "Russia's Conventional Precision Strike Capabilities, Regional Crises, and Nuclear Thresholds," *Livermore Papers on Global Security* 3 (February 2018).

28. Office of the Deputy Assistant Secretary of Defense for Nuclear Matters, *Nuclear Matters Handbook 2020,* p. 27; Office of the Secretary of Defense, *Nuclear Posture Review 2018*, p. 57; Office of the Secretary of Defense, *Missile Defense Review 2019* (Department of Defense, 2019), pp. 20–21.

29. Office of the Secretary of Defense, *Missile Defense Review 2019,* pp. 5–19; Defense Science Board, *Task Force on Defense Strategies for Advanced Ballistic and Cruise Missile Threats* (Office of the Under Secretary of Defense for Acquisition, Technology, and Logistics, January 2017).

30. Office of the Deputy Assistant Secretary of Defense for Nuclear Matters, *The Nuclear Matters Handbook 2020,* p. 27; David A. Deptula, William A. LaPlante, and Robert Haddick, *Modernizing U.S. Nuclear Command, Control, and Communications* (Arlington, VA: Mitchell Institute for Aerospace Studies, February 2019), p. 27.

31. Over the five-year period (FY2017–2021), the Department of Defense spent about $20.3 billion—about $4.0 billion per a year—on sustainment and modernization of U.S. NC2. This includes $4.0 billion in research, development, test, and evaluation; $6.7 billion in procurement; and $9.6 billion in operation and maintenance. This is close to NC2 funding trends in recent previous years. The 10ten-year estimate for NC2 continues the $4.0 billion per a year out to FY26. The comparable number for DoD Defense Department delivery system modernization and sustainment is, on average, about $19 billion per a year over that period. See "Nuclear Weapons Sustainment: Budget Estimates Report Contains More Information than in Prior Fiscal Years, but Transparency Can Be Improved," GAO Report 17-557, July 2017.

32. Information technology systems can be penetrated in several ways. The most obvious is direct access to operating systems and networks through poor password security, unauthorized use of (contaminated) flash drives (à la the 2010 Stuxnet worm), or exploitation by insiders. Broad network surveillance enabling discovery of backdoors into the system is another approach. Once inside, there is opportunity to do immediate damage or to introduce custom malware that sits inertly until activated at some later time to damage or disrupt force or NC2 operations. Finally, there is the opportunity to exploit component supply chains to introduce malware into electronics intended for NC2 subsystems.

33. Paul Bracken, "The Cyber Threat to Nuclear Stability," *Orbis* 60, no. 2 (2016), pp. 188–203; Keir A. Lieber and Daryl G. Press, "The New Era of Counterforce: Technological Change and the Future of Nuclear Deterrence," *International Security* 41, no. 4 (2017), pp. 9–49.

34. For a brief review of the open-system interconnection model, see Vangie Beal, "What Are the 7 Layers of the OSI Model?," April 6, 2021, updated January 27, 2022, www.webopedia.com/quick_ref/OSI_Layers.asp.

35. James M. Acton, "Escalation through Entanglement: How the Vulnerability of Command-and-Control Systems Raises the Risks of an Inadvertent Nuclear War," *International Security* 43, no. 1 (2018), p. 55–99.

CHAPTER 8

Extending Nuclear Deterrence and Assuring U.S. Allies

M. Elaine Bunn

The United States has defense relationships of a distinct type with more than thirty countries. It has made explicit guarantees of extended nuclear deterrence to NATO countries as well as to Japan, South Korea, and Australia. In so doing, the United States has publicly and privately affirmed that aggression against these countries could, under some circumstances, merit a U.S. nuclear response.

While alliances involve more than just military and security relationships, and extended deterrence involves more than just nuclear weapons, the nuclear aspects of these alliances are the focus of this chapter. The decision to make a nuclear deterrence commitment to another country is fraught with strategic dilemmas, as nuclear strategists have long recognized.[1] Less often acknowledged is that extending nuclear deterrence to allies involves a number of operational challenges as well. These include decisions about the forces to be committed in support of an ally; how a nuclear-armed state balances the desire to assure its ally of the depth of its commitment with the requirement to safeguard critical information about nuclear technology and plans; and how the United States would consult with its allies in reaching the decision to initiate the use of nuclear weapons on behalf of those allies.

The management of nuclear operations in support of allies depends fundamentally on the continuous interactions between allies and their respective political and military leaders and professional staffs. These interactions allow for a give-and-take regarding threats (about whom the alliance is worried and what allies are worried adversaries will do). A productive dialogue on threats, in turn, allows for dialogue about responses (how the alliance deals with threats). Thus understanding the role of an alliance's words, deeds, and capabilities—including but not limited to nuclear weapons capabilities—requires understanding the who, what, and how of threats and responses. "Who, what, and how" sounds like a deceptively simple set of questions that could be answered in short order. But threats evolve constantly; allies often have differing perceptions of otherwise shared developments, depending on each ally's history, geography, culture, and domestic politics; and capabilities evolve as well. As a result, the answers to these questions are anything but simple or static.

Understanding nuclear operations in U.S. alliances is about more than just the weapons or what one might think of as military operational details. It is not primarily about, for instance, exactly what happens in annual dual-capable aircraft exercises, when European and American air force crews practice nuclear operations, or precisely what targets might be struck if weapons were to be used. If that is the principal vision of the topic, the essentials of how alliance extended nuclear deterrence and assurance operate will be missed.

As noted, the United States explicitly extends nuclear deterrence commitments to NATO countries, Japan, South Korea, and Australia. While each of these alliances has a treaty foundation, the extended nuclear deterrence commitment derives even more from subsequent practice: official statements from decades of government-to-government meetings; consultations on strategy, policy, planning, and forces; forward-deployed forces (including conventional capabilities and currently, in the case of NATO, nuclear capabilities); and forward-deployable forces, both conventional and nuclear.[2] Much has been written about the Cold War period (1949–1991), particularly with regard to NATO.[3] Here, the focus is on current and recent practice.

There are many differences between that earlier period and the past thirty years—for example, which actors are seen as current or potential nuclear-armed threats; nuclear weapons numbers and types (for both the United States and adversaries); the number of NATO members (from sixteen countries thirty years ago to thirty nations today); heightened nuclear threats to Asia-Pacific allies and U.S. recognition of their importance; the views of different U.S. presidents about alliances; and allies' views of the United States.[4] Many of the underlying principles about the nature of U.S. alliances are the same, but manifestations of extended deterrence have changed. Alliances will continue to evolve, with changes in the security environment, threat perceptions, and domestic politics. And, of course, each alliance is unique, with its own history, concerns, and sensitivities, and thus distinct nuclear operations.

For allies, deterrence is based partly on what they do for themselves, their own capabilities, plans, words, and actions, and partly on those of the United States. Extending deterrence moves beyond trying to prevent attacks on one's own country to trying to extend the deterrence benefits to someone else. To extend deterrence to an ally, the United States must work to deter that ally's potential adversaries (who are also presumably potential U.S. adversaries, as well)—whether that be Russia, China, North Korea, or some other country. Extending deterrence means that the United States considers, and conveys to allies and adversaries, that all its military capabilities, both conventional and nuclear, are available in deterring any attack on an ally.

The audience for extended deterrence is allies' potential adversaries. The audience for assurance is allies and their perception of the U.S. commitment to their defense.

Extended deterrence and assurance are not just about the nuclear components of the U.S. commitment to allies. Both are broader than extended nuclear deterrence and assurance, which are the focus of this chapter and only a subset of alliance relations. But U.S. nuclear forces, whether partially forward deployed (as in Europe) or not (as in Asia), are an essential part of extended deterrence and assurance. And it is the nuclear consultations, dialogues, visits, and exercises with allies that are its instantiation.

The Facts

A factual baseline of current alliance nuclear strategy and policy, forces, consultative mechanisms, and operational practices—which today differ from earlier periods in alliance relations in NATO and in the Asia-Pacific region—provides a foundation for both long-time followers and those new to the subject of extended nuclear deterrence and assurance.

NATO and Extended Nuclear Deterrence: Strategy and Policy

Since the end of the Cold War, NATO has gone through several evolutions in thinking about the threat environment and the role of nuclear weapons in the alliance. The overriding context in 1991 was the dissolution of the Warsaw Pact and the Soviet Union. The "monolithic, massive and potentially immediate threat which was the principal concern of the Alliance in its first forty years" had disappeared.[5] NATO sought to improve and expand security through partnership and cooperation with former adversaries. It also resolved to make "full use of the new opportunities available" and "maintain security at the lowest possible level of forces consistent with the requirements of defence."[6] Regarding nuclear weapons, NATO stated in 1991 that "the Alliance will maintain for the foreseeable future an appropriate mix of nuclear and conventional forces based in Europe and kept up to date where necessary, although at a significantly reduced level."[7]

Given the 1989–1991 changes in the Soviet Union and the Warsaw Pact, one might have thought this was the ideal time for NATO to decide it no longer needed to have nuclear weapons deployed in Europe. But this was not the case; indeed, the alliance's 1991 Strategic Concept reaffirmed the rationale for nuclear weapons in NATO, stating that the fundamental purpose of the allies' nuclear forces

is to preserve peace and prevent coercion and any kind of war. . . . They [nuclear weapons] demonstrate that aggression of any kind is not a rational option. The supreme guarantee of the security of the Allies is provided by the strategic nuclear forces of the Alliance, particularly those of the United States; the independent nuclear forces of the United Kingdom and France, which have a deterrent role of their own, contribute to the overall deterrence and security of the Allies.[8]

The 1991 document continues:

A credible Alliance nuclear posture and the demonstration of Alliance solidarity and common commitment to war prevention continue to require widespread participation by European Allies involved in collective defence planning in nuclear roles, in peacetime basing of nuclear forces on their territory and in command, control and consultation arrangements. Nuclear forces based in Europe and committed to NATO provide an essential political and military link between the European and the North American members of the Alliance.[9]

The alliance committed to "maintain[ing] adequate nuclear forces in Europe . . . at the minimum level sufficient to preserve peace and stability."[10] While this formulation justified the retention of a role for nuclear weapons within the alliance, it also permitted the allies to "significantly reduce their sub-strategic nuclear forces" and shift to a posture of "adequate sub-strategic forces based in Europe which will provide an essential link with strategic nuclear forces, reinforcing the trans-Atlantic link."[11] The short- and medium-range missiles, nuclear artillery, and other tactical weapons deployed on NATO territory throughout the Cold War had been or were being eliminated. Moving forward, those substrategic forces based in Europe would consist "solely of dual capable aircraft which could, if necessary, be supplemented by offshore systems."[12]

By 1999, the threat environment confronting NATO had evolved even further from the overarching "great power" threat of the Cold War, looking at new risks to the broader Euro-Atlantic region and out of the area, which included "oppression, ethnic conflict, economic distress, the collapse of political order, and the proliferation of weapons of mass destruction."[13] But as NATO took on new threats, it repeated that the alliance would maintain for the foreseeable future an appropriate mix of nuclear and conventional forces.

In 2010 yet another NATO review reaffirmed that "*deterrence, based on an appropriate mix of nuclear and conventional capabilities, remains a core element*" of NATO's overall strategy.[14] However, the review continues, "the Alliance does not consider any country to be its adversary," so the object of this "appropriate" mix was left open. The alliance recognized that the "circumstances in which any use of nuclear weapons might have to be contemplated are extremely remote" but went on to state that "as long as nuclear weapons exist, NATO will remain a nuclear alliance."

NATO's 2012 Deterrence and Defense Posture Review elaborated further, saying "NATO is committed to maintaining an appropriate mix of nuclear, conventional, and missile defence capabilities for deterrence and defence." (para. 32)[15] However, it also left the door open to changes: "NATO will continue to adjust its strategy, including with respect to the capabilities and other measures required for deterrence and defence, in line with trends in the security environment." (para. 34)

The 2010 Strategic Concept and the 2012 Deterrence and Defense Posture Review were undertaken in an environment different from the current one. A turning point in NATO's perception of threats came in 2014, with Russia's incursion into Ukraine, illegal annexation of Crimea, and ongoing war with Ukraine, as well as numerous Russian overflights and incursions into allied air space from the United States and Canada to the Baltics and Norway, increased military activities in the waters around Europe and nuclear saber-rattling rhetoric.[16] NATO's response focused primarily on providing non-nuclear reinforcements to Europe, including four brigades to the

Baltic countries and Poland.[17] But the events of 2014 also refocused NATO attention on nuclear issues.

Starting in late 2014, NATO looked afresh at Russia's nuclear doctrine, strategy, posture, exercises, and statements, as well as the implications for NATO overall and for its nuclear policy and posture specifically. The changes in NATO's assessments of Russia over the past decade, as reflected in the NATO summit statements agreed by heads of state of all NATO countries, were notable. In 2012 NATO was still emphasizing cooperation with Russia, and most of the nuclear work in alliance was in the arms control group. By the 2014 summit, the Russian invasion of Ukraine and annexation of Crimea had occurred, but NATO was still debating what it meant and whether there was any nuclear dimension (even a nuclear shadow) in Russia's actions. By 2016, the change had really sunk in; that year's summit statement had language implicitly aimed at deterring limited Russian nuclear use: "Any employment of nuclear weapons against NATO would fundamentally alter the nature of a conflict."[18] This language was repeated in the 2018 and 2021 NATO summit statements.[19]

NATO also recognized the importance of continuing to raise the "nuclear IQ" in NATO or, as the 2016 Warsaw Summit statement put it, the need for "sustained leadership focus and institutional excellence for the nuclear deterrence mission and planning guidance aligned with 21st century requirements."[20] Nuclear deterrence knowledge and culture in NATO had been lost over the previous twenty-five years, during which NATO thought little about nuclear deterrence issues. And some allies had never thought much about nuclear strategy and posture, since newer allies who were once part of the Warsaw Pact did not have the experience of participating in a nuclear alliance with a consultative process.

As part of raising its nuclear IQ, NATO has conducted multiple table-top exercises, seminars and visits by both military and civilians from NATO countries (including the Military Committee and North Atlantic Council ambassadors) to nuclear force facilities, such as dual-capable aircraft bases in NATO, as well as strategic bases at Faslane and Ile Longue (at the invitation of the British and French, respectively).

Consultative Mechanism: NATO's Nuclear Planning Group

The Nuclear Planning Group (NPG) acts as the senior body on nuclear matters in the alliance.[21] The NPG was founded in December 1966 to provide policy consultation on matters associated with nuclear forces in light of the

ever-changing security environment, as well as the safety, security, and survivability of nuclear forces within NATO.[22] Its discussions cover a broad range of
weapons, communications, and information systems and deployment issues.
It also covers wider questions of common concern, such as nuclear arms control and nuclear proliferation. All NATO members, with the exception of
France, which has decided not to participate, are part of the NPG, regardless
of whether they themselves maintain or host nuclear weapons.

The policies agreed on represent the common position of all the participating countries. Decisions are taken by consensus within the NPG, as is the
case for all NATO committees. The NPG meets at least once a year at the
level of ministers of defense and, when necessary, at the level of ambassadors
(permanent representatives). The debates and give-and-take within NATO,
which lead to the policy statements its leaders sign onto, is the stuff of alliances and a key to the durability of NATO.

The Nuclear Planning Group is supported by a senior advisory body, the
High-Level Group (HLG). The group is chaired by the United States (at the
level of assistant secretary of defense) and is composed of national policymakers (at policy director level, or deputy assistant secretary of defense for
the United States) and experts from member country capitals. It meets several times a year to discuss aspects of NATO's nuclear policy, planning and,
force posture and matters concerning the safety, security, and survivability
of nuclear weapons.[23] It relies on the work of several subordinate bodies: the
HLG Working Group, which prepares papers for and otherwise supports
the High Level Group on nuclear posture and policy, and the Joint Theater Surety Management Group, tasked with helping the HLG maintain the
highest standards in nuclear surety (that is, safety, security, and use control).[24]

At NATO Headquarters in Brussels, the work of the Nuclear Planning
Group is prepared by an NPG Staff Group. This group is composed of members of the national delegations at NATO headquarters of all participating
member countries and is chaired by a NATO international staff member
(the director of nuclear policy), who is and has been an American. The Staff
Group prepares meetings of the NPG permanent representatives (nations'
ambassadors at NATO headquarters) and carries out detailed work on their
behalf. It generally meets once a week (sometimes more often, as necessary).[25]
It works closely with the HLG, and for smaller nations, their NPG Staff
Group member sometimes doubles as their representative at HLG meetings
when officials cannot come from capitals.

NATO Forces and Capabilities: Weapons and Delivery Systems

NATO's nuclear forces consist of the U.S. nonstrategic nuclear weapons forward deployed in Europe and the strategic nuclear forces of the United States, as well as the United Kingdom and France.[26] Each of these categories has varying characteristics and consultative processes and needs to be considered separately.

Nonstrategic Nuclear Forces

NATO now has a much smaller set of nonstrategic nuclear capabilities than it had during the Cold War. The variety of U.S. nuclear weapons deployed in NATO in the mid-1980s was striking: four types of air-delivered bombs, depth bombs, long-range missiles (Pershing II and ground-launched cruise missiles), short-range missiles (Pershing 1A, Lance, Honest John), artillery (eight-inch and 155mm), Nike Hercules air defense missiles, and atomic demolition munitions.[27] Since the height of the Cold War, NATO has reduced the size of its land-based nuclear weapons stockpile by more than 90 percent.[28] There is now just one type of U.S. weapon (the B-61 gravity bomb) based in several European NATO countries, for deployment on a limited number of U.S. and allied fighter aircraft.[29]

Dual-Capable Aircraft. Dual-capable aircraft—that is, aircraft that are certified for nuclear as well as conventional missions—include the F-15E, the F-16, Tornado, and in the future, the F-35A and possibly (if Germany decides to replace Tornado dual-capable aircraft with it) the F-18.[30] That a particular aircraft is of the same type or model as some dual-capable aircraft (DCA) is not an indication that the specific aircraft is indeed "dual capable" (nuclear certified with an assigned nuclear role); for example, a particular F-15E, F-16, or F-35 fighter may be conventional only. Members of the alliance may purchase such aircraft for use in a conventional role without participating in nuclear programs of cooperation required (among other things) for nuclear carriage.[31] To be certified as nuclear capable, an aircraft and the aircraft unit's personnel must undergo an extensive training process.[32] Such DCA would carry U.S. weapons if loaded in a conflict; therefore, they would need to meet U.S. nuclear certification requirements.[33]

Some analysts, primarily Russians, have raised questions about whether NATO's approach to nuclear sharing is consistent with the Nuclear Non-Proliferation Treaty (NPT). However, as one expert has written, "The historical record shows that the text of the NPT was crafted by the US and the USSR, in close cooperation, precisely so that NATO's arrangements would be compatible with Treaty obligations—while also constraining the ability of non-nuclear states to acquire nuclear weapons."[34]

The U.S. deployment of nuclear weapons in NATO is also regulated under U.S. law. The United States participates in various programs of cooperation (that is, legal frameworks for international information exchange on nuclear weapons-related issues) with a number of international partners, including the United Kingdom, France, and NATO itself. "Within the United States, the Atomic Energy Act (AEA) governs the exchange of nuclear-related information. Sections 91c, 123, and 144 of the AEA describe the different types of exchanges in which the United States may legally engage. According to the AEA, all international information exchanges are predicated on the existence of an Agreement for Cooperation, such as a mutual defense agreement (MDA), with the individual nation or organization."[35]

The United States concludes bilateral Agreements for Cooperation for Mutual Defense Purposes with NATO members participating in NATO nuclear sharing.[36] Agreements with hosting nations have been described as "bilateral arrangements between the United States, providing the warheads, and European Allies, providing the stationing ground and the means of delivery."[37]

The B-61 Bomb. The U.S. B-61 bomb is the only nuclear weapon forward deployed to NATO and can be carried by U.S. and allied dual-capable aircraft as well as U.S. strategic bombers. Since the first B-61 nuclear gravity bomb entered service in 1968, numerous modifications have been made to improve the B-61's safety, security, and reliability. The B-61 is currently undergoing a life extension program, which will refurbish, reuse, or replace the bomb's nuclear and non-nuclear components to extend the service life of the B-61 by at least twenty years and improve the bomb's safety, effectiveness, and security. This program will address all age-related issues of the bomb and enhance its reliability, field maintenance, safety, and use control. With these upgrades and the addition of a U.S. Air Force–supplied tail-kit assembly, the B61-12 life extension program will consolidate and replace four B-61 weapon designs. When fielded, the B61-12 will balance the greater accuracy provided by the modern tail kit with a substantial reduction in yield, with no overall change in military requirements or characteristics.[38] After several delays, the National Nuclear Security Administration currently plans to manufacture the first refurbished B61-12 nuclear gravity bomb in the first quarter of fiscal year 2022 (that is, in the last three months of 2021).[39] The bomb will be approximately twelve feet long and weigh approximately 825 pounds.[40]

As a rule, neither the U.S. government nor other NATO governments discuss the numbers or locations of U.S. nuclear weapons in Europe; both are officially secret.[41] Some have suggested that new NATO members in Central and Eastern Europe might theoretically be willing to host modern U.S. nuclear weapons on their soil.[42] Such a deployment would be counter to the political commitment known as the Three Nos. In 1996 NATO's foreign ministers declared that the alliance had no intention, no reason, and no plan to station nuclear forces on the territory of new members.[43] This commitment was undertaken in the context of the NATO-Russia Founding Act, which was intended to transform the relationship between the alliance and the Russian Federation.[44] However, as one scholar notes, "Due to the many instances in which NATO assesses Russian behavior to have deviated from the shared values, commitments and norms of behavior enshrined in the [Founding] act, Allies are divided on whether it is still effective."[45]

Storage, Security, and Use Control. U.S. nuclear weapons deployed in Europe (B-61 bombs) are under U.S. custody at all times in a nuclear weapons storage area on a host-nation base. The weapons themselves are stored in underground secure vaults, called weapons security storage systems, inside aircraft protective shelters. The bombs themselves are equipped with permissive action links, which require that a code be entered before the bombs can be armed.[46] Although the Nuclear Planning Group would decide on employment of nuclear weapons on behalf of the alliance, only the U.S. president can authorize the use of U.S. nuclear weapons, including the B-61 bombs and the release codes to unlock the permissive action links. Thus no ally can deliver a U.S. nuclear weapon without U.S. agreement and authorization, and that authorization can only come from the U.S. president.

Cost Sharing. NATO basing nations provide substantial financial support to the nuclear mission. They supply aircraft, aircrews, load crews, and security forces and also provide facilities and much of the supporting infrastructure and equipment for the U.S. munitions support squadrons. In addition, NATO common funding (through the NATO Security Investment Program) has paid for B-61 storage security infrastructure and upgrades in host nations; the U.S. burden-share is generally 22–24 percent of the total program costs, with the rest borne by other NATO members.[47]

Strategic Nuclear Forces

According to NATO documents, the strategic forces of the alliance, and particularly those of the United States, are the supreme guarantee of the security of the allies. U.S. and British nuclear forces are integrated into NATO; France's are not. The final decisions on use of each country's strategic nuclear forces belongs to its leader—the U.S. president, the U.K. prime minister, or the French president.

U.S. Strategic Nuclear Forces. U.S. strategic nuclear forces—the triad of bombers that can carry nuclear weapons, nuclear ballistic missile submarines (SSBNs) with submarine-launched ballistic missiles (SLBMs), and land-based intercontinental ballistic missiles—are described elsewhere in this volume. Of note for NATO (as well as other allies), however, is that they have long had a role in extended deterrence, both in NATO declaratory policy and in exercises and deployments. Since the end of the Cold War, U.S. B-2 and B-52 bombers have flown a number of missions to Europe.[48] U.S. submarines are constantly on patrol, including in the Atlantic, and have from time to time pulled into the U.K. submarine base at Faslane, Scotland.[49]

In addition to the ongoing modernization program to replace the triad, the 2018 Nuclear Posture Review announced that in the near term, the United States would modify a small number of existing SLBM warheads to provide a low-yield option and in the longer term would pursue a modern nuclear-armed sea-launched cruise missile (SLCM).[50] The review notes that "unlike DCA, a low-yield SLBM warhead and SLCM will not require or rely on host nation support to provide deterrent effect."[51] The United States announced in February 2020 that it had fielded the lower-yield warhead, the W76-2, for the Trident II SLBM.[52] (Notably, the United Kingdom, which produces its own warheads, has had a lower-yield warhead for its SLBMs for decades.)[53] The U.S. Defense Department is conducting an analysis of alternatives for the modern SLCM, which may be deployed in a decade if funding is continued.

British and French Strategic Nuclear Forces. NATO has stated since 1974 that French and British nuclear forces would contribute to NATO's overall deterrence.[54] This statement has been constantly repeated since then, including in the most recent Strategic Concept of November 2010, as well as in summit statements in 2016, 2018, and 2021. The independent strategic nuclear forces of the United Kingdom and France and their separate centers of decisionmaking have been characterized as contributing to deterrence by complicating the calculations of any potential adversaries.[55] As one expert notes, "In spite of broadly converging nuclear policies, nuances do exist between Washington, London, and Paris regarding their respective nuclear posture and doctrine. These nuances however contribute to the strengthening of the Alliance overall deterrent by creating additional uncertainties in the mind of any potential adversary."[56] In other words, should an adversary decide to attack NATO, it must not only contend with NATO's decision-making but must also make a judgment about decisionmaking from the leaders of the United States, United Kingdom, and France.

The United Kingdom maintains nuclear weapons for four Vanguard-class submarines, based at HM Naval Base Clyde in Scotland, which will gradually be replaced by the Dreadnought class of nuclear-deterrent submarines. As it has for more than fifty years, the United Kingdom plans to keep one on patrol at all times, known as the continuous at-sea deterrent. The United Kingdom's March 2021 Integrated Review recognizes the changes in the international security environment and lays out a comprehensive framework for U.K. strategic policy through 2025. One means by which the United Kingdom seeks to strengthen its security and defense is through changes to its nuclear deterrent program: it has raised its warhead stockpile cap from 225 to 260 and will no longer place a public limit on the proportion of that stockpile that is operational at any given time, nor will it give any public information on the number of warheads and missiles deployed on its ballistic missile submarines.[57] While the U.K. Trident missiles are a joint procurement program with the United States, the warheads are British and the United Kingdom emphasizes that decisionmaking and use of the system remains entirely sovereign to the United Kingdom: only the prime minister can authorize the launch of nuclear weapons, which ensures that political control is maintained at all times; and the instruction to fire would be transmitted to the submarine using only U.K. codes and U.K. equipment, making the command-and-control procedures fully independent.[58]

France has nuclear weapons for its sea and air delivery platforms. It has forty-eight M-51 SLBMs for its four SSBNs (of which three are in the operational cycle, each carrying sixteen missiles) based at Ile Longue. France's air force has two squadrons of the Rafale aircraft, and the navy's unit of Rafale-M can operate from aircraft carriers. Both Rafale versions can carry the single-warhead nuclear cruise missile, known as ASMP-A (Air-Sol Moyenne Portée-Amélioré, or improved medium-range air to surface missile), giving it a standoff option for air-delivered nuclear weapons.[59] Since becoming a nuclear power in 1960, France has made clear that its nuclear forces are developed and controlled on an independent national basis.[60] But President Emmanuel Macron in a 2020 speech elaborated on current French nuclear thinking:

> [O]ur nuclear forces have a deterrent effect in themselves, particularly in Europe. . . . France's vital interests now have a European dimension. Our nuclear forces also significantly contribute to the overall strengthening of the Atlantic Alliance's overall deterrent, alongside the British and American forces. France does not take part in the Alliance's nuclear planning mechanisms and will not do so in the future. But it will continue to contribute to political-level discussions aiming to strengthen the Alliance's nuclear culture.[61]

Planning, Exercises, and Readiness

During most of the Cold War, NATO nuclear targeting plans were formulated by the multinational NATO staff officers at Supreme Headquarters Allied Powers Europe in Mons, Belgium, under the direction of the Supreme Allied Commander Europe, who has always been an American who is dual-hatted as the commander of U.S. European Command.[62] Among the post–Cold War changes the alliance made was "the termination of standing peacetime nuclear contingency plans," as the 1999 Strategic Concept declared that "NATO's nuclear forces no longer target any country."[63] In place of plans, NATO was to retain an adaptive planning capability.[64] However, NATO's adaptive planning capabilities atrophied through the first decade of the this century.[65]

The end of the Cold War also led to "significant relaxation of the readiness criteria for nuclear-roled forces."[66] Regarding readiness of its nuclear forces, after the Cold War, "NATO took internal measures to reduce the role of nuclear weapons in its planning. The readiness criteria for forces with a nuclear role were significantly relaxed . . . and exercises involving potential nuclear employment reportedly became less frequent and realistic."[67]

As part of NATO's post-2014 reexamination of the alliance's nuclear posture, there has been no public statement about whether NATO nuclear planning has resumed or force readiness times have been shortened. However, there are indications that these issues are being discussed. The 2018 Nuclear Posture Review states that the United States "will work with NATO to best ensure—and improve where needed—the readiness, survivability, and operational effectiveness of DCA based in Europe."[68]

Recent exercises in NATO have included tabletop exercises with alliance civilian and military officials, which allow them to think through as many different feasible scenarios as possible, understand the differing perspectives, priorities, factors, and considerations, and sort them out among allies in peace-time rather than in the midst of crisis. The alliance has also continued to carry out field exercises for the DCA forces. NATO conducts this nuclear exercise in a low-key manner and does not publicize the events. However, nonofficial sources have discussed the exercises,[69] and local aircraft watchers have posted photos on the internet.[70] (These exercises are doubtless observed by the Rus-sians and convey alliance commitment to the nuclear mission and deterrence.)

In addition to hosting U.S. nuclear weapons and acquiring and maintain-ing DCA, there are other ways allies participate in NATO's nuclear mission. These include providing military support for the DCA mission with conven-tional forces and capabilities, known in NATO as SNOWCAT, or supporting nuclear operations with conventional air tactics. Some allies host the annual Nuclear Policy Symposium, held annually since 1992, at which participants (recently including France) focus on a wide range of nuclear issues, including ways to bolster the alliance's deterrence and defense posture, further arms control objectives, and priorities for adapting NATO's nuclear policy.[71]

Asia-Pacific Allies and Extended Nuclear Deterrence

The U.S. alliances with Japan, South Korea, and Australia are in some ways similar to, yet in others very different from, the NATO alliance. They are similar in that they are based on long-standing treaties and subsequent state-ments of commitment; the United States extends nuclear deterrence (the "nuclear umbrella") to them just as it does to NATO allies. But the alliances in the Asia-Pacific region are bilateral, not multilateral. Consultation mech-anisms on nuclear issues are also a more recent development for the United States' Asia-Pacific alliances than for NATO, and these consultations reflect the bilateral nature of U.S. alliances in the region. In contrast to NATO, in East Asia there are no nuclear-armed allies and no nuclear sharing arrange-ments; thus there is no military coordination on potential nuclear deterrence options.[72] The histories of the allied nations there, and the threats that con-cern them, are also different from NATO's.

Consultations with Asia-Pacific Allies

Although U.S. alliances with Japan, South Korea, and Australia go back many decades, official dialogues specifically on extended nuclear deterrence began only in 2010 with Japan and South Korea, and even more recently with Australia. Japan, as the only nation against which nuclear weapons have been used in war, has a bifurcated relationship with nuclear deterrence, which made consultations on nuclear deterrence late in coming: it has a strong anti-nuclear public constituency, but as a non-nuclear nation in Asia concerned about North Korea and China, it needs the extended nuclear deterrence commitment of the United States. One of the first former high-ranking Japanese officials to speak out publicly about the need for more in-depth bilateral discussions of nuclear deterrence issues as one means to demonstrate and buttress the credibility of extended deterrence was Ambassador Yukio Satoh, in an article published in February 2009.[73]

The United States–Japan Extended Deterrence Dialogue (EDD) began in 2010, following discussions between the two countries as the United States was conducting the 2010 Nuclear Posture Review. The Japanese delegation to the Extended Deterrence Dialogue is cochaired by officials at the deputy director general level from the Ministries of Foreign Affairs and Defense; the U.S. delegation is cochaired at the deputy assistant secretary level from Departments of State and Defense.

Recent decades have seen a marked increase in interest on the part of Japanese officials, academics, and experts in discussing nuclear deterrence issues. Even fifteen years ago, it was difficult to find more than a handful of officials in Tokyo who were comfortable discussing nuclear deterrence issues (unlike arms control and disarmament issues, which had long been discussed). The Japanese are now among the most sophisticated and nuanced of allies on nuclear deterrence theory, policy, and posture. The cadre of Japanese officials with a deep understanding of deterrence issues has increased in recent years; many former EDD participants have gone on to other jobs in government (including as vice foreign minister), which strengthens understanding of the complex nature of nuclear and broader deterrence issues.

The formal deterrence discussions with South Korea also began in 2010, in the Extended Deterrence Policy Committee (EDPC); the group was renamed the Deterrence Strategy Committee (DSC) in 2015, when it merged with the Counter-Missile Capabilities Committee.[74] The EDPC/DSC is led by the South Korea's deputy minister for defense and by both a regional and a functional deputy assistant secretary of defense for the United States. The group's work led to a Tailored Deterrence Strategy document agreed to by defense ministers in October 2013.[75] The EDPC/DSC meet as part of the Korea–United States Integrated Defense Dialogue, which was launched in 2011 as a comprehensive defense meeting between the allies that integrates a set of consultative mechanisms.

Both consultative groups meet twice a year, alternating between Japan and the United States for the EDD and between South Korea and the United States for the DSC. Staff-level meetings occur more frequently, to prepare for the committee meetings. Since the EDD and EDPC/DSC began in 2010, there have been dozens of multiday in-depth bilateral discussions with Japanese officials and with South Korean officials. (While the United States has pressed for greater trilateral United States–Japan–Republic of Korea cooperation, historical and current tensions between the two northeast Asian countries have made that problematic.) There have also been dozens of tabletop exercises exploring a variety of scenarios and what the key factors and considerations would be for leaders and their advisers in dealing with them.

The groups have informed themselves on the nuclear forces, and Japanese and South Korean members have seen the forces that are the ultimate guarantors of their security and talked with the operators of those forces. They have visited U.S. intercontinental ballistic missile bases and seen launches and have gone aboard ballistic missile submarines at the Bangor SSBN base and in Guam. They have climbed on bombers and fighters and visited nuclear laboratories, Strategic Command headquarters, and missile defense sites in the United States. The EDD and EDPC/DSC have also visited defense sites in Japan and the Republic of Korea that contribute to alliance conventional and missile defense capabilities. (These are in addition to other meetings and visits Japanese and South Korean officials have had with senior U.S. military and policy officials in the United States and in their own countries.)

In 2016 the United States and South Korea added another group—the higher-level State and Defense Extended Deterrence Consultative and Strategy Committee, which met again in 2019. At the first meeting of the committee in December 2016, the U.S. and ROK participants issued a joint statement, which included the following:

> The United States reiterated its ironclad and unwavering commitment to draw on the full range of its military capabilities, including the nuclear umbrella, conventional strike, and missile defense, to provide extended deterrence for the ROK, and reaffirmed the longstanding U.S. policy that any attack on the United States or its allies will be defeated, and any use of nuclear weapons will be met with an effective and overwhelming response. In particular, the United States emphasized that it remains steadfast in meeting these enduring commitments and providing immediate support to the ROK.[76]

Australia falls under the U.S. nuclear umbrella, but until recently it has not taken up the U.S. offer of a forum for regular, official consultations on extended nuclear deterrence issues, perhaps because of the perceived absence of the sort of nuclear threats NATO, Japan, and South Korea faced. That benign threat perception seems to have changed. As a recent Australian defense white paper explains, "Australia's security is underpinned by the ANZUS [Australia, New Zealand, and United States Security] Treaty, United States extended deterrence, and access to advanced U.S. technology and information. Only the nuclear and conventional military capabilities of the United States can offer effective deterrence against the possibility of nuclear threats against Australia."[77]

Forces and Capabilities: Asia-Pacific Allies

As noted earlier, there are no nuclear-armed allies in East Asia and no nuclear sharing arrangements.[78] The extension of nuclear deterrence to allies in the Asia-Pacific region is underwritten solely by U.S. strategic nuclear forces. In addition, as the 2018 Nuclear Posture Review states, "If necessary, the United States has the ability to deploy DCA and nuclear weapons to other regions [than NATO], such as Northeast Asia" and "the United States will maintain, and enhance as necessary, the capability to forward deploy nuclear bombers and DCA around the world."[79]

Since the emphasis for Asia-Pacific allies is on U.S. off-shore nuclear weapons, the United States has at times made these forces more visible. Although SSBNs are constantly and silently plying the waters of the Pacific (as well as the Atlantic), in November 2016, for the first time in a couple of decades, a U.S. SSBN pulled into port in Guam. The ROK Joint Chief of Staff chair went aboard one day with General Vince Brooks, then commander of the ROK-U.S. Combined Forces Command, and Japanese military and civilian officials went aboard the next. This was a reminder to allies in Asia that nuclear weapons are always in their neighborhood, even if they normally are not visible.[80] Nuclear-capable bombers can be flown there: there were regular bomber assurance and deterrence missions to Asia, and bombers were continuously rotated to Guam from 2004 to early 2020.[81] B-2 and B-52 bombers have been used to signal U.S. commitment to Northeast Asian allies in particularly unnerving times, such as after North Korean nuclear tests or provocations.[82] Some of these flights have included South Korean conventional aircraft escorts for U.S. strategic bombers, handing over the escort duty to Japanese fighters when the U.S bombers entered Japanese airspace. In April 2020, the U.S. Air Force announced it would no longer base strategic bombers outside the continental United States, and thus, for the first time in sixteen years, bombers would no longer have a continual presence in Guam. However, under the dynamic force employment model, U.S. bombers will continue to operate in the Asia-Pacific region from time to time.[83]

The Australian Defence Minister noted in 2019 that "Australia is not only a beneficiary of the U.S. policy of extended nuclear deterrence, it is an active supporter of it, through our joint efforts with the U.S. at Pine Gap and at other facilities . . . Hosting these joint facilities and U.S. strategic capabilities on our soil is Australia's important contribution to the alliance."[84]

An enhanced trilateral security partnership known as AUKUS (for Australia, the United Kingdom, and the United States) was announced by the three nations' leaders in September 2021.[85] AUKUS is intended to deepen cooperation on a range of security and defense capabilities. As the first initiative under AUKUS, the countries committed to support Australia in acquiring nuclear-powered submarines for its navy, leveraging expertise from U.S. and U.K. submarine programs, and embarked on an eighteen-month trilateral effort to seek an optimal pathway to deliver this capability. The Australian submarines would have nuclear reactors for propulsion, but not nuclear weapons. In deciding to acquire nuclear-powered submarines, Australia canceled a contract with a French company for diesel-powered submarines.[86]

Planning, Exercises, and Readiness

There is no history of nuclear planning and field exercises with allies in the Asia-Pacific region, as there has been in NATO. South Korea, Japan, and Australia have extensive non-nuclear military capabilities.[87] There have been a number of non-nuclear field exercises (as there are with NATO) over the past several decades (such as Foal Eagle with South Korea, ballistic missile defense exercises with Japan, and the annual Talisman Saber exercise with Australia) but not nuclear field exercises such as NATO's, since there are no nuclear sharing arrangements with Asia-Pacific allies. They do not deploy dual-capable aircraft, as some NATO allies do, nor other platforms capable of delivering U.S. nuclear weapons. There have, however, been numerous table-top exercises with South Korean and Japanese civilian and military officials that allow them to think through a number of different feasible scenarios involving nuclear crises, to study and understand the differing perspectives, priorities, factors, and considerations, and to sort them out among allies in peacetime rather than in the midst of a crisis.

A Practitioner's Perspective

Writing about extended deterrence, assurance, and alliance nuclear issues, even after forty years working on these issues in the U.S. government, is more challenging than one might think. I began my career working on intermediate-range nuclear issues (NATO's dual-track decision to deploy Pershing II and ground-launched cruise missiles in Europe to counter the Soviet SS-20s, while simultaneously seeking arms control negotiations on them). That entailed frequent trips to NATO headquarters, as well as my first visit to Japan in 1982 to discuss an arms control proposal in the Intermediate-Range Nuclear Forces Treaty negotiations. Ending my government career as deputy assistant secretary of defense for nuclear and missile defense policy, I was the U.S. representative to NATO's High Level Group and the cochair of the Extended Deterrence Dialogue with Japan, and the EDPC/DSC with South Korea. Over the course of that time, I had my own set of experiences and came to my own beliefs about alliances and extended nuclear deterrence. I offer them humbly, not as gospel but as the observations of a practitioner.

The Amazing Nature of Extended Deterrence

One of the things I had read about in graduate school but did not really sink in—at the gut level, not just the intellectual level—until many years later is the nature of extended nuclear deterrence. It is amazing from both extender's and extendee's perspectives. The extendee is a sovereign country that has given up some of its own latitude in high-end situations—including deterring and responding to nuclear use against its people and territory—and relies on another nation for that. And it is amazing that the extender, the United States, takes on the risk and responsibility of putting its own forces, even its population and territory, at peril on behalf of an ally. It is amazing to the point that some in the past—such as Pierre Gallois, André Beaufre, and Charles de DeGaulle—have found it incredible (hence the independent French *force de frappe,* or nuclear strike force). It should be no surprise that allies need constant reassurance, and the question of whether the United States would really trade Boston for Bonn, or Seattle for Seoul, or Los Angeles for Tokyo, has been a subtext in many alliance discussions since modern alliances began after World War II.

Assurance and Deterrence

Assurance—like deterrence—is in the eye of the beholder. A key difference though, is that with deterrence, we cannot just ask adversaries, "What will it take to deter you?" At least if we did, we probably should not believe the answers. But with assurance, we can ask allies what assures them and what factors are most important in their remaining non-nuclear nations.

However, a few cautions: some Americans have a tendency to lead the witness in the ways we talk to allies about extended nuclear deterrence—soliciting the views we think are correct. (For example, asking the Japanese, before 2010, "Would you be concerned if the United States gave up the nuclear Tomahawk cruise missile?" or asking NATO countries, "Would you be concerned if the United States removed DCA bombs from Europe?" or "Aren't you concerned about drastic U.S. reductions?") On the other hand, I find it interesting that we think about shaping adversaries' thinking (that is what deterrence is) but sometimes take our allies' views as immutable. That is not my view: I think we may be able to influence how Japan thinks about nuclear Tomahawk cruise missiles, or Europe about DCA, or other allies about other aspects of extended nuclear deterrence.

Those writing about extended nuclear deterrence often refer to the Healey theorem. The British defense minister Denis Healey noted in the 1960s that "one only needed 5 percent credibility to deter the Russians, but 95 percent to reassure the Europeans."[88] While I do not take the theorem too literally, I do take Healey's point. There is no way the United States could provide too much assurance, whether in Europe or Northeast Asia. It would be like pouring water into a sieve—full for a moment, but it will soon have to be filled again. Both assurance of allies and deterrence of adversaries benefit from constant, ongoing alliance dialogue at all levels and operating and exercising with allies—the instantiation that makes the concept of extended nuclear deterrence real.

Deterring What? And with What?

If you ask allies what threats U.S. extended nuclear deterrence addresses, you will get a variety of responses. Broadly speaking, allies expect the United States will deter nuclear attacks on their country; and that if nuclear attack occurs, the United States will respond in a way that is "overwhelming and effective," which is what the United States has said (in the 2010 Nuclear Posture Review and in subsequent alliance statements). That is the deal many think they have made with extended nuclear deterrence: they have eschewed having their own nuclear weapons and are relying on the United States for the ultimate guarantee of their nation's security. Others believe U.S. extended nuclear deterrence should deter aggression more generally, not just nuclear use. Still others believe it should deter all provocations. One South Korean security expert said to me (circa 2012), "Extended deterrence didn't prevent the sinking of the Cheonan; it didn't prevent the shelling of Yeonpyeong Island; what good is extended deterrence?" Complaints that extended deterrence did not prevent (or avenge) these provocations serve to illustrate a bad tendency of some in allied countries to have unrealistic expectations about the credibility of nuclear threats over secondary issues and to assume that the United States will guarantee security without their countries doing much to take care of themselves. But that seems to be a minority view.

Extended nuclear deterrence cannot be considered in a vacuum. It must take into account the spectrum of adversary threats, including gray-area, hybrid, and conventional actions that could lead to a situation where nuclear weapons move from the background to the forefront of a crisis or conflict. Nuclear use is unlikely to occur out of nowhere. The increasing attention in alliances to information operations and space, cyberspace, and conventional strikes—both ours (United States' and allies') and theirs (potential adversaries')—is the inextricable context for consideration of nuclear operations related to extended nuclear deterrence and assurance.

Deterrence is more than just nuclear, and alliances are grappling with broader questions that are highlighted by recent adversary threats: What is "an attack on one," anyway? Does it include cyberattacks? To which gray-area situations do alliance commitments apply? When do adversaries' use of incremental provocative actions, or salami-slicing tactics, lead to crises or conflicts that do invoke "attack on one" treaty commitments? What is it that allies, as sovereign states, will do, what will they rely on the United States to do, and what will we do together?

Closer Consultations with Japan and South Korea

The deterrence dialogues with Japan and South Korea are incredibly important and were well past due when they began in 2010. Given the dangerous neighborhood they live in, Koreans and Japanese have legitimate concerns about nuclear-armed neighbors. Our extended nuclear deterrence policy is probably the best nonproliferation tool we have with allies. I do not think any ally in Northeast Asia will decide to have nuclear weapons in the next few years. But in fifteen or twenty years, we do not want to be asking, "Why did South Korea and Japan feel they couldn't count on us and needed their own nuclear weapons?" Thus the EDD with Japan and the DSC and the Extended Deterrence Consultative and Strategy Committee with South Korea are forums that merit priority attention from senior U.S. leaders.

That said, there are pluses and minuses to this deeper discussion and understanding on allies' part of deterrence writ large and extended nuclear deterrence specifically. We can no longer say to allies in Northeast Asia, in essence, "Don't you worry your pretty little heads about it, we'll take care of it." However, with sophistication, nuance, and knowledge on deterrence issues comes the realization that deterrence is never guaranteed—it is a goal, not a strategy; that it is difficult to know in any given situation with any given actor what will deter and what will spur; and that the mix of tools for deterrence and the implementation of day-to-day and crisis deterrence is not cut and dried. So it may or may not be assuring to allies. But there is no going back; it is important to exercise and plan and discuss with allies how to deter and, if necessary, how to respond to adversary nuclear use. Sticking one's head in the sand about it does not make such use less likely; it probably makes it more so.

Views within Alliances Are Not Monolithic

Extended deterrence and assurance are very different in different regions (Northeast Asia is not Europe) and even in the same region (Germany is not Lithuania is not Turkey; Poland is not Belgium, and so on). For example, while some in Europe might be happy to see DCA nuclear weapons leave Europe, others would not. Ironically, it is generally those who cannot (under the Three Nos) have nuclear weapons on their territory who do not want them removed from Europe, while some current basing countries (or at least their parliaments or publics) would be generally more relaxed about or even supportive of their removal.

An alliance such as NATO, made up of thirty sovereign countries, is complicated. NATO is a consensus-based alliance; in theory, every decision has to be a unanimous one.[89] There is not—until the final statement is agreed—a NATO position; there are multiple national positions. That means NATO decisions are sometimes derided as lowest common denominator, or "camels designed by committee."

Even getting to a summit statement is a long and arduous process (for example, I spent nine months working toward agreement on four paragraphs—51 to 54—of the 2016 summit statement). Russia is no doubt very much aware of the difficulty of getting thirty democratic nations to agree on anything and may count on NATO being slow and divided in a crisis. But the process of debate, negotiation, and reaching agreement, arduous and frustrating as it may be, is a key factor in the strength of the alliance.

Views within an Allied Country Are Not Monolithic

Even within a single democratic nation, there are many views. I distrust generic characterizations such as "the Japanese think" or "the Dutch believe." I could cite many instances when the foreign ministry and the defense ministry of a country were not in agreement (the same can often be said of the U.S. State and Defense Departments). Even within a ministry, there are often different views—for example, between those working on alliance and deterrence issues and those working on arms control and disarmament issues. If you listen only to those you want to hear, you do not get a full picture of the complexity of alliance issues, whether with NATO allies or with each Asia-Pacific ally. In most cases, there will be an official government position that takes into account all the internal views, so if the question is, for example, "What is the Dutch position?" the response will be the official Dutch government position; the same is true of other countries as well.

Listen as Well as Talk

U.S. consultation at times has consisted of flying in, giving a briefing, and flying out, or calling allies to inform them of new policies the night before we publicly announce them. Genuine consultation takes time, attention, listening as well as talking, and sustained effort (often not U.S. strong suits). Deterrence dialogues with allies are a key piece of that. If the United States is to harness the real potential of alliances, we cannot just say, "This is the way it is." The United States must take into account allies' views and interests. In an alliance, we are all teachers, and we are all students. Governments know their own security situation, their domestic politics, and their needs better than an ally thousands of miles away. They can teach us if we listen.

Differences between NATO and Asia-Pacific Alliances

I have encountered difficulty explaining why the United States has nuclear sharing arrangements with some countries in NATO but not in East Asia.[90] Yes, there are different strategic environments and different histories. But Americans need to be conscious of how their arguments and rationale for taking (or not taking) an action in NATO may affect perceptions of allies in Asia, and the reverse is also true. For example, when NATO supporters argue that the United States cannot withdraw nuclear weapons from NATO because it would decouple European allies from the United States, it logically points to the question for Japanese and South Koreans, "We don't have the same nuclear sharing arrangements with the United States as NATO does. Does that mean we're decoupled?" I often use an analogy for this dilemma: Nuclear sharing is like the wedding ring of the marriage; it can be a sign of commitment, but it is not the commitment itself. In some cultures, wedding rings are de rigueur; in others, not. Some people who do not wear a wedding ring are strongly committed to their spouses, and others who wear them do not have much of a commitment at all. But when a person who usually wears one is seen in a bar without the wedding ring, it means something. The United States can be strongly committed to allies in Asia even without the visible symbol; but removing the sharing arrangement from NATO now would send a negative message about U.S. commitment and undermine assurance and extended deterrence.

Planning

It is not surprising that allies who live in dangerous neighborhoods want to know more and more about how the United States thinks about deterrence planning and about how it might respond—particularly in escalatory high-end situations—to threats to those allies. But there is sometimes too much allied focus on particular scenarios. No one can know what circumstances would eventuate and what the situation would look like in the particular context, and therefore it is impossible to know exactly what the United States would do. This is particularly true with regard to nuclear use. Instead of focusing so much time and attention on U.S. nuclear responses and wondering whether the U.S. president would push the nuclear button, we need to focus our attention on how we could prevent crises and collectively handle the beginnings of a crisis or conflict, including provocations, and work with allies to deal with those. When it comes to potential nuclear scenarios, we need to focus our consultative time and attention on what factors and considerations each leader must take into account.

Some of our allies have expressed a desire for access to U.S. nuclear targeting plans (some in Asia refer to this as wanting a NATO-like process). I believe this is based on a misunderstanding of what NATO's Nuclear Planning Group does. There is a difference between access to policy planning and access to targeting plans, and the NPG is concerned with the former. It is unlikely that allies will have access to U.S. nuclear targeting plans, given the sensitivity of those plans. Such plans can be accessed only on a strict need-to-know basis, so simply having a top secret clearance does not get one access to targeting plans; only a small number of American officials has access to them. More important in carrying out our shared objectives for both deterrence and, if necessary, response in various scenarios is a shared understanding of what adversaries think, what their objectives are, what our alliance objectives are, and the kind of targets that are important to be able to strike.

Allies do need access to conventional plans; without access, each could, for example, undertake its own conventional strikes uncoordinated with allies. While Combined Forces Command Korea provides such a mechanism, there is nothing similar for Japan. I personally think there is a need for some coordination mechanism with Japan on conventional planning.

Nuclear crises do not come out of the blue; they are likely to arise out of conventional crises. Actions we take, individually and together, can make a difference early on to keep us from going to war. For example, in the case of North Korea, we can make sure alliances have a mix of tools—diplomacy, economic sanctions, and information sharing, as well as military capabilities (non-nuclear air, land, maritime forces for offense and defense, and U.S. nuclear weapons as the background but ultimate insurance policy). We can make sure our countries and forces are as protected and resilient as possible against North Korean missiles (whether close, short, medium, intermediate, or intercontinental range) to contribute to deterrence by denial, to lessen or defang the coercive value of those missiles, to take away the cheap shots, and to protect, if necessary. We can ensure that conventional forces can continue to fight through a nuclear environment of North Korea's making. We can have flexible capabilities and processes. We can think through as many situations as are feasible, determine the factors and considerations our leaders would need to take into account, inform ourselves of the views of allies on those factors, and keep talking and exercising.

Do Not Surprise Your Allies

One of the most useful mottoes in my years in government as an alliance practitioner was "Don't surprise your allies." You can disagree, argue, debate, but do not surprise one other. For example, in June 2018, when President Trump suspended major military exercises with South Korea after meeting with the North Korean leader, Kim Jong-un, both South Koreans and Japanese voiced concerns.[91] It was not just that he postponed the exercise: the decision was a surprise to them, and he had called the exercises "very provocative"—the very term Kim had consistently used in criticizing the exercises—and "tremendously expensive" (as though alliance exercises were not worth the monetary cost).

"Do not surprise allies" works in both directions; allies should not announce policies that surprise the United States while implicating U.S. defense of them. For example, after the fifth North Korean nuclear test in September 2016, the ROK government—to the surprise of the U.S. government—announced to the National Assembly and the press its Massive Punishment and Retaliation strategy: South Korea would use its own indigenous conventional missiles to strike North Korea leadership and missiles at the first signs of North Korea's nuclear or missile action. That would not be a problem if there were good coordination and consultation every step of the way. After all, the U.S. government, over many administrations, has urged allies to do more. But we do not want our allies to unnecessarily and independently escalate and entangle us, any more than allies would want the United States to entangle them without their consent. "No surprises" is a good principle for both sides of an alliance.

The Relationship Is Primary

While the nuclear platforms and weapons—the "stuff" of extended nuclear deterrence and assurance—are not unimportant, they are secondary to the peacetime consultations, discussions at various levels, and the web of interaction. Certainly, the nuclear capabilities and forces themselves are necessary. There is a requisite baseline of nuclear forces (which the United States reexamines in each Nuclear Posture Review and about which allies consult continuously). But if there is proper consultation, the precise makeup and characteristics of that nuclear force are not likely to have the greatest impact on allies' views of the credibility of extended nuclear deterrence.

That said, allies' visits to bases to see, feel, and touch "their" nuclear forces—the capabilities that are their ultimate security guarantee—can strengthen assurance. For example, during a visit of the Extended Deterrence Dialogue to the Bangor SSBN base, a Japanese official said quietly to the crew of the SSBN the delegations visited, "Thank you for protecting us." Or as a South Korean expert said at a recent forum, "We hope the United States will continue its modernization of its nuclear forces; your strength is our strength." Forces matter, but the overall relationship and state of the alliance matter more; the "software" is at least as important as the hardware, if not more so.

It is not impossible that allies could doubt the U.S. commitment because of the details of the size or composition or basing of the U.S. nuclear arsenal. This occurred in the late 1970s, when West German chancellor Helmut Schmidt voiced concerns shared by other European NATO nations that the Soviets' SS-20 could decouple the U.S. strategic nuclear force from the defense of Europe. This led to the dual-track decision and the basing of Pershing IIs and ground-launched cruise missiles in Europe, because sea-based nuclear Tomahawk cruise missiles off the coast of Europe were seen as insufficiently coupling to assure NATO allies. So there have been times in history when allies did care greatly about the precise composition and disposition of U.S. nuclear forces.

But at this point, there is nothing to indicate allies are insufficiently assured about the U.S. nuclear arsenal because of any specific technical characteristics of it. Of course, they can be talked into it by U.S. self-denigration of its nuclear capability. In particular, talk of the United States being self-deterred—an argument usually put forward by those who most support new nuclear weapons—is counterproductive from an assurance (and a deterrence) standpoint. Moreover, some aspects of nuclear posture that assure one ally may disturb another, whether that is nuclear weapons deployed on their territory or particular choices in U.S. modernization of its nuclear weapons.

I would recommend that allies not put too much emphasis on any one weapon or platform. At one time, it seems the Japanese saw nuclear Tomahawk SLCMs (on attack subs and on ships that could be deployed in the region but not on land, which would be awkward for Japan) as "their" deterrent. President Bush in 1991 ended day-to-day routine deployment of nuclear SLCMs on ships and attack subs but kept them for contingency deployment. As part of the 1994 Nuclear Posture Review, the United States decided to eliminate the capability for surface ships but retained capability to put them back on attack subs. As one of those tasked with reassuring Japan at the time, I recall our highlighting that with the Japanese government. When the 2010 Nuclear Posture Review eliminated them, I found myself assuring Japan that everything in our nuclear arsenal was part of their extended nuclear deterrence capabilities. Fast forward to 2018 Nuclear Posture Review: SLCMs are back—or at least being considered, with studies to follow on best ways to develop and deploy. But we should not oversell the SLCM to Japan or other allies. It may or may not survive bureaucratic battles or potential arms control negotiations, and it may or may not be funded by Congress. That could be the case for some other nuclear systems as well.

The details of the U.S. nuclear arsenal will change over time, but as long as the commitment remains, the "stuff" is secondary. In the end, if the United States is comfortable with its own nuclear forces and posture and can—and does—make the case to allies that its security commitments, including extended nuclear deterrence, remain strong, then allies are likely to be assured with regard to our forces.

Concluding Reflections

The United States' reputation as a security guarantor is shaped by trends in U.S. behavior in the international arena. To be assured of the U.S. commitment, allies need to have confidence in American judgment and reliability; otherwise, specific capabilities, nuclear or otherwise, do not really matter. To be assured, allies must trust U.S. judgment—and in the case of nuclear weapons, that comes down to trusting the president.

The recent crisis in alliance relationships may be an aberration unique to the presidency of Donald Trump. But while allies' concerns may have been exacerbated by President Trump's disdain for alliances and a transactional approach to them, their extended-deterrence worries are bigger and deeper and of longer standing than transient political administrations. For example, I heard allies say President Obama's red line on Syria chemical weapons use was detrimental to alliances: the United States should not draw red lines it is not going to enforce.[92] (As an ROK expert once said, "After a while, all those red lines begin to look like a red carpet.") Better yet, we should ban the term *red line* from policy discourse.

President Biden's support for rebuilding alliances will be a welcome change after former president Trump's transactional approach to alliances. But there will be no dearth of assurance and extended-deterrence problems for the Biden administration to deal with—some recurring, some new.

In the longer term, there may be a larger question: Will the United States continue to play a major role in the world, in underpinning global stability, and specifically in extending nuclear deterrence to others? But in the near term, as long as there are nuclear weapons in the hands of others, the United States will need to sustain a safe and effective nuclear weapons capability; and as long as the United States plays a leading role in the world, its nuclear weapons will be about more than its own security. The United States has alliances not to be nice but because they are in the United States' interest.[93]

Much can be changed without changing the fundamentals of alliances if each party continues to see its alliance as being in its own interest. As long as the United States is willing to offer extended nuclear deterrence and allies are willing to trust it (or to believe they have no better alternative), it is likely to continue bumping along. If conditions become cloudier and murkier, however, there may be more fundamental shifts, deterioration, and even an end to the U.S. network of alliances—and consequently, more nuclear-armed nations.

Appendix. The Treaty Bases for Extended Nuclear Deterrence Commitments

NATO

Article 5 of the 1949 North Atlantic Treaty states: "The Parties agree that an armed attack against one or more of them in Europe or North America shall be considered an attack against them all and consequently they agree that, if such an armed attack occurs, each of them, in exercise of the right of individual or collective self-defence recognised by Article 51 of the Charter of the United Nations, will assist the Party or Parties so attacked by taking forthwith, individually and in concert with the other Parties, such action as it deems necessary, including the use of armed force, to restore and maintain the security of the North Atlantic area."[94]

Japan

The 1951 United States–Japan Security Treaty was replaced in 1960 by the Treaty of Mutual Cooperation and Security between Japan and United States of America. Article 5 of the latter treaty states: "Each Party recognizes that an armed attack against either Party in the territories under the administration of Japan would be dangerous to its own peace and safety and declares that it would act to meet the common danger in accordance with its constitutional provisions and processes."[95]

South Korea

Article 3 of the 1953 Mutual Defense Treaty between the United States and the Republic of Korea states: "Each Party recognizes that an armed attack in the Pacific area on either of the Parties in territories now under their respective administrative control, or hereafter recognized by one of the Parties as lawfully brought under the administrative control of the other, would be dangerous to its own peace and safety and declares that it would act to meet the common danger in accordance with its constitutional processes."[96]

Australia and New Zealand

Article 4 of the 1951 Australia, New Zealand, and United States Security (ANZUS) Treaty states: "Each Party recognizes that an armed attack in the Pacific Area on any of the Parties would be dangerous to its own peace and safety and declares that it would act to meet the common danger in accordance with its constitutional processes." Article 5 clarifies: "For the purpose of Article IV, an armed attack on any of the Parties is deemed to include an armed attack on the metropolitan territory of any of the Parties, or on the island territories under its jurisdiction in the Pacific or on its armed forces, public vessels or aircraft in the Pacific."[97] The United States suspended its treaty obligations toward New Zealand in 1986, after New Zealand declared its country a nuclear-free zone and refused to allow U.S. nuclear-powered submarines to visit its ports. U.S. secretary of state George P. Shultz and Australian foreign minister Bill Hayden had confirmed that their countries would continue to honor their obligations to one another under the ANZUS Treaty, even though the trilateral aspects of the treaty had been halted.[98]

Notes

1. See, for example, Thomas Schelling, *Arms and Influence* (Yale University Press, 1966); Henry Kissinger, *The Troubled Partnership: A Re-Appraisal of the Atlantic Alliance* (New York: McGraw Hill, 1965); Raymond Aron, *Le Grand Débat* (Paris: Calmann-Lévy, 1963).

2. The treaty language grounding each of these alliances is included in the appendix to this chapter. In addition, more specific references to extended nuclear deterrence are often found in alliance official statements. In the case of NATO, multiple NATO summit statements have consistently stated some variation of the words in the 2021 Brussels Summit Communiqué: "The strategic forces of the Alliance, particularly those of the United States, are the supreme guarantee of the security of Allies. . . . NATO's nuclear deterrence posture also relies on United States' nuclear weapons forward-deployed in Europe and the capabilities and infrastructure provided by Allies concerned." (NATO, *Brussels Summit Communiqué*, issued by the heads of state and government participating in the meeting of the North Atlantic Council, Brussels, June 14, 2021, para. 40). With regard to Japan and South Korea, official

statements in the past thirty years have also elaborated on the nuclear commitment. For example, the statement from the 2016 meeting of the United States–Republic of Korea Extended Deterrence Security and Consultation Group states: "The United States reiterated its ironclad and unwavering commitment to draw on the full range of its military capabilities, including the nuclear umbrella, conventional strike, and missile defense, to provide extended deterrence for the ROK [Republic of Korea], and reaffirmed the long-standing U.S. policy that any attack on the United States or its allies will be defeated, and any use of nuclear weapons will be met with an effective and overwhelming response." (Department of State, "Joint Statement on the Inaugural Meeting of the Extended Deterrence Strategy and Consultation Group (EDSCG)," Washington, D.C., December 20, 2016). Similar statements have been made in meetings with Japan; for example, at a 2019 meeting of the Security Consultative Group, U.S. and Japanese foreign and defense ministers "recognized the critical role that U.S. extended deterrence plays in ensuring the security of Japan, as well as the peace and stability of the Indo-Pacific region. The United States reiterated its commitment to the defense of Japan through the full range of U.S. military capabilities, including conventional and nuclear." (Department of State, "Joint Statement of the Security Consultative Committee," Washington, D.C., April 19, 2019).

3. See, for example, Catherine Kelleher, "NATO Nuclear Operations," in *Managing Nuclear Operations,* edited by Ashton B. Carter, John D. Steinbruner, and Charles A. Zraket (Brookings, 1987), pp. 445–69; and Robert E. Osgood, *NATO: The Entangling Alliance* (University of Chicago Press, 1962).

4. In 1949 there were twelve founding members of the alliance: Belgium, Canada, Denmark, France, Iceland, Italy, Luxembourg, the Netherlands, Norway, Portugal, the United Kingdom, and the United States. The other member countries are Greece and Turkey (1952), Germany (1955), Spain (1982), the Czech Republic, Hungary, and Poland (1999), Bulgaria, Estonia, Latvia, Lithuania, Romania, Slovakia, and Slovenia (2004), Albania and Croatia (2009), Montenegro (2017) and North Macedonia (2020).

5. NATO, *The Alliance's New Strategic Concept,* agreed by the heads of state and government participating in the meeting of the North Atlantic Council, Rome, November 7–8, 1991, para. 5, www.nato.int/cps/en/natohq/official_texts_23847.htm.

6. NATO, *The Alliance's New Strategic Concept,* para. 57.

7. NATO, *The Alliance's New Strategic Concept,* para. 38.

8. NATO, *The Alliance's New Strategic Concept,* para. 54.

9. NATO, *The Alliance's New Strategic Concept,* para. 55.

10. NATO, *The Alliance's New Strategic Concept,* para. 55.

11. NATO, *The Alliance's New Strategic Concept,* para. 56.

12 NATO, *The Alliance's New Strategic Concept,* para. 56.

13. NATO, *The Alliance's Strategic Concept,* approved by the heads of state and government participating in the meeting of the North Atlantic Council, Washington, April 24, 1999, para. 3, www.nato.int/cps/en/natolive/official_texts_27433.htm.

14. "Active Engagement, Modern Defence," Strategic Concept for the Defence and Security of the Members of the North Atlantic Treaty Organisation, adopted

by Heads of State and Government in Lisbon, 2010, para. 17, www.nato.int/nato_
static_fl2014/assets/pdf/pdf_publications/20120203_strategic-concept-2010-eng.
pdf.

15. NATO, *Deterrence and Defense Posture Review*, adopted by heads of state
and government in Chicago, May 20, 2012, www.nato.int/cps/en/natohq/official_
texts_87597.htm. The review also states: "NATO is prepared to consider further
reducing its requirement for non-strategic nuclear weapons assigned to the Alliance
in the context of reciprocal steps by Russia, taking into account the greater Russian stockpiles of non-strategic nuclear weapons stationed in the Euro-Atlantic area"
(para. 26).

16. Thomas Frear, Lukasz Kulesa, and Ian Kearns, *Dangerous Brinkmanship:
Close Military Encounters between Russia and the West in 2014*, European Leadership
Network Policy Brief, November 2014, www.europeanleadershipnetwork.org/wp-
content/uploads/2017/10/Dangerous-Brinkmanship.pdf.

17. Paul Belkin, Derek E. Mix, and Steven Woehrel, *NATO: Response to the
Crisis in Ukraine and Security Concerns in Central and Eastern Europe*, Congressional
Research Service Report R43478, https://fas.org/sgp/crs/row/R43478.pdf.

18. NATO, *Warsaw Summit Communiqué*, issued by the heads of state and government participating in the meeting of the North Atlantic Council, Warsaw, July
8–9, 2016 (para. 54), www.nato.int/cps/en/natohq/official_texts_133169.htm.

19. NATO, *Brussels Summit Declaration*, issued by the heads of state and government participating in the meeting of the North Atlantic Council in Brussels, July
11–12, 2018 (para 36), www.nato.int/cps/en/natohq/official_texts_156624.htm; and
NATO, *Brussels Summit Communiqué*, issued by the heads of state and government
participating in the meeting of the North Atlantic Council, Brussels, June 14, 2021
(para 41), www.nato.int/cps/en/natohq/news_185000.htmhttps://www.nato.int/cps/
en/natohq/news_185000.htm.

20. NATO, *Warsaw Summit Communiqué* (para 53).

21. While the North Atlantic Council is the ultimate authority within NATO,
the Nuclear Planning Group acts as the senior body on nuclear matters in the alliance.

22. NATO, "Nuclear Planning Group," May 27, 2020, www.nato.int/cps/en/
natolive/topics_50069.htm.

23. In 1998–1999, the HLG also took over the functions and responsibilities of
the former Senior Level Weapons Protection Group, which was charged with overseeing nuclear weapons safety, security, and survivability matters.

24. According to the U.S. Department of Defense, Office of the Deputy Assistant Secretary of Defense for Nuclear Matters, *Nuclear Matters Handbook 2020*
(revised), "The JTSMG [Joint Theater Surety Management Group] was established
in August 1977 to seek active participation and consultation among the NATO
Nuclear Program of Cooperation nations to ensure an effective theater nuclear surety
program. The JTSMG serves as the focal point for the resolution of technical matters pertaining to nuclear surety. The group reports to the HLG vice chairman, the
assistant secretary of defense for nuclear, chemical, and biological defense programs
(ASD(NCB)), who provides high-level attention and oversight to JTSMG activities.

The JTSMG is cochaired by representatives from U.S. European Command and Supreme Headquarters Allied Powers Europe. The JTSMG meets in working group sessions four times annually and in plenary sessions twice annually," p. 119, www.acq.osd.mil/ncbdp/nm//NMHB2020rev/docs/NMHB2020rev.pdf.

25. NATO, "Nuclear Planning Group (NPG)."

26. The term *nonstrategic nuclear forces* as used in this chapter refers to those forces that are not part of strategic arms control treaties. Such weapons have in the past also been known as "theater" or "tactical" nuclear weapons. But these terms are unsatisfactory: one country's "theater" is another's homeland, and any use of even "tactical" nuclear weapons would, after seventy-plus years of nonuse of any nuclear weapon, be a "strategic" event. Sometimes, *theater* or *tactical* is used to refer to the range of a system (that is, less than intercontinental range); sometimes, it refers to where it is based ("over there," rather than in one's own country). In the case of B-61 bombs, the ones for carriage on U.S. or other NATO members' dual-capable fighter aircraft are considered "nonstrategic," while B-61 bombs carried on B-2 bombers, with greater unfueled range, are considered strategic, in part because the bombers are limited in New START and previous strategic arms control treaties.

27. Kelleher, "NATO Nuclear Operations," figure 14-1, "NATO Delivery Systems," p. 446.

28. NATO, "NATO's Nuclear Deterrence Policy and Forces," May 11, 2021, www.nato.int/cps/en/natohq/topics_50068.htm.

29. "Several NATO allies also provide DCA capable of delivering U.S. forward-deployed nuclear weapons. The forthcoming B61-12 gravity bomb will replace earlier versions of the B61, and be available for these DCA beginning in 2021 [now 2022]. U.S. and NATO DCA, together with U.S. gravity bombs, are forward deployed in European NATO countries," Office of the Secretary of Defense, *Nuclear Posture Review 2018* (Department of Defense, February 2018), p. 48, https://media.defense.gov/2018/Feb/02/2001872886/-1/-1/1/2018-NUCLEAR-POSTURE-REVIEW-FINAL-REPORT.PDF.

30. The U.S. F-16s gave up their nuclear role in 2016–2017. The 2018 Nuclear Posture Review states, "Current U.S. non-strategic nuclear forces consist exclusively of B61 gravity bombs carried by F-15E DCA, supported by responsive air refueling aircraft," Office of the Secretary of Defense, *Nuclear Posture Review 2018*, p. 48. But some NATO allies still have dual-capable (nuclear-certified) F-16s pending the deployment of follow-on DCA such as F-35. Of the F-16, the posture review states, "We are committed to upgrading DCA with the nuclear-capable F-35 aircraft," p. 54.

31. "North Atlantic Treaty Organization (NATO) Enlargement Costs," Hearings before the Senate Committee on Appropriations, 105th Cong. First Session, October 21, 1997, p. 74.

32. NATO, "NATO's Nuclear Deterrence Policy and Forces," May 11, 2021, www.nato.int/cps/en/natohq/topics_50068.htm.

33. Secretary of the Air Force, Air Force Instruction 63-125, "Nuclear Certification Program," revised January 16, 2020, https://static.e-publishing.af.mil/production/1/saf_aq/publication/afi63-125/afi63-125.pdf.

34. William Alberque, "The NPT and the Origins of NATO's Nuclear Sharing Arrangements," *Proliferation Papers*, February 2017, Études l'Ifri, p. 7, www.ifri.org/sites/default/files/atoms/files/alberque_npt_origins_nato_nuclear_2017.pdf.

35. U.S. Department of Defense, *Nuclear Matters Handbook 2020*, pp. 163–64. The handbook also contains further information on U.S. requirements, including presidential and statutory determinations on weapons-related information sharing with foreign countries.

36. "North Atlantic Treaty Organization (NATO) Enlargement Costs," pp. 73, 85.

37. Dr. Karl-Heinz Kamp and Major General Robertus C.N. Remkes (U.S.A.F., ret.) "Options for NATO Nuclear Sharing Arrangements," chap. 4 in *Reducing Nuclear Risks in Europe: A Framework for Action*, edited by Steve Andreasen and Isabelle Williams, (Washington, D.C.: Nuclear Threat Initiative, 2011), p. 87, https://media.nti.org/pdfs/NTI_Framework_full_report.pdf.

38. U.S. Department of Energy, *2018 Fact Sheet*, www.energy.gov/sites/prod/files/2018/12/f58/B61-12%20LEP%20factsheet.pdf.

39. Charles Verdon, in a question-and-answer session at the ExchageMonitor's annual Nuclear Deterrence Summit, quoted in "After Scheduled Slips, Refurbished Nukes Coming Starting Next Year," ExchangeMonitor Morning Briefing, February 12, 2020, www.exchangemonitor.com/slips-b61-12-first-production-unit-coming-2022-w88-alt-370-2021/?printmode=1. Verdon is the National Nuclear Security Administration's deputy director for defense programs. The agency identified an issue with capacitor components that did not meet reliability requirements; consequently, the B61-12 life extension program will not meet initial production date requirements, according to Lieutenant Richard M. Clark, in testimony, "The Fiscal Year 2021 Budget Request for Nuclear Forces and Atomic Energy Defense Activities," hearings before the House Armed Services Committee, Subcommittee on Strategic Forces, 116th Cong. (March 3, 2020).

40. U.S. Department of Energy, 2018 Fact Sheet, www.energy.gov/sites/prod/files/2018/12/f58/B61-12%20LEP%20factsheet.pdf.

41. As a former U.S. government official whose publications are subject to security review, I cannot cite widely published reports speculating on numbers and locations.

42. See Evan Braden Montgomery, "Extended Deterrence in the Second Nuclear Age: Geopolitics, Proliferation, and the Future of U.S. Security Commitments," Center for Strategic and Budgetary Assessments, 2016, p. 33, https://csbaonline.org/research/publications/extended-deterrence-in-the-second-nuclear-age. Also see tweet by U.S. ambassador to Poland Georgette Mosbacher, May 15, 2020, https://twitter.com/USAmbPoland/status/1261322198008111104.

43. See Warren Christopher, U.S. secretary of state, press conference, December 10, 1996, www.nato.int/cps/en/natolive/ opinions_25112.htm?selectedLocale=en.

44. NATO, *Summary: Founding Act on Mutual Relations, Cooperation, and Security between NATO and the Russian Federation*, May 27, 1997, www.nato.int/cps/en/natohq/official_texts_25470.htm?selectedLocale=en.

45. Katarzyna Kubiac, "Playing Warsaw against Berlin on Nuclear Weapons," European Leadership Network, June 1, 2020, See also Karl-Heinz Kamp, "Nuclear

Reorientation of NATO," p. 8, NATO Defense College Commentary, February 5, 2018.

46. NATO, "NATO's Positions Regarding Nuclear Non-Proliferation, Arms Control and Disarmament and Related Issues," October 22, 2009, www.nato. int/nato_static_fl2014/assets/pdf/pdf_topics/20091022_NATO_Position_on_nuclear_nonpro.pdf.

47. *Fiscal Year 2015 Request for Atomic Energy Defense Activities and Nuclear Forces Programs:* Hearing before the House Armed Services Committee, Subcommittee on Strategic Forces, 113th Cong., April 8, 2014, Bunn response for the record to Sanchez's questions, www.govinfo.gov/content/pkg/CHRG-113hhrg88452/pdf/CHRG-113hhrg88452.pdf.

48. See, for example, "U.S. Air Force B-52s Deploy to Europe," U.S. Air Force Europe, press release 030319, March 14, 2019, www.usafe.af.mil/News/Press-Releases/Article/1784804/us-air-force-b-52s-deploy-to-europe/; "U.S. Air Force B-52s Deploy to Europe," September 5, 2019, www.usafe.af.mil/News/Article-Display/Article/1952419/raf-f-35s-train-with-us-air-force-b-2-bombers-for-the-first-time/; Ryan Pickrell, "A Big Batch of B-52 Bombers Is Flying into Europe amid Heightened Tensions with Russia," *Business Insider,* March 15, 2019, www.businessinsider.com/a-big-batch-of-b-52-bombers-is-flying-into-europe-2019-3.

49. See, for example, "USS Alaska (SSBN 732) Arrives at HMNB Clyde," *U.S. Strategic Command Public Affairs,* July 2, 2019, www.stratcom.mil/Media/News/News-Article-View/Article/1895032/uss-alaska-ssbn-732-arrives-at-hmnb-clyde/; "USS Tennessee Arrives in Scotland for Port Visit," *U.S. Strategic Command Public Affairs,* October 7, 2016, www.stratcom.mil/Media/News/News-Article-View/Article/997925/uss-tennessee-arrives-in-scotland-for-port-visit/.

50. The United States previously had nuclear SLCMs for deployment on surface ships and attack submarines, but they were eliminated on the former in the 1994 Nuclear Posture Review and on the the latter in the 2010 Nuclear Posture Review.

51. Office of the Secretary of Defense, *Nuclear Posture Review 2018,* pp. XII, 54.

52. U.S. Department of Defense Release, "Statement on the Fielding of the W76-2 Low-Yield Submarine Launched Ballistic Missile Warhead," February 4, 2020, www.defense.gov/Newsroom/Releases/Release/Article/2073532/statement-on-the-fielding-of-the-w76-2-low-yield-submarine-launched-ballistic-m/. See also "Strengthening Deterrence and Reducing Nuclear Risks: The Supplemental Low-Yield U.S. Submarine-Launched Warhead," Department of State, *Arms Control and International Security Papers* 1, no. 4, April 24, 2020, www.state.gov/wp-content/uploads/2020/04/T-Paper-Series-4-W76.pdf.

53. Sir Michael Quinlan, *Thinking about Nuclear Weapons: Principles, Problems, Prospects* (Oxford University Press, 2009), p. 127; Austin Long, "Discrimination Details Matter: Clarifying an Argument about Low-Yield Nuclear Warheads," War on the Rocks, February 16, 2018, https://warontherocks.com/2018/02/discrimination-details-matter-clarifying-argument-low-yield-nuclear-warheads/.

54. Kamp and Remkes, "Options for NATO Nuclear Sharing Arrangements," p. 84.

55. See NATO, *Warsaw Summit Communiqué,* para. 53.

56. Camille Grand, "Nuclear Deterrence and the Alliance in the 21st Century," *NATO Review,* July 4, 2016, www.nato.int/docu/review/articles/2016/07/04/nuclear-deterrence-and-the-alliance-in-the-21st-century/index.html.

57. "Integrated Review of Security, Defence, Development, and Foreign Policy, 2021: Nuclear Deterrent," U.K. Ministry of Defence and Defence Nuclear Organization, March 17, 2021, updated April 27, 2021, www.gov.uk/guidance/integrated-review-of-security-defence-development-and-foreign-policy-2021-nuclear-deterrent.

58. Grand, "Nuclear Deterrence and the Alliance in the 21st Century."

59. Bruno Tertrais, *French Nuclear Deterrence Policy, Forces and Future: A Handbook,* Fondation pour la Recherche Stratégique, Recherches & Documents N°4/2020, pp. 3, 55, 58, 62.

60. Corentin Brustlein, "France's Nuclear Arsenal: What Sort of Renewal?" *Politique étrangère,* issue 3, 2017, pp. 113–24.Translated and edited by Cadenza Academic Translations.

61. Élysée Palace, "Speech of the President of the Republic on the Defense and Deterrence Strategy," Paris, February 7, 2020, www.elysee.fr/en/emmanuel-macron/2020/02/07/speech-of-the-president-of-the-republic-on-the-defense-and-deterrence-strategy.

62. Kamp and Remkes, "Options for NATO Nuclear Sharing Arrangements," p. 77.

63. NATO, *The Alliance's Strategic Concept,* 1999, para. 64.

64. Donna Haseley, "Adaptive Nuclear Targeting Is Central to NATO Plan: Draft NATO Doctrine Lays Out Conventional Plan Mirroring Air/Land Battle," *Inside the Army* 4, no. 48 (1992), pp. 1, 6–7.

65. Lorin D. Veigas, "The Revitalization of Theater Nuclear Operations Planning," *Countering WMD Journal,* issue 15 (Summer–Fall 2017), pp. 37–41, www.nec.belvoir.army.mil/usanca/CWMDJournal/Issue%2015%20CWMD%20Journal%2003APR17%20Web.pdf.

66. NATO, *The Alliance's Strategic Concept,* 1999, para. 64.

67. Leo Michel and Matti Pesu, "Strategic Deterrence Redux: Nuclear Weapons and European Security," Finnish Institute of International Affairs, September 2019, p. 51.

68. Office of the Secretary of Defense, *Nuclear Posture Review 2018,* p. 54.

69. See, for example, Julian Barnes, "NATO Launches Its Main Nuclear Drill, Showcasing Its Defenses," *Wall Street Journal,* October 17, 2017, www.wsj.com/articles/nato-launches-its-main-nuclear-drill-showcasing-its-defenses-1508155670; Hans M. Kristenson, "NATO Nuclear Exercise Underway with Czech and Polish Participation," Federation of American Scientists Blog, October 17, 2017, https://fas.org/blogs/security/2017/10/steadfast-noon-exercise/.

70. See, for example, "NATO Nuclear Exercise 'Steadfast Noon, 2014,'" photograph, *The Aviationist* (blog), November 15, 2014, https://theaviationist.com/2014/11/15/steadfast-noon-2014-exercise/.

71. NATO, "NATO Diplomats and Experts Meet in Riga to Discuss NATO's Nuclear Deterrence," September 6, 2019, www.nato.int/cps/en/natohq/news_168595.htm?selectedLocale=en.

72. See Brad Roberts, *The Case for Nuclear Weapons in the 21st Century* (Stanford University Press, 2016), p. 206.

73. Yukio Satoh, "Reinforcing American Extended Deterrence for Japan: An Essential Step for Nuclear Disarmament," *AJISS-Commentary* 57, February 3, 2009, www.jiia.or.jp/en_commentary/pdf/AJISS-Commentary57.pdf.

74. U.S. Department of Defense, "8th Korea-U.S. Integrated Defense Dialogue," press release, September 24, 2015, https://dod.defense.gov/Portals/1/Documents/pubs/Press_Statement_8th_KIDD_Sep24_OSD_FINAL.pdf.

75. Karen Parrish, "U.S., South Korea Announce 'Tailored Deterrence' Strategy," United States Forces Korea, October 2, 2013, https://archive.defense.gov/news/newsarticle.aspx?id=120896.

76. Department of Defense, "Joint Statement for the Inaugural Meeting of the Extended Deterrence Strategy and Consultation Group," https://dod.defense.gov/Portals/1/Documents/pubs/Joint-Statement-for-the-Inaugural-Meeting-of-the-Extended-Deterrence-Strategy-and-Consultation-Group.pdf.

77. Government of Australia, Department of Defense, *2016 Defense White Paper*, para 5.20, www.defense.gov.au/whitepaper/docs/2016-Defense-White-Paper.pdf. For further discussion of Australia and extended deterrence more broadly, see Justin V. Anderson and Jeffrey A. Larsen, with Polly M. Holdorf, "Extended Deterrence and Allied Assurance: Key Concepts and Current Challenges for U.S. Policy," INSS Occasional Paper 69, September 2013, www.usafa.edu/app/uploads/OCP69.pdf; and Stephan Fruhling, Andrew O'Neil, and David Santoro, "Escalating Cooperation: Nuclear Deterrence and the U.S.-Australia Alliance," November 2019, United States Study Center, University of Sydney, https://apo.org.au/node/266586.

78. Roberts, *The Case for Nuclear Weapons in the 21st Century*, p. 206.

79. Office of the Secretary of Defense, *Nuclear Posture Review 2018*, pp. 48, 54.

80. United States Forces Korea, "Ballistic Missile Submarine USS Pennsylvania (SSBN 735) Prepares to Moor in Apra Harbor, Guam," photograph, Image Gallery, www.usfk.mil/Media/Images/igphoto/2001661523/; "U.S. Sends Message to Adversaries with Nuclear Sub Visit, Drills," CNN Politics, October 31, 2016, www.cnn.com/2016/10/31/politics/guam-nuclear-missile-submarine-visit/index.html.

81. Franz-Stefan Gady, "U.S. Air Force Flies Another B-52H Bomber Mission Over South China Sea," *The Diplomat*, March 14, 2019, https://thediplomat.com/2019/03/us-air-force-flies-another-b-52h-bomber-mission-over-south-china-sea/; Amy McCullough, "Bombers on Guam," *Air Force Magazine*, July 27, 2015, www.airforcemag.com/article/bombers-on-guam/.

82. U.S. Air Force, "U.S. Conducts B-52 Overflight in South Korea after Nuke Test," Department of Defense News, January 11, 2016, www.af.mil/News/Article-Display/Article/642180/us-conducts-b-52-bomber-overflight-in-south-korea-after-nuke-test/.

83. Brian W. Everstine, "Air Force Ends Continuous Bomber Presence in Guam," *Air Force Magazine,* April 17, 2020, www.airforcemag.com/air-force-ends-continuous-bomber-presence-in-guam/.

84. "Australia-United States Joint Facilities," speech by Defence Minister Christopher Pyne, February 20, 2019, Australian House of Representatives Ministerial

Statements, p. 1088, https://parlinfo.aph.gov.au/parlInfo/search/display/display.w3p
;query=Id%3A%22chamber%2Fhansardr%2Fe0e7b3e2-2c86-47b4-8de2-de9e8f0f
224b%2F0026%22;src1=sm1. In his speech Pyne also quoted an earlier Australian
official: "As the then Prime Minister, Bob Hawke, noted in his public statement on
Pine Gap in 1984, Australia should not claim the protection of nuclear deterrence
without being willing to make a contribution to its effectiveness."

85. The Hon. Scott Morrison MP, Prime Minister of Austalia, Rt. Hon. Boris
Johnson MP, Prime Minister of the United Kingdom, and Joseph R. Biden Jr., President of the United States of America, Joint Leaders Statement on AUKUS, September 16, 2021, www.pm.gov.au/media/joint-leaders-statement-aukus.

86. An Australian government paper stated, "Nuclear-powered submarines
have superior characteristics of stealth, speed, manoeuvrability, survivability, and
almost limitless endurance, when compared to conventional submarines. . . . This is
about nuclear-powered submarines. The [Australian] Government has no intention
to acquire nuclear weapons." From "Nuclear-Powered Submarine Task Force," fact
sheet, Australian Department of Defence, September 2021, www.defence.gov.au/
about/taskforces/nuclear-powered-submarine-task-force.

87. For example, Japan has deployed a number of missile defense forces, including Aegis interceptors aboard ships and Patriot land-based missile defenses. Japan
has taken primary responsibility for the handling of the dispute over the Senkaku
Islands, conducting its own coast guard patrols to counter Chinese pressure. The
Japanese also scramble their own F-15s from Japanese bases to intercept Chinese and
Russian flights that enter Japanese airspace. South Korea has a strong conventional
military, as well as its own indigenous, conventionally armed ballistic (Hyunmoo-2
and Hyunmoo-3) and cruise missiles (Haeseong II supersonic, ship-launched land-
attack cruise missile) with ranges that can reach deep into North Korea; it is developing intelligence, surveillance, and reconnaissance capabilities and is undertaking
efforts toward an indigenously developed air and missile defense capability. Australia
also has robust non-nuclear military capabilities and prides itself on having fought
alongside Americans in every major military action of the last century.

88. Michael Rühle, "Deterrence: What It Can (and Cannot) Do," *NATO Review*,
April 20, 2015, www.nato.int/docu/review/articles/2015/04/20/deterrence-what-it-
can-and-cannot-do/index.html.

89. In practice, some NATO decisions come with "footnotes" by individual allies.

90. Roberts, *The Case for Nuclear Weapons in the 21st Century*, p. 206.

91. On Trump's visit with Kim Jong-un, see Josh Smith and Phil Stewart, "Trump
Surprises with Pledge to End Military Exercises in South Korea," Reuters, June 12,
2018, www.reuters.com/article/us-northkorea-usa-military/trump-surprises-with-
pledge-to-end-military-exercises-in-south-korea-idUSKBN1J812W.

92. In 2012 President Obama was asked what could lead him to use military
force in Syria. He said, "We have been very clear to the Assad regime that a red line
for us is we start seeing a whole bunch of chemical weapons moving around or being
utilized. That would change my calculus." In 2013 Assad used chemical weapons
against the Syrian population. While the United States considered but did not take

military action, it did reach an agreement with Assad that resulted in the removal and destruction of thousands of tons of chemical weapons. Instead of seeing this as successful coercive diplomacy, many saw it as a failure of credibility. See Derek Chollet, "Obama's Red Line Revisited," *Politico Magazine,* July 19, 2016, www.politico.com/magazine/story/2016/07/obama-syria-foreign-policy-red-line-revisited-214059; and Ben Rhodes, "Inside the White House during the Syrian 'Red Line' Crisis," *The Atlantic,* June 3, 2018 (www.theatlantic.com/international/archive/2018/06/inside-the-white-house-during-the-syrian-red-line-crisis/561887/).

93. Mira Rapp-Hooper, "Saving America's Alliances: The United States Still Needs the System That Put It on Top," *Foreign Affairs,* 99, no. 2 (March–April 2020), pp. 127–40.

94. North Atlantic Treaty, April 4, 1949, 34 U.N.T.S. 24, art. 5, www.nato.int/cps/en/natolive/official_texts_17120.htm.

95. Treaty of Mutual Cooperation and Security between Japan and the United States of America, January 19, 1960, 2 *U.S.T* 1632, art. 5, www.mofa.go.jp/region/n-america/us/q&a/ref/1.html.

96. Mutual Defense Treaty between the United States and the Republic of Korea, October 1, 1953, 5 U.S.T 23602376, art. 3, https://avalon.law.yale.edu/20th_century/kor001.asp.

97. Security Treaty between the United States, Australia, and New Zealand (ANZUS), September 1, 1951, 3 U.S.T 3423-3425, arts. 4 and 5; ANZUS Treaty text available at appendix B of Australian Parliament House of Representatives Joint Standing Committee on Foreign Affairs, Defence and Trade, *Report on the Inquiry into Australia's Defence Relations with the United States,* May 22, 2006, www.aph.gov.au/parliamentary_business/committees/house_of_representatives_committees?url=jfadt/usrelations/report.htm.

98. U.S. State Department, Office of the Historian, "The Australia, New Zealand, and United States Security Treaty (ANZUS Treaty), 1951," https://history.state.gov/milestones/1945-1952/anzus.

CHAPTER 9

Nuclear Operations and Arms Control

Linton F. Brooks

Russia and the United States have the world's most extensive and complicated nuclear operations, and all meaningful arms control agreements to date have been between these two major nuclear powers. Today's Russia is not the Soviet Union of the Cold War but has inherited many operational concepts and ways of thinking from the Soviet era, making examination of Soviet arms control concepts useful even a quarter century after the country's dissolution.[1] Toward the end of the chapter, I discuss some implications for other states. Although the bulk of the chapter is descriptive and analytic, I offer some specific recommendations on potential future arms control issues.

It is important at the outset to understand what is meant here by the terms *arms control* and *nuclear operations*. In both cases I use expansive definitions. In the past few decades, discussion of arms control has largely been limited to legally binding agreements, usually ratified treaties. But the original concept was much broader. Modern U.S. arms control theory can be traced in part to Thomas Schelling and Morton Halperin's seminal work, *Strategy and Arms Control*. Writing in 1961, they say, "We use the term 'arms control' . . . to mean all the forms of military cooperation between potential enemies in the interest of reducing the likelihood of war, its scope and violence if it occurs, and the political and economic costs of being prepared for it."[2] Thus arms control can include treaties, other formal agreements, informal and uncodified reciprocal restraints, military-to-military discussion of doctrine and crisis management, targeting practices, including what are legitimate and illegitimate targets, and provisions for centers to exchange data and norms of behavior accepted by both sides.[3]

Similarly, nuclear operations include more than the movement of military units. Arms control can influence the creation of plans for operations, including targeting plans, can limit where operations can be conducted, and can require advanced notification of such operations. It can influence operations indirectly through constraining the capabilities of individual military units. For purposes of this discussion, all of these various processes are considered operations.

Not everything associated with nuclear weapons, however, is included within nuclear operations. This chapter does not deal with nuclear testing, nonproliferation, or the safety and security of nuclear weapons.

Why Have Russia and the United States Sought Arms Control in the First Place?

In the time it takes to read this chapter, the United States and the Russian Federation can destroy one another as functioning societies. Neither is likely to do so, in part because each side maintains forces that could survive a first strike and inflict devastating retaliation. As a result, nuclear war has become irrational and self-defeating. This condition, called mutual assured destruction, is a frightening and unsatisfactory concept. Many experts have sought a way to move beyond it. They have not found one. That is because mutual assured destruction is not a policy to be embraced or rejected but a fact to be accepted and managed. Arms control is one way of dealing with the implications of mutual assured destruction.

Because neither side can be certain of controlling escalation (especially once the nuclear threshold is crossed), conventional war between nuclear-armed states should also be too risky to contemplate, although it is unclear that this conclusion is universally accepted. Arms control has a role to play here as well.

In managing a relationship characterized by the reciprocal ability to inflict devastation, Russia and the United States have found the concept of strategic stability to be helpful and perhaps central to preventing war.[4] By the end of the Cold War, analysts in both the Soviet Union and the United

States had a roughly similar understanding of the basic premises of strategic stability and of the importance of those principles in avoiding catastrophe. They understood that the concept was primarily bilateral and was primarily about preventing nuclear war. To foster such stability, the two superpowers sought policies, forces, and postures that met three criteria:

- In time of great crisis, there is no incentive to be the first to use military force of any type, nuclear or otherwise ("crisis stability").
- Neither in peacetime, in crisis, nor in conventional conflict is there any incentive to be the first to use nuclear weapons ("first-strike stability").
- Neither side believes it can improve its relative position by building more weapons ("arms race stability").

Many analysts have elected to combine the first two categories into the single term *crisis stability* on the grounds that the reason to avoid crises is the risk of one or another side choosing to use nuclear weapons. This chapter preserves all three terms because the measures to prevent crises are different from the measures to discourage first use and thus must be analyzed separately. While dealing with conventional crises may seem remote from nuclear operations, it is not. The most likely path to nuclear use between Russia and the United States today is not large-scale attack or large-scale war but unintended escalation from a crisis. Because managing escalation is so difficult, it is therefore important to focus on avoiding crises that could result in escalation. Thus crisis stability becomes an important component of preventing nuclear war.

Some assume arms control is an obvious good, but it is not. It is one possible tool to improve national security and enhance strategic stability. Like any tool, it is more useful for some tasks than for others.

Many practitioners (myself included) are skeptical of two of the Schelling and Halperin goals. They doubt nuclear arms control reduces the likelihood of a deliberately initiated war, on grounds that such a decision will more likely be based on political considerations within the attacking state. Arms control can, however, reduce the risk of conflict based on erroneous perceptions that an attack is imminent. Furthermore, the political decision to go to war must consider the size and structure of the military capability of both sides. This can be significantly influenced by arms control. Finally, to the extent that arms control leads to day-to-day first-strike stability, it can decrease the chance that any war is initiated at the nuclear level.

Practitioners also question whether we know how to reduce the scope and violence of war once the nuclear threshold has been crossed. These practitioners have a somewhat different list of what bilateral arms control can do:

- provide public recognition that the two sides regard one another as equals in an area crucial to national survival
- provide communication in difficult times
- provide transparency, which leads to predictability, which, in turn, enhances stability
- avoid an action-reaction arms race in which each side builds new systems in anticipation of or reaction to moves by the other; in some cases, close off militarization of a specific technology
- reduce incentives to preempt with nuclear forces in time of crisis or to escalate to nuclear use in a conventional conflict (provide first-strike stability) by shaping the structure of forces (for example, stressing bombers over missiles, or reducing the role of fixed—and thus vulnerable—intercontinental ballistic missiles with multiple warheads)
- save money by capping expenditures on new systems, either by preventing an action-reaction arms race, precluding the need to build systems to avoid politically important but militarily insignificant differences in force sizes, or improving relations, and thereby reducing the perceived incentive for war
- reduce the chance of inadvertent escalation caused by mismanagement during crises

In addition to these stability benefits, arms control can help improve the overall political relationship. Finally, those who believe that nuclear abolition is a feasible and desirable goal or wish to demonstrate support for Article VI of the Nuclear Non-Proliferation Treaty want to negotiate lower numbers to move closer to zero.[5] The New START Treaty is the latest attempt to pursue many of these goals.[6]

Arms control has recorded some successes that are not normally regarded as related to strategic stability. It has banned nuclear weapons from Antarctica, outer space, the seabed, and several nuclear weapons–free zones.[7] None of these agreements has any impact, however, on nuclear operations (nuclear weapons–free zones to which the United States has subscribed all include rights of transit and overflight even for ships and aircraft carrying nuclear weapons).

Operations Influencing Arms Control and Vice Versa

Operations, as defined above, influence arms control (especially legally binding treaty-based arms control) because the need for effective operations determines the constraints on nuclear forces that a state is willing to accept. Nowhere is this truer than in the targeting necessary to carry out the war plans that may be implemented if deterrence fails. In determining whether to give the U.S. Senate's advice and consent to ratification, senators are interested in the professional military's views on the value of transparency and predictability or the contributions of a specific treaty to the overall political relationship between the two signatories. But what they demand from the military leadership is assurance that the armed forces can still carry out the responsibilities assigned by the president if the proposed treaty is approved and implemented.

While the concepts of deterrence and stability endure, on taking office each administration normally conducts an analysis of how these concepts should be implemented operationally. The result is a classified directive from the president setting forth the required capabilities that must be available should deterrence fail. From this directive are derived, among other things, what target sets must be held at risk by U.S. nuclear forces and with what degree of assurance.[8] Arms control proposals must allow this presidential guidance to be implemented.

There are at least three historic examples that illustrate the relationship between presidential guidance and force structure. In July 1991, the United States and the Soviet Union concluded the first Strategic Arms Reduction Treaty (START I), limiting each side to 6,000 accountable strategic warheads.[9] I was the chief treaty negotiator when START I was concluded. Some officials were proposing a follow-on agreement that would reduce the warhead limit to 5,000. I was inundated with calls from Washington colleagues both inside and outside government explaining why that was impossible and its advocacy unhelpful. Yet in January 1992, the United States and the Russian Federation (the successor to the Soviet Union) reached agreement on a new treaty, START II, lowering warhead limits to 3,500 and tightening the counting rules so the limits would have been much more reflective of actual capabilities. How was this possible?

The reduction was made possible by an extensive study of actual U.S. targeting practices conducted by a senior Department of Defense official, Frank Miller. The results demonstrated that the guidance had been misapplied in a fashion that had resulted in far more targets being covered by far more weapons than were actually required. As a result, the Department of Defense was able to accept dramatically lower limits and tighter counting rules that would have resulted in the limits much more accurately reflecting the requirements to achieve the president's real capability.[10]

A second example occurred in 2010. The initial START Treaty was set to expire, and the United States and the Russian Federation were working to draft a replacement. The new administration had not yet completed its review of nuclear policy and thus had not yet issued presidential guidance on what requirements the U.S. military was expected to meet in the nuclear arena. The administration therefore considered what would be the lowest level it could accept and still meet the previous administration's guidance. The result was the New START Treaty in which the United States sought and gained agreement limiting warheads to 1,550. Following the completion of the administration's 2010 Nuclear Policy Review and the issuance of the resulting presidential guidance, the Joint Chiefs of Staff concluded that the new guidance could be met with roughly one-third fewer strategic nuclear weapons, although it did not prove feasible to negotiate a lower limit with the Russians.

A final example of the relation between presidential guidance and force structure involves past presidents' refusal to adopt a policy of declaring no first use of nuclear weapons. Many arms control advocates favor such a policy. They also argue that the United States should declare that the sole purpose of nuclear weapons is to deter nuclear attack on the United States and its allies. Such a policy could reduce overall U.S. nuclear requirements by eliminating those nonstrategic forces maintained, in part, to support NATO missions in the event of a conventional attack (but which might require compensatory increases in strategic forces). The United States has historically rejected such policies because of concern that U.S. allies will assume that the United States has reduced its commitment to defending them against both nuclear and conventional attack.

These examples show the vital link between implementing presidential guidance and the force structure limitations acceptable in any given arms control treaty. They also illustrate that arms control is one component within an overall national security strategy, not an end in itself.

The need for adequate forces to allow construction of targeting plans (war plans) that meet presidential guidance is not the only factor influencing what constraints a state is willing to accept in formal arms control agreements. Strategic theory also plays a role. It has long been a U.S. belief that bombers and cruise missiles are inherently more stabilizing than ballistic missiles because their long time of flight makes them unsuitable for surprise attack. Thus the United States has been willing to accept counting rules that treat bombers less rigorously. This distinction is often referred to informally as the difference between "slow flyers" and "fast flyers." The United States has also justified such lenient counting rules on the grounds that bombers, unlike ballistic missiles, face significant defenses.[11]

For example, in START I, bombers equipped only with bombs and not cruise missiles were attributed with only one nuclear weapon, even though they could carry significantly more and would have done so in any wartime operation. In New START, all bombers count as a single warhead against the total limit. The Russian Federation today and the Soviet Union in the past have accepted this approach (and in New START insisted on it) not because they share the strategic theory but because they are reluctant to accept the verification inspections that must accompany a more rigid accounting of bomber weapons.

A final constraint is politics.[12] It is obvious that international negotiations are a form of international politics, but domestic politics are also involved. The shape of an agreement, the efficacy of verification, or specific trade-offs between competing objectives often involve subjective political judgments that may not reflect any consideration of nuclear operations. These judgments must reconcile congressional and executive branch perspectives as well as issues of bureaucratic politics. Two examples illustrate this. The first START had elaborate limits on test ranges, static displays of retired systems, training vehicles, and the like because of deep concern by some that the Soviets would use these systems to break out of treaty limits. By the time of New START, it had become obvious that because the Russians could not afford even the forces they were allowed under START I, they were unlikely to use such a breakout option, and so the stipulations were quietly discarded.

START I also allowed the construction on silos for new ICBMs, despite the attempts to constrain Soviet intercontinental ballistic missiles (ICBMs). Advocates for the Peacekeeper (MX) missile, including many in the U.S. Air Force, were convinced that the country would ultimately need to go beyond the fifty MX missiles existing at the time and insisted the option be preserved.

Arms Control and Crisis Stability

Throughout history, states and their military leaders have sought to prevent specific military incidents, sometimes involving loss of life, sometimes not, from escalating into major confrontations. During the Cold War, crisis prevention sought to ensure that innocuous acts of one state were not misinterpreted as hostile by a second state as well as to provide rapid, secure high-level communication to manage and defuse a crisis. Thus the United States and the Soviet Union concluded a number of agreements, of which the most important was the agreement to establish a continuously manned, secure hotline between the two capitals, providing communications that would be both secure and instantaneous, a huge challenge in that bygone era.[13]

To explicitly avoid misinterpretation, the 1991 START Treaty required advance notification of large-scale exercises involving heavy bombers and of training dispersals (exercises) of mobile ICBMs. The provisions on heavy bombers were carried over into the 2011 New START Treaty. Such notifications can avoid misperceptions, although there is always the risk that a training exercise is a cover for preparations for combat. Still, on balance, these notifications were desirable.

Yet in the real world, many crises come because of mistakes in human judgment, especially perceived conflicts of interest. Believing their adversary will not respond, states take provocative actions and then face major conflict when their judgment proves wrong. Future crisis management provisions, therefore, need more and better focus on avoiding misinterpretations and misunderstanding of reactions of other nuclear-armed states.

The Military Role in Crisis Stability

Military-to-military discussions have reduced the risk of incidents at sea, improved mutual understanding of doctrine and procedures, and managed deconfliction of military strikes in Syria. Expanded military-to-military discussions should play an important part in future crisis stability, illustrating the importance of reclaiming the concept of arms control as more than formal treaties. In an ideal world, senior military officers and civilian defense leaders on both sides would routinely discuss the risks of inadvertent escalation owing to miscalculation in crisis as well as the need to clarify ambiguities and misperceptions that could lead to such miscalculations. They would discuss perception and nuclear and conventional doctrines and would engage to avoid inadvertent military clashes and incidents, all of which could indirectly lead to conflict and escalation.

Currently, Russia and the United States do not have the kind of relationship where such robust discussions are possible. Until it becomes feasible for serving military officers to have a candid discussion of inadvertent escalation, it may be necessary to conduct such a dialogue in unofficial channels using retired senior military officers. Ideally participants would include individuals with senior leadership experience in overall strategy, European regional strategy (including the role of NATO), and strategic nuclear forces management. Selection of the right people on both sides would be crucial, as would keeping the discussions private.

Recommendations for discussions between retired officials as a substitute for government-to-government discussions are quite common. I have both advocated and participated in such discussions. Candor requires me to admit that their utility is unclear. Informal discussions have been valuable in understanding the attitudes and positions of the two sides. They have been less valuable in influencing change in those positions. Some useful ideas arise from informal discussions (reputedly, the concept of effective verification in the Cold War). But the best that can be hoped for is that informal discussions will produce ideas that can ultimately be used when government-level discussions begin. To expect more may be another example of the triumph of hope over experience.

Other Forms of Future Crisis Prevention in the Future

There is an enduring requirement for ensuring that innocuous acts are not misinterpreted as hostile by a potential adversary. While military-to-military talks should help avoid misinterpretation of conventional military actions, that alone may not be sufficient. During a crisis, one side might believe the other was seeking to facilitate a first strike by degrading crucial space assets, such as early-warning or communication satellites related to nuclear command and control. Since these systems are often dual use, attacks on them would not necessarily actually be intended as degrading nuclear capabilities but could be perceived that way. To avoid this risk, each side could prepare a list of space assets for which it would regard indications of a possible attack as potentially implying a readiness for a first strike. These lists should be exchanged and discussed and updated annually. As part of this exchange, the sides should individually identify what the relevant orbital dynamics of another space body (for example, a servicing satellite) would need to be to cause concern. Of course, such a procedure does nothing to limit the risk that a state will deliberately seek to attack space assets, but it may prevent an overreaction to innocent actions in time of crisis.

To avoid the false assumption of an imminent cyberattack, Russia and the United States could establish a standing group of cyber experts that meet at six month intervals to discuss possible intrusions into national security networks by third parties and how such intrusions might be detected and attributed. Using this group, the sides should identify what each believes would be indications of a possible preparation for first strike, including both systems and actions. Since both have an interest in preventing inadvertent escalation in crises, they have no incentive to be disingenuous in such an exchange. If one side becomes concerned during a crisis, this group should be convened in parallel with high-level diplomatic or military discussions and seek to clarify the situation. (The purpose of the routine meetings is, in large part, to familiarize the experts with each other's thinking and approach so they will be more effective in preventing misinterpretation.)[14] The obvious risk is that a side will lie during a crisis or that neither side will believe the other, in which case these provisions may be counterproductive.

Summary

Arms control has been a helpful tool for avoiding conflict owing to misunderstanding. It continues to be useful in performing that function today, but there is both a need and an opportunity for it to do more. For the more common and more concerning case of conflict arising from deliberate provocative behavior, arms control thus far has not made much difference.

Arms Control and First-Strike Stability

The term *first strike* can conjure up many images. It can suggest the Cold War concern that the Soviet Union would attempt a surprise attack in peacetime, the so-called bolt out of the blue. Prevention of this depends not on arms control but on deterrence based on the availability of credible, usable, survivable second-strike strategic forces. First strike could also suggest the initial use of nuclear weapons as a deliberate step in a conventional conflict. This section deals with this second aspect of first strike. It examines how the ability to conduct attacks, both nuclear and non-nuclear, on strategic forces and capabilities could threaten stability and what, if anything, arms control might contribute to mitigating that threat.

Discouraging Nuclear Attack

In time of great crisis, particularly if conventional hostilities are already ongoing, each side will fear that the other side is considering nuclear weapons use and will, perhaps, believe that it can limit the damage to itself by striking first. Operationally, the United States and Russia have used two techniques to deter such a first strike. First, they maintain nuclear forces that include an element deemed invulnerable to attack: ballistic missile submarines (SSBNs) and, for Russia and the Soviet Union, difficult-to-locate (and thus to target) land-based mobile missiles. Second, they maintain the ability to launch a portion of their ballistic missile force before incoming warheads can arrive. This launch-under-attack posture applies to ICBMs and perhaps to Soviet/Russian ballistic missile submarines in port. During the Cold War, the United States kept a portion of the bomber force fully loaded with nuclear weapons and ready to take off on short notice to ensure survivability.[15] Although this practice was discontinued after the Cold War, the United States maintains the ability to resume it. (These launches were performed only to assure the survivability of the bomber force; actual strikes would have required additional authorization.)

From the earliest days of the Cold War through today, the United States has considered it necessary to guard against a massive surprise attack in peacetime, the so-called bolt-out-of-the-blue disarming attack. During the Cold War, many believed the Soviet Union might actually be planning such an attack, although most now understand that, at least by the last decades of the Cold War, this concern had more to do with historical memories of Pearl Harbor than with any actual Russian war planning. Because such an attack remains a possibility, as a matter of prudence the United States continues to guard against it, primarily by maintaining much of its operational ballistic missile submarine force (which carries the bulk of the strategic deterrent) in survivable operations at sea.

A major challenge to first-strike stability was highly fractionated ICBMs carrying multiple, independently targetable reentry vehicles (MIRVs). (In such systems, each warhead can be directed at a separate target.) One or two warheads could destroy such an ICBM, which, if allowed to launch, can destroy many targets. This increases the pressure to shoot first in time of great tension. The historic arms control solution for this problem has been to ban or at least limit the number of ICBMs carrying multiple warheads. Except for START II (which never entered into force), no arms control treaty has been successful in implementing this approach. This is because of the historic great dependence of Russia and the Soviet Union on warheads on highly MIRVed ICBMs.

In the 1987 volume that inspired the present work, Michael M. May and John R. Harvey suggest that arms control agreements should seek to "encourage development of survivable basing modes, particularly in their day-to-day alert configurations."[16] This suggestion was never implemented, perhaps because of the continuing but ultimately unsuccessful pursuit of restrictions on heavily MIRVed ICBMs. It deserves to be reconsidered, perhaps by establishing counting rules that treat mobile ICBMs less stringently than fixed ICBMs, in the same way that Cold War treaties treated bomber weapons less stringently than ballistic missile warheads.

Submarine Attacks on ICBMs

During much of the Cold War, submarine-launched ballistic missiles lacked the accuracy to attack hardened silos. As the accuracy of such missiles improved, however, they gained the capability to threaten hardened targets, such as silos or command-and-control facilities. Furthermore, submarine-launched ballistic missiles operating near an adversary's shores can have a much shorter time of flight than ICBMs. Their shorter time of flight made timely response such as launch under attack more difficult. Some arms control analysts in both the United States and the Soviet Union feared that this increased the attractiveness of a first strike, thus decreasing first-strike stability. One proposal was to require that each party keep its ballistic missile submarines outside some fixed distance from the other's shore. Although discussed informally, this never became a serious proposal, because there was no way of verifying compliance with the obligation that did not, in the judgment of the U.S. Navy, involve an unacceptable operational risk to SSBN survivability.

Conventional Attacks on ICBMs

With the deployment of long-range non-nuclear strike capabilities, Russian experts have expressed concern that a first strike on Russia's strategic missile assets and, perhaps, their command and control could be conducted by non-nuclear means. They have suggested the need for an arms control solution—for example, banning long-range conventional strike weapons carried on both ballistic and cruise missiles. The Russians fear that a large-scale conventional cruise missile attack could go undetected and cause substantial damage to their strategic forces.

The United States believes these concerns are overwrought. Most U.S. analysts (myself included) assess the prospects of serious damage to a hardened target (such as a silo) by an individual conventionally armed cruise missile as quite small. Thus an attack would need to involve hundreds, or even thousands, of such missiles, which would need to be carefully coordinated to ensure they arrived at their designated targets simultaneously, since a single detection en route or a single detonation before the bulk of the missiles had arrived would alert Russia to the fact that it was under attack and thus allow a launch of all Russian ICBMs. It is difficult to believe any rational U.S. leader would risk national survival on such an attack.

The United States has sought to conduct unofficial technical discussions with the Russian federation to explain the improbability of such an attack, especially with cruise missiles. Many Russian experts understand this. It is not clear whether the Russian government itself is concerned or whether this is simply a debating point. It has, however, been a stated Russian concern for decades. Large-scale conventional cruise missile attack is an excellent example of where military-to-military discussions could help alleviate a potential concern.

Attacks from Space on ICBMs

For decades, Soviets and now Russians have complained about what they call "space strike weapons," that is, weapons designed to attack targets on the surface of the globe from orbit by deorbiting high-density rods and using the resultant kinetic energy to destroy terrestrial targets, including silos. The idea of such weapons originated in the 1950s and is periodically rediscovered but has never passed beyond the conceptual phase in the United States. The concept was sometimes referred to informally as involving "rods from God."[17]

Historically, the Russian Federation has sought to deal with space-strike weapons through sweeping treaties claiming to prevent an arms race in outer space. The United States has rejected these attempts as unverifiable approaches that would (and probably are intended to) unacceptably constrain U.S. ballistic missile defense and space control programs.[18] It is unclear how serious the concern with space-strike weapons actually is for the Russian government, but to meet the Russian concerns the two sides could agree to ban the testing and deployment of space-strike weapons, to be verified by national technical means (NTM) (an arms control euphemism for intelligence gathering). Space-strike weapons require the ability to deorbit a high-density object and have it strike relatively close to the intended target. While deorbiting might be done without detection, for space-strike weapons to destroy strategic targets they would need to be highly accurate. Developing such accuracy implies a test range that would be detectable.

Attacks on Mobile ICBMs

Systems that are difficult to target and thus less susceptible to a first strike are generally seen as stabilizing. If mobile ICBMs made up the bulk of the survivable second-strike forces of a country, attempts to gain the ability to track and attack such ICBMs could be destabilizing. This is, in many ways, the situation China (and to some extent Russia) faces today. In theory, the United States could unilaterally decide to avoid developing the capability to attack such mobile missiles, thereby increasing strategic stability. That such a proposal has never been seriously considered illustrates two important limitations to the ability of arms control to restrict nuclear operations: First, capabilities that have broad application (such as the ability to attack mobile targets) are unlikely to be constrained under arms control (restricting submarine operations, discussed below, is another example). Second, in debating the choice between improving strategic stability in wartime and improving military effectiveness, improving military effectiveness almost always wins. A plausible explanation is that professional military culture is more likely to value its ability to meet wartime objectives than to favor an abstract concept such as strategic stability. Since a treaty not supported by the Joint Chiefs of Staff has little prospect for Senate advice and consent, there is a tendency to defer to the professional military on major negotiating proposals. It is my impression from extensive dialogue with Russian experts, including those in the military, that a similar dynamic exists in Russia.

National Ballistic Missile Defense

In the late 1960s, many in the United States came to believe that ballistic missile defense of the entire homeland of either the United States or the Soviet Union was dangerous because it might cause one side to believe it could attack the other and absorb the subsequent retaliatory strike. On the other hand, defending national capitals, where decisions would be made, and defending the actual strategic deterrent itself was stabilizing, since it reduced the chance that either side would attempt an attack. It is important to understand that this was not a decision to leave the American people unprotected. Instead, it was a belief, almost certainly accurate, that the technology of the time did not permit a national defense that would be effective enough to prevent a devastating attack.

The result of this line of thinking was the Anti-Ballistic Missile (ABM) Treaty of 1972. The initial treaty allowed defense of two sites by no more than 100 interceptors each. One site would defend the nation's capital, while the other site would defend a single field of ICBM silos within a radius of 150 kilometers. In 1974 the treaty was amended to allow only defense of a single site, with each side able to select what it would defend. Russia chose to defend Moscow, while the United States deployed 100 nuclear-tipped interceptors in North Dakota to protect a portion of the U.S. ICBM force in a complex program called Safeguard. The Safeguard system achieved full operational capability in 1975 but was almost immediately closed at the direction of Congress for cost and effectiveness reasons.[19] In contrast, the Moscow ABM system remains operational to the present date, although with only about 65 interceptors.

Thus throughout the Cold War and until the collapse of the Soviet Union, strategic ballistic missile defenses were limited and did not affect overall strategic stability. The Reagan administration embarked on a Strategic Defense Initiative (SDI) that would shift the basis of deterrence to defense. Although the Soviets were fearful, technical and fiscal challenges limited progress, and the effort faded with the end of the Cold War.

Following the demise of the Soviet Union, many U.S. analysts and policymakers became concerned with the need for a limited national defense, both to deal with unauthorized or accidental use and to counter a growing ballistic missile threat from so-called rogue states—Iran, Iraq, and North Korea. The concept was referred to as Global Protection against Limited Strikes. Such a limited defense would not have required exceeding the ABM Treaty limit of 100 interceptors but was inconsistent with the treaty's mandate against defense of the entire national territory.

Attempts were made by the Clinton administration to negotiate a demarcation agreement, which would allow for some deployments of systems against the rogue-state threat. Russia was unwilling to agree. When it entered office in 2001, the George W. Bush administration (many of whose members had been strong supporters of the strategic defense initiative) immediately moved to withdraw from the ABM Treaty to deploy a defense against rogue states (but not against Russian ICBMs). It announced a national missile defense program based primarily on ground-based, midcourse interceptors deployed in Fort Greely, Alaska, with four at Vandenberg Air Force Base, in California. The total number of interceptors, initially thirty-four, has since been increased to forty-four, with plans to increase to sixty-four (all of the increase has been in Alaska). Future issues associated with this decision are discussed below.

Accidental or Unauthorized Launch

Rather than dealing with the problem of accidental or unauthorized launch through ballistic missile defenses (an initial mission for the Global Protection against Limited Strikes system), Russia and the United States agreed in January 1994 to detarget their strategic missiles. As the White House press statement described the agreement,

> The Presidents announced that they will direct the detargeting of strategic nuclear missiles under their respective commands. This means that by May 30, 1994, no country will be targeted by the strategic forces of either side. . . . Intercontinental and submarine-launched ballistic missiles are capable of being launched against one of several targets or sets of targets stored in weapon system computers. Historically, a target setting associated with actual war plans had been the routine alert assignment of U.S. missile systems. Detargeting will involve changing weapon-system control settings so that on a day-to-day basis no country . . . will be targeted by U.S. strategic forces. Russia has told the United States that their detargeting measures are comparable.
>
> For three of the four U.S. strategic missile systems—the Trident I, Trident II, and Peacekeeper—the missiles will contain no targeting information. The older-technology Minuteman III missile computers, which require a constant alignment reference, will be set to ocean-area targets.[20]

Because China did not keep any of its strategic ballistic missiles on alert, this agreement essentially removed the concern with unauthorized launch. It remains in effect today. It is an example of an arms control agreement made with no formal written text, simply by agreement between two states.

Attacking SSBNs

The most fundamental requirement of first-strike stability is a secure second-strike capability. For the United States, the Soviet Union, and, to a somewhat lesser degree, Russia, ballistic missile submarines provide a major portion of that capability. Thus the ability to threaten the survival of the entire SSBN force would risk major destabilization. It is unrealistic to assume that if a U.S. or Russian warship encounters a ballistic missile submarine of the other navy in time of war, it will not seek to destroy it. Ballistic missile submarines have a self-defense capability that could threaten opposing ships and submarines. At the tactical level, the navy has always believed that a key to victory lies in the motto "attack effectively first." What would be of major concern, however, would be the ability to threaten the entire deployed ballistic submarine force.

In the early days of the Cold War, the short range of submarine-launched ballistic missiles meant that submarines had to operate far from their home ports and close to the territory of their adversary. Early Polaris submarines, for example, operated off the northern coast of Norway to be able to hold Soviet targets at risk. As missile range increased, however, states were faced with two options. They could use the extended range to allow their submarines to patrol in the vast open ocean, where they were largely immune to detection. This was the option selected by the United States, the United Kingdom, and France. Since there is currently no credible threat to a ballistic missile submarine operating in the open ocean, there is no stability issue and thus no need to devise an arms control solution.[21]

The Soviet Union and now Russia took another course. They used the longer range of their missiles to allow them to patrol in bastions near Soviet territory, protected by much of the rest of the Russian Navy, including Soviet attack submarines. The Soviet term for this was "providing combat stability to the ballistic missile submarine force." The decision recognized the growing U.S. superiority in anti-submarine warfare (ASW). Patrolling in bastions also alleviated Soviet concerns with reliable command and control.

In the mid-1980s, the U.S. Navy developed a concept called the Maritime Strategy for use during a war with the Soviet Union. It would use operations on the NATO and Pacific flanks to defend allies, sinking the Soviet Navy wherever it was and not leaving allies such as Norway, Japan, or South Korea unprotected. The attacks would include the forces protecting SSBNs, forcing the Russian Navy to remain in a defensive position, making it easier for NATO to maintain the sea lanes to Europe for resupply of NATO military operations.

The navy leadership accepted the view of a few analysts that there was strategic utility and only limited risk in actually destroying Russian ballistic missile submarines. The notion was that slow destruction of SSBNs would not cause nuclear escalation (no one SSBN being that important) but would alter the overall nuclear balance and induce caution. This view became part of a public debate around the Maritime Strategy in general and the question of attacking SSBNs in particular.[22] Most of the academic community feared that the navy's approach would lead to uncontrolled escalation. The Soviets, not unexpectedly, were quite negative.

From my service on the navy staff at the time, I believe that most operational leaders did not place particular value on actually sinking Soviet ballistic missile submarines. A recent book by the main civilian exponent of the maritime strategy, navy secretary John Lehman, does not mention the term *ballistic missile submarine*.[23]

For those concerned with attacking SSBNs, two arms control solutions were available: a so-called ASW-free zone within the Soviet bastions and informal restraint in declining to conduct operations there. The Soviets had been advocating ASW-free zones as part of a series of naval arms control proposals unacceptable to the U.S. government, in part, because of strong navy opposition.[24] The navy noted that submarines and surface ships equipped for ASW had multiple missions, and it was unrealistic to exclude them from areas important to the outcome of a conflict. Since the navy had resolved the issue of uncontrolled escalation to its satisfaction after significant internal debate and analysis, the flurry of concern in the academic community was largely ignored inside the military. The question of whether the United States should refrain from conducting such operations became moot with the end of the Cold War.

The issue may arise again, however, in the future. China appears to be in the early stages of moving to a major role for ballistic missile submarines in its overall nuclear deterrent, although the rationale for the decision is not entirely clear. When it has acquired sea-based ballistic missiles of significant range, China apparently plans to operate them in protected bastions.[25] The United States will then face the issue of whether to plan on attacking those submarines during the conventional phase of a hypothetical future war. Unlike the Soviet case, pinning down general-purpose Chinese navy forces will be less important (the main threat to navy operations is land-based ballistic missiles). At the same time, the escalatory risks may be greater, since each Chinese SSBN is a larger fraction of its strategic nuclear capability than was the case in the Soviet situation. Because ASW forces, especially submarines, have missions unrelated to SSBNs, ASW-free zones will almost certainly remain militarily unacceptable; strategic restraint may not. Such restraint should be a national decision, not simply a military one. Some would argue it should be communicated informally to the Chinese leadership to reduce the chance of miscalculation.

Attacking Command and Control

Not all challenges to strategic stability can be helped by arms control. As part of a deliberate attack, an adversary might seek to kill the president (the only individual who could authorize a retaliatory response), a tactic called decapitation, or to so degrade the system for transmitting launch authorization that any authorized response order was delayed while authorization for retaliation was sought from the legally designated presidential successor. The purpose would be for an adversary to limit damage to itself by denying any immediate U.S. retaliatory strikes until most U.S. land capability had been destroyed. The presumed hope would be that the threat of further destruction (such as to undamaged cities) would then induce the United States to end hostilities once effective command and control was restored. Arms control can reduce the attractiveness of such a tactic by reducing damage limitation capabilities and preserving a survivable second-strike capability. It has limited direct relevance, however, to preventing such an act of desperation.

There could be a specific area in which arms control might play a modest role. The Soviet Union was obsessed with the prospect of a short-time-of-flight attack on Moscow, which could degrade their national command-and-control system. In particular, Pershing II, with its six-minute flight time from West Germany, terrified the Soviets. Deployment of ballistic missiles or hypersonic boost-glide vehicles on the territory of the Central European NATO allies could result in a time of flight to Moscow as short as four minutes. The Russian Federation would almost certainly see this as destabilizing, whether the weapons were nuclear or conventionally armed (worst-case planners would assume that even if deployed with conventional warheads they could be surreptitiously equipped with nuclear warheads). There might, therefore, be an opportunity to limit or ban such deployments as part of some overall future arms control package with Russia.[26]

A similar concern arose on the U.S. side during the Cold War. As noted, the United States was deeply concerned with the prospect of a sudden Soviet attack in peacetime. Experts calculated that if one of the commonly deployed Russian submarine missiles, the SS-N-6 SLBM with a 3,000-kilometer maximum range, flew a depressed trajectory of about 1,500 kilometers, it could cut four to five minutes off a minimum energy trajectory flight time of about eleven minutes. As a result, many analysts advocate seeking a ban on depressed trajectory flight tests.[27] President Carter proposed such to the Soviets in June 1979, but they did not respond, and the United States did not pursue the topic, although it never tested such trajectories.[28]

Limited Employment Scenarios

During the Cold War, U.S. policymakers assumed that any nuclear use would be on a large scale or would quickly become large scale.[29] Cold War arms control practitioners did not develop any significant approaches to limiting use of one or a few single nuclear weapons.[30] It was assumed that the fear of escalation would make such an approach highly dangerous and therefore uninteresting. In the post–Cold War world, however, many believe that Russia might use a small number of nuclear weapons (perhaps no more than one) if it were involved in a conventional conflict that was going badly.[31] The idea would be to shock its adversary, presumably NATO, into ceasing the conflict on relatively favorable terms to Russia.[32] (This Russia strategy is often called "escalate to deescalate," but the term should be avoided, since it leads to unproductive debates over whether the Russian Federation has or ever had a formal doctrine of that name.) In any case, it has the capability and probably the plans today.

Other rationales for limited uses exist. The Joint Chiefs of Staff publication on nuclear operations states that "adversary nuclear weapon employment could be the result of perceived failure in a conventional campaign, potential loss of control, or perceived threat to regime survival or to escalate the conflict to sue for peace on more-favorable terms. The potential consequences of using nuclear weapons will greatly influence military operations and vastly increase the complexity of the operational environment."[33] Others argue that such an attack or the threat of such an attack might be made by an adversary for whom things were going well to coerce the victim and its potential allies to accept the fait accompli without further resistance.

In responding to such actions, the United States might seek to restore deterrence by responding with a similar limited use. The risk of tit-for-tat response leading to large-scale nuclear exchange is obvious. Thus far, however, the United States has no arms control approach for dealing with such a problem. Instead, it focuses on emphasizing the dangers that escalation cannot be managed after even a limited crossing of the nuclear threshold. Considering arms control as including military-to-military discussions does suggest an arms control approach. Discussing the risks inherent in such a situation between professional military leaders could result in both a deeper understanding of the risks and, perhaps, a mechanism to mitigate those risks. To make these discussions fruitful, they would need to be well prepared, with internal consideration of both risks and options for mitigation (if any).

Summary

Eliminating ICBMs with multiple warheads, the most important arms control objective for maintaining first-strike stability, has not been accomplished, despite decades of effort. The brief exception represented by START

II resulted from unique circumstances of euphoria on both sides following the collapse of the Soviet Union. Both Russia and the United States envisioned a future of partnership rather than confrontation. This euphoria did not last and is unlikely to recur. While other arms control proposals to improve first-strike stability have been made, all have faltered. It appears clear historically that military effectiveness normally prevails over arms control stability objectives.[34] The assumption that enhanced military effectiveness is inevitably superior to arms control measures in advancing national security has not been seriously debated within government. It may be erroneous and should be carefully reviewed in future treaties, including the follow-on to New START.

Arms Race Stability

Arms race stability is, in principle, the easiest to demonstrate of any of the desirable strategic stability attributes. Arms race stability, however, will only be attained if the agreements are actually complied with and both sides have confidence in that fact. This underscores the importance of a verification regime.

Limiting (and ultimately reversing) the buildup of nuclear arms was an important initial motivation for arms control and has arguably been its most important accomplishment. Viewed through American eyes, the Soviet Union seemed gripped by an insatiable desire for more nuclear weapons and their delivery systems. As Harold Brown, secretary of defense in the Carter administration, has frequently been quoted as observing, "When we build, they build. When we stop, they build."[35] Those days are gone, but the possibility of a slow arms race remains. Both sides have a de facto policy of maintaining rough strategic parity with the other country. In particular, the U.S. policy of maintaining strategic nuclear forces that are second to none contributes to reassuring U.S. allies that extended deterrence remains credible. Strategic arms control allows maintaining approximate parity without reigniting an arms race.

Assuming compliance, one significant challenge to arms race stability today is the deployment of exotic systems not covered by the terms of an existing treaty (referred to in strategic arms control treaties as "new kinds" of strategic offensive arms). Although we speak of strategic arms control, there has never been an agreed definition of strategic arms. As a result, treaties typically limit ICBMs, SLBMs, and heavy bombers. Each of these terms has a detailed definition.[36] Difficulties arise when one side develops exotic systems, such as those announced by President Putin in 2017, including a nuclear-powered intercontinental-range cruise missile, a hypersonic boost-glide vehicle that did not meet the definition of a ballistic missile, and an intercontinental-range torpedo.[37]

Even if these systems are ultimately brought into an arms control regime (as is probable if they are actually deployed), they represent a failure of arms race stability. President Putin stressed that their deployment was a response to the (nonexistent) U.S. anti-Russian ballistic missile defense.

Strategic-arms control treaties provide that such systems be discussed within the treaties' compliance body to determine whether and how they will be incorporated into the treaty. (Assuming political agreement, incorporating these exotic systems into a future treaty should be technically easy. Each has a launcher, a delivery vehicle, and a warhead. They thus fit nicely into traditional treaty structures.) Provisions on so-called new kinds of strategic arms date from the first START Treaty in 1991, when the United States assumed that it would be the source of any innovation. Fearing to give the Soviet Union a veto over new deployments, the United States provided that if agreement could not be reached on how to handle an exotic system, deployment could proceed at the discretion of the party that had developed the new system. The United States has interpreted existing provisions on new kinds of strategic arms as requiring that those that are nuclear armed must be included in an existing treaty, while similar systems carrying non-nuclear warheads need not be included. The Russians have never formally accepted this distinction.

A more significant challenge to arms race stability is the existence of so-called nonstrategic nuclear weapons, a term invented to include battlefield and theater weapons and now generally used to identify weapons not subject to any arms control agreement. The term is unfortunate but common; any use of a nuclear weapon will be strategic under any meaningful definition of the word.

Russia has about 2,000 nonstrategic nuclear weapons. About half of these are for naval forces (anti-submarine weapons, air defense weapons, nuclear torpedoes, and various cruise missiles). Land-based weapons include short- and medium-range missiles, coastal defense weapons, air defense weapons, ballistic missile warheads for the Moscow ABM system, and both air-to-surface missiles and bombs for land-based tactical aircraft.[38] In contrast, the United States has only a relatively small number of tactical bombs, some of which are stored in Europe for potential use in NATO nuclear missions.

While strategic weapons can be controlled by limiting the number of delivery systems, this approach will not work for nonstrategic nuclear weapons. Their delivery systems are almost always dual purpose. Therefore, it has long been the view of U.S. analysts that the best way to control such weapons is to limit the total number of nuclear weapons a side possesses, with a sublimit on deployed strategic weapons. Verifying such an approach would be challenging and would almost certainly imply more stringent procedures and more extensive access than any previous agreement.[39] The Russian Federation has historically rejected such an approach, in part because they are unwilling to accept the intrusive verification required.[40]

Failing to deal with this issue is a significant problem for many in the United States, who find it politically and strategically unacceptable for those nuclear weapons of which the United States has a robust arsenal to be constrained by arms control while a different set of nuclear weapons, in which the Russian Federation has a significant advantage, are subject to no limitations. Russian nonstrategic nuclear weapons are also a particular concern because of their threat to U.S. forces in Europe and to America's NATO allies.

Although the best solution to concerns with nonstrategic nuclear weapons would be an aggregate warhead limit on all warheads, if this proved infeasible, Russia and the United States could agree to exchange information annually on the total numbers of so-called nonstrategic nuclear weapons each side possesses, on the types of those weapons (bombs, air defense, cruise missiles, and so forth), and on where such weapons were normally deployed (in general, not specific terms).[41] Such exchanges could reduce uncertainty and worst-case planning. Their principal value, however, would be as a stepping-stone to more formal limits.

It might also be possible to negotiate the elimination of certain types of nonstrategic nuclear weapons. In particular, ground-launched ballistic and cruise missiles with ranges between 500 and 5,500 kilometers were banned by the now-defunct Intermediate-Range Nuclear Forces (INF) Treaty and are now unconstrained. Both Russia and the United States appear interested in some form of regulation of such missiles, especially those with nuclear warhead delivery capability.

The effect on nuclear operations of any agreement on nonstrategic nuclear weapons depends on the details. Most disruptive would be a provision that allows inspections of large storage facilities, such as the Atlantic and Pacific Trident Strategic Weapons Facilities and the large Kirtland Underground Munitions Maintenance and Storage Complex in New Mexico. The Kirtland facility is the largest nuclear weapons storage facility in the United States. It contains both active weapons and weapons awaiting dismantlement. The effect on nuclear operations of having to implement a regime to distinguish between the two is uncertain but likely to be considerable. For their part, Russians have consistently objected to access to their own large storage facilities. Thus reaching agreement is likely to be difficult and contentious and may have significant operational impact.

Verification and Nuclear Operations

Arms control agreements are of limited value unless each side is convinced that the other side is adhering to the agreement. Most of the time spent in arms control negotiations is taken up by verification details. In the United States, the practice is to deal with verification at the same time as we deal with specific restrictions.

It is important to be clear on terminology. There are three broad concepts used to describe the process of ensuring treaties are being adhered to.

Monitoring is a process of gathering objective data. For example, intelligence monitoring may reveal the numbers of systems and their dimensions. Inspection monitors also provide a report of what they observed. Monitoring does not involve judgment; it simply involves gathering data.

Verification is a policy process. It takes the data gathered by monitoring and applies policy judgments to it. For example, verification judgments could consider the past record of a state, reported public statements or disclosures, the general state of relations in the political and military arenas, and similar data. Verification judgments are normally made through some form of interagency process.

Compliance is a condition in which a state is meeting its treaty obligations. The United States normally expresses its judgments in terms of verifying compliance. It only speaks in terms of violation for serious issues. An annual report from the Department of State covers both U.S. compliance and foreign compliance with all existing arms control treaties. This report exists in both classified and unclassified versions, with the unclassified version widely available. Because it is entirely within U.S. control and because of its unique capabilities, the most important (and preferred) way of verifying compliance is through national technical means. Arms control treaties routinely include the obligation not to interfere with NTM. This goes back to the ABM Treaty of 1972 and was aimed at interference with satellites and radars. Cooperative measures are designed to assist NTM, for example by requiring destroyed silos to remain visible for a fixed period or by requiring that mobile missiles at operating base be displayed in the open by opening the garage roofs on short notice in order to verify their location.

NTM, while ideal, is not by itself sufficient to provide all of the information needed to make compliance judgments. A listing of the most important additional verification techniques follows. I have listed these techniques separately but in practice they work together to reinforce one another. For an example of the practical difficulties in negotiating a verification regime, see the account by Rose Gottemoeller, who served as chief negotiator for New START in *Negotiating the New START Treaty*.[42]

Data exchange refers to each side providing detailed information on the numbers (and in some cases locations) of force limited by a particular treaty. With the exception of the 2002 Treaty of Moscow, all post–Cold War arms control treaties have included comprehensive periodic data exchanges, updated continually by an elaborate series of notifications. This aids verification in two ways. First, it is difficult to tell a consistent large-scale lie, and thus the data exchange is usually accurate. Second, these data form the basis for inspections, which validate that the exchanged data are consistent with what is actually present on the ground.

Inspections allow verification of the accuracy of the data the parties have exchanged. Some information (the number of warheads on a specific missile, the number of attachment joints for cruise missiles on a specific bomber, whether facilities declared to have no strategic arms are actually empty) can only be verified by on-the-ground inspections. Such inspections are also used to confirm the data exchange between the sides, as described above.

Remote monitoring has been extensively used in monitoring safeguards agreements between individual countries and the International Atomic Energy Agency, although it has not been used in strategic arms control treaties to date. The techniques used could be relevant to the monitoring of individual warhead storage facilities were that to be included in a future treaty.[43]

Initial displays of new equipment covered by a strategic arms control treaty allow the inspecting side to observe the equipment, make appropriate measurements, and take appropriate photographs. This aids in further inspections and in NTM monitoring.

Monitored destruction allows the parties to verify the destruction and conversion of designated weaponry and equipment. For military equipment for which conversion or elimination cannot be monitored by NTM, treaties provide that destruction and conversion be conducted in the presence of inspectors from the other side. This provision was used extensively for the destruction of launchers under the INF Treaty.

The verification techniques included in a treaty should be those needed to verify the obligations assumed. The absence of a particular verification technique used in an earlier treaty may or may not have any meaning. For example, the 1991 START Treaty employed an elaborate concept called perimeter portal continuous monitoring to verify the number of missiles produced at a specific facility. This was necessary because START limited the number of mobile missiles that either side could possess. The 2011 New START Treaty contained no restrictions on the number of such missiles a side could possess and therefore dropped this monitoring system. This step was erroneously seen by critics as reducing the quality or importance of U.S. verification.

Many political leaders expect that arms control agreements should be enforceable. This sounds wise but actually displays a misunderstanding of geopolitical reality. The only international entity with the legal authority to enforce agreements between states is the United Nations Security Council. But as a practical matter, the Security Council cannot take enforcement action against one of the five permanent members. Thus any treaty with Russia or China cannot in practice be legally enforced.

Instead of depending on external enforcement to deal with violation of arms control agreements, the United States uses the concept of treaties being effectively verifiable. *Effective verification,* a term originating in the 1980s, means that violations can be detected in time for the United States to take effective action to deny the violator the benefits of any violation. This obviously requires that the United States maintain the latent ability to take action to restore the military balance if violations occur.

Requirements for verification have a minor but noticeable impact on nuclear operations. Inspections are usually allowed at short notice, which means, for example, that a ballistic missile submarine preparing to go on patrol might be delayed while an inspection is conducted. While not legally required, it is often the practice to shut down operations at a facility during an inspection. This is both to prevent inadvertent or deliberate intelligence gathering by the inspecting team and also simply a matter of administrative convenience. In theory, cooperative measures could affect operations, but there are no good U.S. examples, since START cooperative measures for the United States involved only destroyed systems. Under START I, Russia was periodically required to open garage roofs for mobile ICBM garages on short notice and display the missile transporter erector launchers stored under them. This may have resulted in some operational problems, but there is no public record of the fact.

The reason verification procedures have not resulted in a significant operational impact is that the military services were deeply involved in drafting and preparing them. Procedures that would have a significant operational effect were, therefore, simply never proposed by the United States. Examples include ASW free zones and submarine standoff zones and the historical navy resistance to limits on sea-launched cruise missiles. While this may have made individual treaties less comprehensive, overall national security was improved. This is an example of the dictum that arms control is not an end in itself but a means to enhance national security.

Because actual drafting is done by the negotiating teams, it is important that those teams have individuals with the relevant operational experience. Two examples from my personal experience as the chief negotiator of first START Treaty illustrate this point. In the first, the negotiating team was drafting language on exercises involving heavy bombers. A relatively junior air force officer assigned to the delegation pointed out that the draft would have required the Strategic Air Command to alter the conduct of some of its major training exercises. The draft was quietly changed.

In a less happy illustration, procedures for shipping stages of the Trident II missile were developed, tabled, agreed to by the Russians, and included in the final treaty. Unfortunately, the procedures were unworkable, given the actual design of Trident shipping containers. While this stipulation was corrected by the Joint Compliance and Implementation Commission, it remains an illustration of the importance of operational knowledge within negotiating teams as well as during the initial drafting in capitals of proposed verification measures.[44]

Current and Future Challenges to Strategic Stability

During the Cold War, the nuclear balance could be assessed largely without reference to other forms of warfare. Ballistic missile defense had been banned by the Anti-Ballistic Missile Treaty of 1972. Conventional capability to damage strategic assets was limited to anti-submarine warfare and air defenses, both of which were well understood. In contrast, today there are significant interactions between nuclear operations and the new war-fighting domains of space and cyberspace. These interactions are not well understood, and, with a few exceptions, arms control approaches for space and cyberspace are not well thought out.

Space

Space is vital for nuclear operations. Space-based assets provide early warning. Space-based communications are an important part of nuclear command and control. Space-based battle damage assessment is an important component of the ability to conduct actual nuclear operations. It is therefore in the interest of both Russia and the United States that there be no interference with those space assets. At the same time, space is probably more crucial to overall U.S. military operations than to the operations of any other state. Consequently, the United States must be prepared to protect its space assets against military attack. This requires both offensive and defensive space control capabilities. The United States has been unwilling to participate in any discussions that could lead to any limitation on space control capabilities, which are generally highly classified and thus would be difficult to discuss in any event.

The Russian Federation has been particularly concerned with the possibility of space-based missile defense, as was proposed in the 1980s under President Reagan's strategic defense initiative. Many U.S. experts believed that the ambitious space-based defenses proposed under that initiative but largely abandoned at the end of the Cold War were impractical and unaffordable. Others argued that the technology was simply immature. Soviets and later Russians (who typically have an exaggerated regard for American technology) believed that such systems were feasible and urged that they be banned. Some in the United States believe that the country is unlikely to be able to afford to deploy such defenses and would therefore lose nothing by banning them, at least for some limited period (for example, ten years). The U.S. government has consistently rejected such ideas in the past. In discussions, Russian proposals often include bans on research. The United States generally rejects the notion of limiting militarily relevant research.

In addition to the provisions to avoid inadvertent crossing of red lines in space discussed earlier and to ban space-strike weapons, there is one other possible arms control provision that has occasionally been considered. Some have argued that testing and deployment of direct-ascent anti-satellite weapons (that is, weapons launched from the earth's surface to destroy satellites in low earth orbit) should be banned. The United States, China, and Russia have each demonstrated the capability for such weapons. Because banning such weapons would do nothing to mitigate against the threat to satellites from cyber weapons, and because it would be difficult to distinguish between weapons designed for regional ballistic missile defense and direct-ascent anti-satellite weapons, this idea has generally not found favor in the past, although there is some current interest in banning such tests to avoid generation of space debris. A further problem is that some strategically critical satellite capabilities rely on a small number of complex and expensive satellites. A limited number of concealed interceptors could create a serious risk. Banning deployment of such a small number of deployed systems appears impractical.

Cyberspace

If the difficulties in applying arms control concepts in the space domain are significant, they pale in comparison with the difficulty of any form of arms control in cyberspace. Neither side has any meaningful concept of how, if at all, arms control might be applied in the cyber domain, and many believe it to be impossible. One logical idea would be to establish a norm (almost certainly not effectively verifiable) that the sides will refrain from attacking nuclear command and control.[45] Discussions of such norms could, at a minimum, help parties recognize the risks in crossing the boundaries being discussed. It may also be useful to implement some form of the procedures discussed earlier for avoiding misunderstanding that a cyberattack is imminent.

Future Challenges

It is impossible to predict what new technologies may emerge that could alter the approach to nuclear operations. One likely candidate is artificial intelligence. There is general agreement in the United States that the decision to launch nuclear weapons should not be made by any form of artificial intelligence but must remain subject to human judgments. Artificial intelligence is expected to play a major role in assembling the data to assist in decisionmaking. This may involve some risks. An artificial intelligence program learned the fiendishly complex Japanese and Chinese game of Go by repeatedly playing against itself until it evolved well enough to beat a human grand master. The approach it took was one no human player would use or understand. Since artificial intelligence by its very nature will evolve, using it as a decision aid means that decisionmakers will not know the actual rationale for how information is presented and what data has been discarded or given a low priority.

A second example: Although the United States is moving rapidly to expand its use of unmanned armed vehicles both at sea and in the air, most analysts believe that anything that delivers a nuclear weapon must include a human in the loop. Probably it is in the U.S. interest to have a similar understanding about the role of humans in nuclear execution and delivery within the minds of potential adversaries, especially Russia and China. There does not appear to be any role for binding rules, but norms, developed through thoughtful strategic stability discussions with Russia and, perhaps, China, including with the uniformed military on both sides, may have value.

A somewhat different technical development would be advances in technology that make a formally unfeasible concept feasible.[46] The most striking example would involve space-based defenses with the ability to significantly thwart a ballistic missile attack, as was envisioned by the Strategic Defense Initiative of the 1980s. What might be the operational response to such a deployment? An initial response might be to simply increase the number of ballistic missile warheads. If it became possible to intercept half of all incoming warheads, doubling the number in the original will ensure targeting objectives are met. This can rapidly become a formula for an arms race, the "winner" of which will depend on the relative costs of adding warheads and adding interceptors.

China has traditionally taken the view that it will increase the size of its force to compensate for United States ballistic missile defense. This does not lead to an arms race only because the United States does not size its national listing missile defense to counter China.

Unlike other nuclear powers, the United States would have the ability to compensate by increasing the number of bombers on alert, although this would come with significant costs, both in conventional missions forgone and in the need for more aviators, more tankers, and more resources for maintaining alert. The assumption is that the threat to ballistic missile forces would be seen as so severe that the additional resources would be forthcoming.

The Russian Federation has already faced this issue because of President Putin's (erroneous) belief that existing U.S. ballistic missile defenses threaten Russia's ability to retaliate. In his 2017 address to the Federation Council, he announced several exotic systems designed to evade ballistic missile defenses (discussed earlier in this chapter). The numbers that will actually be deployed are uncertain.

While there are operational responses to the type of technological breakthrough postulated, they are unlikely to enhance stability. Since the responses of the three major nuclear powers will differ, there also appears to be no useful arms control approach.

Preemptive Arms Control

In theory, it would be a major contribution to strategic stability to look at emerging technologies that could influence the nuclear balance and regulate them in advance. The basic idea is that the time to build the gate is when no one wants to use the road. The only actual treaty that sought to do this was in the non-nuclear area, the 1977 Environmental Modification Convention, which banned military use of modification in weather or climate. Some argue that earlier identification of the risks of developing and deploying MIRVs could have resulted in a ban, thereby avoiding a major source of instability.

While serving as an official in the now-defunct Arms Control and Disarmament Agency in the George H. W. Bush administration, I planned to undertake such an examination in Bush's second term, which never happened. Whatever the merits of this approach in the early 1990s, it is almost certainly no longer feasible. The pace of technology development may be outstripping human ability to understand future implication, let alone preemptively manage such implications.[47]

Confidence-Building Measures

Confidence-building measures can be an adjunct to a given arms control agreement but are not normally considered as arms control. As the name suggests, they seek to increase confidence between two states (or, for purposes of this chapter, two parties to an arms control agreement) that each will act in a responsible matter to prevent conflict. Confidence-building measures can be unilateral or reciprocal. They need not be written down in detail, although they sometimes are. They are usually not verifiable and therefore not legally binding. There is a risk that such measures will be undertaken for their propaganda value, especially one-time gestures such as the January 2019 display of the Russian 9M729 cruise missile (which the United States determined was a violation of the INF Treaty) to foreign observers at a military theme park near Moscow.[48]

Although commonly called an agreement, the detargeting agreement of 1994, discussed earlier in this chapter is an excellent example of a confidence-building measure. The United States and Russia each took steps to reassure the other that there was no risk of starting a war through an accidental or unauthorized ballistic missile launch. Those steps were completely unverifiable and totally under the control of each country. Yet the agreement has endured for a quarter of a century and largely has removed a concern that had been a significant strategic issue. This is true even though the United States has no real idea of how Russia implements the obligation it has taken upon itself. The agreement succeeds because each side believes it is in the other side's interest to adhere to the agreement to reduce the shared risk to both.

Confidence-building measures can take many forms, though they are often not explicitly designated as such. Here are some random examples to illustrate the breadth of the types of measures that can be taken (or at least offered):

- In the 1980s the Soviets argued that U.S. attack submarine operations in the waters where Soviet ballistic missile submarines patrolled risked collision and that therefore ASW-free zones were necessary. The U.S. Navy offered to bring Soviet submariners to U.S. training facilities so that they could understand the precautions American submarine commanders took against collisions. The Soviets declined.
- Russian and American experts took turns observing nuclear accident exercises to gain confidence in the professionalism of the other side.
- Observers are routinely invited to observe military exercises to avoid confusion on how military doctrine is actually implemented.
- The New START Treaty provided for an exchange of telemetric information (even though such an exchange was not required for verification of any treaty provisions) to increase confidence that the sides understood each another's missile development efforts.
- To reduce Russian concern with the ballistic missile defense capabilities of the U.S. SM-3 air defense missile, the United States suggested Russia use its own equipment to measure the missile's burnout velocity (an important parameter in evaluating its capability against ICBMs). The Russians declined.

These examples show the flexibility of confidence-building measures but also illustrate some of their limitations. Even when well conceived, they may fall victim to internal political or bureaucratic barriers. Neither the discussions on submarine safety nor the measurement of SM-3 burnout velocity ever took place. The nuclear accident exercises were clearly scripted (at least initially) to portray Russian forces in the best light. Confidence-building measures can be valuable, but their value should not be overestimated.

Does the Form of Agreement Matter?

This chapter has embraced the Schelling and Halperin definition of arms control as including "all the forms of military cooperation between potential enemies in the interest of reducing the likelihood of war, . . . and the political and economic costs of being prepared for it." Everything from ratified treaties to norms of behavior accepted by both sides has been covered.

That does not mean, however, that we can be completely indifferent to the form of arms control agreements. Many analysts and policymakers have a strong bias in favor of ratified treaties, on the presumption that they indicate a stronger commitment and one more difficult to abandon. Supporters of this view assume that because ratified treaties constitute binding international law, they therefore constitute a more forceful agreement. While this is technically true under the Vienna Convention on Treaties (accepted by the United States as describing customary international law), enforcement of international law depends on the United Nations Security Council, where nuclear states who are likely to be party to arms control agreements have a veto. Thus the distinction between legally binding and politically binding agreements may have only limited meaning.

Historically, it has been more difficult for states to withdraw from ratified treaties in response to internal political pressure. Significant pressure to withdraw from the ABM Treaty, for example, began in the mid-1980s, yet withdrawal came only in 2001. Recent experience with U.S. withdrawal from the INF Treaty may indicate that this precedent no longer applies. To some, the 2019 U.S. decision to revoke its signature of the 2013 Arms Trade Treaty, which the United States had signed but not ratified and which establishes common standards for the international trade of conventional weapons and seeks to reduce the illicit arms trade, further casts doubt on the importance of formal treaties. Despite this, the Russian Federation and many U.S. experts still have a strong bias in favor of ratified treaties that provide legally binding restrictions.

There are, however, equally strong reasons not to favor ratified treaties. They tend to take a long time to negotiate. While in theory they can be amended, that process is often difficult and time consuming. Finally, because of the time they take to negotiate, they often have a lengthy duration. This latter factor is of particular concern in an era in which strategic conditions change rapidly.

There may be domestic legal reasons why a formal government-to-government document is required to implement arms control agreements. Current Russian law requires a ratified treaty to extend privileges and immunities to inspectors or to admit them to Russian military facilities. On the U.S. side, the Atomic Energy Act forbids sharing with Russia such classified information as the number of warheads in a storage location, the number of warheads on particular ballistic missiles, and the location of major weapons storage facilities, except under a ratified treaty. All this information has been shared under New START and would, presumably, be desirable to share under a future agreement.[49]

Laws can be changed, of course. It would be relatively easy for Russia to resume its past policy allowing access as long as there was some overall government-level agreement (not necessarily a treaty). In the United States, the Atomic Energy Act could be amended to create a category of "arms control data" that the president could authorize providing to another state on a confidential basis notwithstanding other provisions of the act. Since this has never been considered by Congress, it is not possible to assess whether it would be found politically acceptable. Even if these changes were made, they would not result in complete flexibility to reach agreements. The Arms Control and Disarmament Act forbids obligating "the United States to reduce or limit the Armed Forces or armaments of the United States in a militarily significant manner, except pursuant to the treaty-making power of the President . . . or unless authorized by the enactment of further affirmative legislation."[50] This restriction may mean that future agreements would need to be politically binding rather than legally binding, a difference that, as noted, may be slight.

It is clear that many of the benefits gained from military-to-military communications could not be achieved under the more cumbersome procedures of ratified treaties. Furthermore, many useful agreements, such as the Detargeting Agreement, were easier to agree on as simple political commitments than they would have been as part of a formal treaty.

If arms control continues to be part of the U.S. approach to international security, the most probable future is that arms control agreements will consist of a package of agreements, some of which must be formalized in a treaty, others of which are simply politically binding agreements, documented perhaps in summit statements, and still others are undocumented reciprocal understandings carried out by each side. Furthermore, it is likely that future agreements may not be exclusively bilateral. An overall agreement might combine bilateral agreements, multilateral agreements, and side agreements involving a limited subset of the parties. Any or all of these might be formally documented. Some elements of the overall agreement may be updated frequently, while others may be intended to endure for a relatively long period. Negotiating such agreements will require the development of skills far beyond those used by Cold War negotiators.[51]

Applicability of Nuclear Arms Control to Other Nuclear-Armed States

Nuclear arms control continues to mean arms control between the United States and Russia. The relevance of their experience to most other nuclear-armed countries is limited now and for the foreseeable future. The one exception may be the nuclear rivalry between India and Pakistan. The parallels are inexact because the short time of flight and the geographic proximity between the two countries, the lack on either side of more than a rudimentary sea-based deterrent, and the aggressive posture called for by Pakistan's concept of full-scope deterrence. Still, given political will, the U.S. experience could, perhaps, lead to agreements that might provide some improvements in regional stability.

Among other nuclear-armed states, Britain and France have no interest in participating in arms control discussions because each considers itself to have a minimal deterrent that cannot be significantly reduced through international negotiations.[52] Their primary concern is that the United States continue to resist Russian attempts in future negotiations to gain some form of compensation for the fact that both France and the United Kingdom are U.S. allies or to place limits on the historic technical and operational cooperation between the United States and each of them.

In looking at the relevance of U.S. and Russian experience, the most complicated case is China. China shows no interest in near-term arms control, insisting that it will join negotiations at an appropriate time once Russia and the United States have made significant further reductions and come much closer to the smaller size of China's arsenal.[53] In the interim, there may be minor steps that can be taken (universalizing the 1988 Ballistic Missile Launch Notification Agreement, for example).[54]

The U.S. and Russian experience is probably of limited relevance for negotiations with North Korea, although if limited inspections become possible, U.S. and Russian experience may provide a template. The most plausible future is that North Korea and other states will formally endorse complete denuclearization of the Korean peninsula when political conditions permit leaving it ambiguous when that may happen. (The United States is unlikely to formally acknowledge the legitimacy of North Korea's permanent possession of nuclear weapons because of concerns for the reaction of regional allies, especially Japan.) Given such an agreement, it may then be possible to negotiate some modest interim measures (restrictions on ballistic missile flight tests, for example) in exchange for economic benefits.

Conclusion

Nuclear operations and arms control are inescapably linked, although their influence on each other is unequal. Arms control is not an end in itself but a tool to enhance national security and international stability. Like all tools, arms control is better at some tasks than at others. From the standpoint of nuclear operations, a good arms control agreement is not necessarily one that lowers forces the most but one that enables those forces to operate more safely and effectively and thus contributes to strategic stability.

The most important impact arms control has on nuclear operations is in setting the size and to some degree the composition of strategic nuclear forces. It is best if nuclear operators and arms control negotiators work closely together to ensure that treaties allow the implementation of nuclear deterrence war plans and that arms control facilitates the maintenance of effective forces at a reasonable cost. An unsolved problem is how to reflect changes in nuclear operations requirements during the period covered by an existing arms control treaty. Our only experience is with reduction in requirements during the Obama administration. But in an era of great-power competition, many believe we may need to increase nuclear forces at some time in the future. Other than the cumbersome amendment process, we have no way to reflect that need in our current arms control approach built around legally binding treaties.

History suggests a number of points about the relationship between arms control and nuclear operations: First, arms control has been a helpful tool for avoiding conflict owing to misunderstanding. It continues to be useful in performing that function today. For the more common and more concerning case of conflict arising from deliberate provocative behavior, arms control thus far has not made much of a difference.

Second, eliminating ICBMs with multiple warheads, the most important arms control objective for maintaining first-strike stability, has not been accomplished, despite decades of effort. The brief exception represented by START II resulted from unique circumstances unlikely to recur. While other arms control proposals to improve first-strike stability have been made, all have faltered. It appears clear that military effectiveness will always prevail over arms control stability objectives, perhaps because professional military, culturally, is more likely to value its ability to meet wartime objectives than to enhance strategic stability.

Third, arms control's greatest contribution may be to arms race stability, but this contribution is critically dependent on effective verification. Verification measures can have a modest and acceptable impact on nuclear operations, but only if experts in those operations participate in the drafting of verification proposals. Operational knowledge is needed within negotiating teams as well as during the initial drafting in capitals of proposed verification measures.

Finally, confidence-building measures, while valuable, are inherently limited and are not a substitute for formal arms control.

Future arms control agreements will be more complex than those today, both because of technological factors—space, cyber capabilities, artificial intelligence—and because of the more complex geopolitical situation compared with the Cold War. New approaches to agreements will be required, probably including a mix of commitments in different formats (treaties, informal agreements, unilateral steps) and involving multiple parties. Negotiating such agreements will require the development of procedures and skills far beyond those used by Cold War negotiators and will require new understanding and new approaches for both nuclear operators and arms control negotiators. It is not too early to begin thinking about the implications of that future world.

Notes

In addition to the collective review by other chapter authors, Ambassador Brooks is grateful for individual comments from James Acton, Charles Glaser, Rose Gottemoeller, John Harvey, James Timbie, Michael May, Frank Miller, Robert Soofer, Perter Swartz, and Jon Wolfstahl and for research assistance by Mary Chestnut and Brian Radzinsky. He alone is responsible for the use he has made of their insights.

1. Some of the early part of this chapter, especially the discussion on strategic stability and the benefits of arms control, were previewed in Linton F. Brooks, "The End of Arms Control," *Daedalus* 149, no. 2 (2020), pp. 84-100.

2. Thomas C. Schelling and Morton H. Halperin, *Strategy and Arms Control* (New York: Pergamon-Brassey's Classic, 1985), p. 2.

3. Targeting is also influenced by the provisions of the law of armed conflict, especially the requirements of discrimination (for example, between combatants and noncombatants or between civilian and war-supporting infrastructure) and proportionality (requiring, among other things, minimizing collateral damage). For a discussion of these influences, see Charles J. Dunlap Jr., "Taming Shiva: Applying International Law to Nuclear Operations," *Air Force Law Review* 42 (1997), pp. 157–71. When he wrote this article, Dunlap was legal counsel to the commander of the U.S. Strategic Command. For an alternate view casting doubt on the ability of nuclear use to ever be proportional and discriminant, see Newell L. Highsmith, *On the Legality of Nuclear Deterrence,* Livermore Papers on Global Security 6, Lawrence Livermore National Laboratory Center for Global Security Research, April 2019.

4. The term *strategic stability* is subject to varying interpretations. See Elbridge A. Colby and Michael S. Gerson, eds., *Strategic Stability: Contending Interpretations* (Carlisle Barracks, Pennsylvania, U.S. Army War College Strategic Studies Institute, 2013). The Russian government uses an expansive definition that sometimes seems to be a synonym for national security policy. This chapter uses *strategic stability* because, narrowly defined in the terms indicated below, it remains the most useful concept for assessing the contributions of arms control to the prevention of nuclear war. For a challenge to the entire concept of using the concept of strategic stability to evaluate arms control, see Keith B. Payne and Michaela Dodge, *The Strategic Stability Dialogue: Think Before You Speak*, National Institute for Public Policy Information Series 495, July 8, 2021.

5. Article VI obligates all parties to the Nuclear Non-Proliferation Treaty "to pursue negotiations in good faith on effective measures relating to cessation of the nuclear arms race at an early date and to nuclear disarmament." This remains a binding obligation on the United States. Progress toward this goal is an important political restraint on proliferation. Lack of interest in actual abolition among most nuclear weapons–possessing states, coupled with the increasing tension among the major powers, suggests that the conditions permitting serious consideration of total elimination are unlikely to be present in the coming decades. As a result, implications on nuclear operations of reduction to very low levels are not considered further in this chapter. Treaty on the Non-Proliferation of Nuclear Weapons (NPT), Article VI, www.un.org/disarmament/wmd/nuclear/npt/text/.

6. The New START Treaty (or New START) is officially the *Treaty Between the United States of America and the Russian Federation on Measures for the Further Reduction and Limitation of Strategic Offensive Arms*, signed in Prague, The Czech Republic on April 8, 2010. New START replaced 1991's *Treaty Between the United States of America and Union of Soviet Socialist Republics on the Reduction and Limitation of*

Strategic Offensive Arms, signed in Moscow on July 31, 1991, and referred to as the START Treaty, START, or START I. START is an acronym (Strategic Arms Reduction Treaty). As such, the formulation "START Treaty" is illogical and ungrammatical ("Strategic Arms Reduction Treaty Treaty"). It has become common practice, however, including in official government documents and congressional testimony, to treat START as though it were a normal word. The terms *START Treaty* and *New START Treaty* have become universally accepted in the policy community. This chapter follows this common usage despite its ungrammatical underpinnings.

7. The Antarctic Treaty, December 1,1959; Treaty on Principles Governing the Activities of States in the Exploration and Use of Outer Space, including The Moon and Other Celestial Bodies, January 27, 1967; Treaty on the Prohibition of the Emplacement of Nuclear Weapons and Other Weapons of Mass Destruction on the Seabed and the Ocean Floor and in the Subsoil Thereof, February 11, 1971. Countries in nuclear weapons–free zones commit themselves to not manufacture, acquire, test, or possess nuclear weapons. Five such zones exist today: Latin America (the 1967 Treaty of Tlatelolco), the South Pacific (the 1985 Treaty of Rarotonga), Southeast Asia (the 1995 Treaty of Bangkok), Africa (the 1996 Treaty of Pelindaba), and Central Asia (the 2006 Treaty of Semipalatinsk). Nuclear weapons states are invited to sign protocols stating that they will respect the status of the zones and will not use or threaten use of nuclear weapons against states that have signed. The United States has signed and ratified the protocol to the Latin America nuclear weapons–free zone and has signed but not ratified protocols to the South Pacific, African, and Central Asia zones. Arms Control Association, "Nuclear-Weapon-Free Zones (NWFZ) at a Glance," Fact Sheet, July 2017, www.armscontrol.org/factsheets/nwfz.

8. For the most famous example, see the Carter administration's PD-59 document, George Washington University National Security Archives, https://nsarchive2.gwu.edu/nukevault/ebb390/docs/7-25-80%20PD%2059.pdf). The Reagan version (NSDD-13) is available at the Federation of American Scientists website, https://fas.org/irp/offdocs/nsdd/nsdd-13.pdf.

9. Although START I was described as limiting each side to 6,000 warheads, those were not actual physical objects. Ballistic missiles were counted with the maximum number of warheads that they could carry. Bombers were counted more flexibly, depending on whether they carried cruise missiles. The result was that START I could have resulted in each side deploying perhaps 8,500 actual warheads.

10. For details, see Frank Miller's chapter 3, in this volume.

11. It is also true that in the past, lenient counting rules favored the United States, which had more robust bomber forces.

12. In February 2022, as this volume was in final preparation, Russia invaded Ukraine in violation of both international law and of obligations it had assumed. However the conflict is resolved, this action will complicate (or perhaps eliminate) prospect for further arms control. It does not, however, invalidate any of the analysis in this chapter about what arms control can and cannot do and its influence on nuclear operations.

13. For a complete list and discussion, see United States Arms Control and Disarmament Agency, *Arms Control and Disarmament Agreements: Texts and Histories of the Negotiations* (Washington, D.C., 1990).

14. The suggestions on space and cyber weaponry are drawn almost verbatim from Brooks, "The End of Arms Control."

15. Before 1968, bombers loaded with nuclear weapons were maintained on airborne alert. The practice was ended after a series of high-profile crashes.

16. Michael M. May and John R. Harvey, "Nuclear Operations and Arms Control," in *Managing Nuclear Operations*, edited by Ashton B. Carter, John D. Steinbruner and Charles A. Zraket, pp. 734–35 (Brookings, 1987).

17. For discussion of some problems with the concept, see Richard L. Garwin, "Space Weapons: Not Yet," discussion paper, meeting 283, Pugwash Workshop on Preserving the Non-Weaponization of Space, Castellón de la Plana, Spain, May 22–24, 2003. For further background, see Robert Preston and others, *Space Weapons Earth Wars* (Santa Monica, CA: RAND Project Air Force, 2002).

18. The Department of Defense *Dictionary of Military and Associated Terms*) defines *space control* as "operations to ensure freedom of action in space for the United States and its allies and deny a threat freedom of action in space." Office of the Chairman of the Joint Chiefs of Staff, *DOD Dictionary of Military and Associated Terms* (Washington ,D.C.: The Joint Staff, November), p. 19.

19. The Safeguard system deployed thirty long-range nuclear-armed Spartan missiles intended to intercept attacking warheads outside the atmosphere and seventy shorter-ranged nuclear-armed Sprint missiles for close-range intercept. See Sharon Watkins Lang, U.S. Army Strategic Missile Defense Command historian, "SMDC History: Safeguard Achieves Full Operational Capability," September 27, 2017, www.army. mil/article/194445/smdc_history_safeguard_achieves_full_operational_capability.

20. "Detargeting of Strategic Nuclear Systems," statement released by the White House, Office of the Press Secretary, Moscow, Russia, January 14, 1994.

21. Predictions that some new technology or new operational concept will turn the oceans transparent have been common over the past fifty years. Thus far, none have been borne out. Since the late 1960s, the navy has invested in a Strategic Submarine Security Project to examine what the laws of physics might allow in making a submarine vulnerable. They have made a number of technical and operational changes to guard against these hypothetical threats. Some analysts have recently suggested that the ability to analyze massive amounts of data using artificial intelligence might compromise submarine security. There is little reason to believe a major breakthrough is imminent, although the possibility is one reason for maintaining a triad of strategic forces.

22. For the rationale for anti-SSBN operations, see Linton F. Brooks, "Naval Power and National Security: The Case for the Maritime Strategy," *International Security* 11, no. 2 (1986), pp. 58–88. Virtually all public support for this position came from mid-level navy officers. For a summary of the arguments against an anti-SSBN strategy, see James J. Wirtz, *Strategic Anti-Submarine Warfare: Risk, Leverage, and Coupling in the Post–Cold War Era,* Defense Nuclear Agency Technical Report

DNA-TR-92-77, January 1993. The document includes a list of all the major articles against the concept, all of which were written by academics or former government civilian officials. Although supportive of the maritime strategy concept generally, Wirtz concludes that the strategy should not be used against post–Cold War Russia because of concerns with escalation control.

23. John Lehman, *Oceans Ventured: Winning the Cold War at Sea* (New York: W.W. Norton, 2018).

24. Lehman, *Oceans Ventured,* pp. 227–43. Ironically, ASW-free zones had been proposed to the Soviets by President Carter in 1979, President Carter to Soviet General Secretary Brezhnev, Vienna, June 17, 1979, *Foreign Relations of the United States, 1977–1980,* vol. 6, *Soviet Union,* edited by Melissa Jane Taylor, Document 202.

25. The People's Republic appears to have a number of operational questions about ballistic missile submarines for which it has not yet decided on answers. For a summary of China's probable approach, see Tong Zhao, *Tides of Change: China's Nuclear Ballistic Missile Submarines and Strategic Stability* (Washington, D.C.: Carnegie Endowment for International Peace, 2018).

26. I am indebted to Sergei Rogov, of the Institute of U.S. and Canadian Studies, in Moscow, for this thought.

27. May and Harvey, "Nuclear Operations and Arms Control." A minimum-energy flight profile uses the smallest amount of fuel for a given range. A depressed trajectory achieves a shorter flight time and a lower apogee compared with a minimum-energy trajectory.

28. President Carter to Soviet General Secretary Brezhnev, June 17, 1979.

29. There were extensive discussions of limited options and limiting escalation, but in fact even the smallest use would have been quite extensive.

30. This de facto view was not shared by all. Thomas Schelling regarded limited countervalue strikes as rational and potentially controllable. I am indebted to Charles Glaser for this insight.

31. NATO had significant plans in this regard during the Cold War. "Overall Strategic Concept for the Defense of the North Atlantic Treaty Organization Area," MC 14/3, para 22(a), January 16, 1968, states that, "NATO must be manifestly prepared at all times to escalate the conflict, using nuclear weapons if necessary." This remained NATO's formal strategic concept until the end of the Cold War.

32. For a discussion of a possible Russian "theory of victory," including limited Russian nuclear use, see Brad Roberts, *The Case for U.S. Nuclear Weapons in the 21st Century* (Stanford University Press, 2016), especially chap. 4.

33. *Joint Nuclear Operations, April 17, 2020* (Washington, D.C.: Joint Staff), Joint Publication 3-72.

34. Under the limits of New START, the United States has elected to deploy ICBMs with only one warhead. Given the widespread assumption that two warheads are required to ensure adequate destruction of an ICBM within a silo, this deployment significantly reduces Russian incentives to conduct a strike on the ICBM force. It does nothing, however, to reduce the destabilizing effect of Russian MIRVed

ICBMs, especially the new SS-28 (Sarmat) heavy ICBM. Some constraints on Russia are provided by overall treaty limits.

35. This quotation by Secretary Brown has been extensively cited and widely repeated. I have, however, been unable to identify its original source.

36. For example, the definition of a ballistic missile in New START reads as follows: "The term 'ballistic missile' means a missile that is a weapon-delivery vehicle that has a ballistic trajectory over most of its flight path." Under this definition, hypersonic "boost-glide" vehicles would be excluded, since they do not have "a ballistic trajectory over most of [their] flight path."

37. For a technical analysis of these systems see Jill Hruby, *Russia's New Nuclear Weapon Delivery Systems: An Open-Source Technical Review*, Nuclear Threat Initiative, November 2019; and Amy F. Woolf, *Russia's Nuclear Weapons: Doctrine, Forces, and Modernization*, March 21, 2022, Congressional Research Service R45861, https://crsreports.congress.gov. This report is updated periodically.

38. Hans M. Kristensen and Matt Korda, "Russian Nuclear Forces, 2022," *Bulletin of the Atomic Scientists* 78, no. 2, pp. 98–121.

39. There has been extensive analysis of warhead-level verification outside government but often under government sponsorship. See, for example, National Research Council, *Monitoring Nuclear Weapons and Nuclear-Explosive Materials: An Assessment of Methods and Capabilities* (Washington, D.C.: National Academies Press, 2005), https://doi.org/10.17226/11265; Department of Defense, *Assessment of Nuclear Monitoring and Verification Technologies* (Defense Science Board, January 2014); International Partnership for Nuclear Disarmament Verification, *Phase I Summary Report: Creating the Verification Blocks for Future Nuclear Disarmament* (November 2017).

40. The idea of a total warhead limit was first advanced about twenty-five years ago. At that time, the United States had more spare warheads that could, in time of crisis, have been reloaded on U.S. ballistic missiles. The Russians were concerned with this imbalance. The notion of a total warhead ceiling was to essentially allow a trade-off between U.S. upload potential and Russian nonstrategic nuclear weapons. In recent years, Russian concern with the U.S. advantage in uploading its missiles has faded.

41. The locations of U.S. weapons stored in Europe are widely known from various leaks but are treated as classified within the United States. The United States would need to consider whether increased transparency from Russia was worth formally declassifying these locations. The views of the host nations would obviously be a critical factor.

42. Rose Gottemoeller, *Negotiating the New START Treaty* (New York: Cambria Press, 2021).

43. The agency's techniques include, for example, remote cameras monitoring entrances to storage facilities and high-technology seals verifying that containers have not been opened.

44. The Joint Compliance and Implementation Commission was established under the START with, among other things, the responsibility to make changes "as may be necessary to improve the viability and effectiveness of this Treaty." This

allows correcting minor problems, such as the one described, without resorting to the amendment procedure. Bodies such as the commission have been included in all recent nuclear arms control treaties to which the United States is a party. The New START version is called the Bilateral Consultative Commission.

45. In recent years, there has been considerable work on norms in bodies such as the United Nations Group of Government Experts and the NATO Cyber Security Center of Excellence. None of this work has gained widespread support in the U.S. national security community.

46. I am indebted to one of the anonymous Brookings reviewers for pointing this out.

47. For a detailed argument, see Thomas L. Friedman, *Thank You for Being Late: An Optimist's Guide to Thriving in the Age of Accelerations* (New York; Picador, 2017).

48. Neil MacFarquhar, "Russia Shows Off New Cruise Missile," *New York Times,* January 24, 2019.

49. The logic here is that treaties and legislation are both considered part of the supreme law of the land under the U.S. Constitution. When enacted laws conflict, the standard presumption is that the latter law enacted takes precedence over the former. Applying this logic, a treaty ratified after the enactment of the Atomic Energy Act would take precedence over that act. This logic has never been tested in court, nor is it clear who would have standing to bring a case. Nonetheless, it would appear to limit what can be agreed to without a treaty.

50. 22 U.S.C. 35, sec. 2573.

51. For a detailed discussion see James Timbie, "A Way Forward," *Daedalus* 149, no. 2 (2020), pp. 190–204.

52. Israel is widely assumed to possess nuclear weapons, although neither Israel nor the United States acknowledges this fact. If there is an Israeli nuclear deterrent, it is probably directed at its hostile non-nuclear neighbors, not other nuclear states. Nuclear arms control would thus be irrelevant.

53. In 2018 a knowledgeable mid-level Chinese official told me that this meant U.S. and Russian total stockpiles of no more than 1,000 warheads each, a condition unlikely to be met for decades, if ever.

54. In its November 2021 annual report to Congress (Office of the Secretary of Defense, *Military and Security Developments Involving the People's Republic of China,* Washington, DC), the Defense Department states that China "has commenced building at least three solid-fueled ICBM silo fields, which will cumulatively contain hundreds of new ICBM silos" (p. vi). There has been no public acknowledgment by China that these are in fact new silos, and it is unclear whether they are intended to be completely filled. If there are to be hundreds of new silos it will increase both the opportunity and the need for traditional arms control. It is unlikely, however, that these forces will come to fruition within the next two decades. Thus, they have not been considered in this chapter.

Contributors

AMBASSADOR LINTON F. BROOKS is an independent consultant on national security issues and a member of the National Academy of Sciences Committee on International Security and Arms Control. He has over six decades of experience in national security, much of it associated with nuclear weapons. He served from July 2002 to January 2007 as administrator of the U.S. Department of Energy's National Nuclear Security Administration. His other government service includes service as Deputy Administrator for Nuclear Nonproliferation at the National Nuclear Security Administration, Assistant Director of the United States Arms Control and Disarmament Agency, Chief U.S. Negotiator for the 1991 Strategic Arms Reduction Treaty, Director of Defense Programs and Arms Control on the National Security Council staff and several Navy and Defense Department assignments as a thirty-year career naval officer.

M. ELAINE BUNN, a consultant on strategic issues, is a nonresident fellow at the Center for Strategic and International Studies' Project on Nuclear Issues, the National Defense University's Center for the Study of Weapons of Mass Destruction, and the Royal United Services Institute. She served as Deputy Assistant Secretary of Defense for Nuclear and Missile Defense Policy from March 2013 to January 2017. Previously, she worked in international security policy at NDU's Institute for National Strategic Studies (2000–2013) and in the Office of the Secretary of Defense (1980–2000). She has published articles and book chapters on deterrence, assurance of allies, strategic planning, nuclear policy, and missile defense, and speaks frequently on these issues at U.S. and international conferences.

MICHAEL S. ELLIOTT is a retired member of the Senior Executive Service. Elliott's twenty-five years of military service included a distinguished flying career in the B-1, B-52, and FB-111. He entered government as a civil servant in 2003, culminating with a tour as the USSTRATCOM Deputy Director for Strategic Plans and Policy. From 2009 to 2010, Elliott was the Chairman's representative to the new START negotiations. From 2010 to 2015 he was the Deputy Director for Strategic Stability, The Joint Staff. In this capacity he was a senior advisor to the Chairman for shaping and implementation of nuclear plans and policy. In 2015 the president conferred upon him the rank of Meritorious Executive.

CHARLES L. GLASER is professor of Political Science and International Affairs at George Washington University. He was the founding director of the Elliott School's Institute for Security and Conflict Studies from 2009 to 2019, and is now the co-director. Previously, Glaser was the Emmett Dedmon Professor of Public Policy at the University of Chicago. His books include *Rational Theory of International Politics* (2010) and *Analyzing Strategic Nuclear Policy* (1990). In 2018 he was awarded the International Studies Association, Security Studies Section, Distinguished Scholar Award. In 2021 he was awarded the National Academy of Sciences' William and Katherine Estes Award for behavioral research toward the prevention of nuclear war.

DR. JOHN R. HARVEY is a physicist with over forty years of experience working nuclear weapons and related issues, first at Lawrence Livermore National Laboratory, then at Stanford University, and in senior positions in the Department of Defense (twice) and the Department of Energy. From 2009 to 2013, he served as Principal Deputy Assistant Secretary of Defense for Nuclear, Chemical, and Biological Defense Programs. He was Undersecretary Ash Carter's lead for the 2010 Nuclear Posture Review, and for engaging the National Nuclear Security Administration (NNSA) on joint oversight of the U.S. nuclear stockpile. Dr. Harvey helped oversee DoD acquisition programs to sustain and modernize nuclear weapons delivery systems and nuclear command and control. He has written and spoken extensively on these issues. On retiring from government service, he consults with, among others, the Defense Science Board, Institute for Defense Analysis, Strategic Command's NC3 Advisory Panel, and NNSA's Defense Programs Advisory Committee.

GENERAL C. ROBERT KEHLER retired from the United States Air Force on January 1, 2014. In his last assignment he commanded United States Strategic Command where he was directly responsible to the secretary of defense and president for nuclear deterrence, global strike, space, and cyberspace operations. Prior to that, he commanded Air Force Space Command (predecessor to United States Space Force) and several major space and nuclear ballistic missile operational commands. Kehler is the recipient of numerous military awards, has two master's degrees, and is a graduate of executive development programs at Carnegie-Mellon, Syracuse, and Harvard Universities. He continues to serve as a senior fellow of the National Defense University, private consultant, and corporate director.

AUSTIN LONG is Deputy Director for Strategic Stability in the Joint Staff J5 (Strategy, Plans, and Policy).

The Honorable FRANKLIN MILLER is a principal at the Scowcroft Group in Washington, DC. He dealt extensively with nuclear policy and nuclear arms control issues during his thirty-one-year government career, which included senior positions in the Defense Department and on the National Security Council staff. He was directly in charge of U.S. nuclear deterrence and targeting policy from 1985 to 2001 and also chaired NATO's senior nuclear policy committee, the High-Level Group, from 1997 to 2001. He is a member of the Strategic Command Advisory Board and served on Defense Policy Board from 2008 to 2020. He also served on the 2008 Secretary of Defense Task Force on DoD Nuclear Weapons Management (Schlesinger Task Force) and on the 2013–2014 Congressional Advisory Panel on the Nuclear Security Enterprise (Mies-Augustine Panel).

DR. JAMES N. MILLER is Assistant Director for Policy and Analysis at the Johns Hopkins University Applied Physics Laboratory, and serves concurrently as a special government employee on the Defense Science Board and as US Coordinator for Australia, United Kingdom, and United States (AUKUS) Initiatives on the National Security Council. Dr. Miller served previously in the Department of Defense as Deputy Assistant Secretary of Defense for Requirements, Plans and Counterproliferation, Principal Deputy Under Secretary of Defense for Policy, and Under Secretary of Defense for Policy. He holds an A.B. degree in economics from Stanford University and master's and PhD degrees in public policy from Harvard University.

BRIAN RADZINSKY is a postdoctoral fellow at the Center for Global Security Research at Lawrence Livermore National Laboratory. He previously served under Janne Nolan as Deputy Director of the Nuclear Security Working Group at the George Washington University.

JOHN K. WARDEN is a research staff member in the Strategy, Forces, and Resources Division at the Institute for Defense Analyses, where he contributes to studies and analysis in support of the Department of Defense. He is the author of numerous studies and articles related to nuclear weapons and deterrence, including *Limited Nuclear War: The 21st Century Challenge for the United States* (Livermore Papers on Global Security, No. 4, July 2018) and "North Korea's Nuclear Posture: An Evolving Challenge for U.S. Deterrence" (Proliferation Papers, Ifri, March 2017). He holds an M.A. in Security Studies from Georgetown University and a B.A. in Political Science and History from Northwestern University.

Index

Bush (G. H. W.) administrations, 60–62; SIOP Review and, 62–65 Civil-military relations in nuclear war planning, 8–9, 71–93; declaratory policy in NPR, 75–78; increase in, 10; New START Treaty limits negotiations and, 72–75; nuclear commanders and, 147–52; nuclear employment guidance and, 78–87; planning guidance detail and, 110–12; reflections on, 87–90
Clausewitz, Carl von, 89
Clinton, Bill, 68, 255
Clinton, Hillary, 84
Cold War: Air Force bombers on alert during, 27, 105–06, 171, 251; arms control during, 259–60; common sense of purpose during, 134; continuous airborne alerts during, 27–28; crisis prevention during, 187, 248; damage-limitation capabilities, 18; delegation of authority to use nuclear weapons during, 32, 156; end of, 106–09, 134–35; launch-on-warning policy, 26; mutual assured destruction capabilities and, 20–21; NATO nuclear weapons during, 180, 227; nuclear decision process, 158; nuclear deterrence during, 17, 36; nuclear operational planning during, 103–06, 112; SSBNs and, 257; survivability of nuclear forces during, 19–21; targeting during, 38, 53–54
Columbia-class submarines, 22–23, 169
Command-and-control. *See* Nuclear command-and-control
Communications technologies: advancements in, 5–6, 11; command vulnerabilities and, 31–33; cyberattacks and, 6, 11; NC2 system and, 173, 177–79, 178–79*f*; survivability of nuclear forces and, 177, 190. *See also specific types*
Compliance with treaty obligations, 264–65
Confidence-building measures, 271–72
Congress: arms control and, 245, 247; New START Treaty and warhead limits, 72–73, 78–79; on presidents' sole authority for nuclear use, 160–61; Safeguard system closure and, 255

Constitutional checks and balances, 162
Conventional war: escalations of, 187, 188, 225, 242–43, 260; non-nuclear attacks, 34, 76–77, 85
Costs of nuclear weapons, 1, 84–85, 129, 210, 244, 255, 270
Cotter, Donald R., 4
Course of action development, 114–16, 115–16*f*
Credibility: damage-limitation capabilities and, 39; delegation of authority to use nuclear weapons and, 32; first-use policy and, 40; globally integrated campaigns and, 151; limited nuclear options and, 18–19, 39; nuclear command-and-control and, 30; nuclear deterrence theory and, 16–19; nuclear personnel and, 143; readiness of forces and, 133–34
Crisis prevention: allies and, 225; arms control and, 242–43; during Cold War, 187, 248; cyberattacks and, 192, 249–50; early-warning systems and, 172, 174, 175*f*, 190, 192, 193, 249; during modern conflict, 187–89; for nuclear accidents, 5, 30, 33–34, 181, 247–48, 272; for unauthorized nuclear use, 33–34, 181
Crisis stability, 243, 247–50
Cruise missiles: air-launched, 1, 23, 28, 104, 124; defense against, 186; sea-launched, 23–24, 185, 211; strategic theory and stabilization, 247
Cyberattacks: challenges to arms control and, 269; communications vulnerabilities and, 6, 11; crisis prevention and, 192, 249–50; deterrence of, 34; NC2 system and, 188, 191–93, 268–69; NPR and nuclear retaliation for, 40

Damage expectancy (DE), 125–26
Damage-limitation capabilities, 18, 21, 34, 39, 57, 259
DCA (dual-capable aircraft), 23, 154, 208, 214
De-alerting, 159–60
Decapitation strikes, 31–33, 156, 185, 258–59
Deconfliction of nuclear weapons, 125